Selected Writings
on Anarchism
and Revolution

Edited, with an Introduction, by MARTIN A. MILLER

The M.I.T. Press
Cambridge, Massachusetts, and London, England

Selected
Writings
on Anarchism
and Revolution
P. A. Kropotkin

Introduction and new material copyright © 1970 by The Massachusetts Institute of Technology

Set in Monophoto Ehrhardt. Printed in the United States of America by Halliday Lithograph Corp. and bound by The Colonial Press Inc. Designed by Dwight E. Agner.

ISBN 0 262 11037 7 (hardcover)
ISBN 0 262 61010 8 (paperback)
Library of Congress catalog card number: 73-107994

Title page drawing by Margaret Agner.

Contents

Preface   vii

Introduction, *Martin A. Miller*   1

Essays   Must We Occupy Ourselves with an
Examination of the Ideal of a Future
System?   46

The Commune of Paris   118

The Russian Revolutionary Party   134

Expropriation   160

The State: Its Historic Role   210

The Revolution in Russia   266

Letters   To Nettlau   292

To Steffen   308

To Brandes   318

Kropotkin and Lenin   Conversation with Lenin   324

Two Letters to Lenin   334

Glossary of Names   341

Chronology of Important Dates in
the Life of P. A. Kropotkin   357

Selected Bibliography   360

Name Index   363

Subject Index   366

Preface

This collection of political works by Peter Kropotkin is intended to make some of his most representative writings on anarchism and revolution more accessible. The material contained in this book consists of essays and letters which either have not been previously translated or which have been out of print since their original publication. While the entire scope of Kropotkin's political thinking cannot possibly be projected in a single volume, it is hoped that many of his most fundamental conceptions have been exemplified in the following pages.

The essays have been selected to provide an understanding of Kropotkin's interpretation of the role of anarchism in modern history, his criticism of capitalism, his conception of revolution and his views on the ideals to be realized in the postrevolutionary society of the future. The articles dealing specifically with Russia supplement these theoretical writings by supplying the reader with a concrete analysis of a society confronted by an authentic revolutionary opposition. This analysis can be followed to its conclusion in the section on Kropotkin's meeting with Lenin and his letters to the Bolshevik leader after the 1917 revolution. The letters to Nettlau, Steffen, and Brandes present additional concerns which are closely related to the large themes of anarchism and revolution described in the essays.

The material has been arranged chronologically in order to stress the development of Kropotkin's ideology. All of the essays and letters have been reproduced in their entirety. Explanatory notes have been incorporated into the text, although these have been limited as much as possible. Kropotkin's essays were meant to be read directly, without the distractions from the issues at hand which scholarly footnotes frequently produce. For this reason, biographical data on the numerous personalities mentioned by Kropotkin—statesmen, scholars, and revolutionaries—have been placed in a glossary of names at the end of the book. Kropotkin's own notes have been retained in the text.

I wish to express my gratitude to Vernon Richards of the Freedom Press for his cooperation in the preparation of this anthology and also to Professor Richard Wortman of the University of Chicago for his astute criticism of the introduction to this volume. Needless to say, the errors that may remain are due solely to my own intransigence and not to the critical comments I have received. I am especially grateful to my wife Ylana, who has been of great aid in the various stages of the preparation of this book. Finally, concerning Russian transliteration, I have adopted a slightly modified variant of the Library of Congress system (names most familiar in English have not been systematized strictly: hence, Peter, instead of Petr, Kropotkin) and Russian dates are in the old style (the Julian calendar used in Russia until February 1918 was twelve days behind the Western calendar in the nineteenth century and thirteen days behind in this century).

MARTIN A. MILLER
Stanford, California
June 1969

**Selected Writings
on Anarchism
and Revolution**

Introduction

I

The conception of a society without authority, of a civil order without any form of constitution or government, has fascinated man almost as long as he has possessed the power of speculative thought. Among the ancients, political philosophy was rooted in the idea that the quest for justice and the good cannot be separated from the existence of the state. Aristotle in particular had harsh words for those who would live beyond the confines of the state, whom he referred to in his *Politics* as "lawless, dangerous beasts." So too Pericles before him had clearly stated to the Athenian citizenry that people who do not participate in the affairs of state have no business in the state. However, a reaction developed to these views under the Macedonian hegemony when the Greek polis was finally shattered: Stoics looked beyond the civil state to the world of universals in nature, Cynics who followed the example of Diogenes became disgusted with society and celebrated the natural authority of the individual over that of the civil order. Other early examples of the revolt against the state must include the Essenes' monastic retreat from Jerusalem in the first century B.C. to escape the rigid authority of Rome on the one hand and the static institutionalization of Hebrew monotheism on the other. An episode frequently cited as a precedent for modern anarchism is the brief sixteenth century Anabaptist commune in Münster which transformed itself from an antiauthoritarian movement to a ruthless dictatorship before being crushed by the united (temporarily) forces of the Reformation and Counter-Reformation.

Precedents, however numerous, are never quite the same as that which follows. The anarchist movement did not really develop until the middle of the nineteenth century and did not produce its brilliant theorists until that time. It is not accidental that the revolutionary extremity of opposing all civil authority did not arise until the nation-states in Europe had become completely consolidated, until the organizational framework of political and economic centralization had become predominant in Europe, and until technology had developed to such highly complex levels of production that men could begin to dream of utopias where machines would labor instead of human beings. Without these factors, the anarchist rebellion would probably not have gained a mass following around the globe and talented men such as Pierre Joseph Proudhon, Michael Bakunin, and Peter Kropotkin would not have felt compelled to compose their philosophies of antiauthoritarianism.

The centralization of political authority, a process which had been occurring for centuries, reached a new level of development at this time. This process was accompanied by the formation of national ideologies which attempted to create an identification between the citizenry and the abstract entity of the state. As popular demands for political participation grew, the myth of the state as the seat of progress became more widespread. At the same time, the industrial revolution brought even greater power to the service of the state. The growing capacity of governments to mobilize men and resources, however, provoked critics to challenge the expanded use of political power. Although some critics accepted the progressive role of the nation-state and questioned only its uses, others produced ideologies which attempted to counter the notion of the state as salvation. A breed of alienated men who believed neither in the inherent virtues of industrial capitalism nor in the chauvinistic loyalty of nationalism attacked these aggressive developments. Thus, despite the derivative aspects of anarchist theory, the essence of its critique is specifically tied to the intellectual forces and political events of the latter part of the nineteenth century. The distinction to be drawn before and after this era is the difference between anarchist aspects of other phenomena and anarchism itself.

In its broadest perspective, anarchism is a total assault upon all the institutions of authority and upon every attitude and theoretical position based upon the acceptance of authority. As governments have always been the supreme source of secular authority, anarchists centered their attack upon all govern-ments, regardless of the form under which they ruled. Anarchism demands nothing short of absolute liberty, a highly moral and just community where man can decide his own destiny, and the guarantee both of egalitarian human relationships and the basic necessities of life for all.

Unavoidably, efforts to implement such demands brought out painful contradictions. While much of anarchist theory contained an implicit assumption that life was best lived in small, rural communities away from corrupting centers of power, some of its most striking successes and most of its support were to be found in large urban areas as well as in the countryside. Anarchism sought to realize the ideal of equality, yet its leaders and major theorists were not infrequently aristocrats and sons of landowners (Tolstoy, Bakunin, Kropotkin, Cherkezov, and Malatesta, to name only a few of the most prominent examples). It strongly opposed organization and hierarchy, yet anarchist groups and leagues from various countries periodically gathered for congresses to discuss the tactics of revolution which often included precisely these concepts. Proclaiming internationalism and unity without ideological doctrines, the movement found itself split from within due to both national affiliation and questions of ideology. Concerning the latter, the varieties include anarchist communism, anarcho-syndicalism, as well as mutu-alist, collectivist, and individualist anarchism. Perhaps most significant, anarchist theory posits a belief in man's reason, goodness, and perfectibility while in practice it gave birth to such illegitimate offspring as the terrorist excesses of assassination and a strong current of anti-intellectualism among many of its adherents. The reaction to the image created by the bomb throwers and assassins has been vividly described by Conrad. In the introduction to a novel on anarchists, he related a conversation with a friend on the subject which reflects his attitude:

> I remember, however, remarking on the criminal futility of the whole thing, doctrine, action, mentality; and on the contemptible aspect of the half-crazy pose as of a brazen cheat exploiting the poignant miseries and passionate credulities of a mankind always so tragically eager for self-destruction. That was what made for me its philosophical pretenses so unpardonable. Presently, passing to particular instances, we recalled the already old story of the attempt to blow up the Greenwich Observatory; a blood-stained inanity of so fatuous a kind that it was impossible to fathom its origin by any reasonable or even unreasonable process of thought. For perverse unreason has its own logical processes. But that outrage could not be laid hold of mentally in any sort of way, so that one remained faced by the fact of a man blown to bits for nothing even most remotely resembling an idea, anarchistic or other.[1]

Such tragedies—and there were a staggering number of them in Europe at the turn of the century—led to the common association of anarchy with violent chaos. But it was precisely the opposite image that most anarchists labored to create. Indeed, it was Kropotkin himself who vigorously attempted to redefine anarchism in such a way as to convince the public that the movement was not espousing a philosophy antithetical to civilization. In this regard, it is interesting to note that although Kropotkin was invited to write the anarchism entry for the eleventh edition of the *Encyclopaedia Britannica* (1910), the editors found it necessary to add a lengthy footnote describing the terrorist acts and assassinations which in their view were an inherent part of the anarchist movement not included by Kropotkin.

The connection between the anarchist and the criminal out-

---

1 Joseph Conrad, *The Secret Agent* (Garden City, New York: Doubleday Anchor, 1953), p. 9. The quote is from the introduction written in 1920. The novel was originally written in 1907.

law continually haunted the movement and its adherents. One of the earliest studies of the anarchist mentality, based on actual interviews with a variety of persons associated with the movement in France at the end of the nineteenth century, found that often the anarchist was expressing "a simple protest against the contemporary social organization." These men, who functioned beyond and against the law of the state, were characterized as

individuals, social outcasts [*déchets sociaux*] in defiance of a society of which they are the victims, by whose laws they feel burdened—these are the outlaws who adorn themselves with the name of anarchists. They assert themselves as such without knowing what anarchy is.[2]

The social composition of the movement was, in part at least, made up of discontented people who had little notion of what opposition politics was about. They were attracted by the pamphlets which poured forth from the anarchist printing presses stressing the ideology of retribution against their common enemy, the state. Their terrorist behavior was the result of a "disequilibrium" produced by the propaganda: "their minds were not able to comprehend the true grandeur of the [anarchist] morality."[3]

In this way, anarchism combined within itself the extremes of intellectuals such as Kropotkin and Tolstoy, surrounded by an aura of unimpeachable moral conduct, together with assassins and bandit-outlaws such as Ravachol and Sazonov. What these widely disparate individuals shared was a common attitude toward society and the state. It was an attitude of profound alienation cutting across all social class lines from urban aristocrat to rural peasant. Anarchists, in thought and deed, were striking out against centralized authority in favor of a primitive, simplistic, somewhat romantic culture based on the fulfilment of need. There was in addition a strong belief that customs and morals native to a people (*moeurs*) are superior and provide more

2 Augustine Hamon, *Psychologie de l'anarchiste-socialiste* (Paris: P. V. Stock, 1895), p. 15.

3 Ibid., p. 284. For a recent treatment of anarchists as social bandits, see E. J. Hobsbawm, *Primitive Rebels* (New York: Norton, 1965).

liberty than the legislated legal systems of state institutions. Laws must be destroyed, not obeyed, in order for man to be free. Yet one can ask with Camus, "is a world without laws a free world?"[4]

II

In the general history of anarchism, the name of Peter Alekseevich Kropotkin dominates the latter part of the nineteenth century. After Bakunin's death in 1876, Kropotkin was unquestionably the most widely read and respected anarchist theorist. Yet, although his revolutionary activities are extremely important in any consideration of the Russian revolutionary movement or of the history of European socialism, no scholarly biography of Kropotkin exists in any language. Prolific though he was in writing, his complete works have never been collected and published in their entirety. Many of his books, articles, and pamphlets—not to mention an infinitely large correspondence, much of which remains unpublished—are scattered in the pages of relatively obscure journals and newspapers in Russia, France, Switzerland, England, North and South America.[5]

Kropotkin's career as a revolutionary can be divided into three segments: his formative years in Russia (1842–76), his

4 Albert Camus, *The Rebel* (New York: Vintage, 1956), p. 158. Camus is concerned with the interrelationship between revolutionary terror and the "military socialism" of the victorious opposition. For a consideration of anarchism and the avant-garde, see Renato Poggioli, *The Theory of the Avant-Garde* (Cambridge, Mass.: Harvard University Press, Belknap Press, 1968), pp. 98–100.

5 Aside from a number of short biographical propaganda pamphlets by anarchists, often written hastily and under difficult conditions, there is George Woodcock and Ivan Avakumovic, *The Anarchist Prince* (London and New York: T. V. Boardman, 1950) and Jean Delphy and Fernand Planche, *Kropotkine* (Paris: Editions S.L.I.M., 1948). The most thorough Kropotkin bibliography is in Aleksei Alekseevich Borovoi and Nikolai Konstantinovich Lebedev, eds., *Sbornik statei posviashchennyi pamiati P. A. Kropotkina* (Moscow-Petrograd: Golos truda, 1922), pp. 190–249. One should also consult the entries in Max Nettlau, *Bibliographie de l'anarchie* (Paris: P. V. Stock, 1897), pp. 72–86, 238–9. For a complete bibliography of Kropotkin's published and unpublished works prior to 1876, see Martin A. Miller, *The Formative Years of P. A. Kropotkin, 1842–1876: A Study of the Origins and Development of Populist Attitudes in Russia* (Ph.D. diss., University of Chicago, 1967), pp. 391–404.

mature years while living as an émigré in Western Europe (1876-1917), and his last years in the Soviet Union to which he returned after the revolution (1917-1921).

Prince Kropotkin was born in Moscow on December 12, 1842, the youngest of four children. His ancestry was aristocratic on both sides, but his paternal ancestry could be traced back to the original ruling dynasty of Russia, the Riurik house. His father owned several estates and an estimated twelve hundred serfs, a sufficiently large number for a landowner in the twilight years of legal serfdom. As a child, he was subjected to a rigid upbringing.[6] Virtually his entire waking day was regulated according to his father's will. Private tutors, both foreign and Russian, supervised his formal education, which included not only a knowledge of European languages and culture but also manners, dress, and even recreation.

In a sense, Kropotkin's life was a fusion of Russian and European cultural influences. Growing up in Russia, he continually reached out for European culture; later in Europe, he could never forget the Russia he had left behind, and his later writings were unmistakably colored by his formative years in that country. Fundamentally, his anarchist ideology was a reaction to the experiences he had at home as a child and in the Russian military service. This reaction later assumed a political configuration, rooted as it was in a curious mixture of the revolutionary populism and philosophical materialism which were persuasive intellectual currents in Russia during the 1860s and 1870s.[7]

Kropotkin's years of school at the exclusive Corps of Pages in St. Petersburg (1857-62) and his years in the Russian military and civil service (1862-72) were in many ways a preparation for

6 See Nikolai Konstantinovich Lebedev, ed., *Perepiska Petra i Aleksandra Kropotkinykh* (Moscow-Leningrad: Academia, 1932), vol. 1, *passim* and Peter Kropotkin, *Memoirs of a Revolutionist*, ed. James Allen Rogers (Garden City, New York: Doubleday Anchor, 1962), pp. 1-54.

7 This argument is documented and analyzed in detail in Miller, *The Formative Years*, chap. I.

the revolutionary career he was to choose. He had an opportunity (rare for revolutionaries among his contemporaries) to witness the mechanics of government administration and military discipline firsthand. For a year he was *page de chambre* of Emperor Alexander II, toward whom Peter initially felt a strong sense of admiration before becoming completely disillusioned with court politics. At the same time, he began to channel and articulate the sense of emotional discontent he felt during these years. Just before entering school, he had edited a handwritten journal called *Vremennik* (after Chernyshevskii's *Sovremennik*) which he and his brother distributed to a small number of sympathetic friends; later while in military service in eastern Siberia he became a newspaper correspondent for the *Moskovskiia vedomosti* (1862-67). These were his first experiences in critical writing on aspects of Russian society and served as the foundation for his radical journalism later as the editor of the anarchist organ *Le Révolté*, and as a collaborator on numerous other anarchist publications in Western Europe.[8]

Other lessons were learned during these preparatory years. After graduating first in his class from one of the most prestigious military schools in Russia, Kropotkin could have chosen virtually any ministry or guard regiment to begin his service and eventually could have risen to the rank of a high functionary. Instead he chose a Cossack regiment in remote eastern Siberia to serve as a military administrator. He felt his education had been largely wasted and his major concern at this time was to occupy himself in a "useful" pursuit. He considered entering the university as "a boring two years" of listening to lectures given by "various fools." He wrote to his brother on May 10, 1861: "I truly desire to be someone useful," and he was con-

---

8 *Le Révolté*, published in Geneva and Paris between 1879 and 1887, has been called "the most influential anarchist paper since the disappearance of Proudhon's *Le Peuple* in 1850" by George Woodcock, in *Anarchism* (Cleveland: Meridian, 1962), p. 198. Kropotkin's articles in "Sovremennaia letopis'," a supplement to the *Moskovskiia vedomosti*, have never been translated or republished. Collections of his later journalism can be found in *Paroles d'un révolté* (Paris: Flammarion, 1885) and in *The Conquest of Bread* (New York: Vanguard Press, 1926).

vinced that this goal was unattainable in a "glorious post" in a ministry.[9]

The years in eastern Siberia were years of self-discovery which led ultimately to a career not in the service of the Russian state but in the service of revolution directed against all national states. Kropotkin at first believed that reform in Russia was possible, but his experience serving on penal reform committees proved to him the hopelessness of legal measures for improvement. The administrative committees which had been established as part of the 1861 peasant emancipation decrees either became functionally impotent or were entirely abandoned. Kropotkin was particularly disturbed when General Kukel, the liberal administrator under whom he served, was removed because he had been involved with revolutionaries exiled to Siberia. Before his departure however, Kukel sent Kropotkin on a mission to warn the exiled radical publicist Mikhailov that police agents from the capital were investigating the conditions of his confinement. During the visit, Kropotkin became friendly with Mikhailov, who gave him a copy of a book by Proudhon with the publicist's own marginal notes. This was Kropotkin's first acquaintance with anarchist ideas.

After renouncing his administrative duties, Kropotkin spent much of his time on geographical expeditions. His scientific interests were important nonetheless for his later interests. Aside from an original hypothesis on the formation of the Ice Age which was well received in scientific circles, he succeeded in formulating the basis for his theory of cooperation among the species of nature. This was later developed into the theory of mutual aid which Kropotkin posed as a challenge to the Darwin-Spencer conception of the survival of the fittest. Kropotkin's view was that the element of struggle was common to all species; but instead of being directed into competition among members of the same species, the struggle was "against all natural conditions unfavorable to the species." From this struggle, all species found that mutual protection and cooperation rather than

9 Lebedev, ed., *Perepiska*, 1: 222, 253.

competition against one another were critical for survival. Those who did not cooperate became extinct. "The unsociable species," Kropotkin wrote, "are doomed to decay."[10]

Also at this time Kropotkin began to deal with the question of authority over the masses, a conception which had great significance for his later thought. The following incident illustrates this attitude. During a brief visit to one of the towns along the Amur River, Kropotkin recorded in his diary the terrible living conditions he witnessed. The workers of these Siberian towns (many of whom were convicts and exiles deported there to work) appeared to him as an alienated and exploited class used for the profit of the state. The authorities could not deal with the immense disciplinary problems created by the workers, who were completely hostile to the political and social structure of the area. They stood apart from the Russian authorities as well as from the non-Russian natives. To the astonishment of the local administrators Kropotkin at one point intervened on behalf of some workers who had been severely punished for drunkenness. For Kropotkin, the system was wrong because it stripped away liberty and self-respect from the workers. The punishments were useless since they had nothing to do with solving the problem.[11] The basis of the conflict was the effect of authority itself. Kropotkin saw authority exercised by government as an unnatural condition. Government had created its own legitimacy, rather than being rooted in the natural needs of society. Man—and society—was in fundamental opposition to this authority. Left to their own devices, even these hardened laborers could learn to respect their own work and become socially responsible individuals. So long as they remained enslaved to a system which punished them for being what the system made them, they would never be able to alter their situation appreciably.

10 Peter Kropotkin, *Mutual Aid* (London: Heinemann, 1907), p. 293. In the introduction (pp. vii–ix) Kropotkin relates the Siberian experience to his later theories.

11 The incident is clearly described, together with Kropotkin's attitudes, in his *Dnevnik P. A. Kropotkina* (Moscow-Petrograd: Gosudarstvennoe izdatel'stvo, 1923), pp. 149–150.

Kropotkin finally resigned from military service in 1867. He found he could no longer accept the responsibilities or perform the obligations which his position demanded. Later, in his memoirs, Kropotkin explained his position at this time and related it to his upbringing.

Having been brought up in a serf owner's family, I entered active life, like all young men of my time, with a great deal of confidence in the necessity of commanding, ordering, scolding, punishing, and the like. But when, at an early stage, I had to manage serious enterprises and to deal with men, and when each mistake would lead at once to heavy consequences, I began to appreciate the difference between acting on the principle of command and discipline and acting on the principle of common understanding . . . Although I did not then formulate my observations in terms borrowed from party struggles, I may say now that I lost in Siberia whatever faith in state discipline I had cherished before. I was prepared to become an anarchist.[12]

Although older than most of those of the mid-century generation who turned to the growing revolutionary movement, Kropotkin threw himself into it in the early 1870s with all the passion of a convert who had at last committed himself to a career in opposition to the ruling regime. In the spring of 1872, he traveled briefly to Switzerland where he met many Russian émigrés closely identified with the Bakuninist section of the First International, read all the radical literature he could obtain, and attended numerous meetings of workers affiliated with the International. Returning to Petersburg, he was admitted to the Chaikovskii Circle, the most active revolutionary populist organization of the period. Because of his age (thirty at this time), his years as a government administrator, and his princely ancestry, Kropotkin was not accepted without suspicion on the part of many members of the circle.

Nevertheless, Kropotkin proved himself a loyal revolutionary despite ideological disagreements with a majority of the members. One memoirist, for instance, records that Kropotkin frequently engaged in "heated arguments on the question of the

12 Kropotkin, *Memoirs*, p. 148.

state and anarchy."[13] Kropotkin took a more extreme position in opposing the existence of the state (which few of his comrades were willing to accept), although he was in fundamental agreement with the major premises of the populist group; these included the necessity of revolutionary change and a belief that the primary force which could bring about change was that of the people. The best evidence for analyzing Kropotkin's political philosophy at this time is his 1873 manifesto. (See page 46.) Entitled "Must We Occupy Ourselves with an Examination of the Ideal of a Future System?," the manifesto was composed with the intention of providing a platform of views which could be accepted by the group as a theoretical foundation for revolutionary strategy and tactics. Interestingly, Proudhon appears in this essay as the only anarchist influence explicitly mentioned, although the influence of Bakunin's ideas is evident throughout.

III

The 1873 manifesto is Kropotkin's first major essay on politics. Many of the ideas which Kropotkin developed later can already be seen in an earlier form in this document. Fundamentally, the conceptualization of what he later called anarchist communism was a combination of economic egalitarianism and political liberty. Put in another way, he believed man had to be liberated from capitalism and the state in order to be free. It was on the issue of the state that Kropotkin's anarchism distinguished itself most markedly from other varieties of socialist (and populist) thought. He attempted to prove that the state was unnecessary for the accomplishment of the most vital functions needed for survival and defense. On the other hand, the existence of the state was the cause of most of society's evils. Reforming a

13 Leonid Emmanuilovich Shishko, *Sergei Mikhailovich Kravchinskii i kruzhok Chaikovtsev* (n.p., n.d. [St. Petersburg, 1906]), p. 11. On the Chaikovskii Circle, see Martin A. Miller, "Ideological Conflicts in Russian Populism: The Revolutionary Manifestoes of the Chaikovskii Circle, 1869-1874," *Slavic Review*, vol. 29, no. 1 (March, 1970), pp. 1-24.

basically corrupt institution was futile; it had to be entirely swept away in revolution if true progress was to occur.

This line of reasoning led Kropotkin in this essay to a critical examination of all forms of government. He had to refute the presumed benefits of republican and democratic systems of authority as well as to show why the tsarist autocracy in Russia needed to be overthrown. His picture of Western constitutional government was one of acquisitive and egotistical individuals skilled at maneuvering the political party in power to greater exploitation of the masses. The parties themselves were unrepresentative of the people since the majority of the citizens were disenfranchised or ignorant of the realities of politics. Worse, the constitutional parties acted as a bulwark against radical change: by machinations and clever rationales, the parties convinced the masses that they possessed political rights, which in turn served to diminish their revolutionary initiative. Such governments dominated the press, controlled opinion and froze the unequal social class divisions which were a necessary part of any bourgeois system.

Several other subjects which find fuller elaboration in later writings are discussed in detail in the 1873 essay. Kropotkin was quite concerned about the role of education in society. He felt that education as it was institutionalized in contemporary societies was one of the major factors responsible for preserving political, economic, and social inequalities. Students were predominantly from the upper classes and aspired to the highest ranks of the state to receive the rewards it offered. Education was an intellectual luxury unconcerned with the needs of the people at large. Transformed through revolution, education could be adapted to train everyone in a society to perform a necessary task which would in turn dignify the nature of labor and end the class divisions of educated elites and uneducated masses. The focal point for the newly trained masses would be rural communes (*obshchiny*), each of which could produce various products necessary for the welfare of society in general. These small units would voluntarily unite for purposes of exchange or defense for mutual benefit. All of this was to be established without any government, administration, or legal system.

These conceptions received more sophisticated expression in Kropotkin's later essays.[14] A historical dimension was added to indicate the influence of anarchy in the past and to show how the whole of history was moving in the direction of the worldwide destruction of governments (see page 210, "The State: Its Historic Role"). While the 1873 manifesto was one of Kropotkin's most graphic illustrations of the postrevolutionary society under anarchism, he returned to this theme in the later essay "Expropriation" (see page 160). Here he described in detail the revolutionary tactic of seizing the means of production and all private property, and the methods of reapportioning this as "common property" on an equitable basis among the people. The necessity of abolishing the wage system and the means of replacing it were also considered. Taken together, the 1873 essay and "Expropriation" present the clearest picture of the anarchist society of the future which Kropotkin had in mind.

In the later essays Kropotkin introduced conceptions that can be found in other forms in the 1873 manifesto. His stress on the *obshchiny* as the basic units of the future revolutionary order was later superseded by the concept of the free commune. The major difference was that the *obshchina* was primarily a rural agricultural collective community in Russia whereas the commune for Kropotkin was an institution that could operate in an urban setting as well as in the countryside. In theory, the commune served the same function as the Russian *obshchiny*, that of providing a locus for the organizing centers of activities during the revolution and of acting as the foundation for the postrevolutionary society of decentralized, autonomous, and

14 In later essays, Kropotkin returned frequently to his critique of democratic systems of government. See "Representative Government," *Commonweal* (London), nos. 312–21 (1892) for a biting criticism. For his later views on education, see his article "Integral Education," *Freedom* (London), September 1901, p. 49. His position here was that education should combine "brain work" and "manual work" so that society would be composed of people with a knowledge of science and trades. Learning must have a purpose, which is first and foremost to aid the masses in improving their material conditions.

voluntarily cooperating units. Kropotkin also believed that the commune had been the historical force which had stood against the encroaching effects of the state in the past. (See his essay "The Commune of Paris," page 118.)

Another conception which underwent such an evolution was the notion of the revolutionary party. In the 1873 essay Kropotkin emphasized the importance of a radical party dedicated to populist ideals which was to aid in bringing about the revolution. In his later writings, he was critical of parties because he became convinced that control of the masses by a party elite would lead to worse problems once the revolution was victorious, namely, the establishment of a revolutionary government by a party or faction. Past revolutions had failed precisely because the masses had been convinced by their leaders to establish a representative body which would organize a new revolutionary government. This for Kropotkin was a contradiction in terms. Such a representative body inevitably assumed political authority and thereby degenerated into an obstacle to the realization of a true revolutionary society. Thus, government and revolution were incompatible; "outside of anarchy there is no such thing as revolution" and revolution could only be accomplished by the initiative of the people themselves. Revolutionary authority was no better than the authority it had overthrown.[15]

Two final concepts should be mentioned in connection with the origins of Kropotkin's ideology and the 1873 essay. First, the kind of revolution Kropotkin called for was a social revolution. The concept was already present in the 1873 manifesto and was subsequently expanded. By his use of this term, Kropotkin meant a complete transformation of society. It was intended to go beyond a mere *coup d'état* or even replacing a reactionary

15 Peter Kropotkin, *Revolutionary Government* (London: Freedom Press, 1923), p. 7. Recognizing the strength of trade unions in Europe, Kropotkin later tried to transform them into agents of revolution. The time had come, he wrote, for trade unions "to enter a new period of constructive activity." They must aspire to "take possession" of the cities and the land, and not be satisfied with piecemeal reform. ("The Development of Trade Unionism," *Freedom*, March 1898, pp. 9-10.)

government by a so-called revolutionary government. The social revolution was the violent destruction of all governmental forms of legal authority and the transition to autonomous free federations of communes ruling themselves without the state and without capitalism. To achieve this stage of free or anarchist communism, it was imperative to recognize "that the material guarantee of existence of all members of the community shall be the first act of the social revolution."[16] The justice of and rationale for the social revolution was evident from Kropotkin's belief that it was the means of reconquering that which had originally belonged to the people, that which had been usurped from them by princes, priests, and property owners throughout history.

Second, when discussing the mechanics of radical change, Kropotkin repeatedly referred to the people as the basic motivating force. This aspect of his thinking was intimately associated with his experiences in Russia and specifically with the ideology of populism. As has been mentioned, Kropotkin had come to identify with the plight of the people from an early age in a specific manner. The antithesis between authority and freedom which he encountered in eastern Siberia was conceptualized as a conflict between man and the state. In addition, during the early 1870s while in the Chaikovskii Circle, he accepted the Bakuninist position on the role of the people in the revolutionary struggle. This meant giving priority to the spontaneity of the masses rather than to the consciousness of the intelligentsia as the primary factor in a revolt. The people already possessed the instinct for revolution; intellectuals had to try to understand how the revolutionary potential of the masses actually functioned and how to encourage its expression, but could not attempt to direct or control the drive of the people to rebellion. Kropotkin never lost this unquestioned faith in the revolutionary instinct of the masses. He assumed that they would know what tactics to employ during the actual revolution and that, aside from occasional exceptions, they would be capable of running the new society with justice and without vindictiveness

16 Peter Kropotkin, *Anarchism: Its Philosophy and Ideal*, Freedom Pamphlets, no. 10, 1897, p. 16.

toward their old masters. Examples of the corollary of this position, an intolerant anti-intellectualism, abound in Kropotkin's writings.[17]

IV

In addition to Kropotkin's leading role as a theorist for the Chaikovskii Circle between 1872 and 1874, he was also one of the the group's most successful propagandists. At many meetings arranged by the circle for workers, Kropotkin lectured on various revolutionary themes and discussed these ideas with his audience. He also helped establish the Moscow branch of the Chaikovskii Circle and was on the verge of moving into the countryside to agitate among the peasantry when he was arrested in March 1874. After a two-year confinement in the notorious Peter and Paul Fortress in St. Petersburg, Kropotkin secured a transfer to a military prison hospital on the basis of his declining health. The hospital's system of surveillance was far less stringent than that of the fortress, which enabled him to communicate with his friends still at large and to organize a plan for escape. The escape, boldly and masterfully executed in broad daylight on June 30, 1876, created a scandal in the government and was justly celebrated by revolutionaries as one of the most sensational of the century. Kropotkin secretly made his way to England by ship where he began a period of emigration that was to last over forty years.

Although Kropotkin managed to overcome the suspicions of his comrades in the Chaikovskii Circle during his revolutionary activities between 1872–74, he was always considered somewhat apart from the other members because of his background. One comment that appears frequently in the memoir literature is that Kropotkin seemed more European than Russian. This was partly due to the fact that few of the revolutionary populists in Russia had traveled abroad as Kropotkin

17 On the arguments over consciousness and spontaneity in Russia, see Franco Venturi, *Roots of Revolution* (New York: Alfred A. Knopf, 1960), chap. 17 (pp. 429–68). On the theme of anti-intellectualism, see Paul Avrich, *The Russian Anarchists* (Princeton, N.J.: Princeton University Press, 1967), chap. 4 (pp. 91–119).

had in 1872 and few possessed his ability to read European languages. One of the circle members who knew Kropotkin wrote later that he considered him "a European from head to foot."[18] Russian émigrés who saw Kropotkin in Europe shortly after his escape in 1876 from imprisonment in St. Petersburg attest to his adjustment to European culture and to a lessening of his concern for the Russian revolutionary movement.

> Soon after his arrival abroad, he went totally into the International movement, and the problems of the revolutionary struggle in Russia, such as they were, fell into the background for him. Having a mastery of European languages, he immediately immersed himself in the Western European movement . . .[19]

In reality, the adjustment was not without some difficulties (for example, in England he was reduced to communicating by writing notes in restaurants and rooming houses since he could not speak English clearly enough) and he did not completely disengage himself from the Russian movement, as his European writings and letters clearly show. He did realize, however, that he could not live in Russia except underground and illegally, and he was unwilling to undergo the hardships of that life. His decision to remain abroad was prompted also by his belief that the revolution would probably occur in Europe before Russia and by a disagreement over the tactics employed by the leading radical parties which had succeeded the Chaikovskii Circle.[20]

Kropotkin quickly rose to a prominent position in the anarchist movement, initially through his participation in the congresses of the late 1870s and, later, through his radical

18 (Leon) Lev Tikhomirov, *Vospominaniia* (Moscow: Gosizdat, 1927), p. 79.

19 (Paul) Pavel Borisovich Akselrod, *Perezhitoe i peredumannoe* (Berlin: Grzhevina, 1923), I: 183–4.

20 The focus of the Russian revolutionary movement had shifted in the late 1870s from arousing the peasantry to organizing a direct struggle against the tsar. Of this change Kropotkin wrote: "I always believed that revolutionary agitation ought to be carried out mainly among the peasants for the preparation of a peasant uprising . . . I could not convince myself that even the successful assassination of the tsar could have any significant direct results even in the sense of political freedom." (Kropotkin, *Memoirs*, p. 327).

journalism which extended over several decades. Kropotkin was present at the St. Imier International Congress at Verviers in Belgium in September 1877, which consisted of the anti-Marxist faction of the First International, and also at the International Socialist Congress held in Ghent a week later. These meetings pointed out clearly that the dissension between the followers of Marx and Bakunin was too great to bring about the unity that many socialists hoped for. Kropotkin's role in these gatherings was cut short by the threat of arrest, and he left the Ghent Congress abruptly to return to England where he had been residing since his escape from Russia the year before.

At the Jura Congress of 1879, Kropotkin's ideas received greater notoriety. In his speech, Kropotkin discussed the concept of expropriation of all land and property, which was to be carried out by local communes. He emphasized the role of the commune in the transition period between the destruction of the state and the beginning of the anarchist society. He was at this time quite conscious of specific problems in different countries and attempted to take them into consideration.[21]

In 1881, an effort was made to reconstitute permanently the anarchist sections of the First International. The International Anarchist Congress met in London and passed many resolutions to this end, although the unification was not to be realized and the next anarchist congress on an international level was not held until 1907. The 1881 congress did, however, codify the tactic which was to dominate the movement for many years: "propaganda by the deed." The interpretation of this position was not unanimous partly because there were differences of views on what deeds should be carried out and who should initiate them. Kropotkin, one of the more prominent participants at the congress, presented a viewpoint which

21 The speech, entitled "Idée anarchiste au point de vue de sa réalisation practique" was subsequently published in Kropotkin's paper *Le Révolté* (Geneva), November 1, 1879 and as a separate pamphlet. See also Max Nettlau, *Der Anarchismus von Proudhon zu Kropotkin* (Berlin: Der Syndicalist, 1927), pp. 289-95 and Charles Thomann, *Le mouvement anarchiste dans les montagnes neuchâteloises et le Jura bernois* (La Chaux-de-Fonds: Imprimerie des cooperatives réunis, 1947), pp. 134-39.

stopped short of justifying individual terrorism but which gave implicit justification for mass action against the state:

> If we believe that it is sufficient to overthrow the government, then we will become an army of conspirators, but we in Jura and in Lyon at least, do not conceive of the revolution in this way. The next revolution must from its inception bring about the seizure of the entire social wealth by the workers in order to transform it into common property. This revolution can succeed only through the workers, only if the urban and rural workers everywhere carry out this objective themselves. To that end, they must initiate their own action in the period *before the revolution*; this can happen only if there is a strong *workers' organization*. The revolutionary bourgeoisie can overthrow a government but it cannot make the revolution; this only the people can do.[22]

Kropotkin went on to outline the role of the anarchists in this connection. He urged the formation of small revolutionary groups which were to "submerge" themselves in the workers' organizations, to arouse the revolutionary aspirations of the people. This formulation was clearly reminiscent of the Russian populist concept of "fusing with the people" which the Bakuninists of the Russian movement had favored in the middle 1870s. In the language of the report of the committee on resolutions for the 1881 congress, it became a concept meant to activate popular discontent specifically against governmental authorities: "the simplest deed performed against existing institutions is better for the masses than thousands of publications and a flood of words."[23]

The interpretation of what acts were permissible under the heading of "propaganda by the deed" became a subject of much debate as assassination and terrorism became increasingly important as tactics employed by anarchists and anarchist sympathizers in the last quarter of the nineteenth century.

22 Max Nettlau, *Anarchisten und Sozialrevolutionäre* (Berlin: Asy Verlag, 1931), p. 208.

23 Ibid., p. 221. Kropotkin's paper had already accepted the concept: "Permanent revolt by word of mouth, in writing, by the dagger, the rifle, dynamite . . . Everything is good for us which goes beyond legality." (*Le Révolté*, December 25, 1880; quoted in Jean Maitron, *Histoire du mouvement anarchiste en France* (1880–1914) [Paris: Société universitaire, 1951], p. 70).

The assassination of Emperor Alexander II of Russia on March 1, 1881 (itself preceded by other terrorist acts), was a dramatic introduction to the leitmotiv of *attentats* which haunted ministers and government leaders of all countries. Explosions became more and more frequent, reaching a peak around the turn of the century: Ravachol allegedly was responsible for eleven dynamite blasts in Paris between 1892 and 1894 in which at least nine people were killed in the name of anarchism, and six heads of state were assassinated between 1894 and 1912 by persons frequently associated with anarchist ideas.[24]

Terror did not always work from Left to Right. Kropotkin found himself the object of an assassination plot organized in Russia by the government in the aftermath of the emperor's murder. In 1881, Kropotkin, then living in Geneva, discovered that tsarist agents had been sent abroad to kill him. The plan was never carried out primarily because Kropotkin publicly exposed the names of the individuals involved and the details of the attempt to murder him. In addition to being printed in his own paper, the story was carried by several British newspapers including the *Times*. Kropotkin claimed later that the well-known Russian writer Saltykov-Shchedrin learned of the plot and traveled abroad to aid Kropotkin. Eventually the information got to the revolutionary émigré Peter Lavrov who passed it on to Kropotkin. Officials of the Russian police and government were implicated in the disclosure.[25]

Moreover, the anarchist movement was constantly being infiltrated by police agents. One agent named Serraux in Paris even managed to run an anarchist journal (*La Révolution Sociale*)

24 These were President Carnot of France (1894), Premiers Canovas (1897) and Canalejas (1912) of Spain, Empress Elizabeth of Austria (1898), King Humbert of Italy (1900), President McKinley of the United States (1901). On the career of Ravachol, see Jean Maitron, *Ravachol et les anarchistes* (Paris: René Julliard, 1964).

25 On this incident, see Kropotkin's letter in *Russkiia vedomosti*, no. 251 (October 31, 1912), p. 3, and Nikolai Konstantinovich Lebedev, "P. A. Kropotkin i narodovol'tsy," *1 Marta 1881 goda* (Moscow: Politkatorzhan, 1933), pp. 128-9. See also Kropotkin's *Memoirs*, pp. 277-83 where he describes this affair in the context of what he calls "the golden age of the Russian secret police."

financed by the police which contained articles by some of the most outstanding theorists of the movement; Kropotkin, to his credit, consistently refused to contribute to this journal. One of Kropotkin's most interesting published correspondences is the exchange of letters with Vladimir Burtsev concerning espionage in the movement during the first decade of this century. Burtsev, a Russian refugee and editor of a radical journal dedicated to the Russian revolutionary movement, uncovered information which implicated many members of the revolutionary parties (including the anarchists) as *agents provocateurs*. At first, Kropotkin refused to believe what seemed preposterous and criticized Burtsev for soiling the image of the Left with his exposures. However, on July 10, 1909, Kropotkin congratulated Burtsev on the exposure of the celebrated spy Azef. By this time he had come to realize that the police had planted many of the bombs attributed to revolutionaries and that the anarchists "had been used (*byl ogurachen*)" as "their tools." A little later he admitted that there was a need for "cleaning house" among revolutionaries because the Jacobin tactics of terror had caused mistrust and had "gotten to the point of making our action useless."[26]

Kropotkin's attitude toward terror was highly ambiguous. He is usually depicted as a man of angelic humanism and high ethics who was disgusted by the assassinations and bombings. The evidence indicates, however, that although he found violence abhorrent as a tactic, he frequently accepted it in the context of desperate acts committed by men responding to unbearable conditions. He justified the assassination of Alexander II in the clearest of terms. In his newspaper *Le Révolté* he wrote that "the events of March 1 are an enormous step toward the approaching revolution in Russia; and those who have prepared and carried out this deed, who have imprinted their blood upon this heroic act, have not sacrificed themselves in vain."[27] Upon learning of the assassination of the Austrian

26 "Pis'ma P. A. Kropotkina k V. L. Burtsevu," *Na chuzhoi storone*, VI (1924): 131 and 141–2 (letter of February 28, 1911).

27 Quoted in Lebedev, "Kropotkin i narodovol'tsy," p. 124.

Empress Elizabeth, Kropotkin wrote to his friend Georg Brandes, the Danish literary critic, that the guilt and responsibility for the crime belong to society: "Individuals are not to blame; they are driven mad by horrible conditions. Such a man was Luccheni, the assassin." These acts will go on "so long as contempt for human life shall be taught to men and so long as they will be told that it is good to kill for what one believes to be beneficial for mankind."[28] In a letter to his friend Nikolai Vasil'evich Chaikovskii (after whom the Russian revolutionary circle had been named in the 1870s) on February 2, 1895, Kropotkin wrote that terror can only be understood by those "who have experienced the effects which called it into being." He also approvingly quoted a phrase of his old comrade Kravchinskii's: "Terror is horrible; there is only one thing worse than terror and that is to submissively suffer violence."[29]

On the other hand, Kropotkin did oppose strongly what he considered mindless and purposeless terror. When faced with extreme positions such as the proposal of mass violence and terror, he vigorously denounced these tactics from both a practical and ethical viewpoint. In one article, he considered the possibility of violently exterminating the middle class as a means of destroying the state but rejected it outright. He argued that a revolutionary minority could not massacre the middle class because it composed the majority in most nations and because such bloodshed could not be justified by any rational objective. In rejecting mass violence, he needed a convincing alternative.

In order to conquer, something more than guillotines are required. It is the revolutionary *idea*, the truly wide revolutionary conception which reduces its enemies to impotence by paralyzing all the instruments by which they have governed hitherto.

Very sad would be the future of the revolution if it could only triumph by terror.[30]

28 Letter of Kropotkin to Georg Brandes, *Freedom*, October 1898, pp. 68-9.

29 "Pis'ma P. A. Kropotkina k N. V. Chaikovskomu," *Russkii istoricheskii arkhiv* (Prague) I (1929): 307.

30 P. Kropotkin, "Revolutionary Studies," *Commonweal* (London), vol. 7, no. 296 (January 9, 1892).

The alternative to the impulse for massive terror was a spirit and an idea of revolution which was to guide the masses toward constructive tasks. The role of the people, central as it was to any revolution, "ought to be *positive* at the same time as it is destructive."[31]

On another occasion, Kropotkin discovered that an anarchist periodical had justified mass terror as a revolutionary tactic and he wrote an angry letter to a friend on the subject. He called the article "outrageous" and feared that this type of propaganda would turn away potential converts among the youth. Worse was the fear that "terror may become the *only* kind of propaganda, which would be a horrible result."[32] According to a memoirist who knew and worked with Kropotkin in Paris in 1905, he accepted terror as a tactic but "only in exceptional instances when it provides a great stimulus for the revolutionary arousal of the masses."[33] Kropotkin's equivocal attitude toward this problem has rarely been stated so aptly.

Nevertheless, Kropotkin himself suffered as a result of the identification of anarchism with terrorism. In 1881, Kropotkin was expelled from Switzerland under pressure from the Russian government. He took refuge in France but ran into worse problems. The following year, after a series of explosions and riots in central France, the police arrested a number of anarchists including Kropotkin. In January 1883 in Lyons, sixty-five anarchists (of which only fifty-one had actually been arrested) were accused of having been responsible for the acts. When it became clear in the course of the trial that there was insufficient evidence to convict the accused of these crimes, the prosecution resorted to an old law against joining the International.

31 Ibid., no. 300 (February 6, 1892).

32 "Pis'ma P. A. Kropotkina k V. N. Cherkezovu," *Katorga i ssylka*, 1926, no. 4 (25), pp. 15–16. (Letter of January 8, 1904). The article which aggravated Kropotkin appeared in *Khleb i volia*, no. 5, 1903 (December) anonymously and was entitled "K kharakteristike nashei taktiki." The article claimed that all individual terrorist deeds were "heroic acts" and led to "the one menacing massive terror" which would bring down "the entire capitalist structure."

33 Ivan Knizhnik, "Vospominaniia o P. A. Kropotkine i ob odnoi anarkhicheskoi emigrantskoi gruppe," *Krasnaia letopis'*, no. 4 (1922), p. 33.

Actually, the International was defunct, and of the accused only Kropotkin had ever belonged to it. Before his conviction, Kropotkin gave an eloquent and passionate defense speech in which he charged the prosecution, as representatives of the legal authority of the state, with creating the disorders themselves through the persecution of revolutionaries and workers. In a moment of excessive optimism, he declared to the court: "Believe me, gentlemen, the social revolution is near. It will break out within ten years. I live among the workers and I am sure of it. Take inspiration from their ideas, join their ranks and you will see that I am right."[34] Nevertheless, Kropotkin, who was then forty, was sentenced to prison in Clairvaux for five years.

Kropotkin did not serve the entire sentence however. After a series of protests from French and British intellectuals on his behalf, Kropotkin was released on January 15, 1886. He proceeded to England where he resided for the next thirty years. Photographs from the early nineties show him to have aged beyond his years and his health grew increasingly worse. He began to appear less frequently at political meetings and public gatherings, and aside from his trips to America in 1897 and 1901, he rarely left his residences in Harrow and Bromley.

V

During the years when his international reputation as the leading anarchist theoretician was at its zenith, one of Kropotkin's major concerns was his critique of social democracy. Kropotkin's hostility to Marx developed during his first trip to Switzerland in the spring of 1872, when he became attracted to the Bakuninist faction of the International. There was evidence of this feeling in the 1873 manifesto, particularly when Kropotkin discussed the dangers of authority in any form and the threat posed by the concentration of power. In his memoirs, he alluded to his initial encounter with *Das Kapital* while a member of the Chaikovskii Circle in St. Petersburg.

34 For the entire speech, see *Freedom*, vol. 28, no. 13 (April 29, 1967).

He claimed to have found the book pretentious and unscientific. "The excursions of Marx into the realm of quantitative expression and algebraic formula were ridiculous," he wrote. [35]

Whether or not Kropotkin underestimated Marx and Marxist theory in the 1870s is difficult to establish, but the challenge of Marxism and social democracy became undeniably apparent to him once he became a resident of Western Europe. Virtually every issue of his newspaper contains critical articles on Marxism. Indeed, some of Kropotkin's most enduring anarchist polemics were fashioned out of his appreciation of the threat posed by the social democratic Left. Aside from his bias against dialectical theory which presumed to express certain social and economic laws, Kropotkin believed the greatest danger in the popularity of Marxism to be its principle of authority and power. He labeled German social democracy "state socialism" and criticized it for cooperating with Bismarckian policies. This was merely another form of authority to be imposed upon the people. Just as revolutionary government was a contradictory term to him, so was state socialism. Revolution and socialism could not be truly realized or completed unless all authority was ended, whether of the Left or the Right. Kropotkin put his hopes for transformation in the masses, not in socialist parties: "everything which issues from the life of the people must move against this statist course" in the socialist movement.[36] He even claimed that Marxists did not really desire revolution and tried to indicate how they were in fact working against the coming revolution. He believed that the organizational tactics of social democracy were smothering the revolutionary instinct of the people. For a revolution to be successful, it was necessary to have "fatal encounters" between the masses and the representatives of power. These encounters which constitute the prelude to revolution in the

35 Kropotkin, *Memoirs*, p. 319. One contemporary was suspicious of Kropotkin's actual knowledge of Marx's work and was doubtful "if he had familiarized himself with Marx's theories at that time." (Akselrod, *Perezhitoc*, I: 183).
36 "Pis'ma P. A. Kropotkina k N. V. Chaikovskomu," p. 311. (Letter of April 22, 1897).

form of riots, strikes, and uprisings could occur only when unencumbered by socialist doctrines and rigid control by intellectuals. According to Kropotkin, social democracy would interfere with these outbreaks: "that is its historical function. For that it was created"[37].

Kropotkin was not convinced of the originality of Marx's theories. When Cherkezov wrote that he thought he had proved Marx's eclecticism and plagiarism, Kropotkin heartily concurred. Kropotkin also believed that Marx's ideas could be traced back to Adam Smith, Blanqui, and other earlier writers.[38] He thought it was unfortunate that Marx's followers refused to see this and chose instead, as Kropotkin noted in the case of Russia, to propound these theories as original and messianic. His comment after reading the articles of Plekhanov and Lenin in *Iskra*, the Russian social democratic organ, was that they were slavishly ignorant. He pitied the revolutionary youth of Russia "who have not escaped the light of Liebknecht" and who did not "wish to know any other light."[39]

Kropotkin realized the significance of the ideological schism between Marx and Bakunin over control of the First International. The critical juncture had been reached in 1872 when Bakunin and his followers were expelled from the organization. Marx's victory had been expensive: the International was unable to survive and the entire movement never completely recovered from the wounds incurred in the struggle. The vicious arguments and polemics continued, with the anarchists feeling themselves pure and noble outcasts who had been out-maneuvered and overpowered by a more unscrupulous and less moral foe. As a result, the anarchists shifted to the tactics of "propaganda by the deed" in the early 1880s in a desperate

37 Ibid., pp. 315–16 (Letter of August 21, 1901). For a Marxist response to Kropotkin's views of social democracy see Henry M. Hyndman, *The Record of an Adventurous Man* (New York: Macmillan, 1911), pp. 240–45.

38 "Pis'ma P. A. Kropotkina k V. N. Cherkezovu," pp. 9–10 (Letter of May 25, 1900). Cherkezov felt that Marx had actually plagiarized the work of Considérant, the disciple of Fourier.

39 Ibid., pp. 13–14 (Letter of November 28, 1902).

effort to win support from the masses. The logic of this ideology pushed some anarchists to extremes that neither government nor socialist would tolerate. Kropotkin chose the pen as his major weapon to strike back at the Marxist wing, depicting their tendency toward authoritarianism as corrupt, evil, and unrevolutionary. The warfare continued between anarchists and social democrats, largely on a polemical level in the pages of party organs, until the socialist triumph in Russia in 1917 brought the combat to the level of physical violence as well. Despite this, the expression used by the anarchist historian Nettlau to describe Marxist social democrats is particularly revealing: "our friends the enemy."

Kropotkin also considered other forms of socialist thought. His attitude toward syndicalism was generally sympathetic. He did accept the tactic of the general strike as a means of securing the revolution. The goals, however, had to remain antiauthoritarian. Kropotkin would not tolerate new economic power centers as a result of the general strike but did see the possibility for strong workers' organizations in the syndicalist movement. Perhaps the most appealing aspect of syndicalism for Kropotkin was the stress placed on the need for workers themselves to make decisions concerning revolutionary action and the new organization of society. He also accepted the federalized, cooperating nature of the *syndicats* and labor unions but was wary of the syndicalist tendency to concentrate on the urban proletariat and thereby ignore the interests of the rural peasantry.[40]

Kropotkin distinguished his own anarchist communism from the collectivism of other anarchists. He had first proposed the need for anarchists to abandon the collectivist idea at the 1880 congress of the Jura Federation of the International. In his presentation, he argued that the goal of complete public ownership of both the means and the fruits of production was

40 For his attitude on this subject, see his article "Sindikalizm i anarkhizm," ed. Grigorii Maksimov, *Internatsional'nyi sbornik posviashchennyi desiatoi godovshchine smerti P. A. Kropotkina* (Chicago: Federatsiia russkikh anarkho-kommunisticheskikh grupp, 1931), pp. 88–98.

best described as communist. The major bone of contention with collectivists was the method of remuneration of labor and the distribution of necessities in the new society. Kropotkin's position was the following:

Collectivists begin by proclaiming a revolutionary principle—the abolition of private property—and then they deny it, no sooner than proclaimed, by upholding an organization of production and consumption which originated in private property.[41]

By this he meant that collectivists would merely reestablish what they had worked to destroy through revolution if they introduced payment by labor checks as renumeration. Instead of wages, collectivists desired to use these checks which would be used to procure the necessities for the worker. This however was another wage system for the benefit of "the great collectivist employer—the state." A society which takes possession of all social wealth ought to proclaim free distribution for all and abolish all systems of remuneration and wages. The problems of determining the value of labor would merely reintroduce exploitation and competition. Kropotkin was against the notion of "to each according to his deeds" and desired instead "to put the needs above the works."[42]

In addition to the concept of communism, Kropotkin elaborated on other themes which his predecessors had neglected. Just as he tried to show the historical significance of anarchism, he attempted to outline its scientific and ethical foundation. To prove this, he claimed that anarchism was an explanation of the processes of nature and that "its method is

41 Kropotkin, *The Conquest of Bread*, p. 156. For the Jura Congress speech see *Le Révolté*, October 17, 1880.

42 Kropotkin, *The Conquest of Bread*, p. 164. Kropotkin's concept of anarchist anarchism was not completely original; Malatesta and others had formulated similar ideas as far back as 1879–1880. The position expressed here represents a shift from the 1873 manifesto where, under the influence of Proudhon and Bakunin, Kropotkin accepted the idea of labor value and remuneration notes. Although he differed with his predecessors on the issue of labor remuneration in all of his major works after leaving Russia, there are of course many points of agreement in their thinking. Nettlau's volumes should be consulted for any comparative analysis.

that of the exact sciences" in that all of its conclusions could be scientifically verified.[43] Certain laws concerning the operation of the civil order were deducible from natural phenomena; this in turn indicated how anarchist tendencies were part of the natural order. Basically, Kropotkin believed that an analogy could be drawn between the behavior of animal and human species on the one hand and the functions of nature on the other. His examples were connected to his conviction that, by nature, all societies rested on principles of harmony, solidarity, and cooperation. This for him was demonstrable and a scientific fact. Imbalance occurred when other forces were applied to established and natural equilibriums. Revolutions for human society were therefore as natural as volcanic eruptions in that each will always seek to reestablish the lawful natural equilibrium.

Force will accumulate its effect; it *must* come to light, it must exercise its action, and if other forces hinder its manifestation it will not be annihilated by that, but will end by upsetting the present adjustment, by destroying harmony, in order to find a new form of equilibrium and to work to form a new adaptation. Such is the eruption of a volcano, whose imprisoned force ends by breaking the petrified lavas which hindered them to pour forth the gases, the molten lavas, and the incandescent ashes. Such, also, are the revolutions of mankind.[44]

Kropotkin related his conception of the morality of anarchism directly to such scientific examples. In an essay devoted to this problem, he defined good as what is useful for the preservation of the species and evil as what is harmful to it. Morality was defined therefore, as "a natural need of animal races." Man's natural needs as an individual were identical with those of the whole society. The moral conflict arose in discovering how to combat the forces which sought to maintain inequality and exploitation. Immorality was whatever existed as compulsory. One could not convict murderers without attempting to discern the causes of what drove the individuals to kill. Morality,

43 Peter Kropotkin, "Modern Science and Anarchism," ed. Roger N. Baldwin, *Kropotkin's Revolutionary Pamphlets* (New York: Vanguard Press, 1927), p. 152.

44 Kropotkin, *Anarchism: Its Philosophy and Ideal*, p. 6.

Kropotkin continued, could not be legislated. Brutality and deceit existed only insofar as inequality existed, and the natural solidarity of society remained stifled by authority. Kropotkin argued for "the full and complete liberty of the individual" as the ethical basis of anarchism.[45] He stopped short of falling into the trap of having to accept egoism and extreme individualism only because he believed in the innate sociability and passivity of man, when allowed to be free without constraint from above.

The issue that proved to have the most damaging effect on the anarchist movement from within, aside from the problem of terror, was Kropotkin's position on World War I. Prior to 1914, his statements on war seem to follow consistently the position of most socialists and anarchists who viewed all war as a means for ruling classes of governments to increase their wealth and power at the expense of the masses. He spoke out against the Boer War at a time when patriotic fervor in England was high. On one occasion, he tried to indicate the responsibilities of workers in bringing wars such as this to an end. If the labor force unanimously refused to fight and demanded an end to the war, it would stop, he argued. Instead, they were blinded by the propaganda of the state and the middle classes who urged them to fight a war from which they could gain nothing. Kropotkin called for an international federation of trade unions "irrespective of political opinions and nationality" which would stand united against participation in war.[46]

In a letter of 1904, during the Russo-Japanese War, Kropotkin wrote that war and revolution were in opposition to one another. The war against Japan, he said, brings "great suffering to the Russian people and distracts its attention from domestic tasks." The revolutionary movement, which had been making great strides, "will be slowed down, perhaps even halted by this war." He went on to state that "every war is evil, whether it ends in victory or defeat; an evil for the belligerent

45 Peter Kropotkin, *Anarchist Morality*, Freedom Pamphlets, no. 6 (London, 1892), pp. 13, 17.

46 *Freedom,* September 1901, p. 50. (Letter read at a meeting on June 21, 1901.)

countries, an evil for the neutrals. I do not believe in 'beneficial' wars."[47]

Yet, these very pronouncements were reversed ten years later to the shock and embarrassment of many anarchists who maintained a pacifist position on the war. He published open letters in numerous newspapers and journals in various countries making his views quite explicit; he went so far as to have open letters published in Russian newspapers in which he argued for the necessity of defeating Germany.[48] The historian Mel'gunov took issue with the thesis of these letters, arguing that Kropotkin was only arousing militarism and chauvinism in Russia and elsewhere which would lead to the acceptance of war by workers and have disastrous consequences for the future of revolution. Kropotkin's reply is interesting. The same fear of damage to the coming revolution by war voiced in 1904 was now used to accept the framework of war for the purpose of securing the anticipated social revolution. If Germany triumphs, all revolutions will be put down, he wrote. This "horrible influence" would be limitless. In Europe and Russia, the revolutionary movement would be set back, crushed, and the power of governments would become even more repressive. Germany, therefore, had to be defeated. Kropotkin's image was of a Manichaean apocalyptic struggle, the outcome of which would determine whether Europe would descend into barbarism under German militarism or survive to continue progress toward revolution under Anglo-French hegemony.[49]

His arguments on the war were as doctrinaire as any of those of the socialists he had criticized earlier on other issues.

47 *Khleb i volia*, no. 7 (February 1904), p. 6. (Letter of February 18, 1904.)

48 "Pis'ma o sovremennykh sobytiiakh," *Russkiia vedomosti*, no. 206 (September 7, 1914) and no. 229 (October 5, 1914).

49 Sergei Mel'gunov, "Kropotkin et la culture française," *Le Monde Slave*, I, (January 1925), pp. 59–61. Later, once the Russian revolution had become a reality, Kropotkin wrote that revolution was "the primary episode of the war," and as such, would liberate the people and end Prussian militarism. Entirely reversing his 1904 statement, war and revolution were now seen as inseparable components of a single process. (Peter Kropotkin, "O sovremennoi anglii," *Vestnik obshchestva sblizheniia s Angliei* [Moscow], February 1918, p. 6).

He was obsessed by the spectre of a more terrible reoccurrence of the bloodshed in Paris in 1871 when victorious Prussians had stood over the slaughtered Commune. Yet, as difficult as it was for many of his associates to comprehend the dramatic shift of an anarchist urging victory for the allied governments, there was much in his background to make his war position comprehensible, if not logical. For one thing, his indecisive attitude on terror permitted him to justify violence under certain conditions, of which this war proved to be one. Also, Germany had always represented two of the most oppressive forms of authority for him: Prussian militarism on the Right and Marxist authoritarian socialism on the Left. Faced with German military aggression, he was barely able to distinguish between the two phenomena.

There were some attempts by anarchists close to Kropotkin to explain the origins of his war posture. In 1906, according to one memoirist, Kropotkin already exhibited signs of his later position on World War I. During the planning and organizing of the anarchist congress held in London in the fall of that year, Kropotkin raised the issue of a possible military campaign by Germany against Russia. He spoke of Wilhelm II as "the crowned gendarme" who was plotting the invasion. Kropotkin admitted that "if a war between Germany and Russia begins, I would haul a rifle on my old shoulders and go off to kill Germans."[50] This was a pledge he was to utter again once the war he feared became a reality in 1914.

Rudolf Rocker described a meeting with Kropotkin in 1896 in which his war position was already clearly outlined. He was "convinced that the Kaiser's government was working in a direction which made war inevitable" and that "only an inner change in the political and social life in Germany itself could save Europe and the world from this disaster." In another conversation which took place a year before the war, Kropotkin was already thinking of the settlements which could emerge after the fighting. In one particularly prophetic statement, he told Rocker:

50 Knizhnik, "Vospominaniia o P. A. Kropotkine," p. 35.

If Germany loses the war she will be a problem to the victors, and the problem may not be solved without a European revolution. If Germany is broken up by the victors, it will create an irredenta that will give Europe no peace. . . . If the Germans are defeated, they will brood over their wounded national pride . . .[51]

Rocker describes the confusion among anarchists which resulted from Kopotkin's stand on the war. Rocker himself managed to oppose Kropotkin, but only with great difficulty. Kropotkin's books had shaped his life and he felt indebted to his teacher whom he had admired for years. This was not an untypical experience. Battles developed within the movement. One example of the tragic circumstances which resulted was the argument between Cherkezov, who supported Kropotkin, and Malatesta, who opposed him, in the office of *Freedom*, the London anarchist journal Kropotkin helped to establish. The journal editors turned against Kropotkin while Malatesta and Cherkezov, who had been old friends, angrily attacked each other. "Such were the bitter arguments at this time among comrades," Rocker concluded.[52]

The most significant and penetrating criticism of Kropotkin's position came from the pen of Errico Malatesta. In a series of articles written during the war years, he attempted to point out the contradictions in Kropotkin's argument by showing that taking sides in the war was tantamount to accepting militarism, nationalism, and statism, all of which anarchists had always opposed. Only if "the 'fatherland' really became the property of all the inhabitants" and not merely the possession of the ruling classes could an anarchist join such a battle. In contrast to Kropotkin, Malatesta saw no particular benefit from an Anglo-French victory.[53] The state was incapable of good; it was a criminal aggressor and anarchists could make no common

51 Rudolf Rocker, *The London Years* (London: Robert Anscombe and Co., 1956), pp. 148, 150.

52 Ibid., p. 248.

53 Errico Malatesta, "Anarchists have Forgotten their Principles," *Freedom*, November 1914. This article has been reprinted in Vernon Richards, ed., *Malatesta: His Life and Ideas* (London: Freedom Press, 1965), pp. 243–7.

cause with it. Malatesta sharply condemned Kropotkin and his
followers for having renounced "the spirit and all the traditions
of liberty; they have Prussianized England and France; they
have submitted themselves to tsarism."[54] In a memoir written
some years later, Malatesta expressed the difficulty of opposing
Kropotkin, whose stature was virtually beyond question among
anarchists: "it was one of the saddest, most painful moments
of my life (and, I dare to suggest, for him too) when, after a
more than acrimonious discussion, we parted like adversaries,
almost as enemies."[55]

VI

In the midst of the war that Kropotkin had predicted with grave
apprehension came the revolution he had anticipated with hope.
He had often written that Europe would determine the progress or regress of Russia (his war position was also based on
this premise) and many of his articles seemed to indicate that he
expected the social revolution to break out in London or Paris
first. Yet, his relativism had always allowed for local peculiari-
ties and varieties of revolution. The overthrow of the Russian
autocracy was not unexpected but was nevertheless an event of
unparalleled significance for him.

During the long years of emigration, Kropotkin had never
lost his emotional attachment to his native land. This feeling
is expressed in his articles (particularly those in Russian), his
correspondence, and in his activities. In numerous writings and
public speeches, Kropotkin had presented to Europeans the
image of Russia as a battleground where noble revolutionaries

54 Errico Malatesta, "Pro-Government Anarchists," *Freedom*, April 1916, p. 28.
In this article, Malatesta was attacking the Manifesto of the Sixteen, a public
statement of support for the Allies signed by Kropotkin and other prominent
anarchists. For this manifesto, see Maksimov, *Internatsional'nyi sbornik*, pp.
341-343 and Sébastien Faure, ed., *Encyclopédie anarchiste* (Paris: La librairie
internationale, 1934), IV: 2543-2544.

55 Errico Malatesta, "Peter Kropotkin: Recollections and Criticisms of an Old
Friend," Vernon Richards, ed., *Malatesta*, p. 260. See also M. Pierrot, "Kropotkine et la guerre," *Les Temps Nouveaux* (Paris), March 1921, pp. 9-10.

fought against a reactionary system of government. His description of the prison system in Russia and the barbarity of punishments meted out to rebellious intellectuals and workers was for many Europeans their initial exposure to the details of tsarist justice.[56] When it was announced in the spring of 1909 that Nicholas II of Russia was planning to visit England, Kropotkin prepared an "indictment against the Russian government" which he published in a London newspaper. He also was instrumental in organizing English parliamentary committees to aid the cause of Russian revolutionaries. Thus, one must take this background of concern into account in understanding Kropotkin's decision to return to Russia after he learned of the February Revolution. In addition to this, his decision was based on a feeling that he could be of more use in a republican Russia than in Europe where his image as the patriarch of the anarchist movement had been severely undermined by his position on the war.

The route he took to Russia was by sea via several Scandinavian ports—a route not very different from the one by which he had left Russia forty-one years before. He traveled as inconspicuously as possible to avoid attracting the attention of the Germans, though he had published a farewell letter to the English people in the *Times* of London and was greeted by crowds of sympathizers at every port. Upon arriving in Russia, he gave a prepared speech before a large crowd in Petrograd where he described "the happiness of returning to a renewed, free Russia—free not by the grace of a monarch but by the will of the Russian people." In the speech he attempted to sketch the historical significance of a Russian republic, viewing it as the outcome of the revolutionary movement's struggle against autocratic rule since the Decembrist uprising in 1825, as well as

56 See especially *The Terror in Russia* (London: Methuen and Co., 1909) and *In Russian and French Prisons* (London: Ward and Downey, 1887). See also Kropotkin's article "The Present Crisis in Russia," *North American Review*, 172 (1901): 711–23 and Konstantin P. Pobedonostsev, "Russian and Popular Education (A Reply to Prince Kropotkin)," *North American Review*, vol. 173, pp. 349–54.

part of the same process of transformation undergone by seventeenth-century England and eighteenth-century France. He demanded two things for the guarantee of full liberty in Russia: (1) internally, the decentralization of power and the corresponding realization of equality for all citizens, and (2) externally, the defeat of Germany. "This war must liberate Europe from the sword that has been hanging over its head for the last twenty to thirty years" and "thereby secure our new republic."[57]

One of the best records of this period of Kropotkin's life comes from his correspondence with Professor Sergei Tiurin, an old friend from London whose name he had used in traveling incognito to Russia. The earliest letters, written during the first months after arriving in Russia, express Kropotkin's enthusiasm: visitors coming at all hours, public speeches being given, the sheer excitement of being in his homeland again at the moment of such a tremendous political upheaval. It was not long, however, before the mood changed. He realized the enormous problems facing the new government, particularly the war and the internal instability. He sharply criticized the Bolsheviks for their ties to the German Social Democratic party, which he condemned for supporting Germany's war policy. In early August, about a month after his return to Russia, he wrote:

I hope all intelligent people can understand what a profound transformation Russia is undergoing, and know the consequences of the German government's use of the influence of the German Social Democratic party in all of Europe; especially in Russia where they [the Bolsheviks] look to Berlin as Catholics look to Rome . . .[58]

He lamented over the disorganization and lack of adequate food in the Russian army. The fact that he considered this "the

57 *Tsentral'nyi gosudarstvennyi arkhiv oktiabr'skoi revoliutsii* (TsGAOR). *Fond* 1129, *opis'* 3, *yed. khran.* 461, *listy* 1–14. This dossier is part of the Kropotkin collection of unpublished papers preserved in the state archives in Moscow.

58 Sergei Petrovich Tiurin, "Ot'ezd P. A. Kropotkina iz Anglii v Rossii i ego pis'ma," *Na chuzhoi storone,* 1924, IV, pp. 226–30 (Letter of July 26/August 8, 1917).

main misfortune of Russia" attests to the priority he placed on the war issue. The attacks of Kornilov on the Right and of Bolshevism on the Left seemed secondary to this.[59] To be sure, although Kropotkin rejected positions offered to him in the Kerensky government, he was interested in its continued existence at least until an anarchist alternative appeared viable. He proposed the establishment of a federal republic and was busy working on plans for local, autonomous, self-governing units apart from the centralizing influences of the capital. He also became involved with a Federalist League at this time, which consisted of a small group of scholars who were engaged in preparing for publication a multivolume study of the various aspects of federalism, under the editorship of Kropotkin.

Whatever hopes Kropotkin had for the realization of the social revolution and an anarchist society in Russia were ended by the October Revolution. The optimism of Kropotkin's earlier writings is all but absent in the letters and scattered pieces of evidence from the last few years of his life. His last home was Dmitrov, a small provincial town some forty miles north of Moscow where he was relocated after his previous residences in the city had been nationalized. He continued to maintain his outspoken criticism of Marxism and of the Russian Marxists who were then in control of the government. According to a sympathetic observer who had been close to Kropotkin years before, the aging anarchist leader "had lost touch with the events which had occurred and lived with values of the past."[60] Whether of the past or of the future, Kropotkin's values were distinctly at variance with those of the new revolutionary government—the realization of the very theoretical contradiction he had warned against. In his last letter to his old friend Burtsev, he explained how he was attempting to carry on various projects dealing with federalism and nongovernmental internationalism, but added that he was hampered by "the social

59 Ibid., pp. 231-3. (Letter of September 4, 1917). For translated exerpts of this correspondence, see Kropotkin, *Memoirs*, pp. 306-11.

60 Knizhnik, "Vospominaniia o P. A. Kropotkine," p. 47.

democratic method of autocratic decision by decree on all questions."[61]

As for his political writings from this period, most of his time was spent editing republications and translations into Russian of his previous works which had been banned under the tsars. The one major work of these years remains his unfinished *Ethics*, the research and conceptualization for which he had virtually completed before returning to Russia in 1917.[62] He attempted to launch a journal in 1918 which was based on a notion of friendship and cooperation between Russia and England that he hoped could be fostered. His argument in justifying such a relationship was similar to the one he posed in defending his war position. He still believed the influence of European ideas upon Russia to be of supreme importance, the advance of the socialist revolution notwithstanding. There were two possible currents of influence, the Anglo-Latin and the Germanic, and Russia had historically been more susceptible to the most noxious of the two (the Germanic). Thus, in working out new forms of life based on freedom and equality in a revolutionary society, it was crucial to realize that "England and France stand far ahead of Germany and Austria in this respect." In addition, Kropotkin believed that "the necessity of a fundamental reconstruction of mutual relations of labor and capital in agriculture and industry" was understood in England and that the English people would undoubtedly move toward a resolution of this vital social question.[63]

There is also an unfinished essay from these years in which Kropotkin admitted that Russia had strayed from the path of authentic revolution primarily because "the lofty social ideal" of the early Russian revolutionaries, which is necessary for any revolution, had been replaced by "teachings of economic

61 "Pis'ma P. A. Kropotkina k V. L. Burtsevu," pp. 154–5. (Letter of February 1, 1918).

62 Peter Kropotkin, *Ethics* (New York: McVeagh, 1924). A second volume was to be published but Kropotkin died before this was completed.

63 Peter Kropotkin, "O sovremennoi Anglii," *Vestnik obshchestva sblizheniia s Angliei* (Moscow), pp. 3–6. There were no further issues published after no. 1 in February 1918.

materialism emanating from Germany." In this article, Kropotkin's mood was almost desperate in considering the future course of the revolution:

> Only one thing remains: to live by the hope that this type of revolution was accepted only under the pernicious influences of the last years of autocratic orgy (*vakkhanaliia*) and that the common sense of the Russian people will rise to the top and deliver [us] from the ulcer (*iazva*) which threatens to cripple the Russian revolution and render it useless.[64]

Despite this pessimism, Kropotkin refused to entertain the possibility of outside interference to overthrow the Bolshevik regime. In his much publicized open letter to the workers of the West, he strongly argued that the Russian revolution must be allowed to follow its own course and that, despite its initial errors, it had already introduced many progressive measures. He called on all Western workers and intellectuals to "put an end to the support given until now to the enemies of the revolution." Referring to the civil war then raging in Russia, Kropotkin wrote that any aid to the anti-Bolshevik armies was aid to the restoration of the monarchy and total reaction. He was critical of the revolution because of its dictatorial and centralizing character but urged that the lesson of the revolution for the West should be both positive and negative. Party control of revolutions should be avoided, but fundamental social reconstruction by local forces was possible only through revolution.[65]

Kropotkin's last years were not easy ones. Aside from ideological problems, there were problems of obtaining provisions and physical necessities, which were extremely scarce during the civil war. When offered a position by the faculty of geography at Moscow University in 1920, Kropotkin declined politely, answering that "my health, especially after surviving two winters [in Russia], does not permit the regular routine

64 Peter Kropotkin, "Ideal v revoliutsii," *Byloe*, no. 17, 1921, pp. 39–41.

65 "Letter to the Workers of Western Europe," Roger N. Baldwin, ed., *Kropotkin's Revolutionary Pamphlets*, pp. 252–6. See also Camillo Berneri, *Peter Kropotkin. His Federalist Ideas* (London: Freedom Press, 1943), pp. 13–14.

which a profession demands."[66] Yet, although physical privation sapped his health, he was most concerned about the fate of the revolution. It was this concern that drove him to arrange a meeting with Lenin and to write the two letters of protest to the Bolshevik leader which are included in this anthology.

At the end of January 1921 Kropotkin contracted a serious case of pneumonia. For days he lay mortally ill. Doctors were personally sent to Dmitrov by Lenin and daily bulletins were published in the government newspapers on his declining condition. Finally, on February 8, Kropotkin died. A large funeral, organized by the anarchist organizations still functioning, carried Kropotkin's remains to be buried. The black and scarlet flags of anarchism were publicly displayed in the procession for one of the last times in Moscow and "speakers of many political tendencies" paid tribute to the anarchist revolutionary.[67] Lenin had offered to provide a state burial, but the anarchists refused on ideological grounds in the memory of their teacher.

VII

Kropotkin's personality has been veiled by accolades of tribute to his qualities of warmth, honesty, and selfless devotion to the cause of the people. This is a useful approach toward understanding him if one is interested in countering the image of bomb throwers and of the fiery Bakunin as prototypical anarchists, but it is only part of the truth. Kropotkin was a highly cultured and gentle individual who, judging from the memoir literature, impressed most people who met him regardless of their political positions. Gentle natures and violent revolutions, however, do

66 N. P. Krainer, "O priglashenii P. A. Kropotkina na kafedru geografii Moskovskogo universiteta," *Izvestiia vsesoiuznogo geograficheskogo obshchestva,* 1968, no. 2, p. 173.

67 Emma Goldman, *My Further Disillusionment in Russia* (Garden City, New York: Doubleday, Page and Co., 1924), p. 64. See also *My Disillusionment in Russia* (Garden City, New York: Doubleday, Page and Co., 1923), pp. 53–56, 153–159 for Emma Goldman's description of her meetings with Kropotkin shortly before his death.

not mix easily, and Kropotkin had another side to his personality which has often been overlooked. At least two of his close associates managed to perceive this side at widely separate periods of his life. Kravchinskii, who knew Kropotkin as a young revolutionary in Russia as well as later in Europe, tried to explain why Kropotkin decided to remain abroad in 1876 and concluded that his talents and interest could best be expressed "in the vast public arena and not in the underground regions of secret societies." Kravchinskii saw Kropotkin as a man unable to fit himself into the disciplined and rigorous life of the conspiratorial party which demanded virtually complete obedience to common means and ends, and the ability to function effectively in the tightly communalized brotherhood of such a group. "He is too exclusive and rigid in his theoretical convictions. He admits no departure from the ultra-anarchical program," Kravchinskii wrote.[68] Kropotkin was, in the late 1870s, too individualistic and too committed to his own conceptions to continue work in the Russian revolutionary underground.

The other piece of evidence to consider is Malatesta's memoir on Kropotkin. Malatesta, writing after Kropotkin's death, had been deeply wounded by the ideological split with his old comrade over the war, and his memoir was an effort to come to terms with Kropotkin's motivations as an anarchist. He probed Kropotkin's scientific work and found that his method was a systematic effort to "explain everything with one principle and reduce everything to unity." Kropotkin tended to use science "to support his social aspirations" and was unable to "observe facts with objectivity."[69] He began with a hypothesis, collected facts to support it, and refused to entertain evidence contrary to it. This was particularly true of issues and problems that directly affected his deepest concerns about society. These concerns involved a debt which Kropotkin believed all privileged classes owed the oppressed classes of society. The emancipation of the workers was conceived of as an obligation owed to them because

68 Sergei Kravchinskii, *Underground Russia* (New York: C. Scribner's Sons, 1892), p. 89.

69 Malatesta, "Peter Kropotkin," p. 261.

of the exploitation carried out by the well-born. Kropotkin's conflict, then, was an effort to harmonize a highly rational philosophical system with an acutely sensitive and emotional response to social injustice. Kropotkin's theory of anarchism, according to Malatesta, illustrated the failure to resolve this conflict. The theory was neither scientific nor objective since it was based ultimately not on demonstrable evidence but on faith. Kropotkin was convinced that the coming revolution would be a storm led by the impulse and spirit of the heroic masses, whose inherent virtues he accepted totally and unquestioningly. Kropotkin's anarchism is therefore weakened by its "fatalism" and its "excessive optimism" concerning the coming revolution.[70] Malatesta further charged that these "errors" induced many comrades to passivity since the notion of the spontaneity of the people left intellectual radicals with little to do.

Malatesta's criticism, although somewhat exaggerated, was essentially correct. In assessing Kropotkin's thought, several points must be mentioned in this regard. First, he frequently refused to consider the complexity of human nature and stubbornly maintained his faith in the supreme goodness of man. The aspects of human irrationality were completely disregarded. Man's destructive capacity was interpreted in terms of insidious conditions under the political authority of the state and the exploitative system of capitalism. Free of these dehumanizing influences, Kropotkin believed man would be capable of living peacefully and cooperatively in an anarchist society. Second, his philosophical system was based on a totalistic conception of authority. Kropotkin did not feel the need to examine the areas of life where men found authority necessary and positive. Man was redemptive, but any external authority was corrupt by definition. Third, he never outlined principles of organization, control, and hierarchy since he believed that such principles were contrary to anarchism and that the oppressed masses knew best how to arrange and administer the functions necessary for survival, defense, and, ultimately, the enjoyment of life. Consequently, anarchist groups found themselves at a tremendous

70 Ibid., p. 267.

disadvantage in their attempt to challenge effectively the formidable and sophisticated apparatus of the state. The frustration that this neglect fostered led to the widespread recourse to violent deeds which preoccupied many of Kropotkin's followers.

On the other hand, Kropotkin's anarchism provided an incisive critique of the awesome power of the modern state, its tyrannical control over men, and its destruction of the natural community in human society. Among his books one can find many practical proposals for the improvement of agriculture and industry in both urban and rural communities. Kropotkin's anarchism was an effort to delineate the progressive future of human evolution where custom and habit natural to man would predominate over the artificial, prescriptive norms of the state. In this way, he attempted to introduce ethical principles into the entire structure of society.

The romantic and apocalyptic imagery of anarchist theory remains, questioning the legitimacy of every form of government, criticizing the injustice of every institution based on authority. Kropotkin once considered the question of whether men would be able to live without authority, even if the social revolution were successful. He posed the problem by speculating that "anarchy may be good for a higher humanity, not for men of our own times."[71] Yet he believed not that anarchism was beyond the reach of ordinary men but that it was every man's natural inclination to strive to live apart from prescribed morality and imposed authority. Emma Goldman, an anarchist who was present at Kropotkin's funeral, had another view. She wrote that if one defined aristocracy not in terms of birth or wealth but according to a higher spirit, "all true anarchists were aristocrats."[72] One may still fruitfully ponder the question, while reading Kropotkin's essays, of whether anarchism is impractical and an impossible condition for humanity or whether humanity is not yet able to take on the responsibilities of a higher form of social life called anarchism.

71 Peter Kropotkin, *Anarchist Communism* (London: Freedom Press, 1920), p. 29.

72 Emma Goldman, *Living My Life* (New York: A. Knopf, 1931), I, 194.

Essays

"Must We Occupy Ourselves with an Examination of the Ideal of a Future System?" was written by Kropotkin in November 1873. From the manuscript and from the discussions of this period by memoirists, it is evident that the essay was composed for consideration by the members of the Chaikovskii Circle, the leading revolutionary group at that time in St. Petersburg. There is conflicting evidence as to whether Kropotkin was asked to write the essay as a general ideological manifesto which would express the collective viewpoint of the circle or whether he composed it on his own initiative in the hope of imposing a minority viewpoint as the circle's official ideological position. In any case, the manifesto was discussed at several meetings. However, before any final decision could be reached, the police began a series of arrests which broke down the operations of the circle. The unsigned manifesto was seized at the apartment of one of the circle members, I. I. Gauenshtein, still in its first draft form. Kropotkin's notations and corrections which line the margins of the manuscript indicate that he had planned to make fairly extensive revisions. His own arrest followed soon after, on March 12, 1874, and the manifesto was left to accumulate dust in the archives of the tsarist police. Kropotkin made no references to the essay in his later writings, and there is no mention of it in his memoirs (with the single exception of one very brief mention of it in a supplementary chapter of a posthumous Russian edition [*Zapiski Revoliutsionera* (Moscow, 1929), II, p.219]).

The essay is significant not only in terms of Kropotkin's own intellectual evolution (which is discussed in the Introduction to this book) but also in connection with the ideology of the Russian revolutionary movement. It should be recalled that many revolutionary populists in the early 1870s were divided between loyalties to the positions of Peter Lavrov and Michael Bakunin. Lavrov urged a gradualist approach to revolution, with a preparatory period in which radical intellectuals would seek to educate the people and develop their "consciousness." Bakunin argued for a direct approach of inciting revolt among the discontented masses in any form. Kropotkin's manifesto stands decisively in the Bakuninist camp.

The manifesto was first published in a commemorative issue of a Russian journal after Kropotkin's death in 1921, although in an abbreviated form (*Byloe*, no. 17 [1921], pp. 3–38). The first complete publication of the document is in *Revoliutsionnoe narodnichestvo*, edited by Boris S. Itenberg *et al.* (Moscow: Nauka, 1964), I, 55–118. The following version of this essay, the first in English, has been translated from this complete text by Victor Ripp. The manifesto appears here in its entirety, with the exception of the marginal notes and crossed out phrases which have been omitted for the sake of clarity. The words *obshchina*—plural, *obshchiny*—(rural peasant community) and *mir* (institutional form of self-administration in peasant communities, usually concerned with taxes and land distribution) have been retained because of their specific meanings in the context of Kropotkin's argument.

Must We
Occupy Ourselves
with an Examination
of the Ideal of
a Future System?

I

I believe that we must.

In the first place, in the ideal we can express our hopes, aspirations and goals, regardless of practical limitations, regardless of the degree of realization which we may attain; for this degree of realization is determined purely by external causes.

In the second place, the ideal can make clear how much we are infected with old prejudices and inclinations. If some aspects of everyday life seem to us so sacred that we dare not touch them even in an analysis of the ideal, then how great will our daring be in the actual abolishment of these everyday features? In other words, although daring in thought is not at all a guarantee of daring in practice, mental timidity in constructing an ideal is certainly a criterion of mental timidity in practice.

In speaking about the definition of the ideal, we of course have in mind the definition of only four or five prominent features of this ideal. Everything else must inevitably be the realization of these fundamental theories in life. Therefore these things cannot be a subject for discussion now. The forms of the realization cannot be derived by scientific means. In practice they can be derived only by means of repeated practical discussion shortly before and during the realization on the spot, in the *obshchina*, in the artel, but not now at the beginning of things.

There is not the slightest doubt that among different socialists of the most varied shades there does exist a rather complete agreement in their ideals, if these are taken in the most general form. Those social conditions which they would hope to realize in the more or less near future are generally quite the same; their differences proceed not from fundamental differences in the ideal, but rather from the fact that some concentrate all their attention on that ideal which can, in their opinion, be realized in the immediate future; others concentrate on the ideal which, in the opinion of the former, is more remote.

In fact, all present-day socialists strive toward the fullest possible equality in the conditions of development of private individuals and societies. They all desire the realization of such a system so that everyone would have the same opportunity to earn his livelihood by his own labor, that is, so that everyone would have the same right to use those instruments of labor and those raw materials without which no labor is possible; so that everyone would be compelled to earn his livelihood by his own labor; so that the distribution of useful occupations in society would be such as to make impossible the formation of a class occupied for life (and moreover, because of heredity) exclusively with *privileged labor*, that is, labor more pleasant, less difficult, and less protracted, but giving the right to the same, or greater prosperity as others; so that everyone would have the same opportunity, on a level with all others, to receive that theoretical education which now constitutes the lot of only a few; so that the relations of a private individual to all others would be such that he might be happy and at the same time bear the least amount of restraint on his personal freedom and personal development. In a word, to state these positions briefly, today's socialists are striving for equality: in rights to work; in labor; in methods of education; in social rights and duties, with the greatest possible room for the development of individual characteristics; in those capabilities which are harmless for society.

Such is the program of the immense majority if not all of the socialists of our time. Even those who evidently advocate a completely different ideal, those who, for instance, advocate as the ultimate ideal a state communism or a hierarchical system and so forth in the end desire the same thing. If they concentrate strong power in the hands of either a ruling minority or elected representatives and, by this means, sacrifice individual initiative, this is by no means because they attribute no value to it or consider it detrimental, but only because they do not consider possible the realization of such a system in which all four forms of equality would be realized in equal measure, and they sacrifice one form for the attainment of the others. Moreover, not one of the *active* followers of these learned socialists believes that any social form whatever could ossify and resist further development.

We will now examine all the above-mentioned various forms and conditions of equality separately, and we will see how compatible they are with one another and how necessary a common realization of all of them is for the durability of each. We will examine in particular the practical measures which now seem useful for the realization of each of these ideals.

The first condition of equality is self-evident and is least subject to dispute.

If each member of society is to have the possibility of earning his livelihood by his own labor—without, as a result, enslaving himself to anyone else, neither to a private citizen, nor to a company, nor to an artel—he must obviously always have the possibility of acquiring that shovel with which he intends to dig, that cotton from which he intends to spin a thread or to weave a fabric, that bread, those clothes, that room where he must live, that place where he will work, before he manufactures anything having an exchange value for society. It is apparent that in former times production was so simple that all this did not require a vast accumulation of the initial products of personal labor, that anyone, although working only with the instruments of labor available in his family, on those raw products which he took free of charge from nature, could produce useful exchange values. But now—and the progress of society consists in this—the preliminary accumulation of the products of labor for the creation of the instruments of labor and the storing up of raw material must be so great that it can no longer be the business of a private individual or a private group of individuals. It is clear therefore that if it is desirable that a person beginning to work not enslave himself, not yield part of his labor, his strength, his independence, either permanently or temporarily, to private individuals whose arbitrariness always will determine how great that part should be, then it is necessary that private persons control neither the instruments of labor (tools, machines, factories), nor the places of cultivation of the raw products (the earth), nor the raw products stored up beforehand, nor the means for storing up and conveying them to a given place (the means of communication, warehouses, and so forth), nor the means of existence during work (the supplies of the means of subsistence and housing).

Thus we arrive at the elimination, in that future system whose realization we desire, of any personal property, of any property of an associated joint stock company, an artel, and so forth.

Those writers of a former time who came to this same conclusion saw no way out other than the transfer of all the capital of society to the state, that is, to a powerful organization representing in itself the interests of society and managing all matters which concern the whole society in total.

It was left to it [the state] to guarantee each member of society the opportunity to obtain the necessary instruments of labor, and so forth; it was also left to it to distribute among the members of society those products made by them. But precisely because of this, the brilliant dreams of the followers of these scholars did not find enough adherents among those who would have to realize these dreams in actuality. In the very ideal of these scholars only one aspect of life is considered, the economic. Those who were accustomed to thinking in a concrete manner understood very well that no matter what combination of conditions was contrived in order that this government might express the views of the majority, that no matter how mobile, fluctuating, and susceptible to change its composition might be, the group of individuals to whom society cedes its rights would always be the power, separate from society, trying to broaden its influence, its interference in the business of each separate individual. And the wider the circle of activity of this government, the greater the danger of enslavement of society, the greater the likelihood that the government would stop being the expression of the interests and desires of the majority.

Thus, both the masses and many individual thinkers long ago realized that the transfer of this most essential element of the life of society into the hands of any elected government whatsoever would be the source of the most essential inconvenience, if not simply the suicide of society.

From this realization the most natural transition was to the idea that all capital, no matter how accumulated by preceding generations, must become the property of all, of the whole society, which must itself be the fully empowered manager of it.

The expression of this ideal in its most immediate, direct form, consists of: (1) the recognition of all available capital, whether or not gained through labor, as the property of all members of that territorial unit (group of districts, nations, countries), where the socialist revolution is occurring; (2) the recognition of all public capital which can be worked (arable land, exploitable ore, factories, railroads operative and under construction, apartment houses, and so forth) as given over for use (for a certain period of time) to those individuals who now exert their labor; (3) the taking of necessary measures so that the unprofitable conditions in which separate working groups find themselves would be equalized within the various small territorial units (the town, the province) by means of the mutual agreement of these groups—without eliminating the possibility of a further redistribution to equalize disproportionate conditions within the more extensive unions of small territorial units.

But still clearer is the second condition of equality, namely, that everyone should be compelled to earn his livelihood through his own labor. This aspiration is common to all socialists and is expressed with perfect clarity by them. Disagreements arise only in regard to what is rightfully to be considered personal labor. But this disagreement is to a significant degree the result of a simple misunderstanding. All economists have long since distinguished productive labor from useful labor, counting as the latter the labor of scholars, writers, artists, administrators, and so forth. But this subdivision is hardly appropriate in the present case, and it hardly distinguishes labor *necessary* for a given group and that which is *unnecessary*. We believe that only that production should be considered as labor which all society can make use of, and which the significant majority *wants* to make use of. Thus, we would have to include in our formula: "labor for which there is a demand by the majority of society." Clearly, the classification of the different types of labor involving the mutual relations of members within a given group of society must be the business of only that group—but all relations of this group to other, similar groups is the business of those groups with which it enters into union or into an exchange of products. Thus, in the *obshchina*, where not all members of the society can read and write, and not all can acquire more advanced knowledge, the teaching of higher algebra can be designated not as labor but as a leisure activity. On the other hand, if the whole society is so developed in musical matters that hearing music has become a necessity for it, then the performance of these pieces can be designated as labor, liable to payment in other equivalent labors—if this designation was made by the *majority* of the group. It is obvious, however, that other groups less developed in musical matters may not recognize the musical instruments manufactured by the first group as a product of labor necessary for themselves, and may not agree on an exchange of them for an equivalent quantity of labor of the type they acknowledge as useful. The immense difference between such a state of affairs and the present one is obvious, in that now a handful of individuals, controlling the labor of others, have the right to make use of it without supervision for the satisfaction of their own needs, and thus use the labor of all to pay for the production and actions necessary to themselves alone. This evil is being eliminated.

But it has often been stated that such an order of affairs as we have in mind in our ideal has another inherent shortcoming. It has been said that the requirements of the majority are not at all the essence of the requirement for the progress of human society; that progress in society always results because some minority, having accidentally fallen into especially favorable circumstances, developed more than all the rest and discovered and laid down to the world new truths, which were absorbed by those individuals who were relatively prepared. Though we doubt (for reasons developed below) that such was the path of progress in society in the majority of cases or that it must always have been like this, yet even if we grant that such was the sole possible path of progress in a given direction, albeit only in some rare, even unique instance, we must then of course consider whether the classification of labor which we propose in the ideal might not extinguish *this* gleam of progress.

It is clear, however, that those who reasoned in this way were imagining an *ideal* evaluation of labor in *present* society, and assuming the contemporary situation, with its present suffocating conditions in the workshops, with its debilitatingly heavy work, with that unbearable tedium of machine labor which now is necessary in order to have even shelter and a crust of bread. But it is obvious that the classification of labor of which we speak is possible only in a society which has been subjected to that change mentioned in connection with the first condition of equality. And for such a society a lack of considerable leisure time is unthinkable. If some economists asserted that the equal division of all the present income of society's nonworking sector among all members of society would raise each member's average salary only five sou (eight kopecks), these economists once again assumed an impossible condition, that is, they imagined a sharing impossible in present society, one which was to occur while preserving present conditions and forms of production. Now, of course, it is impossible even to define how much time would be required for each member of society to labor on the production of those objects necessary to provide all members of society with comfort, [a comfort] equal to that of people in the lower part of today's middle class. But it can be stated directly that if each worker now supports on the average (in Germany and France) three people besides himself (in France almost four people) of whom only one is a member of the worker's family, whereas the other two (almost three in France) are parasites on the family—then in a better organized society, where the worker need only support one, or more usually two people (that is, in sum, two to three people counting himself, instead of four to five), he can work half as much (five and a half hours instead of eleven hours a day), in all thirty-three hours a week, and moreover without in any way diminishing his prosperity. Recalling further all the unproductive expenses of society, caused mainly by social disorder (troops, wars, jails and courts, lawsuits, and so forth), recalling further what immeasurable quantities of labor are spent on the production of objects not leading to an increase in the productive power of of the people—we, of course, will understand how much leisure there would be in a correctly organized society, leisure even for the satisfaction of such intellectual pleasures as a middling nobleman does not even dream of at present; we will understand then how much closer to the truth was Owen, who was convinced that for this, as well as for much else, three hours labor by all the members of society would be sufficient.

Here is why we believe that (granting the progressive influence of the minority) separate individuals would have the full opportunity to formulate all those progressive ideas which separate individuals can formulate, to disseminate them, to invent all those mechanical tools which could facilitate man's satisfaction of his needs, and to invent and perfect all those pleasures which promote the further development of the individual. The preparation of the groundwork in a society which would consist of members who have since childhood had the opportunity to receive that training which now is the lot of only the fortunate few; the capability of this society, given the elimination of present obstacles, to comprehend all that is good; the ability to identify the good with the socially useful and the bad with the socially harmful; finally, an extension to the presently inactive masses of the spheres of vocational, scientific and artistic creativity—this is the guarantee of progress in the future society, and it is not only not less than any existing today, but ten, even a hundred times greater.

Therefore, we consider our second condition both a necessary condition of equality and the most immediate; but, in addition, we consider that a great stride towards attaining this part of the ideal is the acknowledgement of *social* exchange value only for such objects as will be acknowledged as useful for society by the *majority* of a given group, or a given union of groups.

All the preceding now leads us as well to a belief in the feasibility and the practical expediency of an organization of useful occupations which lacks those groups of individuals occupied exclusively with privileged labor (intellectual labor, the management of some business of industry, the factory, the *obshchina*, and so forth). There can be no doubt that the existence of such a class of people is a manifestation of inequality, in itself obviously undesirable. There can be doubt and objection only in the sense that: (1) the existence of such a class is necessary for the further development of the very society; (2) from the point of view, held by many, that the division of labor is necessary.

We said above that we find it neither just nor useful that public labor should pay for objects useful or necessary only to a minority. We said also that there would be sufficient leisure to produce these objects after the completion of that work required by society, and that the likely extent of this leisure, together with the increase in basic training and an increase in the number of people having the opportunity to use this leisure for every possible occupation would promote society's progress. This would be a sufficient guarantee against stagnation in the culture and civilization of the society.

Now we proceed. We say that among those occupations which will be acknowledged as necessary by a given group of people there may be occupations which are, so to speak, privileged. From the first, every *obshchina* will require a schoolteacher, a doctor, a bookkeeper; after some time there will be a need for a professor, a scholar, a technician, perhaps a banker, and so forth. It will be asked, will it be more advantageous for the *obshchina* as a whole that this schoolteacher concern himself solely with the education of children for those seven or eight hours which every member of the society must devote to a socially useful occupation, without devoting himself to any other work whatsoever; or should he as well daily or regularly perform other duties of so-called unskilled labor, for example chop wood for the school (if that is necessary), wash or scrub the floors, fire the stoves, sweep the school-yard, provide school supplies, and so on? Should a professor—in such an *obshchina* where it is required—concern himself solely with delivering lectures during the designated seven or eight hours, or should he concern himself as well with the preparation of the physical layout? Should he concern himself, together with the metal-worker and the mechanic, with cleaning up the dirt in the university building, and so forth? We believe that, yes, he must perform the latter. Since the formation of a class of intelligentsia, the formation of an aristocracy of skilled labor alongside the democracy of unskilled labor is completely undesirable, the whole question, consequently, is only how profitable for society is such a division of occupations wherein separate individuals do not specialize as now. It seems absurd to people that [someone like] Darwin should concern himself with cleaning up, only because they are unable to rid themselves of the conceptions which they have accepted whole from contemporary society. They forget that for such an individual as Darwin to appear, [a man] who in his intellectual development outstripped his society by a whole century, a certain selection of especially favorable, exceptional conditions was necessary over the course of many years. They assume (without proof, of course) that if Darwin and Wallace had not put forth the hypothesis of natural selection in 1859, then humanity would have remained ignorant of it for many centuries, and that there is no combination of social conditions such that would have allowed this hypothesis to be stated not merely in 1859 but even considerably earlier. They consider the natural or most advantageous path of progress for humanity to be the revelation by separate individuals of those ideas which outstrip those of the mass of society by a whole century or even a millenium. All these opinions and views are, however, utterly untrue.

In the light of all that has been said, we consider absolutely necessary, in the first place:

The acknowledgment of the superfluity of that class which enjoys a privileged type of occupation; in other words, the acknowledgment of the necessity of manual, muscular labor for all members of the society, along with the acknowledgment of complete freedom for each individual in choosing those occupations—if he can prove his capability in the selected type of occupation.

The realization of these two conditions of equality and the transfer of them into actuality guarantees the realization of the fourth condition, equality in education—not merely the possibility of equality in education, but actually, in fact.

Unconditionally denying that the most advantageous, progressive movement in society is by means of the development of a minority which receives a far greater education than the rest of society, we by no means wish to subsidize such a minority with public funds: thus we do not need universities or academies maintained by the public funds, if they are not to be used by every member of society without exclusion. If private individuals, wishing to use their leisure for the further development of intellectual capacities, should establish institutes of higher learning, study societies, conservatories, and so forth—let them maintain these with the products of their leisure, let them visit them during their leisure hours, during that time which the other members of society will spend on entertainment or pleasure-making; but the society which does not want to disturb those conditions of equality which it achieved through its own efforts must not spare even one unit of public labor for their maintenance.

We do not want the educational process to act in the direction of dividing people, from childhood onward, into those who are led and those who lead, of whom the former are mainly familiar with the unskilled labor necessary for their daily lives—and the latter mainly with the methods of management and the so-called higher manifestations of the human mind. Therefore, we have absolutely no need of universities which produce doctors, when the majority of those working in this field are destined to fulfill the duties of watchmen, nurses, orderlies; or lawyers when the majority will be only clerks; or professors—along with office watchmen, or skilled technologists—along with miners.

Repeating the formulation of Proudhon, we say: if a naval academy is not itself a ship with sailors who enjoy equal rights and receive a theoretical education, then it will produce not sailors but officers to supervise sailors; if a technical academy is not itself a factory, not itself a trade school, then it will produce foremen and managers and not workmen, and so on. We do not need these privileged establishments; we need neither universities nor technical academies nor naval academies created for the few; we need the hospital, the factory, the chemical works, the ship, the productive trade school for workers, which, having become available to all, will with unimaginable speed exceed the standard of present universities and academies. In eliminating all the necessary ballast of useless occupations, in devising accelerated methods of education (which always appear only when a demand for them arises which cannot be put off), the school will train healthy workers equally capable of both further intellectual and physical work.

How many hours the student will have to concern himself with actual *production* at each age level (not play at production as in current technical and secondary schools) and how many hours with theoretical studies—and up to what level the latter will be required—will be decided independently by each *obshchina* and district; and, of course, this decision will not be accidental as it is now, but based on rational principles.

We must say, finally, several words about compulsory

education, which has been the subject of so many arguments. We believe that the source of these arguments was that those who argued against this requirement always had in mind the contemporary state, with all its attributes. But, obviously, we speak not of compulsory education in present society with its present government, but of a future society with those institutions which will fulfill those useful functions (or, more accurately, potentially useful) which the government now fulfills. Therefore we of course consider that in a future society, education—which up to a certain limit will be defined by the society itself—will and must be compulsory.

In the light of what has been said, we consider necessary for the realization of this fourth aspect of the ideal of equality the recognition of the necessity to close all universities, academies, and other institutes of higher learning, and to open everywhere trade schools, whose volume of instruction will in a very short time surely increase to the level of present universities and surpass them.

To achieve agreement on the fifth point of political equality was always the most difficult of all for all socialist schools. For several decades the learned representatives of socialism could find no other alternative for realizing their ideals than by means of a strong centralized government, a strong government which would have fixed and regulated all social relations, which would have interfered with all the details of people's private lives. These conceptions were particularly developed among the writers of France and Germany. But this caused a natural aversion to other, correct, principles of communism, both among the masses and among especially sincere socialists.

It is clear, however, that all this is the consequence of a simple misunderstanding. Freed of the always dangerous idea of an all-powerful government, communism quickly began to spread even in Western Europe—in an altered and limited form— under the name of collectivism.

On the other hand, many excellent thinkers of the present century have tried to define in their writings the combination of conditions in which private individuals could be guaranteed the greatest freedom of activity and development along with the least restraint. It is clear, however, that as long as these thinkers limited themselves to working out only purely political relations, they could not achieve any practical results. But with the transferring of the issue to the area of economic relations, the problem is much more simply resolved. The most ideal form devised by the defenders of the idea of the state is a federated republic with the *obshchina* autonomous and deciding independently as much business as possible, with as much independence as possible from the district and ultimately from the state. We see such a form in the United States of America. In Europe one necessary addition to this form is held to be that certain laws must be brought to a vote of all the people, all citizens, as we see in certain cantons in Switzerland, and in the Swiss Union at large for laws concerning the alteration of the Code of the Union. Finally, the putting of *all* laws to a vote by the people, while granting the government only the right to promulgate them, is considered a further improvement of this form.

To enumerate here all the inconveniences of these forms, all the infringements of liberty to which they lead, all the inability of these forms to express the will and desire of the majority—even in the majority of cases—would be inappropriate. This criticism has been made many times, and it is sufficient to say that its conclusions proceed not from a logical analysis of the *possibilities* but from a criticism of the actual, contemporary phenomena. Finally, it is sufficient to say that this whole analysis led to the following positions. Apart from all those qualities and characteristics of any government which result from an economic inequality of rights, all the indicated forms lead to this: (1) that the centralized government of a district, state, and union is not the expression of the will of the majority of the population; (2) that growing constantly stronger, it usurps the rights of the state, district, *obshchina*; (3) that separate individuals, possessing great energy, can, even if only for a time, seize great power into their hands and paralyze all the necessary measures which the majority wishes to take;

(4) that in creating a highly complex state machine, and requiring long practice to become acquainted with the mechanism, such a system leads to the formation of a class especially concerned with state management, which, using its acquired experience, begins to deceive the rest for its personal advantage; (5) that, finally, the boundary between law and decree cannot be ascertained even with approximate accuracy and that it thus is necessary, given the impossibility of daily convening the entire populace for voting, to transfer considerable power to the centralized government of a district or state.

All this criticism led Proudhon to the rejection of any government and to *anarchy*.

One feature, common to every government, is that the members of the *obshchina*, district, and state are deprived of a part of their right to decide their own personal matters, and this right is given to several individuals. Moreover, precisely which matters are to be decided by those individuals who make up the local government is defined in general terms. A feature no less central is that this group of individuals is permitted to decide not only any private matters whatsoever but all those matters which arose or could arise in the management of public matters; and they are limited in deciding those matters only by quantity. Another feature common to every government and just as basic is that this same group of individuals, or even a still smaller group, chosen either by the first [group] or by all of the remaining population of the state, district, or *obshchina* in total, is permitted to execute the decisions of either the general meeting or the elected government. For this a whole hierarchy of executive organs is created which is obliged to submit to the directions of the executive power of the *obshchina*, district, or state. For the sake of expediency, the executive power of the *obshchina* subordinates itself to the district [power], and this one—in its turn—to the state [power]. Such, in general features, is the essence of all governments. The differences consist only in this—in one place the *obshchina*'s circle of activity is wider, in another, more public matters are handed over to the district or central government; in some places the authorities are wholly or partially elected, in others, they set themselves above the people, and so on.

The inconveniences which arise from such a state of affairs are too well known for it to be appropriate to pause over them. But more important here is not whether these inconveniences are great or small, but that they lie in the most basic conception of the institution, in its very essence, and so cannot be eliminated by any measures such as limitations, control, and so on as long as the very essence of the institution continues to exist.

And as a matter of fact we know that any group of people entrusted with deciding a certain set of activities often of an organizational quality always strives to broaden the range of these activities and its own power in these activities. And the more intelligent, energetic, and active these people, the greater will be this striving on their part to usurp those activities not entrusted to them. The more energetic, active, and conscientious these people, the more the remaining society becomes accustomed to not overseeing them, to not checking on them. It becomes easier, consequently, for a dishonest but talented person, who has accidentally gotten into the government, to direct the activities of this group for the attainment of his personal aims.

It is well-known that to apply some general principle to the business at hand is most difficult. The newer this general principle and the less familiar its particular applications, the easier it is, with the application of this general principle, to make concessions which can completely paralyze the principle itself. Moreover, in a system of elected leaders who must decide for a certain group of people, they may find themselves forced to make a decision which corresponds to the general principle in theory, but not to its particularities [in practice]. In short, the most difficult part of the decision, which most of all requires the assistance of various opinions, is left by the group to a separate person. Any central authority of the district, state, or country must consist of a small number of persons, and the larger this unit, the fewer the possibilities that the elected persons were known to the majority, the less, consequently, is the election of reliable, worthy people assured.

Finally, any government created in the present form must have in its authority the power to execute its decisions. But it is clear that if the decisions of the government were each time considered useful by the majority of citizens possessing equal rights, then there would be no need of such power at all. If there were found small, isolated deviations by separate persons or small groups from the fulfillment of the will of all, then these persons or groups either should be abandoned or should be forced to that fulfillment by the disadvantages of such a deviation, without any physical power. This physical power, which every government possesses, is only necessary because no government whatsoever can be the expression of the will of the vast majority. The closer it is to this expression, the less is the physical power at the disposal of the government (example: the United States of America with forty thousand troops).

But again all these arguments lead to the idea of the harmfulness of any central authority and, consequently, to anarchy.

But let us imagine a country organized without such central authority, without a government, and we will see in what practices of society the need for such a government can be found.

Let us imagine groups of rural *obshchiny* engaged in agriculture and producing grain, cattle, and so on. Let us imagine, that by the commom consent of all the inhabitants of a given country these *obshchiny* are not considered the owners of the lands occupied by them, but only the users of them. Let us suppose, that in a separate *obshchina* there appears a parasite who shirks his work and wishes to live without working. He does not now [in present society] receive money, and without money he cannot live. Then [in future society] he will not receive money or that certification that every day he finished his portion of required labor, and without this he will also be unable to live.

Let us suppose that he begins to steal and so on. Now they send him to the district police officer. In the future, an autonomous, communal court will deal with him—by itself or through elected representatives.

In short it is clear, and about this there can be no dispute, that in all its own internal affairs the *obshchina*, just as now, is and will be able to be in command without creating a government.

But let us suppose that one *obshchina* seizes the land of another, drives its own cattle onto its meadows or plows its field. Now from this arises a whole *case* which is decided in all sorts of government courts. How would it be without these courts? In the first place, no *obshchina* of plowmen can live alone. It necessarily must enter a union of agricultural *obshchiny*, which in its turn must be in union with unions of artisans, factory workers, and so forth. It is clear that the *offended obshchina* has to appeal with the complaint to its own union of agricultural *obshchiny*. *How* must this appeal be accomplished, *how* can the union decide the issue? For this there are dozens of methods, each of which is a hundred times better than present ones. The *obshchina* can, for example, immediately summon to the location of the event the elected representatives from all the *obshchiny* of the union, and supposing that every *obshchina* is so interested in its public affairs that it gathers for the resolution of them in several days, the representatives could be on the spot and decide the dispute in about ten days. It is apparent that this is not the time to decide how to do this more conveniently. The important question is whether this method is quicker and whether it leads more truly to the goal than the existing ones.

Every decision must be implemented. Who will implement it if there are no district police officers and neighboring officials with throngs of troops? We believe that if there were an *obshchina* unreasonable enough to oppose the decision of the union it had joined voluntarily, then the union would always have a very powerful weapon against it—to exclude it and to deprive it, consequently, of the exchange of services for which this *obshchina* joined the union, [while] in addition informing all the other unions of the reasons for the expulsion. If it did happen that the reasons were erroneous, then the *obshchina* would be accepted in some other union.

It is precisely thus in the disputes among the unions of plowmen and the unions of carpenters, coal miners, iron-workers, and so on. Just as the unions of farmers cannot exist alone, so also the separate *obshchina* cannot, and they must enter into unions of a second order with other artisans, just as all the groups of workers of a given trade must [unite] among themselves.

In short, we do not see what the legal function of the state could be in such a system nor in what instances the need for it could be found.

But one can also find little need in all other matters. For this we will touch upon the main functions of the present day state: taxes (for the needs of this state); an army (for the support of this state and for protection from foreign enemies); institutions for the collection of taxes; institutions for the means of communication, the post and telegraph; institutions for the people's education; institutions for national economy, institutions for the police.

Armies, as the guardians of order, become less necessary the closer the decisions of the government express the interests of the majority. In the absence of a government they become necessary only for protection from foreign enemies. But experience has shown that regular armies have never been sufficient for protection from the invasion of enemies. Still less would they be sufficient if the invasions were accomplished by the will of an entire nation. If the whole nation wished to invade foreign regions, then only an armed populace could oppose it. The German-French war [1870] serves as the best proof. Only an armed nation could stop an army of seven hundred thousand; that is why the Germans were so afraid of a people's war, as much as, if not more than, the French government, and so harshly prevented its inception. The only means of stopping such an invasion would have been the armament of entire unions, the expedient distribution of duties in the unions and so on. Authority and command would be required only for directing a standing army and for providing it with stores and supplies; and with the disappearance of the army the authority disappears.

Means of Communication. Now, when these are located in the hands of private companies which try as much as possible to exploit private persons, it is apparent that their transfer into the hands of the government is an inconvenient measure (England). But if the very construction of railroads is the result of agreement between the producing groups of railroad workers and those *obshchiny* across whose lands the road passes, then it is apparent that such exploitation is out of the question. If the measure of any product is the amount of labor spent on it, and if the railroad association raises the transport fee above this cost, then it would be profitable for all the various unions having business with it (all the plowmen who supply the grain) to break their agreement with this association, thus forcing it to return to former relations.

The Posts and Telegraphs. It is clear that this branch presents still fewer reasons for the intervention of the state. At the same time the posts and telegraphs present an excellent example of how much can be achieved by independent development and free agreement. The whole present international system of post offices is the product of such agreement. It would have been considered an absurdity if two hundred years ago it were said to someone that a letter would circle the entire globe in several days, that it would be possible to observe its path almost around the whole globe, that it would pass among scores of sovereign states, and that the several kopecks paid for it would be distributed fairly among all these states (the smallness of the unit does not act as an obstacle, for example: the former Germanic customs union), and that all this would be the product of a free union (federal) agreement. But it is in fact so. And here, consequently, we do not see what could constitute the role of the state.

Thus, having touched upon the various functions of contemporary governments, we do not see the necessity for arranging daily life on the social foundations of government and state. Therefore, in connection with the above remarks about every government's inability to act fairly and about its harmfulness, we believe that if the fifth condition of equality is to be realized it is necessary to recognize the necessity of the abolishment of any government existing now and to give the producing *obshchiny* and artels themselves the opportunity to manage absolutely all matters concerning their members, to unite spontaneously in unions on the basis of free agreements as much as necessary, and in these unions, to decide all matters concerning the separate artels and *obshchiny*.

If the positions cited above are acknowledged, then with the total realization of all of these conditions, the ideal is depicted roughly in this way:

The population of a given territory is grouped in the villages and *obshchiny*. In all *obshchiny* the communal cultivation of the land is gradually introduced.

All the plants, factories, and workshops in the cities, all the raw materials of the owners of these factories are consigned to the use of those who worked in them. Production is on the artel basis. The distribution of occupations among the members of the artel takes place according to the voluntary agreement of the artel members.

All the houses in the cities are consigned to the common use of the whole city. In all quarters the committees determine the number of apartments needed, lock or alter the worthless ones, and construct new ones. The distribution of apartments is done by categories, depending on the number of families, and within the categories, by lot.

All the capital of urban capitalists, in hard cash or valuable items, is declared the property of all members of the territory; all promissory notes are destroyed.

At first in every factory work continues as before—let us suppose nine hours a day. Each member of the artel or *obshchina* who works this amount of time according to the assignment of the artel receives in return a receipt from the artel.

All the artels of a given trade are grouped at first in a given city, in one or in several unions, and either these unions or the artels independently enter into unions for the exchange among themselves of the products of their manufacture. Having need of farmers, bakers, herdsmen, shoemakers, and so forth each artel, of necessity, has to enter a union of all the artisans of a given city, which in its turn has to enter a union that possibly has a greater number of agricultural unions. Convinced that each artel's checks for nine hours actually represent nine hours of work of roughly equal difficulty, these unions let each other have their products on the basis of this calculation. If the farmers do not agree to enter these unions and to accept the town checks in exchange for their products, then obviously there has to be a meeting of the elected representatives from all the artels to engage in a sale of their products and in the conversion of them into hard cash. Business with all the other producing groups will proceed on the usual sale and purchase principles exactly as with all foreign trade, for as long as they do not join the union.

All the children receive instruction, vocational and theoretical, from the artel or *obshchina* itself. Since it is necessary to raise the level of education, the artels enter unions and through their combined efforts open institutes for more extensive higher education to be attended by all the youths of the union.

In every agricultural *obshchina*, in every trade artel, exact accounts will be kept. In them will be written the number of working members, the expenses for the purchase and maintenance of the instruments of labor and raw materials, the amount of products manufactured daily; thus, one can determine, on the basis of the simplest calculation, how many measures of rye, wheat, oats, plows, shovels, nails, boots, and so on represent one hour of the *obshchina's* labor. This figure serves as the standard in the exchange among the members of the *obshchina*. Guided by this and convinced of the correctness of the calculation, two or several agricultural *obshchiny*, two or several artels of various trades enter a union for the exchange of products among themselves.

According to the rules of the formation of the union the calculation will be common for the whole union; it is determined by what is equal to one hour of union labor, expressed in nails, pens, hats, grain, wine, and so forth.

Every union will have to receive many items from the outside (for example, tea, kerosene, and so on). Foreign trade is necessary for this. If this union itself exports something, then it has the opportunity by this means to receive hard cash. If not, then it can enter into alliance with the unions of the gold mine owners, in order to receive gold from them according to the same value of production; or, during a time of social upheaval, a union of gold-mine workers can be founded under the supervision of a committee of representatives elected from all the people to manage the working of gold. Clearly, the administration of the exchanges will by no means be entrusted to such a committee, but merely the accurate bookkeeping, the control for the determination of the value of production of a pound of gold. The inventory and custody of all state wealth can be entrusted to other committees, for example the unemployed capital in the museums, the conversion of jewels into national wealth, the inventory and custody of state weapons of the fleet, battle supplies, gold and silver bars, and the banks and mints, and so on.

It is apparent that all these committees will perform some of the actual or possible functions of the present-day government, but it is no less apparent that they will not at all resemble the present-day government.

One of the difficult problems of the exchange is the following: let us suppose, that the union of Viatka farmers came to the conclusion that ten hours of labor, with their soil and climate, amounts to ten measures of rye, but the union of Tambov farmers found that ten hours of their labor is equal to eleven measures of rye. And since it seems unprofitable for them to enter in common union, they do not enter a common union where this difference would be equalized. Therefore, the ironworkers and others prefer to exchange their products with the Tambov [farmers] and not with the Viatka [farmers]. Hence the source of all kinds of dissensions. This difficulty, however, is resolved rather simply by several means.

In the first place, no one ever even supposes that all the difficulties which arise could be settled at once. There is no doubt that it will be possible to solve these and many other difficulties only by means of many trials, failures, redistributions, even quarrels. The question can only be what system gives the most leeway so that ultimately, the correct exchange of the products of labor may be arranged—the present system or the one proposed? But the answer to this question cannot be open to doubt.

In the second place, even now it is possible to foresee some ways out of this difficulty: (1) It is impossible even to suppose that it would be convenient to alter the social system in such vast units as the present states of Russia. There is no doubt that such a state has to be divided into several large unions. Then each of these unions will possess a sum of manufactured riches capable of providing the opportunity to arrange a more equitable exchange. (2) If the value of production in the Viatka province is greater than in Tambov, then the value of iron, firewood, and so on will be greater in the latter. This is already one condition for the restoration of the equality of the value of grain. Finally, if in the Viatka province the production of grain costs more than in Tambov, then it will not even be set aside for export from this province. The grain is expensive here because the cultivation of the land produces so little of it that it cannot be an item of export. Therefore, grain will not even figure in the exchange of the products of the Viatka province with the others. But within the local economy of this province the difficulty in grain production will be balanced by the capacity for the production of other items. Therefore, in sum, the Viatka province will not be poorer than the others. It is well-known that mankind is not, generally speaking, poorer in one district than in another from purely physical conditions (with the exception of some arctic savages). The differences in the wealth of various provinces now depend more on relative, everyday causes than on natural ones, as do the differences in the wealth of separate persons.

Finally, it is well-known that people now cultivate unprofitable lands and work at the most unremunerative trades only because they are forced to do this, since they cannot pass on to other lands and cannot establish another trade. Therefore, perhaps one must even preserve the inequality in the exchange, since it will serve as a reason for people, too attached to the native land by sentimental affection, to abandon it sooner for resettlement to other, more convenient locations.

In general, we are not writing a scheme for the structure of a society many years in the future. If we even speak about how society could be structured in the future it is only in order to show that the destruction of presently existing obstacles will expedite the chance for a more equitable structure, only in order to jot down an outline of this future system in the most general terms. We are even deeply convinced that any attempt to define this system more precisely is a fruitless expenditure of time. And here is why. To define a system in which there is absolutely no room for any injustice whatsoever means to jump ahead many thousands of years. Such work is already fruitless, because with the abolishment of some injustices that exist now even the conception of justice, of good and evil, of the good and bad, of the useful and harmful, will be modified. Therefore, there does not even exist now that mind which could comprehend all the future moral ideas of mankind. Consequently, any contemporary idea will be a manifestation of present-day conceptions of morality, a manifestation which will be impossible, because before it is realized, in its totality, new conceptions of justice will be created and *begin to be realized*.

Consequently, it is impossible to construct theoretically an ideal which could be realized even approximately.

But no matter how good the theoretical ideal, it has no value whatever if it does not have guarantees of realization. And it can have a guarantee of realization only when it is the expression of the existing aspirations and hopes of the majority. Meanwhile, one can say only that the aspiration of the majority is the realization of the above-mentioned ideals of equality. In what practical form these ideals will be shaped no one can now decide, least of all, of course, the scholar. For this it is necessary to know the quantity and forms of the integral of the total aggregate of the system of ideas, the degree of development, the tendencies of each separate person. We need not speak of the scholar, who cannot know this (for neither statistics nor history is, and for a very long time will not be, the expression of this aspect of life); yet even the man standing closest to the people can determine only in the most general features what could now satisfy mankind.

Our concern is to express this general striving, to elucidate it for those to whom it is still more vague than to us; to show that these hopes can be realized; to encourage this belief in those in whom it is weakening; to show that the main obstacles to the realization of these hopes are not in their vagueness but are external obstacles; to point out the weak aspects of these obstacles, to create around ourselves groups for the ruthless destruction of this whole armor of obstacles, and to fall [in battle] in the breaking of this armor.

But to work out the particulars of these ideals, that is, to work out the fine points of *one's own* dialectic, to exercise *one's mind* with logical rigor—this is the concern of idle parasites. It must not be *our* concern.

In light of all the foregoing, we believe that the realization of the future system must proceed simultaneously in all its aspects, that is, that along with the destruction of the economic nobility must go the destruction of the contemporary state system.

Further, proceeding from the principle that the more clearly defined the goals and character of the revolution, and the more socialist these goals, then the more it will have adherents, we believe that the revolution must strive to realize all these goals at once, as a whole, bearing in mind that limitations and compromises will inevitably be provoked by the activity itself.

Therefore, we would believe it necessary to take the following steps immediately after the disorganization of the present government:

The land should be declared the property of all, of the whole Russian people.

Every village and countryside settlement should receive the use of those lands which they now control.

All the lands taken by the whole countryside or by separate peasants of the village or countryside should become the possession of this village or countryside.

All the landowner's lands which are lying fallow should become the possession of the former peasants of this landowner.

All the lands bought by separate peasants for themselves should become the possession of the whole community of the village where this peasant is registered.

All the workers living off the wages of the landowners or leaseholders should register in the village which formerly was in the possession of the landowner. If there are more than ten of them, they should form a special settlement, having received from the *mir* a strip equal to those of the other members of the village. The landowners who survive should work the land of the *mir* on an equal basis with the other peasants of the village or countryside.

No recompense whatsoever for the expropriated land is due: nothing special from the village community allotment is due. If the *mir* should designate them [the landowners] as incapable of any work it should be empowered to fix them a stipend at its discretion, equal to that of the aged.

All the landowner's farmsteads, gardens, draft animals, instruments, and machines should become the possession of the former peasants of that landowner. If the landowner's land is bought by someone after the emancipation of the peasants, then it goes to the former peasants with all that is on it. If the estate is constructed in a new place where there are no peasants, then it is allotted to the workers on the estate.

In every district a committee should be named from the elected peasant representatives, in order to make the lands equal among the peasants of that district, to draw up the boundaries and to place posts.

The subsequent redivision of land should occur in three, five, and ten years.

Every plant or factory should become the possession of the workers in that plant or factory, along with all the machines and supplies of raw materials.

The workers must select from themselves a manager, foremen, and so forth.

In every factory a strict calculation must be made of how many people worked every day and how much was done.

At first, for a certain time, every worker should receive some pay for every hour of work.

From all factories of every region, honest workers must be chosen to ascertain how many people work every day in each factory and how much and what is made.

Everything that is manufactured by every factory should be pooled in stores and for a certain period should not be sold.

The former masters of the factories who survive should be accepted equally with all in any factory—given the consent of the workers of that factory—at a post to which they are assigned.

All former officials, from ministers to copyists, should be accepted with equal rights into any artel, given the consent of the artel.

All former soldiers should be dispersed to their homes, having received a certain sum for the journey.

In each village an artel guard of some size should be formed.

All former criminals should return to their homes.

The offences of each should be judged honestly in that artel where he is registered.

All the houses in the cities should become the possession of the whole city.

In each quarter, committees should be named for the calculation of how many apartments are needed for the inhabitants of this quarter, for the subdivision of them into unmarried, artel, and family [apartments]. All those registered in apartments for the unmarried receive them by lot from those listed in this category. The same holds for the artel and family [categories].

All cash capital of separate persons, institutions, palaces, churches, and monasteries must go into a common treasury into which it must be placed according to schedule. After some time it will be divided among the provinces or districts without exception.

All ships should become the possession of the sailors who work on them.

Committees should be named for appraising the value of transporting [cargo] for a given distance on each ship. All the promissory notes either of individuals or of the state should be destroyed by burning on the square.

All *ownership* records and serf books in the courts must be burned, but all account books in the stores must be preserved.

All wares in the stores must be registered in detail and records made thereof. After a certain time they should be given out to artels selected from among those of the city.

In each city a committee should be named for the purchase of all those provisions the peasants bring to the marketplace. For a certain time the distribution should be free, but subsequently this committee should make the transaction with hour-receipts.

We move now to the question on which the greatest division exists among the various schools. This question is whether the realization of the stated ideal is possible by peaceful means or whether it will necessarily be achieved by means of revolution, upheaval?

Very many believe that this realization must be achieved by peaceful, gradual means. Very many go further and say that gradual [development] of some aspects of this ideal must take place first, at least in part, and subsequently the remaining (that is, not only each of the aspects of the ideal gradually, but also each one separately).

The most usual way indicated is first of all the acquisition of political rights by the people, that is, the freedom of assembly, freedom of the press, freedom of the composition of societies. And subsequently, the establishment of a government of the people (and even of voting by the people). The origin of this way of thinking is obvious. It has blown over directly from Western Europe.

However, there are many extremely weighty objections against this path.

It goes without saying that they [those who favor peaceful means] proceed from that utterly unproven position that every people must inevitably pass through all those phases of development which other peoples have passed through. But what is important for us is not its origin, but the fact that it assumes that the people's use of political rights is a better condition for the acceleration of social upheaval than the absence of these rights. By now one can show a priori that this supposition is false. If the question were what condition of the people is more advantageous for peaceful progress, then there is no doubt that it is the one in which the people can freely align themselves, discuss their affairs, and execute their decisions. But the matter takes on quite another aspect if one assumes that the social transformation cannot occur by peaceful means, but inevitably must occur by means of insurrection. If one admits this position as fundamental, then the question becomes this: what condition most hastens social insurrection—the one in which the people enjoy the freedom of meetings and societies, the freedom of speech and of the press, or that in which it enjoys not one of these guarantees, not even individual security? What position most encourages the revolutionary spirit of the people? If that is the way the question is stated there can be no doubt of the answer. Not we, but the very defenders of the acquisition of political rights who assert that the use of these rights is the best guarantee against revolutionary outbreaks, answer the question by themselves. But this position can be corroborated by many other considerations. We are ready to admit that the freedoms of speech and assembly extraordinarily assist the elucidation of all considerations and ideas; it also stands to reason that the clarity of the consciousness in a large measure assists its realization. But we know very well that the intellect and the will operate in every action. And the significance of the latter is incomparably greater than that of the former in all ordinary life and the more so in any unusual action. Indeed, by no conclusions whatever is it possible to convince a man that it pays for him to take up arms at a given moment, since such an appeal is an appeal for self-sacrifice. By no conclusions whatever is it possible to convince a man that it will be best of all for him to risk his life, in order to gain possible prosperity for his neighbors and children, [as] in a lottery (that is, in a gathering of facts where it is impossible to weigh *all the pros and cons*). Between a clear consciousness and a fervent desire to realize the good (though necessarily vague) ideal, [there is] a terrible abyss. And this abyss explains all those facts which can lead to the corroboration of the stated position.

Indispensable for the beginning of any revolution are, first of all, the realization of dissatisfaction with the present, the consciousness of the endlessness of this condition and of its irreparability by customary means, and finally, a readiness for risk in order to change this condition.

For the success of the revolution, the force of pressure, weakness of the government, and clarity of the aspirations are indispensable.

The people's enjoyment of political rights for all these indispensable elements (not excluding even the last) acts in the reverse direction.

The less secure a person feels in his most sacred rights, the greater is his inclination to revolutionary methods of action, the greater is his animosity towards the contemporary order. Examples: the mass uprisings in China and Spain on the one hand, and, [on the other], the obtuse satisfaction of the citizens of the Swiss republic with their condition. In fact, all large-scale uprisings occur when the people can bear it no longer (after hunger, disease, and so forth). The Spaniards declared that if the government began to take drastic measures, this would provoke an uprising of vast dimensions.

The less measures are taken which arouse hopes for further improvements, the less futile prove to be any beginnings on which the hopes at first were placed, the stronger is the consciousness of the endlessness of the condition, the irreparability of it by the usual reforms, the stronger is the readiness for revolutionary action.

It is necessary to keep in mind at this point that the more trivial the reforms, the more clearly evident is their triviality to the entire mass. And the reforms are the more trivial the less they enlist the energies of gifted people. We know what a mass of rather clever people took great interest in the judicial reform in Russia, because this reform was most cleverly arranged; and we also know that the revolutionary attitude of the Russian youth in a large measure is supported by the fact that Russia lags behind contemporary states and that this youth cannot apply its energies to such pursuits which it knows from the life of Western Europe. Under the conditions in Germany, they would turn into learned professors trying to solve a question of metaphysics, of science, but not of life.

It goes without saying, finally, that the more precarious the material and political condition of the people, the stronger is the readiness for risk on their part.

We see, consequently, that the possession of political rights acts on all sides as a diminution of revolutionary initiative.

Thus, it is clear that this fact weakens the main condition of the success of a revolution, that is, the force of pressure. Besides, the power of the government is increased. The less the government violates various rights of the individual, the more it assures the protection of property, the better [and] more popular it is, the stronger it is, the more easily it can suppress an uprising. The less popular it is, the weaker it is. Soldiers, although tyrannized during the time of Alexander I, were in many places ready to follow their own humane officers. The Muscovite *khozhalyi*[1] of the good old times would never refuse the government those services which the Petersburg police officer refuses and will refuse.

All these positions are so obvious and their corroborating facts are so generally well known that there is no need to pause over them. We proceed to the clarification of the views. It is said to us: the more free the discussion of the questions, the better will the vague strivings be explained and the easier it will be to realize them. In an abstract form, this is indisputable. But here again is the same everlasting confusion of the idea of the future system with the idea of the present one; the same everlasting habit of thinking in abstract ideas, without hitting upon their real, ordinary forms. Let us suppose that this position is true. But where and when? In the future system— *yes!* In the present one—absolutely *not*. Indeed, those main-

1 Military police.—*Editor*.

taining this position forget that the primary condition for the clarification of a view is its certainty, its delineation from others, the truthfulness of those views with which it conflicts. But if the acquisition of political rights gives the socialists the complete freedom to express themselves, then it gives no less a freedom to their opponents; together with the propagation of social ideas goes the propagation of antisocial ones. But still worse: there arises the propagation of whole billions of intermediate opinions, each of which tries to disguise one or another side of the common evils, to cover it with this or that rag, to distract from it with this or that trinket. If all the opinions were stated with something approaching candor, they would be almost harmless. If this whole net of trinkets was proposed through error and not with cunning, if it were proposed with force, with intellectual clarity, then the truth would emerge from the conflict.

But under [present] circumstances it fully achieves its aim; it actually deprives less developed people of the possibility to confront matters squarely. And to this intellectual and cultural superiority, to the general servility before self-imputed knowledge, to all the forces which heighten this servility—to this is added the strength of capital, which provides the opportunity to spread one's ideas by newspaper propaganda, by cajolery, by bribery (direct and indirect) of the gifted and influential individuals from the mass, as well as in other ways. What kind of socialist propaganda can endure competition with newspapers with an initial expenditure of 140 million rubles of capital in two years, issued in a hundred thousand copies (like *The Times* and *Daily News* [of London]), and having the powerful support of the entire civilized bourgeois public? It is worthwhile to remember how much each such newspaper corrupts people every day so as to curse this freedom of speech in contemporary society—which provides no opportunity for a socialist counterbalance. And this propagation is terrible not because of the filth, not because of the abomination of its opinions; it is terrible because it does not in the least propound its opinions, but simply enfolds a man in the mist of a world foreign to him. This is not the sting of a snake, this is the captivating glance of a boa constrictor, this is the slime which engulfs the helpless man.

And these gentlemen forget still more. They forget the available time and the available brainpower of each man and of each society in total. When tomorrow it is necessary to select a collector of taxes in the *obshchina*, when the day after tomorrow one will have to decide between this and that candidate for the chamber of state or government, when tomorrow it is necessary at a meeting to speak out against the tax on tobacco and in answer to the speech of an agitator to adduce just as many facts, when, even, it is simply necessary to know what the Virginians think about the tax on tobacco, when tomorrow one will have to listen to the lofty speech of a learned orator and so on, and each somewhat honest man will outdo himself on these "issues"—then will there remain much time and ready brainpower to think about the social revolution, about the *future* system, when in the *present one* . . .[2] and when the first ten hours of the working day are spent before the puddling furnace with a very heavy poker in [one's] hands?

And after all this can one still speak about the acquisition of political rights? No, there is no other way for us: there, where there are not these rights—there is no need for us to trouble about them; there, where they are—we must not use them, employing the law of Rostopchin with respect to the French army of 1812: *faire de vide devant eux.*

II

We proceed now to the most difficult but at the same time the most essential question of our program, the question about the practical measures which should be taken for the realization of our ideal.

We have already stated that in our opinion the realization of this ideal must occur by means of a social revolution. In this we do not at all flatter ourselves with the hope that with the first revolution the ideal will be realized in all its completeness; we are even convinced that for the realization of the equality we have sketched, many years are still required, and many limited, perhaps even general, outbursts. But we are also convinced that the more completely, the more widely the demands of the masses are established from the very first revolution, the more clearly and practically these demands are expressed— then the more the first step will destroy those cultural forms which hinder the realization of the socialist system, the more disorganized those forces and attitudes to which present-day social and state daily life adhere will be; then, the more peaceful the successive upheavals will be, and the sooner will follow successively large-scale improvements in the attitudes of people.

Therefore, our goal must be to apply our powers to hastening this outburst, so as to elucidate those hopes and aspirations which exist in the vast majority in vague forms, so that in good time one can take advantage of those circumstances under which an outburst could have the most favorable outcome, so that, finally, the outburst itself would occur in the name of clearly expressed demands, and precisely in the name of those cited by us above.

We must, consequently, set forth the sum total of measures by which, in our opinion, these goals can best be reached.

If with the working out of our ideal we could proceed largely by logical means, then here our main support will be experience. While speaking about the ideal, we could proceed from the common aspirations and hopes of the masses, and deduce that social structure which could be the best way to use these aspirations (of course, not contradicting the character of the views of our people) and which could be the expression of conceptions about justice that are always inherent in all the masses. Here we cannot be satisfied with the general hopes and aspirations of our people; we must take into account the entire range of private notions, ways of thinking, attitudes, actions, and so forth; it is not possible to foresee in advance which ones; it is possible to find out only by means of experience.

Further, in the general aspirations of the masses of all peoples there is very much in common; that is why the aspirations and hopes expressed by Western European workers are, in many respects, accepted sympathetically by ours. But in questions of revolutionary practice the Western European examples must be introduced only with extreme caution, since it is extremely difficult to weigh in each given instance the totality of everyday conditions which cause this or that result.

But these considerations also define the one common trait of the whole second half of our program. On the one hand we now consider our ideals finally settled, we consider the fundamental principles of our ideals invariable, and we will make any particular concession only when we see the final impossibility of realizing some aspect of our ideal in practice, and then, nevertheless, will consider this concession forced and temporary. On the other hand, since the program of our practical preparatory measures must be determined not only by their expediency in view of the common ideal, but also by the totality of the everyday conditions of the milieu in which we act, then we will not consider this part of our program something invariable; on the contrary, we will be ready for any change in it, if only life will show us that such methods of action will better and more directly lead to the proposed goal.

There are, however, several fundamental positions which we consider possible and necessary to maintain unchanged in all our practical, preparatory work. This is the rejection within the revolutionary organization of such relations among people, and of such ways of conduct, as directly contradict the ideal for the sake of which they are introduced. Thus, we absolutely reject the introduction into the revolutionary organization of a hierarchy of ranks which enslaves many people to one or several persons; an inequality in the interrelations of the members of one and the same organization; mutual deception and coercion for the attainment of our goals. It goes without saying, of course, that we consider all similar means completely permissible and even necessary in all our relations with the government with which we enter into battle.

We will still return to these questions when we elucidate the character of the organization proposed by us.

First of all, we are deeply convinced that no revolution is possible if the need for it is not felt in the people themselves. No handful of people, however energetic and talented, can evoke a popular insurrection, if the people themselves, in their own best representatives, do not achieve the realization that they have no other way out of the position with which they are dissatisfied except insurrection. Consequently, the business of any revolutionary party is not to call for insurrection but only to pave the way for the success of the imminent insurrection, that is, to unite the dissatisfied elements, to promote the acquaintance of separate units or groups with the aspirations and actions of other similar groups, to assist the people in defining more clearly the true causes of dissatisfaction, to assist them in determining more clearly their actual enemies, removing the mask from the enemies who hide behind some decorous disguise, and finally, to contribute to the elucidation both of the nearest practical goals and the means of their realization.

Therefore, first of all, are there these dissatisfied elements among the Russian people? Does there exist that mood which is necessary for the success of any revolutionary organization?

We can boldly answer that there are. All our personal observations, all the information we receive, irrefutably indicates that among our peasantry and factory workers there is a smoldering discontent; that with the systematic destruction of the masses of people this discontent is growing; that in the first period after the emancipation of the peasants it was incomparably weaker than now; that the hope continues to live among the peasants that by some means the landowners and the peasants will be made equal in regard to the land, taxes, and natural duties; that the hope that this equalization will proceed from above is gradually being lost; that the worship of the person of the tsar is in some places being undermined noticeably; that this worship, about which so many have spoken before, is in general extremely fragile and very easily gives way to completely different attitudes, especially among the peasant youth; that the belief in the fact that the tsar is completely powerless among the lords surrounding him is constantly strengthening and thus leads inevitably to the fact that the people, once their patience is exhausted, will undertake to destroy these lords mercilessly (and without their support the tsar will become a powerless figurehead); that this discontent of the peasantry is noticed not in any one locality, but to a greater or lesser degree everywhere; that only those who have never been closely associated with the peasantry or factory workers deny this, and, on the contrary, all those who have been in some manner close to the peasantry or factory workers confirm it; that the observations of the same people lead to the conclusion that the readiness for insurrection, for risk, is much greater than even the optimists could believe; that finally, this is confirmed by the local uprisings which are constantly recurring. So much for the attitudes in the economic sphere.

As for the state [sphere], we see on one hand the greatest indifference to all reforms of government, on the other—a general hostility towards any representative of state interests; this hostility constantly grows with the increase of state extortions.

Yet there is a divergence between the nobility and the people; the development of senseless luxury among the nobility, the rapid development among the nobility of an unimaginable avidity and depravity which accompanies the decline of creation, talent, and serious thought, and the development of cruelty, of the mad pursuit of easy gain, and so on, all attest that the nobility on its part will not decide in time on the necessary concessions and will not be able to satisfy the people with them.

Finally, the development in Europe of the military-predatory element, the senseless increase of regular armies, and the inevitability of large scale wars in Europe, indicate the inevitability of such a development of state power as must rapidly lead many states of Europe, beginning with the poorest, to complete bankruptcy, and the people to further ruin. In short, all that we see around us leads to the unquestionable conviction that to begin organizing a revolutionary party is quite timely and that the tasks of this party are significantly eased by the assistance it meets everywhere.

For the convenience of survey, the tasks of this party can be subdivided into two branches of activity, which, however, must in fact proceed simultaneously and inseparably: on one hand is the dissemination of its views and the increase in the number of like-minded persons, and on the other hand, the unification of them into one common organization.

For convenience we will examine these two activities separately.

First of all, where must our activity be directed, where must we chiefly spread our views and seek for ourselves like-minded persons—among the student youth and nobility in general or among the peasantry and urban workers?

We answer this question categorically, and we consider this answer the fundamental position in our practical program: unquestionably among the peasantry and urban workers. Here must we spread our views, here must we seek comrades who would aid the further dissemination of these views; with these comrades we must enter into a friendly, closely united organization. We do not wish to sever any relations with the educated milieu and especially not with the milieu of student youth; but, refusing to take upon ourselves the permanent role of tutoring this youth in the stated direction, we will enter into close relations only with those circles or individuals who immediately inspire the confidence or the almost complete hope that they will direct their subsequent activity among the peasantry and urban workers. For the mass of educated youth we are ready to do only one thing: to disseminate, and (if the cause cannot spread without our assistance, and also if we have enough extra energy) to prepare those books that directly assist the explanation of our ideals and our goals, that make available those facts which show the complete inevitability of the social upheaval and the necessity to unite, to organize the *people's* awakened strengths.

We came to these conclusions by means of experience, by means of life itself, but we can also confirm them with several considerations. We will set forth both these and others.

First of all, the insurrection must proceed among the peasantry and urban workers themselves. Only then can it count on success. But no less necessary for the success of the insurrection is the existence among the very insurrectionists of a strong, friendly, active group of people who, serving as a bond between the separate localities and having clearly determined *how* to formulate the demands of the people, how to avoid various traps, how to secure its victory, are agreed on the means of action. It is clear, moreover, that such a party must not stand outside the people but among them, must serve not as a champion of some alien opinions worked out in isolation, but only as a more distinct, more complete expression of the demands of the people themselves; in short, it is clear that such a party cannot be a group of people alien to the peasantry and workers, but must be the focus of the most conscious and decisive forces of those peasants and urban workers. Any party standing outside the people—especially one of the nobility—however it be inspired with a desire for the well-being of the people, however well it expresses the demands of the people, will inevitably be doomed to ruin, together with all the rest, as soon as the rebelling people with their first deeds lay open the chasm between the nobility and peasantry. And we see in this only an entirely justified retribution for the fact that those of this party were earlier not able to become comrades among the people but rather remained supreme guides. Only those whose former way of life, whose previous deeds are wholly of a character which merits the faith of the peasantry and workers will be heeded by them; and this will be only the activists of the peasantry itself and those who will wholeheartedly surrender themselves to the people's affairs and prove themselves not with heroic deeds in a moment of enthusiasm, but with all their previous ordinary life; those who, having cast off any shade of nobility in life, now will enter into close relations with the peasantry and urban workers, tied by personal friendship and confidence. Finally, once the necessity of the unification of the people's awakened forces is recognized, then we definitely can not understand how it would be possible to avoid the conclusion that the only possible place is one among the peasantry and workers themselves. Such a way of life serves as direct proof to one's associates that professed convictions are not simple verbiage, but a matter of one's whole life. Such is the main reason which prompts us to transfer our activity to the midst of the peasantry and urban workers. But there are still several secondary considerations which lead to the same conclusion.

Most important is the relatively mild acceptance by our students of the propagation of the socialist revolution and of an active participation in this direction. Moreover, it is clear that such a rejection is evoked not by a deficiency of those facts which might lead to a belief in the intolerable nature of today's social order—these facts are too generally known—nor by the impossibility of being convinced that any useful reform in this direction cannot be peaceful—in this respect as well, contemporary history is too rich in facts. [It arises] simply from not being receptive to any sort of extreme views, an inability to renounce the tradition of scholarly learning and, finally, simply an unwillingness to accept in theory that sort of conclusion whose fulfillment in life is by no means desired. Besides that, all the educated youth is so infected by an awe of authority, so corrupted by the habit of demanding hundreds of facts to be convinced, facts twisted and presented in all sorts of ways, dug out from the same various, authoritative sources, when there already exists a whole aggregate of facts illustrating the argument (just like those scholars who maintain that the variability of species *still* is unproven). Finally, they are so accustomed to demanding that the path of the future development of mankind be scientifically deduced for them, when to deduce this scientifically is not possible either now or in the very distant future—that, generally speaking, any propagandizing among the educated youth requires so much erudition and dialectics that it involves a terribly unproductive waste of time, and a distraction of energy from incomparably more urgent matters. Moreover, those of the young who sincerely seek a way out of their doubts, will, on finding out the necessary facts, inevitably come to the same conclusion themselves concerning the necessity of revolutionary activity.

For this reason, our responsibility regarding these individuals should only be to give them the opportunity to learn certain facts, that is, to acquaint them with the main events of the most recent history of the working-class movement in the West and at home; with the relation of the nobility and the government to this movement; and, finally, with the results which we ourselves are approaching in our activity—but even here only as much as our assistance can *promote* the appearance and distribution of such books. Thus, we, of course, will keep up an acquaintance with such circles where it is possible to meet with people who, uncorrupted by the aristocratic-scholastic spirit, willingly agree with the necessity of transferring their activity to the worker's milieu; and we will try not to miss the opportunity of drawing near such people and arranging things with them. But to take on oneself the role of tutor, to concern oneself with the education and training of the individuals working among the people—this we positively decline, since we can always find like-minded people of much greater reliability, in many respects more useful, and in any case more deserving if we turn directly to the milieu of the peasantry and the urban workers. Finally, we must acknowledge that even the very best representatives of civilized society, once they have managed to get used to its corroding conditions, never provide such solid representatives of propaganda among the people as one would wish. They are so accustomed to the accepted form of life and thought, and to a certain type of world view, that [few] isolated individuals ever completely give them up.

Finally, there is one other feature of activity among the peasants and urban workers which should not be left without comment. The necessary and primary condition of any success whatsoever among the peasants and the workers is the full renunciation of any signs of nobility, the lowering of one's material circumstances almost to the level of that of the milieu where one intends to act. And one must work, do actual work, which each worker and each peasant can understand precisely as work. On the other hand, we know that every revolutionary activist is required to have a moral strength, a stubborn, steadfast strength of will. And every party actually always did strive to instill this quality in its members, but for the most part they strove to achieve this largely by mutual moral influences. Without denying the effectiveness of the latter, we consider it insufficient, and believe that a better school for instilling this will is the voluntary assumption of pleasant, useful (though not easy) persistent labor and the rejection of material well-being. A person unable to renounce these comforts, when he sees the usefulness of such renunciation, is not capable of persistent, tedious labor, and never will be capable of persistent revolutionary activity. He might be the hero of a moment, but we have no need of heroes: in moments of passion, they appear of themselves, from among the most ordinary people. We need people who, once having come to a certain conviction, are for its sake ready to withstand all possible deprivations day in and day out. But activity among the peasants and workers demands precisely this rejection of every comfort of life, a lowering of one's prosperity to a level attainable by the worker, and—work, without fail, work. Thus, we see in the activity indicated by us both an unavoidable educational significance and, beyond that, the best means of testing people. If any sort of deprivation was to be assumed expiatory penance or exclusively a means of education, then we, of course, would not consider it; we are not a monastic order. But in our century of lying and deceit by others and ourselves, we consider it not superfluous to note that activity among the peasants and the workers, though provoked by entirely different considerations, does have, coincidentally, this meaning and this significance.

On the other hand, we see that the search among the peasantry and the urban workers for individuals who might serve as centers for further propagandizing the idea of the necessity of a socialist upheaval (in the direction indicated above) gives results far better than even the most daring innovator could have expected several years ago. We could draw a picture here of the results achieved in several corners of Russia, but in order not to give a fuzzy, incomplete picture instead of the one it would be appropriate to trace we will restrain ourselves once and for all. Anyone sincerely desiring to learn these results can always find the opportunity to do so orally, from us or from our friends.

Here is why we set forth the basic position of our practical program—we intend to disseminate our views and to search out those who think as we do almost exclusively among the peasantry and the industrial workers.

We now pass to the possible objections to this position. It may be pointed out to us: it is too soon to undertake such activity. We are few; when we gather a number sufficient so that our activity among the people might have noticeable results, then we, of course, will set out to the peasantry and the workers' milieu. Till that time, let us gather friends from among the educated youth.

In part we have already answered this objection by pointing out that we will sooner find like-minded people in the peasant and working-class milieu than in the students' milieu. But we could introduce even more particular arguments against this objection.

First of all, this objection assumes as proved one proposition which, however, is not proved, and indeed is not true. This is that the most productive propagandists and organizers among the people apparently are, and will be, the so-called intelligentsia. We consider this position completely false. Even if a man from the intelligentsia is better educated, more skilled in argumentation, more capable of finding in each fact a particular side, then it still by no means follows that such a person is necessarily a better agitator than a person from the milieu of the people. Experience up to now leads to the conclusion that agitators as devoted to the task can arise from the milieu of the people as arose from the intelligentsia. As concerns the persuasiveness of the arguments of these [educated] agitators, it must be remembered that they will have dealings not with scholars, who are always ready to hide behind every barrier, behind every bush, if only to uphold some traditional idea, but with people not prejudiced against the truth of social views. If the arguments of such agitators could not persevere against the argument of some philosopher, then this is proof of the idea that the existing structure is so bad and so inflexible that it is necessary, and possible, to change it only through revolution— [an idea] which, once instilled, transforms itself into belief among these agitators, and does not give way before any argument; after this a person sooner seeks the motivation of what is being said to him than the logical proof of what is being asserted. Thus, we are convinced that to be persuaded of the injustice of the present system, of its inability to alter itself without pressure on the part of the oppressed, and, finally, of the possibility of its change by this means, in no way requires the extensive preparation which the civilized youth supposes. But once having acknowledged that the preparation of the social revolution requires incomparably less training than that which we receive, if only it be directed expediently—and that the training of such people who are not at all prejudiced requires no great amount of time—we must accordingly acknowledge further that, because of the range and type of his activity, an agitator from the people will be incomparably more useful than an agitator from the civilized milieu. This last assertion is already so clear that we will not enlarge on it.

Further, we consider it a central mistake to set up a goal of creating agitators among the people who hold themselves at a distance from the people and move in the circle of their own intelligentsia comrades. It is impossible to suddenly cross at some given moment from the spheres of the intelligentsia to the milieu of the people, just as one pleases. The spheres of the intelligentsia pervasively place on the people who move in them a characteristic stamp, which it is first necessary to renounce in order to have success among the people. To become a populist agitator in several days is impossible; it is necessary to be trained in this activity. For this reason, we consider the best means for the achievement of *this* aim of ours to be to proceed immediately to activity among the people, no matter how small the circle of individuals who have arrived at this same conclusion. We are also convinced that rallying people in the name of a future activity is impossible, or at least, extremely inconvenient, and that it is much easier to rally people in the name of an activity in whose possibility and appropriateness everyone can believe now, and in which one can immediately engage oneself. By showing the results achieved and acting on people not merely by words, but by words and deeds, it is considerably easier to convince them of that of which one is oneself convinced. Since it is necessary to have dealings with the most ordinary people, and since any undertaking must be built with the assistance of precisely these people, it is necessary to keep in mind that any unification in the name of an activity proposed for the future, in which it is not possible to be immediately engaged, will lead to the formation of a circle of such people whose mutual inclination and influence on one another will more quickly provide the main business, and they will sooner completely forget about their future goal. Finally, in immediately setting off for activity among the people (and we suggest that the educated youth with whom we are in agreement do this), we at once give them the opportunity to test and prove their strengths in that endeavor which demands the rejection of many previous traditions. Moreover, this is at the same time an act in the service of the future revolution, for each one of the educated youth, even though he might not consider himself prepared for agitation among his educated fellows, always has so many facts already in reserve that he can share them with the people of the peasantry and the workers. Even if his ideals about the future are not so clearly understood by them as to serve as an object of dissemination, he always can assist the development among the workers and peasants of a criticism of existing conditions and the elucidation of the reasons for all the evils of contemporary life. Such contact with the peasants and workers not only does not hinder the development of ideals of the future in him [the educated youth] but even will promote the development of precisely those ideals which result directly from a rejection of the falsity of all aspects of existing conditions.

In short, we believe that: (1) to unite in order to proceed immediately to activity among the people is the most direct route; (2) to unite in the name of some future enterprise is extremely inconvenient; (3) to unite in the name of an enterprise already under way is considerably more expedient and useful; (4) any result achieved in activity among the people is already a result achieved in the cause of the social revolution; (5) activity among the people is activity which gives the opportunity to every honest person to apply his strengths; (6) this activity offers the most satisfactory conditions for his further personal development and excludes the possibility of being distracted from his ultimate aims; (7) finally, such activity, conducted jointly, is the best means of harmoniously encompassing the varied shades of opinions, which will always exist, and to bring them to a more direct expression of the aspirations for equality which are inherent in the people.

For this reason we consider as a definite mistake a program which demands full agreement among the participants of all details of the ideal and, besides that, the organization of an extensive group of participants before proceeding to activity among the people.

For this reason we say to each honest man, no matter how isolated he might be in some corner of Russia: assume that position in which it will be possible for you to come together with the peasants and urban workers on an equal level; begin to gather like-minded people from among them, and try to train populist agitators devoted to the undertaking from among the better people of this milieu; then, in the name of the incipient undertaking, gather around yourself friends from the intelligentsia who have not been contaminated by the nobility.

This is the direct expression of our views on this question. We can only add that daily experience indicates that a very great number of activists in all parts of Russia have come to the same conclusion, completely independent of one another.

The question arises, then, in what situation can activity among the people be most useful? In what situation should the populist activist begin?

To these questions we can give one general, categorical answer. Most important is that the [situation] in which a man lives in these circumstances be such that any worker or peasant entering his house and speaking with him sees in his form of life a worker or peasant just like himself, and if he [the worker] feels a difference between himself and the other, it is only in the degree of development. Thus, any such situation in which a person in order to retain his place is required to live in the manner of the nobility, we consider definitely disadvantageous.

We, therefore, positively reject the possibility [that persons] in the positions of any government officials, landholders, and so on will have success. We believe, then, that the most advantageous situation is the situation of the peasant or the industrial factory worker. But we believe that there are also many other situations which do not exclude the possibility of activity in certain cases, as, for example, a village doctor's assistant, sometimes a teacher, even perhaps a district clerk, and so forth. This would not be the place to go into an analysis of the relative advantages of these situations; guided by a self-established aim, each can weigh the advantages and disadvantages of any situation better than we.

We now pass to the most immediate definition of what must properly comprise, in our opinion, the activity of everyone placed in such a situation. In its general features this activity is clear. It is: (1) to elucidate to one's associates the central deficiencies of the existing system; (2) to elucidate that masked and obvious exploitation to which the worker is subjected by all the higher strata of the society and the state; (3) to point out the means of escaping this condition, that is, to convince others that this system of society will not change without strong pressure from the oppressed, that any concession from the nobility can be forced only by strength; finally, that to strive to achieve, even [successfully] to achieve, some one particular concession would not have any significance, given the solidarity of the economic and state exploitation; (4) to convince others that the forceful appropriation of the nobility's and the state's means of exploitation is possible, and that there are facts to confirm [the view] that an agreement will be established between the peasants and the workers of various localities when this results; (5) finally, to unite the most active individuals into one general organization, that is, to present the opportunity for activists of different localities to become personally acquainted, to find out, in this way, about the course of affairs in different places, to confer and to arrange among themselves relatively general measures.

If it is agreed that this must be the character of any activity which is located among the peasants and urban workers, then one disputed issue is resolved: should propaganda be directed at the separate individual or at the masses? In other words, what sort of propaganda should be conducted—*personal* or *mass*? We do not now have sufficient experience to decide this question definitely, but we will propose here several considerations regarding both possibilities.

We believe that if the uprising does not occur immediately, in a very short interval of time, then conducting propaganda which is overt, ubiquitous, and directed to one and all is impossible and indeed useless. Going among the villages, sowing on the run ideas about the necessity of an uprising, creating momentary impressions (granting that a person is in such a position that the peasantry listens to him), we consider useless, and, most important, relatively ineffective at the present moment. Any momentary influence in this direction will not endure; it will very soon fade if the same idea is not subsequently enforced constantly by local populist agitators. Finally, to produce a coordinated impression of some strength on the immense expanse of Russia would require considerably more activists than could be gathered now.

For this reason we would consider a permanent influence more useful, and given this, an influence both on opinion in general in a given village or even neighborhood, and an influence on separate individuals. But in this [latter] case the influence [must be] so strong and complete that, with the departure of the activists from the village, those separate individuals who remain would continue to explain to their fellow villagers the same views and would continue to gather the better individuals for the expansion of the undertaking. Moreover, we consider it necessary, of course, that this village or rural area should subsequently be visited constantly (and the oftener the better) by the one who previously lived in it, or by those who through him acquire an acquaintance with a circle of selected people of that village. We consider as no less necessary, then, that the circle of this village should be acquainted not only with that agitator who lived there, but with people from circles formed in other villages. Perhaps periodic meetings will be necessary for this, which we consider completely feasible. If these meetings had to be limited only to delegates' stories of what was happening in the various places, they would still be useful. But it is more likely that at those meetings some general questions concerning the general undertaking will be raised.

We believe, then, that it would be useful for every village circle to create some similar organization, that is, it should meet for the discussion of the general business of the circle (and there always is such general business, and the more zealous the agitator, the more there will be), it should create some division of responsibilities according to general agreement, and should communicate with other village circles with which it is familiar. We would suggest that it is never necessary to stop because of the possible insignificance of a circle's composition or of the issues available at a given moment. A circle might consist of only three people, but if these people should be united by a close, personal friendship, then they would find general issues; and once having acknowledged themselves mutually bound by the general enterprise, they would have more inclination to activity. If a meeting consisted only of representatives from four to five circles and if the result was only a realistic, graphic description by each of these four to five people, assembled from different places, that this and that was being done in this and that place— then, still, this result might be worth a certain expenditure of time and means, if only its significance not be exaggerated.

Such are our reasons for a united propaganda and organization.

But if a circle is formed only to engage in personal development and indoctrination, if new friends are acquired only to conduct idle talk about important matters safely in a large group, then it is clear that this turns into the worst and most harmful inactivity. Moreover, an exclusive circle, if it intends to reach decisions merely within itself, unavoidably comes to this if its members have not sufficiently developed any worthwhile features; but one must always expect precisely that in the majority. It is just here, in our opinion, that what we have called mass propaganda offers assistance. If the aim of such a circle is the further dissemination of its views not only among the circle of adherents, but rather among all inhabitants of the same village, then such a circle will be incomparably better insured against disintegration and against moral corruption, and moreover it will be preparing for the undertaking of the populist movement.

Indeed, if the more intelligent individuals (honest and sincere—these conditions we consider to be recognized as the most important requisites) will constantly remember to read today such and such a book and to conduct such and such a conversation concerning it, to provoke talk about it tomorrow at a gathering and so on—then they will achieve three goals at once: they will better discover the attitude of separate individuals and their own ability to advocate their beliefs to the people; encourage certain attitudes of the majority; and, besides, protect themselves against idleness and empty chatter. We confess we somehow do not always believe those people who acquire beliefs for themselves alone or to share them with special individuals. Thus, we come to the conclusion that in order for individual propaganda and organization to proceed somewhat successfully in peasant and workers' milieus, it is necessary that the populist agitators who come from the intelligentsia, or from the people's milieu itself, should by no means limit themselves to communication among adherents; rather they should also try to influence the general opinion of all the masses by any means considered useful. Thus, the proponents of propaganda and organization directed at individuals will acknowledge that mass propaganda is useful even for the most individually oriented propaganda and agitation.

But mass propaganda has a tremendous significance in itself. Indeed, if a fleeting influence cannot seriously be acknowledged as useful, then no one will begin to deny that an influence and activity constantly repeated on a large scale and in a definite direction could achieve a definite result, modifying general opinion in a definite direction. Thus, it cannot but be acknowledged that such a modification is not only useful but highly desirable, and this for many reasons.

First of all, though it is doubtlessly true that the social viewpoints are so just and follow so easily from very simple considerations that they are inherent in all people, nevertheless we know that it is still very far from a vague comprehension—and it is of course vague—to a comprehension so clear that the village would agree with those measures proposed by the better, energetic individuals. It is still further to immediate action. Therefore, let us grant that in the village a circle could be formed from the better people, that they could be esteemed by society, and that they could convince the village—considering it in the totality of its present unpreparedness—to take up arms (once it is clear to the village that other villages as well have taken this course). Nevertheless it cannot be asserted that the village—considering the unpreparedness of the masses— definitely would take those ultimate measures which would ensure and secure victory for it. But not only that; it cannot even be guaranteed that, taking up arms, it would begin to destroy precisely that (and precisely to that degree) which requires destruction. Therefore, besides the training of separate people, it is extremely necessary not only that *certain* conscious ideas about the totality of general relations and about the possible means of restructuring them should reach the masses, but as many as possible, as clearly as possible.

In saying this, we, of course, do not at all wish to state that it is necessary that the social revolution wait while these clear, conscious ideas penetrate the masses. But we do say that the more of these that penetrate, the better, and that, consequently, it would be extremely strange and inconsistent to let pass any occasion for disseminating these ideas to the masses. It is precisely among the masses that it is necessary to develop the spirit of criticism, the spirit of dissatisfaction, an understanding of the hopelessness of peaceful reforms, the spirit of courage and faith in the possibility of united activity. The more developed this spirit is in every person, the more united with others each separate individual who enters into an organization of the people will feel, the stronger his faith in the possibility of a transformation will be, and the more clearly will his view of the future system take form. Finally, every individual is a product of the views surrounding him, and the more that certain opinions reach the masses, the more there will stand out from the masses new people who devote themselves to the common undertaking, and the more radical will these people be.

This is why we think that any populist activist must utilize every occasion, and even must seek out all occasions, to influence one and all in the understood direction. He must never forget this goal, not in a single conversation, not in a single act, and, in fact, he cannot forget it if he but applies himself with enthusiasm to his work. Suppose a man is oppressed, not educated, capable of considering only the most immediate events and totally incapable of discussing their causes. But even here it will always be possible, by assuming the point of view of this man, to analyze phenomena in a more general way and to lead him to considerations of general causes. With each separate individual it will be necessary, of course, to speak differently; to one it will be necessary to develop social views and the inferences from them more fully, to another, in the most primitive form. But, at least, all these conversations should be aimed at developing a receptivity for these views, a sensitivity for feeling the yoke, and the realization of the necessity of counterposing peasant unity against it.

How to proceed with each person, what chord to touch, how openly to state your ultimate ideas—all this will depend on the training of that person, of that society with which you are dealing, and the caution which is necessary in this or that instance. One thing, however, should be remembered: a receptivity to these ultimate goals must be prepared in one and all; consequently, it is necessary to act in this direction. Of course, people will be found everywhere in whom personal egotism is stronger than anything else, and to bother with them, even in passing, would mean to spend time and energy fruitlessly. But we are not speaking of them; we are speaking of all the masses who have neither the occasion nor the time to be consciously concerned with their surroundings, but who, precisely, will be required to act at some time. Not to try to influence these masses would be simply a mistake.

In the light of what has been said, we consider that efforts directed at individuals and efforts directed at masses must proceed simultaneously, hand in hand; to try to influence only the general opinion of the masses, without creating an intimate circle of several people which could be made into a general organization, would be just as much of a mistake as to try to form only an intimate circle but to let pass the opportunity to influence the general attitude of the masses. The interests of the whole undertaking demand both the one and the other influences simultaneously.

It is clear that all that has been said applies completely to the urban workers as well. We note, in addition, that our urban workers present several essential differences from those of Western Europe, and that these differences explain why activity among urban workers, despite their small number in Russia, has serious significance. The fact is that alongside the workers who are turned into constant city dwellers and have a defined trade, that is, skilled workers, there exists a considerably more extensive class of workers, so-called unskilled workers. This is made up entirely of peasants, mostly youths, who have not mastered a defined labor trade and who go to work at all sorts of textile factories.

They all have a land allotment in their native district and are closely tied to their fellow villagers; none live in the city constantly, but gather from the various corners of Russia for a time, and then, once again, after some two years, and often every year in times of unemployment, they return to their villages to do peasant labor.

This mobile element from the peasant milieu in most cases represents both a highly receptive ground and means for the dissemination of social ideas: they are free of the conservative influence of the family, somewhat more observant of various relations in life and, moreover, they continually return to the village. Furthermore, they all live not in isolation, as the skilled workers do, but in artels, which considerably facilitates an acquaintance with a large circle of people. The culling out from them of separate individuals capable of further agitation is facilitated, moreover, by the wide range available for the selection of the best people; and the aid of the educated youth who conduct studies with these workers significantly facilitates the choice, since it provides the possibility of maintaining an acquaintance with very many workers. Since these workers in no way sever their ties with the village and do not in the least alter their previous, peasant form of life, it is easiest of all to train from among them the people who will later serve as the nuclei of peasant circles in the villages.

This is not the place to set forth the practical methods of this propaganda, but we will pause over one circumstance which, in our opinion, many treat too lightly. This is that we consider it necessary and useful to impart to the workers information regarding the field of scientific knowledge. We were often asked before, as a favor, to concern ourselves with the teaching of reading and writing and arithmetic. If this is a natural means to become acquainted with an artel and if it is to be expected that people will be found in this artel who will become rather interested in social propaganda then we, of course, will not refuse such lessons; or, if there are other, more productive studies, then we will try to seek out people who, though not wishing to concern themselves with social propaganda, would, however, concern themselves with [these studies]—knowing the aim with which these lessons are conducted. When we see, on reading some book in the course of these studies and conducting a general discussion about the reading, that separate individuals take the common interest to heart, we will try, by more frequent conversations, to lead these people to the idea that the study of arithmetic or writing does not at all lead to the goal; we will then begin to acquaint them with the totality of the social viewpoint and will try to enter into personal, friendly relations with them. Those who see the study of arithmetic as their exclusive goal, we will, of course, leave in a certain time, as we understand very well that it is impossible to teach arithmetic to all those who want to learn it, and that there are things more important. If we meet a person who is receptive, energetic and gives promise of becoming a useful agitator, who does not even know how to read, we, of course, will unfailingly consider it a *necessity* to teach him reading and writing, understanding very well that a literate person can more easily conduct agitation than can an illiterate; so that those things about which there was no time to talk, he will discover both from the proper books and from the personal reflections about what was read.

We also consider it necessary to impart to those better people who will become populist agitators more detailed information about history (that, of course, which serves as the basis of our conclusions) concerning so-called political economy, that is, a criticism of existing relations between labor and capital. We know it takes more than a day or two to transform a peaceful worker, who for a century has stood behind a machine revealing his energy, honesty and lack of egotism solely in personal or artel relations—into a convinced, active, populist agitator. We know further that the transformation is the more durable and the guarantee of ultimate success is the greater, the larger the accumulation of facts which a man possesses and the more the sphere of phenomena provides him with arguments to strengthen his ideas. For this reason, we must impart to such a person the material he requires and we must attempt to sharpen his capability to use any fact to strengthen his views. Since in a three to four month period there will always be found more than enough time for such conversations, and since an exposition of necessary historical facts or an elucidation of economic relations is often more convenient in continuous form, we consider it positively necessary to impart this information by reading them a course of history and political economy (if one can designate as a course a score of serialized stories in which every fact supports a particular set of views, and every conclusion serves as an object of general discussion on a particular topic). For this reason, we affirm that it is necessary to train populist agitators. To train them in a period of weeks is impossible if one wishes to leave anything which endures after one departs. During a period which lasts several months, time will always be found to familiarize them in detail with those facts which later will be very useful to them in their agitational activities.

Consequently, it is necessary to conduct these discussions, and it is necessary to be concerned about the more extensive education of these agitators, always strictly avoiding, of course, burdening their minds with any superfluous ballast whatsoever.

It is clear that in any undertaking no specific boundaries can be set. It is only necessary that each activist should clearly understand his goal and not deviate from it because of irrelevant inducements.

From all that has been said, it is already clear that we set aside the main position in our propaganda for personal, *oral* and not *written* propaganda, both in view of the goals and in view of the illiteracy of the Russian people. But by this we by no means deny the necessity of written propaganda, and we consider it necessary for the very same goals.

About the character of written propaganda in the so-called civilized milieu we have already spoken above; the possibilities of our relations to [this milieu] were defined. But far more necessary is the appearance and dissemination among the workers and peasantry of such books as would satisfy the aims set forth above. Books of this type we consider positively necessary.

Those books are necessary which would give those who are unable to raise and formulate certain questions easily the opportunity to broach these questions nevertheless. A book especially written for this purpose provides the opportunity to raise and subject to general discussion such questions. Further, those books are necessary which would give the populist agitator the necessary material and facts with which to convince his interlocuters. Such facts are provided by books about the history of the people, by books which explain the means by which capital has accumulated in private hands, the seizure of land, the seizure by the government of the people's rights, and so forth. Moreover, those books are necessary which arouse the spirit of independence, the consciousness in the people of its strength and of the impotence of the nobility; and those which enforce the feeling of world unity, a consciousness of the common interests and the common enemies of all the separate parts of the Russian land, of all the separate classes of the people; and those which make clear the mutual interests of the tsar, nobility, merchants, extortionists and clergy. In short, fictional stories are needed as occasions for discussion; stories are needed about the strong personalities who emerge from the peasant milieu; historical and realistic stories are also needed which elucidate all the desperation of the contemporary way of life, which arouse a consciousness and spirit of strength, elucidating the necessity, the possibility, and the means of preliminary organization. For this reason, we set as our essential task the preparation and dissemination of such books. We are certain that everyone occupied with propaganda in the peasant and workers' milieu who possesses creativity and talent can always find time to write such books, without interrupting personal propaganda; and we are always ready to apportion a part of our energies to the printing and dissemination of these books.

It is clear that almost all such books must be uncensored. We also need, however, short, censored stories touching on various aspects of social life, since it is impossible to appear before an unknown group of peasants or workers for the first time with an uncensored book; for this reason we will always try to get our writers to produce—and we will always try to find in earlier publications—those stories, which, since they are at least not harmful, could provide the basis for necessary discussions. It is clear that all this requires the most insignificant expenditure of time; and means always can be found even from outside sources.

Finally, we believe that it would be highly useful to have a periodical publication, not large, written in language understood by the peasants and workers, which would act in this same direction, while introducing a contemporary element into it.

It remains for us, finally, to examine one type of propaganda which we call *factual*.

Here we place all those activities which promote, in our and others' opinion, the spread of the views stated by us, as well as the organization of a revolutionary party of the people. Here we will examine, consequently, all such institutions which propagandize the social viewpoint, as for example, local disturbances in the factories or in the towns with some particular aim, directed against some local abuses; finally, local, popular movements with a broad, socialist goal.

We begin with the *artel*. After everything stated above, it hardly needs mention that as a means of improving the social mode of life we consider the artel to be completely inapplicable and inexpedient. As an educational measure for the preparation of the social revolution we consider it not only not useful, but even completely harmful. Any temporary improvement of the material mode of life of a small group of people in the present, criminal society unavoidably leads to a strengthening of their conservative spirit. All their further activity is directed to preserving, to holding this, *their* privileged position, and for just this reason they must, as if fated, dissipate any impulse and in part even the actual possibility of spreading this improvement to others. Absorbed in matters of their artel, they are occupied with them first and foremost, and become less capable of using their time for active social propaganda. Then, little by little, they lose any desire to concern themselves with this undertaking; the improvement of circumstances leads only to the effort to retain these circumstances, to preserve them from the hazard of any movement, of any political interference, and so forth; it leads to self-aggrandizement and a supercilious attitude to one's other less-fortunate brothers; that which in significant measure is the result of fortunate accidents is ascribed to one's personal energy, and so on. In short, we are convinced that any artel, no matter how successful, is the best means of attracting the most intelligent workers to a semibourgeois situation, and, often of taking useful energy from the revolutionary agitation. For this reason, we do not consider the artel a means of social propaganda.

Such are the most natural, general conclusions; but each of them can be supported and developed by scores of proofs taken from experience. All the procedures in Western Europe and to some extent in Russia provide rich material for this. Naturally, we attribute just as little educational significance to consumer artels. Those of the German agitators who are delighted by the results of low prices in some communal kitchens[3] and attribute an educational significance to the common management of kitchens could be convinced, precisely in Russia, where each artel of unmarried factory workers represents such a consumer union, how simple and comprehensible this principle is, apart from any propaganda, and how easily it is realized in practice, if it does not encounter some external or historical obstacles. They would similarly be convinced of how slow is the path they have chosen, if they consider the establishment of consumer societies a step towards revolutionary activity. We view mutual-aid funds, mutual assistance, and so on in the same way we view consumer artels. All the previous considerations apply unconditionally to them, and all of these could be supported by a still greater quantity of facts, proving both their impotence and their harmful influence. We would even consider personal help by means of collections each time it is necessary (for example, a friend suffering from an

3 The reference is to the effort made by socialists to establish inexpensive eating places for workers. Aside from providing food, these communal kitchens also served as a means of radicalizing the workers. Kropotkin believed this could succeed in Russia. For a fuller discussion of this subject, see Peter Kropotkin, "Communist Kitchens," *Freedom*, September 1914, p. 68. See also "Expropriation," pp. 185–186 in this volume.—*Editor*.

accident) as more moral than a fund which becomes some sort of tax for the poor. For this reason, we will never advocate these funds and are always ready to dissuade our friends.

But, nevertheless, we do consider useful any *fund for social propaganda*, for the acquisition of books which provoke criticism of the existing situation and a realization of one's own strengths; for assistance to agitators who give up their jobs in exchange for a life devoted to the aim of propaganda; for the maintenance of apartments, and so on. Of course, we very well understand the insufficiency of such funds (except for the exceptional workers with means) and thus would not begin to exaggerate their significance. Clearly it would be most desirable if these funds were to be established in accordance with the necessities of propaganda and organization. Finally, among a number of similar educational methods, we consider as positively useful the *community of workers built on communistic principles*, that is common ownership of all earnings. But we know very well how great the difficulties are which attend any such institution, due to the impossibility of building a communist spirit in present society, and partly because of local conditions (the sending off of one's earnings to the village, and so on). We believe, for this reason, that one ought to recommend this measure as an excellent educational means for agitators, but that to bring it to fulfillment will be possible only to a limited degree and with special individuals; and [that] only, in large part, when the workers live with those members of the young intellegentsia who have been educated in this spirit. In any case, if persons of such similar inclinations do build such a community, then, in our opinion, they should not be disregarded.

We regard any local disturbances with some particular aim (for example, a demonstration against a foreman or manager at a factory, a demonstration against some restraining measure, a disturbance in a village with the aim of removing the foremen, the clerks, the middlemen, and so on) as a means of educating the masses and as a means for the populist agitators to get to know the people better, to know the outstanding individuals, and finally, for these individuals to acquire local influence and, in part, to be educated in the spirit of opposition, of more or less dangerous protest. The significance of particular movements, of course, is impossible to deny, and since they always occur apart from the will of separate individuals, it remains for the agitator merely to utilize them in order to know the people better. It is impossible not to acknowledge that such disturbances, if they do not lead to cruel suppression, always reinforce the spirit of dissatisfaction and irritation in the masses.

Acknowledging this usefulness, however, we clearly must decide whether it is in the interests of organization to provoke and support such disturbances. We believe that a general answer to this question cannot be given. It is only necessary to have in mind, in each particular case, how much each disturbance can promote or hinder the success of organization and propaganda. If it is possible to foretell that such a disturbance will provide the opportunity to know the people better, while not entailing the removal of agitators from the area with which they have already familiarized themselves and where they have already gained a certain confidence—and if along with this it gives the masses an opportunity to feel the strength of comradely protest—then, of course, it is necessary to support and call forth such a disturbance; if it is possible to foretell that, though gaining its particular goal, the disturbance may entail the removal of the agitators from the area where it would be desirable for them to remain, then it would be appropriate to avoid such a disturbance. It is appropriate for activists, in our opinion, to protect their efforts and not to expose themselves to risks for trifles or for results which will be useful to no one. It is necessary to remember, besides, that all the governments of the West, and ours as well, will not hesitate to adopt the same program, namely, always trying to provoke these local disturbances in order to seize the better people, tear them from their places, or shoot them and plant terror among the populace. For this reason, such a movement becomes a two-edged sword. On the one hand, the relations between the government and the people are made clear; on the other hand, it draws too heavily on the strengths of the revolutionary party and on the better people of a given district.

There is one more consideration, concerning, however, only people from the so-called civilized milieu. This is that in many disturbances they will by no means suffer all those consequences which such a disturbance inflicts on the peasantry and the urban workers. No matter how morally heavy the punishment is which befalls a person from the intelligentsia in such a case, it is incomparably lighter materially than the punishment which befalls the others (and appropriately so, in the eyes of the people). Though it be in the name of general principles, this circumstance, however, obviously undermines for the future the credibility of agitation in certain localities by a person from the intelligentsia. Finally, any means not leading directly to an end, becomes very quickly itself an end of a new undertaking, and we would consider it necessary in any similar undertaking always to consider prevalent, general opinion concerning a particular question in formulating a decision. Not less essential is that any [misdirected] agitation detracts attention and time from the more essential agitation.

But there can also appear another consideration. Any agitation not reinforced by action soon ceases to sustain the courage of the activists. Activists cannot so calmly bear the injustice surrounding them, and they inevitably strive to enter the battle against this injustice, in whatever form it appears. To try to abstain from protest when it insistently suggests itself means to develop an indifference to surroundings, and even a type of Jesuitism. We think, however, that such an objection would be incorrect. First of all, it would be very desirable if the propaganda and the organization of agitators were looked on precisely as a business, and that a battle with a manager or foreman should not be considered a more serious "enterprise." Any person looking at any fact presented to him just from the point of view of propaganda and organization will always be able to utilize it in order to explain it to those around him as a particular manifestation of the whole, and to transfer to the common enemy the passionate abhorrence aroused by it. Further, any activist and sensitive man is, even without external interference, sufficiently inclined to protest against any particular outrage, and with such people it is sooner necessary to restrain outbursts of passion against a particular event, pointing out the opportunity to use it for organizing the people, than it is to inflame this passion against the actual event. Finally, as concerns that fact which [is true] of any effected protest, no matter how clear its damage and no matter what might be said against it at the time of preliminary discussion—in any risk the agitator must be in the forefront; there is no need to discuss this elementary fact. All that has been said also applies completely to the question of *strikes*. So much has been written and said about them already that we can limit ourselves only to general conclusions.

First of all, it is clear that strikes, just as any palliative measures, cannot essentially improve the position of the workers. That small improvement which a strike sometimes achieves in either a shortening of the workers' hours or in an increase of the workers' pay is always temporary and is very soon wiped out. Further, one can adduce the fact that a strike in Western Europe is always the sole means of raising the income somewhat, when, with the increase in the cost of living, this becomes absolutely inadequate for existence. For this reason, in Western Europe the strike became a common weapon in the fight between labor and capital, both in the industrial and in the agricultural spheres, and the organization of the strike was for a long time the sole goal which occupied (and till this time occupies) a great many workers' societies and a great many agitators. In Russia, a strike is a manifestation incomparably more rare for a great many reasons, about which this is not the place to speak. Must the strike, consequently, be propagandized here in the same way it has been propagandized for the past twenty to thirty years in Western Europe? Can we not achieve with its help the same results as were achieved by Western European workers and which indisputably promoted social propaganda in several respects?

It would be extremely improper to compare our position in

this respect with that of Western Europe. In Western Europe strikes are not a phenomenon of recent years, nor even of the last century. In England, that is, precisely in that country where they [strikes] have achieved both the highest wage and the lowest number of working hours, they were already begun and organized in the thirteenth century. Workers' unions were already so widespread and so strong in the last century thanks to the strike that whole decades would be necessary for the development of such unions now [in Russia]. That is why England could outstrip other countries in the rate of raising wages and decreasing working hours, which, however, is noticeable everywhere in the last century, although to a lesser degree than in England. The power of the workers' unions for strikes cannot be acquired quickly—it requires long years of strikes unimpeded by the government and long years of training.

Now new ideals, new goals, new aspirations are appearing among the workers. The problem of the labor question has already become not the partial improvement of daily life, but the question of the transfer of the instruments of labor to the workers themselves. In this form, the problem also has arisen in Russia. Consequently, the question about the organization for strikes also becomes the question of whether or not we must now, when this problem is so widespread, work to create an organization which was established in the West at the time when the problem was raised about the [partial] improvement of daily life, and not about radical change. The answer is inevitable and clear: *no!* Can it really be useful to oppose evil in its particular form when the general cause of evil is already known? Do we really have the right to hide this general cause? Indeed, once the general cause of evil is known, once hope and belief in its eradication have appeared, can we and the workers introduce into the propaganda of the organization for strikes that belief which was introduced into this propaganda by those who saw in the strike the sole possible weapon of the struggle with capital? It is clear, consequently, in Russia, where the workers' movement is beginning at this time, that the strong organization for strikes which exists in many places of Western Europe cannot be created. It is clear that if the workers' movement retains its faith in the attainment of the ultimate goal, it will not apply itself to strikes with that energy applied up to recent times in Western Europe.

But if the strike cannot be a goal in itself for us, might it nevertheless be a useful means towards the attainment of a given goal? Offering a practical impetus for organization accessible to all, cannot the strike lead those into the organization who would not join without this impetus? Will it not serve as a good opportunity for social propaganda?

But here, in turn, we again encounter the same question: how useful for the attainment of a given goal is it to place some secondary goal in the forefront? Or, in other words, how useful is it to attract to an organization which seeks a social transformation people who still do not agree with the necessity of a transformation? But the answer to the question in such a form cannot be open to doubt. Of course it is not useful because these people will only obstruct the organization in the attainment of its goals; consequently, it is necessary to act on them by other means. In general, we consider it not only careless but quite impractical to recruit people for one goal while presenting them with another. As to the fact that the strike can serve as a good occasion for social propaganda, it is necessary to remark that there is always an opportunity for criticism of the mode of daily life, and the strike is not the most opportune. The strike serves as a good method for arousing the consciousness of one's power only when it ends in victory. Speaking about the form which has attained the greatest development in the West we will refer here to the example of Western Europe. All who have dealings with strikes confirm exactly this. But the strike is only crowned with success when the workers have other funds beforehand (disregarding for the time being the interference of the government, and even supposing that it does not exist). We have already stated above why we think that we do not now intend to form another organization for strikes.

As to the consciousness (of solidarity) of unity, of community, which mutual assistance during strikes so promotes, we think that the same consciousness is achieved in the same degree by the constant intercourse of the groups which are indispensable for an organization; and the more lively and intimate the intercourse, the more homogeneous their composition. An extensive organization for the sake of strikes does not at all assist this last condition but rather hinders it by introducing the extreme heterogeneity of agitational training into the structure of circles which are necessary for these goals. This is why we think that for us an extensive organization for strikes would not be an expedient means for attaining our goals.

There remains, then, the educational element of the strike, which is unquestionable in many respects. Any strike trains the participants for a common management of affairs and for the distribution of responsibilities, distinguishes the people most talented and devoted to a common cause, and finally, forces the others to get to know these people and strengthens their influence. For this reason we assert that it would not be appropriate if forces were available to let one strike pass without the populist activists taking the opportunity of active participation in it. But for the sake of this, to provoke strikes purposely, with all their terrible consequences for the workers in the case of failure (deprivations, hunger, the spending of the last meager savings), we consider positively inadvisable.

Finally, we move to the last category of instances for factual propaganda. This is the local movement with a definite, common socialist goal. Let us suppose that there is a basis for thinking that in some province an insurrection could arise *with a clear goal to expropriate all the lands, factories, houses, and capital in the possession of the mir, and to organize itself in its own way.* But also, it is expected that this movement will not be supported and will be crushed by the troops. Should one assist this movement, should one support morally and physically those who gather to begin this movement, or should one make all efforts in order to refrain from this? It is evident that many considerations arise here. Let us disregard the fact that such disturbances, begun with goals clear to all, can lead also to arousing the neighboring districts. Even when all the determining circumstances are apparently known, no one can guarantee the outcome of such a movement, especially when everywhere there are some dissatisfied elements. History is full of such surprises, which not one of the most gifted and knowing contemporaries foresaw at all. Therefore, we would never take it upon ourselves to decide this question except as we are acquainted with the local conditions of a given case and according to a discussion of them at a full meeting of the populist activists. But we point out this question now because it determines the party's plan of action. If it were decided that *such* a local movement were desirable, then the choice of the locality would make it possible to direct all the available forces there, instead of scattering them across all of Russia. Therefore, we will state only several considerations which might appropriately motivate one to ask this question, since a knowledge of the local conditions of different parts of Russia will allow us to talk about it.

What the oppressed, local socialist movement consists of is well known. What bacchanalia are played out by the eternal predators of the people over the corpses of all that is honest, bold, intelligent in a defeated locality—all this is scorched with shameful marks on the bestial faces of these predators. That this devastation overwhelmingly oppresses even the largely indifferent majority is also well known. But something else is clear as well: those of the survivors in whom the spark of the human spirit is not extinguished by bestial needs will be driven to curse all of life with enmity. It is clear that the eyes of anyone not blind will be opened by this drama when the masks are removed and frenzy drives the impotent and base to wreak their anger on the strong and honest caught in the trap. Let the nobility and the tsar be displayed at least once in all their bestial nakedness, and the rivers of blood spilled in one locality will not flow without consequence. Without the rivers of blood the social upheaval will not be accomplished; subsequent [upheavals] will replace the first ones, if only the first will let loose the flood for the future ones. But, nevertheless, these first rivers, perhaps streams, are already flowing now, and they flow, trickle, uninterrupted through all the recent decades. Perhaps it would be folly on our part even to dream about how to hold them back, and perhaps there is no better outcome for us than to drown ourselves in that first river which bursts the dam.

Our relations to all parties are quite clearly defined in what has been said. We will state them, however, in a few words.

First of all our relations to the International. To unite with the International, not in principle but in fact, we consider impossible to discuss now. As long as we have no strong organization among the peasantry and workers, our relations will only be personal and not businesslike; it is hardly worthwhile to discuss such relations. Consequently, [the question] of whether to join the International or not is still in the future. We can only say that due to the vast difference [between] the way we think (the character of our ideas and aspirations) and the characteristics of the Western European workers, due to the difference of language and to our economic isolation, we do not think that in the near future our relations could be in any way intimate and active, except among separate individuals. No doubt every socialist movement in the West will be quickly echoed in our people, any large scale success of Western International organizations will be received with sympathy and interest by us and will encourage us. It is also highly probable that the decisions of the International will be discussed here not only by educated youth, but also by workers' groups. All this however does not yet constitute that intercourse which must exist among the parts of *one* party. And this can hardly be arranged quickly. Therefore we limit ourselves only by the declaration that in principle (as evident from all that has been said), we fully agree with the branch of federalists in the International and we deny the statist principles of the other branch.[4]

As to our Russian parties abroad (since we agree in principle with the Russian representatives of the federalist division of the International), we completely remove ourselves from any

4 Kropotkin is here identifying with the Bakuninist faction and against the Marxist faction of the International.—*Editor.*

interference in their dissensions because they have a personal character and because, living here, we cannot have any precise understanding of the character of these dissensions. We must say in regard to their periodical publications that we cannot recognize any of them as the organ of our party.

Deeply respecting some representatives of our Russian emigration and their activity in the International, we nonetheless do not intend to enter into a close organized union with any of them, because we see no possibility whatever to make this union functional. We intend to develop here autonomously, without any guidance from foreign parties, since we believe that the emigration can never be the exact expression of the needs of our people, except in their most general features: a necessary condition for this is a stay among the Russian peasantry and urban workers. Finally, a necessary condition for the full unification of individuals is the opportunity to engage in uninterrupted, intimate relations—which is impossible at the present moment.

"The Commune of Paris" was originally published in Kropotkin's newspaper, *Le Révolté*, on March 20, 1880, to correspond with the ninth anniversary of the 1871 Paris Commune. In the article, he places the 1871 uprising in a specific evolutionary perspective. He sees the Commune as the "forerunner of the social revolution" which will finally realize the original revolutionary objectives of the Communards. In a final page which is not included in this translation, there is a brief discussion of the necessity to carry the revolution into the countryside as well as the cities: "the emancipation of the proletariat will not even be possible so long as the revolutionary movement does not encompass the villages."[1] For the success of the social revolution, urban communards must help propagandize in rural areas, he continues, by forming an agrarian league which would have branches in every village. This concept was also put forth in the 1873 manifesto.

The following version is from *The Commune of Paris*, Freedom Pamphlets, no. 2 (London: W. Reeves, 1895). Reprinted by permission of the publisher.

1 Peter Kropotkin, *Paroles d'un Révolté* (Paris: Flammarion, 1885), p. 140.

The
Commune
of Paris

I. THE PLACE OF THE COMMUNE IN SOCIALIST EVOLUTION

On March 18, 1871, the people of Paris rose against a despised and detested government, and proclaimed the city independent, free, belonging to itself.

This overthrow of the central power took place without the usual stage effects of revolution, without the firing of guns, without the shedding of blood upon barricades. When the armed people came out into the streets, the rulers fled away, the troops evacuated the town, the civil functionaries hurriedly retreated to Versailles carrying everything they could with them. The government evaporated like a pond of stagnant water in a spring breeze, and on the nineteenth the great city of Paris found herself free from the impurity which had defiled her, with the loss of scarcely a drop of her children's blood.

Yet the change thus accomplished began a new era in that long series of revolutions whereby the peoples are marching from slavery to freedom. Under the name "Commune of Paris" a new idea was born, to become the starting point for future revolutions.

As is always the case, this fruitful idea was not the product of some one individual's brain, of the conceptions of some philosopher; it was born of the collective spirit, it sprang from the heart of a whole community. But at first it was vague, and many of those who acted upon and gave their lives for it did not look at it in the light in which we see it today; they did not realize the full extent of the revolution they inaugurated or the fertility of the new principle they tried to put in practice. It was only after they had begun to apply it that its future bearing slowly dawned upon them; it was only afterward, when the new principle came to be thought out, that it grew definite and precise and was seen in all its clearness, in all its beauty, its justice and the importance of its results.

During the five or six years that came before the Commune, socialism had taken a new departure in the spread and rapid growth of the International Workingmen's Association. In its local branches and general congresses the workers of Europe met together and took counsel with one another upon the social question as they had never done before. Among those who saw that social revolution was inevitable and were actively busy in making ready for it, one problem above all others seemed to press for solution. "The existing development of industry will force a great economic revolution upon our society; this revolution will abolish private property, will put in common all the capital piled up by previous generations; but, what form of political grouping will be most suited to these changes in our economic system?"

"The grouping must not be merely national," answered the International Workingmen's Association, "it must extend across all artificial frontiers and boundary lines." And soon this grand idea sunk into the hearts of the peoples and took fast hold of their minds. Though it has been hunted down ever since by the united efforts of every species of reactionary, it is alive nevertheless, and when the voice of the peoples in revolt shall melt the obstacles to its development, it will reappear stronger than ever before.

But it still remained to discover what should be the component parts of this vast association.

To this question two answers were given, each the expression of a distinct current of thought. One said the popular state; the other said anarchy.

The German socialists advocated that the state should take possession of all accumulated wealth and give it over to associations of workers and, further, should organize production and exchange, and generally watch over the life and activities of society.

To them the socialists of the Latin race, strong in revolutionary experience, replied that it would be a miracle if such a state could ever exist; but if it could, it would surely be the worst of tyrannies. This ideal of the all-powerful and beneficent state is merely a copy from the past, they said; and they confronted it with a new ideal: an-archy, that is, the total abolition of the state, and social organization from the simple to the complex by means of the free federation of popular groups of producers and consumers.

It was soon admitted, even by the more liberal-minded state socialists, that anarchy certainly represented a much better sort of organization than that aimed at by the popular state. But, they said, the anarchist ideal is so far off that just now we cannot trouble about it.

At the same time, it was true that the anarchist theory did need some short, clear mode of expression, some formula at once simple and practical, to show plainly its point of departure and embody its conceptions, to indicate how it was supported by an actually existing tendency among the people. A federation of workers' unions and groups of consumers regardless of frontiers and quite independent of existing states seemed too vague; and, moreover, it was easy to see that it could not fully satisfy all the infinite variety of human requirements. A clearer formula was wanted, one more easily grasped, one which had a firm foundation in the realities of actual life.

If the question had merely been how best to elaborate a theory, we should have said theories, as theories, are not of so very much importance. But as long as a new idea has not found a clear, precise form of statement, growing naturally out of things as they actually exist, it does not take hold of men's minds, does not inspire them to enter upon a decisive struggle. The people do not fling themselves into the unknown without some positive and clearly formulated idea to serve them, so to say, as a springboard when they reach the starting point.

As for this starting point, they must be led up to it by life itself.

For five whole months Paris had been isolated by the German besiegers; for five whole months she had to draw upon her own vital resources and had learned to know the immense economic, intellectual, and moral strength which she possessed. She had caught a glimpse of her own force of initiative and realized what it meant. At the same time she had seen that the prating crew who seized power had no idea how to organize either the defense of France or its internal development. She had seen the central government at cross purposes with every manifestation of the intelligence of the mighty city. Finally, she had come to realize that any government must be powerless to guard against great disasters or to smooth the path of rapid evolution. During the siege her defenders, her workers, had suffered the most frightful privations, while her idlers reveled in insolent luxury, and thanks to the central government she had seen the failure of every attempt to put an end to these scandals. Each time that her people had showed signs of a desire for a free scope, the government had added weight to their chains. Naturally such experiences gave birth to the idea that Paris must make herself an independent commune, able to realize within her walls the wishes of her citizens.

The Commune of 1871 could be nothing but a first attempt. Beginning at the close of a great war, hemmed in between two armies ready to join hands and crush the people, it dared not unhesitatingly set forth upon the path of economic revolution. It neither boldly declared itself socialist nor proceeded to the expropriation of capital nor the organization of labor. It did not even take stock of the general resources of the city.

Nor did it break with the tradition of the state, of representative government. It did not seek to effect *within* the Commune that very organization from the simple to the complex which it inaugurated *without*, by proclaiming the independence and free federation of communes.

Yet it is certain that if the Commune of Paris could have lived a few months longer, it would have been inevitably driven by the force of circumstances toward both these revolutions. Let us not forget that the French middle class spent altogether four years (from 1789 to 1793) in revolutionary action before they changed a limited monarchy into a republic. Ought we then to be astonished that the people of Paris did not cross with one bound the space between an anarchist commune and the government of the spoilers? But let us also bear in mind that the next revolution, which in France and Spain at least will be communal, will take up the work of the Commune of Paris where it was interrupted by the massacres of the Versailles soldiery.

The Commune was defeated, and too well we know how the middle class avenged itself for the scare given it by the people when they shook their rulers' yoke loose upon their necks. It proved that there really are two classes in our modern society; on one side, the man who works and yields up to the monopolists of property more than half of what he produces and yet lightly passes over the wrong done him by his masters; on the other, the idler, the spoiler, hating his slave, ready to kill him like game, animated by the most savage instincts as soon as he is menaced in his possession.

After having shut in the people of Paris and closed all means of exit, the Versailles government let loose soldiers upon them; soldiers brutalized by drink and barrack life, who had been publicly told to make short work of "the wolves and their cubs." To the people it was said:

You shall perish, whatever you do! If you are taken with arms in your hands—death! If you use them—death! If you beg for mercy—death! Whichever way you turn, right, left, back, forward, up, down,—death! You are not merely outside the law, you are outside humanity. Neither age nor sex shall save you and yours. You shall die, but first you shall taste the agony of your wife, your sister, your mother, your sons and daughters, even those in the cradle! Before your eyes the wounded man shall be taken out of the ambulance and hacked with bayonets or knocked down with the butt end of a rifle. He shall be dragged living by his broken leg or bleeding arm and flung like a suffering, groaning bundle of refuse into the gutter. Death! Death! Death![2]

And after this mad orgy, these piles of corpses, this wholesale extermination, came the petty revenge, the cat-o'-nine-tails, the irons in the ship's hold, the blows and insults of the jailers, the semistarvation, all the refinements of cruelty. Can the people forget these base deeds?

Overthrown, but not conquered, the Commune in our days is born again. It is no longer a dream of the vanquished, caressing in imagination the lovely mirage of hope. No! the "commune" of today is becoming the visible and definite aim of the revolution rumbling beneath our feet. The idea is sinking deep into the masses, it is giving them a rallying cry. We count on the present generation to bring about the social revolution *within* the commune, to put an end to the ignoble system of middle-class exploitation, to rid the people of the tutelage of the state, to inaugurate a new era of liberty, equality, solidarity in the evolution of the human race.

II. HOW THE COMMUNE FAILED TO REALIZE ITS TRUE AIM AND YET SET THAT AIM BEFORE THE WORLD

Ten years already separate us from the day when the people of Paris overthrew the traitor government which raised itself to power at the downfall of the empire; how is it that the oppressed masses of the civilized world are still irresistibly drawn toward the movement of 1871? Why is the idea represented by the Commune of Paris so attractive to the workers of every land, of every nationality?

The answer is easy. The revolution of 1871 was above all a popular one. It was made by the people themselves, it sprang

2 Arthur Arnould, *Histoire populaire et parlementaire de la Commune de Paris.* [Bruxelles: H. Kistemaeckers, 1878. 2 tomes en 1 vol.]

spontaneously from the midst of the mass, and it was among the great masses of the people that it found its defenders, its heroes, its martyrs. It is just because it was so thoroughly "low" that the middle class can never forgive it. And at the same time its moving spirit was the idea of a social revolution; vague certainly, perhaps unconscious, but still the effort to obtain at last, after the struggle of many centuries, true freedom, true equality for all men. It was the revolution of the lowest of the people marching forward to conquer their rights.

Attempts have been and are made to change the sense of this revolution, to represent it as a mere effort to regain the independence of Paris and thus to constitute a tiny state within France. But nothing can be more untrue. Paris did not seek to isolate herself from France, any more than to conquer it by force of arms; she did not care to shut herself within her walls like a nun in a convent; she was not inspired by the narrow spirit of the cloister. If she claimed her independence, if she tried to hinder the interference of the central power in her affairs, it was because she saw in that independence a means of quietly elaborating the bases of future organization and bringing about within herself a social revolution; a revolution which would have completely transformed the whole system of production and exchange by basing them on justice; which would have completely modified human relations by putting them on a footing of equality; which would have formed our social morality anew by founding it upon equality and solidarity. Communal independence was then but a means for the people of Paris; the social revolution was their end.

And this end might have been attained if the revolution of March 18 had been able to take its natural course, if the people of Paris had not been cut to pieces by the assassins from Versailles. To find a clear, precise idea, comprehensible to all the world and summing up in a few words what was needed to accomplish the revolution, this was really the preoccupation of the people of Paris from the earliest days of their independence. But a great idea does not germinate in a day, however rapid the elaboration and propagation of ideas during periods of revolution. It always needs a certain time to develop, to spread throughout the masses, to translate itself into action, and this time the Commune of Paris failed. It failed mostly because as we have before observed, socialism ten years ago was passing through a period of transition. The authoritative and semi-religious communism of 1848 had no longer any hold over the practical, freethinking minds of our epoch. The collectivism which attempted to yoke together the wage system and collective property was incomprehensible, unattractive, and bristling with difficulties in practical application. Free communism, anarchist communism, was only beginning to dawn upon the minds of the workers and scarcely ventured to provoke the attacks of the worshippers of government. Minds were undecided. Socialists themselves, having no definite end in view, did not dare to lay hands upon private property; they deluded themselves with the argument which has lulled the activities of many an age: "Let us first make sure of victory, and then see what can be done."

Make sure of victory! As if there were any way of forming a free commune without laying hands upon property! As if there were any way of conquering the foe while the great mass of the people is not directly interested in the triumph of the revolution, by seeing that it will bring material, moral and intellectual well-being to everybody! They tried to consolidate the Commune first and defer the social revolution until afterward, whereas the only way to go about it was *to consolidate the Commune by means of the social revolution.*

The same thing happened with regard to the principle of government. By proclaiming the free Commune, the people of Paris proclaimed an essential anarchist principle, which was the breakdown of the state. But as the idea of anarchism had then but faintly dawned upon men's minds, it was checked half way, and in the midst of the Commune the ancient principle of authority cropped up and the people gave themselves a council of the Commune, on the model of municipal councils elsewhere.

And yet, if we admit that a central government to regulate the relations of communes between themselves is quite needless, why should we admit its necessity to regulate the mutual relations of the groups which make up each commune? And if we leave the business of coming to a common understanding with regard to enterprises which concern several cities at once to the free initiative of the communes concerned, why refuse this same free initiative to the groups composing a single commune? There is no more reason for a government inside the commune than for a government outside.

But in 1871, the people of Paris, who have overthrown so many governments, were only making their first attempt to revolt against the governmental system itself; consequently they let themselves be carried away by the fetish worship of governments and set up one of their own.

The result is a matter of history. Paris sent her devoted sons to the town hall. There, shelved in the midst of files of old papers, obliged to rule when their instincts prompted them to be and to act among the people, obliged to discuss when it was needful to act, to compromise when no compromise was the best policy, and, finally, losing the inspiration which only comes from continual contact with the masses, they saw themselves reduced to impotence. Being paralyzed by their separation from the people—the revolutionary center of light and heat—they themselves paralyzed the popular initiative.

The Commune of Paris, the child of a period of transition, born beneath the Prussian guns, was doomed to perish. But by its eminently popular character it began a new series of revolutions, by its ideas it was the forerunner of the social revolution. Its lesson has been learned, and when France once more bristles with communes in revolt, the people are not likely to give themselves a government and expect that government to initiate revolutionary measures. When they have rid themselves of the parasites who devour them, they will take possession of all social wealth to share according to the principles of anarchist communism. And when they have entirely abolished property, government, and the state, they will form themselves freely, according to the necessities indicated by life itself. Breaking its chains, overthrowing its idols, humanity will march onward to a better future, knowing neither masters nor slaves, keeping its veneration for the noble martyrs who bought with their blood and suffering those first attempts at emancipation which have enlightened our march toward the conquest of liberty.

III. THE TEACHINGS OF THE COMMUNE IN MODERN
SOCIALISM

The public meetings organized on March 18 in almost every town where there is a socialist group are well worthy of careful attention, not merely because they are a demonstration of the army of labor, but also because they afford an opportunity for gauging the sentiments of the socialists of both worlds. They are a better opportunity for "taking a poll" than could be given by any system of voting, an occasion when aspirations may be formulated uninfluenced by electoral party tactics. The workers do not meet simply to praise the heroism of the Parisian proletariat or to call for vengeance for the May massacres. While refreshing themselves with the memory of the brave struggle in Paris, they have gone further and discussed what lessons for the coming revolution must be drawn from the Commune of 1871. They ask what the mistakes of the commune were not for the sake of criticizing the men who made them but to bring out clearly how the prejudices about property and authority, which then reigned among workers' organizations, hindered the bursting forth of the revolutionary idea and its subsequent developments into a beacon to light the world.

The lesson of 1871 has benefited the workers of every land, enabling them to break with their old prejudices and come to a clearer and simpler understanding as to what *their* revolution is to be.

The next rising of communes will not be merely a "communal" movement. Those who still think that independent, local self-governing bodies must be first established and that these must try to make economic reforms within their own localities are being carried along by the further development of the popular spirit, at least in France. The communes of the next revolution will proclaim and establish their independence by direct socialist revolutionary action, abolishing private property. When the revolutionary situation ripens, which may happen any day, and governments are swept away by the people, when the middle-class camp, which only exists by state protection, is thus thrown into disorder, the insurgent people will not wait until some new government decrees, in its marvelous wisdom, a few economic reforms. The people themselves will abolish private property by a violent expropriation, taking possession in the name of the whole community of all the wealth accumulated by the labor of past generations.

They will not wait to expropriate the holders of social capital by a decree which necessarily would remain a dead letter if not accomplished in fact by the workers themselves. They will take possession on the spot and establish their rights by utilizing it without delay. They will organize themselves in the workshops to continue the work, but what they will produce will be what is wanted by the masses, not what gives the highest profit to employers. They will exchange their hovels for healthy dwellings in the houses of the rich; they will organize themselves to turn to immediate use the wealth stored up in the towns; they will take possession of it as if it had never been stolen from them by the middle class.

And when the industrial baron who has been levying blackmail upon the worker is once evicted, production will continue, throwing off the trammels which impede it, putting an end to the speculations which kill and the confusion which disorganizes it, transforming itself according to the necessities of the movement under the impulsion given to it by free labor. "Men never worked in France as they did in 1793, after the soil was snatched from the hands of the nobles," says the historian Michelet. Never have men worked as they will on the day when labor becomes free and everything accomplished by the worker will be a source of well-being to the whole commune.

An attempt has been made of late to establish a distinction between various sorts of social wealth, and the socialist party is divided upon the question. The present collectivist school, substituting a sort of dogmatic theory of collectivism for the collectivism of the old International (which was merely anti-authoritarian communism), has sought to establish a distinction between capital used for production and wealth supplying the necessities of life. Machinery, factories, raw material, means of communication, and the soil are on the one side, and dwellings, manufactured produce, clothing, commodities, on the other. The first are to be collective property, the second are designed, by the professors of this school of socialism, to remain private property.

There has been an attempt to set up this distinction, but popular good sense has got the better of it; it has found it illusory and impossible to establish. It is vicious in theory and fails in practical life. The workers understand that the house which shelters us, the coal and gas we burn, the fuel consumed by the human machine to sustain life, the clothing necessary for existence, the book we read for instruction, even the enjoyments we get, are all so many component parts of our existence, are all as necessary to successful production and the progressive development of humanity as machines, manufactories, raw materials, and other means of working. The workers are arriving at the conclusion that to maintain private property for this sort of wealth would be to maintain inequality, oppression, exploitation, to paralyze beforehand the results of the partial expropriation. Leaping over the fence set up in their path by theoretical collectivism, they are marching straight for the simplest and most practical form of antiauthoritarian communism.

Now in their meetings the revolutionary workers are distinctly stating their right to all social wealth and the necessity of abolishing private property in articles of consumption as well as in those of reproduction: "On the day of the revolution, we shall seize upon *all* wealth stored up in the towns and put it in common," say the speakers, and the audiences confirm the statements with their unanimous approval. "Let each take from the pile what he needs and be sure that in the warehouses of our towns there will be enough food to feed everyone until free production has made a fair start; in the shops of our towns there are enough clothes to dress everyone, kept there in reserve while outside there is nakedness and poverty. There are even enough luxuries for each to choose among them according to his liking."

Judging by what is said at commune commemoration meetings in France and elsewhere, the workers have made up their minds that the coming revolution will introduce anarchist communism and the free reorganization of production. These two points seem settled and in these respects the communes of the next revolution will not repeat the errors of their forerunners, who so generously shed their blood to clear the path for future progress.

There is, however, a third and no less important point upon which agreement is not yet reached, though it is not so very far off. This is the question of government.

As is well known, there are two sections of the Socialist party, completely divided by this point. "On the very day of the revolution," says the one, "we must constitute a government to take possession of the supreme power. A strong, powerful, resolute government will *make* the revolution by decreeing this and that, and forcing all to obey its commands."

"A miserable delusion!" says the other. "Any central government, taking upon itself to rule a nation, must certainly be a mere hindrance to the revolution. It cannot fail to be made up of the most incongruous elements, and its very essence as a government is conservatism. It will do nothing but hold back the revolution in communes ready to go ahead, without being able to inspire backward communes with the breath of revolution. The same within a commune in revolt. Either the communal government will merely sanction accomplished facts— and then it will be a useless and dangerous bit of machinery; or else it will wish to take the lead to make rules for what has yet to be freely worked out by the people themselves if it is to be really viable. It will apply theories where all society ought to work out fresh forms of common life with that creative force which springs up in the social organism when it breaks its chains and sees new and larger horizons opening before it. The men in power will obstruct this outburst, without doing any of the things they might themselves have done if they had remained among the people, working with them in the new organization instead of shutting themselves up in ministerial offices and wearing themselves out in idle debates. The revolutionary government will be a hindrance and a danger; powerless for good, formidable for ill; therefore, what is the use of having it?"

However natural and just, this argument still runs counter to a great many prejudices stored up and accredited by those who have had an interest in maintaining the religion of government, side by side with the religions of property and of theology.

This prejudice, the last of the three, still exists and is a danger to the coming revolution, though it already shows signs of decay. "We will manage our business ourselves without waiting for the orders of a government, we will trample underfoot those who try to force us to accept them as priests, property owners or rulers," the workers have begun to say. We must hope that the anarchist party will continue to combat government worship vigorously, and never allow itself to be dragged or enticed into a struggle for power. We must hope that in the years which remain to us before the revolution the prejudice in favor of government may be so shaken that it will not be strong enough to draw off the people on a false route.

The communes of the next revolution will not only break down the state and substitute free federation for parliamentary rule; they will part with parliamentary rule within the commune itself. They will trust the free organization of food supply and production to free groups of workers—which will federate with like groups in other cities and villages not through the medium of a communal parliament but directly, to accomplish their aim.

They will be anarchist within the commune as they will be anarchist outside it—and only thus will they avoid the horrors of defeat, the furies of reaction.

"The Russian Revolutionary Party" was one of Kropotkin's earliest efforts to bring the nature of the revolutionary struggle in Russia to the attention of Englishmen. The article is essentially a historical sketch of the movement from the 1860s up to the assassination of Alexander II in 1881. Indeed, it was the tsaricide which prompted Kropotkin to defend and justify the movement which was responsible for this crime. His argument is that the revolutionaries were increasingly driven to more radical alternatives because of the regime's rigid refusal to accept gradual and reformist change.

With regard to the term *revolutionary party*, Kropotkin is not speaking of a single political party in the parliamentary sense (they were prohibited in Russia) but rather of an opposition movement composed of numerous and widely varying ideological circles, groups, and parties. So too, the term *reactionary party* should be understood to mean the influential statesmen in the government having reactionary views.

The article is reprinted with permission of Associated Book Publishers Ltd. from its original publication in *Fortnightly Review*, n.s., vol. 31 (1882). The footnotes are Kropotkin's, unless otherwise indicated.

The
Russian
Revolutionary
Party

During the last half-dozen years the Russian revolutionary party, improperly called nihilist, has continually attracted the attention of the public and of the political writers and thinkers of Western Europe. A good-sized library might be filled with what has been written on the subject, including, with the hasty and superficial stuff produced for the daily press, not a little work that shows a studious perusal of Russian history and literature. But still we meet daily, both in the press and in society, with opinions so varied, with statements so erroneous, and with such fantastic hypotheses about what are called "the fanatics, the nihilists," that it might be supposed we were dealing with some religious upheaval in the remote highlands of central Asia rather than with a political crisis in a country whose capitals are but four or five days' journey from the capitals of Western Europe.

Many causes have contributed to this effect; the want of knowledge of the Russian language; the secret character of the movement; and a variety of prejudices, political, social, and national, certainly must be mentioned among them. But the chief cause is that the origin of the movement and the explanation of those features which distinguish it from former revolutionary movements in Europe have been sought either in the action of circumstances of little moment (such, for instance, as the condition of higher schools in Russia), or in influences too vague and ineffective. Thus, for explaining "nihilism," there has been much talk about Hegel, Schopenhauer, and the writings of a few Russian authors. But the social and political conditions of Russian life were taken into account too little or not at all. Of course philosophical schemes and the writings of able men exercise a certain influence on the development of political parties. But even if we admit that the Russian revolutionary party was influenced by the philosophy of Hegel or Schopenhauer (the truth is that the works of J. S. Mill, Comte, Buckle, Darwin, and Spencer are far better known among the Russian youth than either Schopenhauer or Hegel), we should have to ask why these schemes of philosophy were preferred to others? Again, each scheme of philosophy having followers who belong to quite different political schools, we should have to ask why the Russian revolutionists have drawn such extremely practical conclusions from a given school of philosophy, and not the very reverse conclusions? And with regard to Russian political writers, ought we not to inquire, before all else, what circumstances have determined the appearance of works of a given kind—these works being themselves the product of the medium which the author lives in, and which he is able to modify but to a very slight extent? To answer such questions would have been to begin with a thorough study of social conditions and political life in Russia, and that study was never undertaken.

Another very common cause of errors is the confusion often made between distinct periods of development of the Russian revolutionary movement. The nihilism of 1861—a philosophical system especially dealing with what Mr. Herbert Spencer would call religious, governmental, and social fetishism —is confounded with the peaceful socialism of 1872 and with the terrorism of today. In this way we get that mythical and psychologically impossible personage, the "nihilist" of the European press, who, chancing to become discontented with the dean of his university, takes to making bombs and killing the tsar. Life and evolution move quickly during revolutionary times, and the Russian revolutionary party, young as it is, already has a whole history. Of course each phase of its development has had its influence on, and has bequeathed some of its features to, the following phase. But to confound them one with another is necessarily to arrive at erroneous conclusions. To direct attention to these two subjects, and especially to the second (for the first is too large and important to be adequately dealt with in an article), is the purpose of this paper.

The whole reign of Alexander II, the first five years alone excepted, presents an uninterrupted series of revolutionary conspiracies. From the moment when on the eve of the emancipation Alexander II surrendered to the reactionary party, neutralized the effects of the Emancipation Act by entrusting with its application in life its very enemies, and condemned beforehand to sterility all reforms which were in way of elaboration at that time—since the end of 1860, in fact—secret societies have begun to appear, and have operated until now. No prosecutions, deportations, nor executions have arrested their development. No sooner have wholesale arrests destroyed one society than another has already appeared and begun to spread its ramifications all over Russia. The development of them all is the same. At the outset the program of the young society is theoretical, wide, but at the same time moderate as to its means of action. Theoretical propaganda of reforming principles, persuasion, but no direct action against the government, no revolutionary proceedings characterize the nascent secret society. But, as it develops, as it comes into contact with new and varied elements, as it tries to apply its principles to life, its program becomes more definite and receives a decidedly political bent. The direct struggle against government by revolutionary means becomes an important part of the program; and, in proportion as the prosecutions directed against the society increase in violence, its means of action are modified accordingly. In this way four strata of secret societies have succeeded each other. Immediately after the dispersion of those which led in 1861 and 1862 to the condemnation of

Chernyshevskii and Mikhailov, a new group of secret societies, those of Karakazov and Ishutin, made their appearance. They were broken up after Karakazov's attempt against the tsar in 1866, but were soon followed by the circles of Nechaev. And as soon as these last were destroyed in 1870, we saw the appearance of very numerous "circles" instituted in 1871–1873, either in the shape of one vast organism, or in the shape of several separate but friendly societies. These last were the common source from which arose all the numerous societies which have stood at the bar since 1873 in the trials. Of course, the great majority of those who joined the secret societies of 1871–1873 have either died in prison and on the gallows, or are languishing in Siberia or in central prisons. But among those who appeared before the courts during the trials of the last four or five years we continually met with men and women whose names have been well known in the revolutionary circles for ten years. Vera Zasulich, Sophie Perovskaia, Tat'iana Lebedeva, Hesse Helfman, Kviatkovskii, Solov'ev, Morozov, and many others, were active members of the "circles" started at that time. If, therefore, we wish to have a correct idea of the present movement, we must necessarily revert to the circles of 1871–1873, and consider the conditions under which they came into being and the evolution they have undergone.

Their character was determined by the miserable circumstances of the country. Serfdom was abolished; peasants had acquired a certain amount of personal liberty which certainly will not be underrated by those who have themselves witnessed, as the author of these lines has, the horrors of serfdom. But it was easy to foresee what subsequent facts have proved. Having been admitted a heavy redemption of "the souls" of serfs in the shape of a redemption of allotments of land (these last being quite insufficient for the peasant's support) and taxed to twice and thrice their value, the peasantry must, of necessity, be speedily brought to the verge of starvation. The famine of 1867, with all the shortcomings and administrative bribery that it unveiled, was a solemn advertisement; and in 1870 it was already obvious that the Russian peasantry would soon be brought to such despair that a peaceful settlement would be very difficult, if not impossible. The so-called self-government of peasants had already become a word without any real meaning, the authority of the landlord having been replaced by the authority of a horde of brutal officials (each village-commune being under no less than forty-one different authorities) who brought to life again the worst reminiscences of the reign of Nicholas I. The provincial "self-government" or *zemstvo*[1] had been converted into a simple additional branch of the St. Petersburg chancelleries for levying additional taxes, and was deprived of all means of doing anything for the welfare of the provinces. To quote one conservative's opinion, Mr. Suvorin confesses in his *Almanack* for 1882 that "the meaning of all reforms was modified by subsequent ministerial circulars," that "the zemstvo was being undermined in all directions," that "its requests were never taken into account," and that "it was only tolerated."[2] Public instruction was in the hands of Count [Dmitrii] Tolstoy—"the most despised man in Russia," say the Russian newspapers—whose whole system, briefly and accurately described, was to render superior, secondary, and primary education as inaccessible as possible, and to obstruct by all imaginable means the establishment of schools by private persons and by zemstvos. The reform of the courts was proclaimed; the new code of criminal procedure was, perhaps, the most liberal in Europe; but no sooner had it become law than it was ruined by ministerial circulars. The guarantees as to preliminary inquests and as to freedom of defense were abolished; public opinion became a dead letter; and there were thousands of prosecutions and sentences yearly that remained unknown not only to the people but even to the judicial authorities themselves. The press was gagged. "To write anything about the situation of the peasants

1 Institutions of local self-government concerned with public health, education, and regional administration established in 1864 through state reform.—*Editor*.

2 The paper which contains these appreciations, entitled "The Statesmen of the Last Reign" (pp. 273-288 of the *Almanack*), was cut out by the censorship, but a few copies of it are in circulation in St. Petersburg, and one of them has reached London.

was a crime," says Professor Kavelin, formerly tutor in the imperial family. To denounce administrative corruption, to condemn Count Tolstoy's system of education, to protest against the robbery of crown lands was a crime. Even to write about the rural community was a crime. The arbitrariness of the executive had no limits. The governors of provinces were all-powerful. They simply robbed peasants of their lands; they prevented the few well-intentioned men who had remained in the zemstvos from doing anything useful; they would induce the ministry of interior to deport to Siberia men of high and low social standing, to "more or less remote provinces of the Russian empire," under the mere pretext that they were "quarrelsome persons."[3]

The worst was that there remained no hope of improvement while Alexander II was alive. He was completely in the hands of the reactionary party. Fear of revolution eternally haunted him and was cleverly exploited by his advisers: he completely

---

3 I am aware that these statements will be considered by many of my readers as one-sided, if not untrue. But to these I shall merely recommend the perusal of documents published in Russia itself, either by the government or by men who have nothing to do with revolution or with nihilism (especially during the dictatorship of Count Loris-Melikov, when a little liberty was given to the press). Professor Yanson's statistical work on the economic conditions of peasantry (analyzed in the *Quarterly Review* of April 1881, and perfectly true with regard to the facts, whatever be the conclusions drawn out of them by the author), and the works of Count Valuev's land commission, will give an adequate idea of the steady impoverishment of the peasantry and of how they are ruined by taxes. The stenographic reports of the trial before the senate of Messrs. Tokarev and Loshkarev, both members of the council of the ministry of the interior [show that they have been] convicted of having illegally deprived peasants of their own lands and afterward having flogged them to death for refusing to pay rents arbitrarily imposed on them for the land they were robbed of. This, as well as the information published in Russian daily papers on the wholesale robbery of crown lands under General Kryzhanovskii's rule in Orenburg, may serve as an instance of the misdoings of administration. Mr. Golovachev's work, *Ten Years of Reforms,* and the numerous documents published in Russian moderate-liberal reviews and papers (*Vestnik yevropy, Otechestvennyia zapiski, Golos, Poriadok,* and even *Novoe vremia*) during Loris-Melikov's rule, on public instruction, on the zemstvos, on the judiciary reform, and so forth, will show how far the real meaning of all reforms of the last reign was altered by the ministers of interior, hostile to any liberal reform.

renounced liberalism and reforms. Several reforms, elaborated at the beginning of his reign, received the shape of law; but a few days or weeks later he yielded to the influence of Count Shuvalov or General Trepov, and by one stroke of his pen he destroyed all the good which might have been expected from the new law. The most necessary reforms, as for instance that of taxation, were refused, notwithstanding the unanimous representations of the zemstvos, under the pretext that they would imply an appeal to the nation for the control of state expenses. In Western Europe when the reactionary party takes the upper hand there is always the hope that in a few years the country, having become enlightened, will refuse to submit to its guidance. But nothing of the kind was to be expected in Russia. We have not a liberal party, for anything like political action in common is considered conspiracy, and that is a peril that Russian liberals were not, and are not until now, bold enough to risk. Most of them preferred to take the various opportunities of money-making that were offered by the rapid development of trade and manufactures in Russia during the last twenty years. They tried their fortunes as speculators in stocks, railways, and banks, or as lawyers. A new generation of men absorbed exclusively by their own mercantile interests, which the Russian satirist Mr. Shchedrin has so perfectly well described under the name of "Heroes of Tashkent," replaced the sincere liberals of 1861. What, in such an atmosphere as this, was left for the young men and women who were inspired by an earnest wish to work for the improvement of their country?

The whole period from 1861 to 1870 was characterized by a series of attempts to achieve this end in every way that was lawful. Public education, attempts at cooperation, public service as justices of the peace or in the new courts, medical work in villages, public service in the peasants' "self-government," all were tried; and in every case the conclusion was forced that nothing could be done while the form of government remained unchanged. A crown prosecutor, that is, an official of high and independent position, Mr. Sil'vanskii, published a few years ago a narrative of his own experience—an awful story of the struggle in which he engaged for defending his right not to be compelled to act against his conscience. The same story is true of many of those who afterward became revolutionists. Before they joined the revolutionary party, Osinskii and Kviatkovskii (hung in 1880) served in the zemstvo; Voinaral'skii was a justice of the peace; Kravchinskii, Dubrovin, Shishko, Sukhanov, Yemel'ianov, were officers; Weimar was a distinguished surgeon; and the present writer was for several years a public official naïvely believing in the good intentions of his government. And how many of us have left a scientific career, after opening our eyes to the fact that nothing could be done in this way for the welfare of the people! Nearly all those who have taken an active part in the revolutionary agitation, before joining the revolutionary party, have tried to work in peaceful and law-abiding ways. "When the history of the last fifteen years becomes possible," said Professor Stasiulevich a few months ago in the *Herald of Europe*, "it will show a long series of individual efforts which have all broken against insuperable obstacles, which have been killed in their germs, or deadened by the steady and abiding pressure of a heavy, all-suffocating atmosphere. The brutal arbitrariness of the subordinate agents of the government together with the suspicious fears of their superiors poisoned even residence in a village or provincial town and made it downright impossible."

Many—very many, indeed—have found an issue. They have retired from public life and, folding their hands, they have set themselves to wait for "some improvement," without troubling themselves how and whence it might come. But theirs were not the feelings which inspired the majority of our young men and women. The doctrine "everybody for himself, and God for all" found little favor among them. There are periods when whole generations are penetrated with the noblest feelings of altruism and self-sacrifice; when life becomes utterly impossible—morally and physically impossible—for the man (or woman) who feels that he is not doing his duty; and so it was with young Russia. It undertook the enormous task of awakening society from its deadly sleep, and of diffusing among the masses the principles of freedom and socialism, no matter what terrible sacrifices the effort might entail upon it.

The circles which originated at that epoch proceeded with the utmost caution. They began by founding societies for mutual instruction and the education and development of character. Together with scientific studies they pursued the mutual development of self-sacrifice, of an unlimited devotion to the cause of the people, and of such qualities as are necessary for a successful action in common—sincerity, perfect morality, and no eagerness for personal preeminence. Numerical strength was considered far less important than the moral qualities of members; and this carefulness in selection explains the universal equality of members, the unanimity of circles, and the good faith by which these circles are distinguished. It is obvious that women have taken an important part in all recent Russian revolutionary action, and that they were always the firmest and most devoted members of Russian secret organizations. A special study should one day be written of their share in the movement. Here it must suffice to say that the guiding principles of the Russian revolutionary movement—that is, the welfare of the masses and the need of an absolute self-sacrifice in those who pursue this end, the perfect equality of men and women in the circles, and the thorough respect toward women with which the relations with them were imbued—have persuaded the noblest women of young Russia to devote themselves heart and soul to the revolutionary cause.

Education being considered a most important item in the program, the circles which afterward became the most important (in Russia they are usually called the circles of Chaikovskii) began their work by helping the education of young men. They bought directly from publishers whole editions of certain books and distributed them either gratuitously or at cost price. The books thus circulated were all published in Russia and all authorized by censorship. They were the works of Flerovskii and Scheller on the situation of the working classes in Russia and Europe; those of Chernyshevskii, Dobroliubov, Lassalle, Marx, J. S. Mill, and so forth. In this way, the circles established wide and deep relations in the provinces. But the government considered these proceedings criminal. Arrests were made, publishers suspected of doing business with the propagandists were ruined, and the censorship prohibited and completely stopped the sale of all such books. This peaceful undertaking had thus to be abandoned and recourse had to be to other means.

The three foregoing groups of secret societies, namely, those of Chernyshevskii, of Ishutin, and of Nechaev, already had understood that the chief aim of any political party in Russia ought to be to get into close relations with the great mass of the people. Their attempts had failed. But the idea remained, and about the end of 1873 the attempts to form closer relations with working people were renewed in several parts of Russia by men sufficiently prepared for that difficult task. They were successful. Thus began this remarkable movement, whose motto was *V narod!* ("to the people!") and which has imparted to the socialist movement in Russia those peculiar features that mark it as radically different from all that has been known in Western Europe. Hundreds and thousands of young men and women broke with their past—with rank, education, family, customs— and inspired by the motto *V narod!* went forth as artisans to artisans, as peasants to peasants, to live the life of the poorest, to work side by side with them, to feel in their own persons their misery and suffering, and to teach them, to help them, to give them courage and strength, to awaken them from their apathy, and to bring them to a better understanding of their place in society and their duty towards themselves and their neighbors.

All former attempts from above to wrest concessions from our absolute government had failed because of the inertia of the masses. On the other hand, the popular movements of other times have failed likewise, as the people were unorganized and had no definite political idea. It was only natural, therefore, to seek to establish an intimate connection between the two movements, that from above and that from below, and to achieve a fusion between the several elements concerned. To awaken the conscience of the people, and to help them to express their wants, seemed the party's first duty. Further, the ambition of the party being the improvement of the condition of the poor and oppressed—which is so bad in Russia that Western Europe cannot even imagine the like of it—it was quite natural that the propagandist should live with the poorest and the most cruelly oppressed, and there endeavor to increase the knowledge, to awake the sentiment of self-respect, and teach the hope for a better state of things. But nowhere in the West is the chasm between the upper and lower classes so wide as in Russia. They are two different worlds, ruled by different laws (written law and common law); with different conceptions of property (Roman law and communistic customs of Indo-Germanic races), of the state (Byzantine law and Slavonic communalistic and federative principles), of self-government, of taxes, of commercial relations, of marriage, of inheritance. That being the case, was it not necessary to begin by knowing the peasant, his ideals, his conceptions, and his wishes, and not by imposing on him schemes elaborated on purely theoretical bases? Until of late, however, the Russian peasant has always regarded the man who wears broadcloth and neither plows nor hews, neither hammers nor digs side by side with him, as an enemy. We wanted faith and love from them; and to obtain them it was necessary to live their life. It was hard, of course. The peasant feeds on rye bread and water—when he is lucky enough to have rye bread, which he often lacks; his home is a miserable hovel; the vilest official can beat and ill-use him with impunity. The workman labors fourteen and sixteen hours a day at the factory, earning very little; he dwells, with twelve or fifteen of his kind, both male and female, in a single room. It was hard to live a life of this sort; but hundreds of the party did live it, for all that. Young men left their classrooms, their regiments, and their desks, learned the smith's trade, or the cobbler's, or the plowman's, and went out to work and to teach among the villages. Highborn and wealthy ladies betook themselves to the factories, worked fifteen and sixteen hours a day at the machine, slept in dogholes with peasants, went barefoot as our working women do, bringing water from the river for the house. Vulgar souls may sneer at this; but fifty years hence the women of Russia will animate and inspire their children with the story of these lives.

The ideal of the circles was mainly socialistic. But, although it was staunchly and ardently upheld, the majority were of the opinion that a preconceived ideal was premature while the mass of the people had had no opportunity of expressing its wishes. Our final aim was the same as that of the socialists of Western Europe, and a few of us warmly advocated the achievement of a violent social revolution. But the great bulk of the party were decidedly opposed to strong measures and shrank from the possibility of a peasants' uprising. Later on, when it became obvious that the government would not permit even peaceful propaganda, the idea of a general revolution gained ground. But it is certain that, could it have developed freely from the outset, the development of this party would have been pacific, as has been the development of the socialistic party in Western Europe, or of the Peasants' party in Norway. But the government thought fit to make this impossible.

At this time the reactionary party had no more moral force in Russia. Its influence depended mainly upon the support it received from the emperor, and this support might fail it any day. To maintain itself in power it was compelled to play on the emperor's terror of revolution, and to keep him persuaded that his life and his dynasty were in danger. But in reality the life of the tsar was never safer than then. The party was quite opposed to any idea of violence, and I can say now that when one young man came to St. Petersburg from a remote province with the firm resolution of making an attempt against the tsar, the socialists used all their might to prevent him from achieving his object. Crowded jails and incessant prosecutions, however, were necessary to the reactionary party to maintain its influence at the court; and 1874, 1875, and 1876 were years of wholesale domiciliary search and arrest. According to official figures, more than a thousand persons were arrested in connection with the Trial of the Hundred and Ninety-Three,[4] not to speak about

4 Largest of the trials held in the late 1870s to convict revolutionaries. The trial lasted from October 1877 to January 1878.—*Editor*.

those arrested in connection with another dozen trials; and the majority of the arrested passed three and four years in prison before they were tried—three years of cellular detention in the damp casemate of the fortress of Peter and Paul or in the cells of other prisons, without ever speaking a human sentence, without paper, without news from kinfolk, with nothing but the few books of the prison library, read over and over again in the twilight of the blinded windows.[5] Of some three hundred men and women who were kept thus for several years, eleven died of consumption and scurvy, four cut their throats with broken glass, many attempted suicide, and nine went mad. To prove the general quality of the charges, it may be added that of the hundred and ninety-three, ninety were positively acquitted as there were no charges against them, and this by a court so bent upon severity that it condemned all those who were considered as most active in the propaganda to seven, nine, and twelve years of hard labor, with loss of civil rights and transportation for life to Siberia. In other trials of the same epoch the sentences were so harsh that women were condemned to nine years' hard labor for having given a single socialistic pamphlet to a workman. I hardly need add that nearly all acquitted were immediately exiled "to less remote provinces" of Russia—such as the peninsula of Kola or the northern Ural; and that they are there until now, literally starving in hamlets where no skilled labor is wanted, receiving a meager salary from the government.

The proceedings of the government in the prosecution it started with against our party are so extravagant and so little known in England that the thick volume which would be necessary to tell them in would probably be a popular book. The treatment in central prisons—where prisoners remain year after year without any occupation in their cells—is so bad that, according to the public statement of the priest of one of these prisons, the mortality one year exceeded twenty

5 I was the only one to whom paper and ink were allowed in the fortress until sunset daily. This was at the special request of the Geographical Society, as I was finishing for it a book on the glacial period.

per cent. The famine insurrections in the Kharkov prison and in the St. Petersburg fortress; the employment of administrative banishment (without trying the exiles) on such a scale that there is hardly a hamlet in the north of Russia and Siberia from Kola to Nizhne-Kolymsk that does not have its exiles;[6] such sentences as that imposed on Miss Gukovskaia, who was but fourteen years old at the moment of her "crime" (exciting the crowd to deliver Koval'skii) and was condemned for life to exile to Siberia, where she drowned herself in the Yenisei; the practice of imprisoning by wholesale on simple denunciations of paid spies, who can prove themselves useful only by denouncing somebody; all this ought to be told with all the awful details, but in the present article I can only refer to these facts. The reader may judge for himself what a part they have played in the ulterior development of the party.

The typical case is that of Vera Zasulich. Everybody knows now what had brought her to attack the chief of the St. Petersburg police, General Trepov. What she wished to do was simply to direct the attention of public opinion in Russia and in Europe on what is done in Russian prisons; to make known how Bogoliubov, one of the prisoners of the house of detention (a prison for those who wait trial), was outrageously and cruelly flogged in the prison for not having greeted the almighty chief of the St. Petersburg police, and how all other political prisoners who protested with cries and groans against the punishment executed at the very doors of their cells were beaten and kicked by dozens of policemen ordered for that

6 As to administrative exile I cannot do better than quote the following words of E. A. Shakeev, pronounced at the sitting of the assembly of the St. Petersburg nobility on March 1, 1881. He said, "Often for a simple acquaintance, or for being the relation of a compromised person, for belonging to a school which was disliked by the administration, for an impudent expression used in a letter, or for a photograph, young men were sent to exile. The *Courts Herald* formerly published the number thus exiled on a simple order of the administration, and this number varied from 250 to 2,500 per year; but if we take into account the number of those exiled by the executive during these last years—a number which we can only suppose—this exile will appear as a hecatomb of human beings." (*Golos*, March 3, 1881).

purpose by General Trepov. The fact that she could bring these proceedings to public knowledge only by shooting the powerful general is of itself enough to exemplify the situation in which the party was placed. The Bogoliubov affair was common talk in St. Petersburg, but not a single journal dared say a word about it. And when we told and published the story in pamphlet form, and sent it to the more important European papers, expecting that, not interested in concealing the truth, they would publish the whole evil business, not one of them took any notice of the communication. Then it was that Vera Zasulich took a revolver, and, without saying a word of her purpose to anyone, did what we know. "I did so because I saw that it was otherwise impossible to bring the fact to the knowledge of the public," she said before the court; and she added: "I was very glad to learn that Trepov was not killed, as that was not my intention." So announced itself in Russia the first act of "terrorism." Public opinion, in the persons of the jury, acquitted Zasulich; but it is known that the government ordered her rearrest at the very doors of the court, and rearrested she would have been if the crowd had not rescued her.

In the development of the movement, the case of Vera Zasulich was decisive. Ever since, Russian revolutionists, seeing that they are outlaws whom nobody defends, have taken to defending themselves. The first result of this recognition and the necessities entailed thereby was to protect themselves against spies who delivered men to a sure death in prisons and in Siberia merely to earn a little money; and the second was to defend their homes from the raids of the secret police. I say "raids," for no milder expression can be applied to the descents of the secret police in Russia. At two or three in the morning the door-bell is rung, and no sooner is it answered than a dozen officers, soldiers, and porters swarm into the rooms. The women are ordered out of bed and made to dress before a gendarme; if they protest, they are dragged out bodily. If they happen to be dressed, they are made to undress before the raiders, or they are undressed by them, and searched for papers and letters. The children are moved from their beds; the beds themselves are examined, and so forth. I speak with full knowledge of the facts, and not on mere hearsay, as every one of my relations who has a weakness for liberal opinions has been subjected to one or more such experiences. One was bold enough to tell the raiders what he thought of them. He was arrested there, and lay five months in jail. Then he was sent straight to a miserable hamlet in eastern Siberia. His exile began in May 1875; it is not ended yet.[7] Is it necessary to add that scores and scores of like cases could be produced?

It was quite natural, I think, to reason in some such terms as these: "In other countries men have courage enough to defend their homes. An Englishman or an American would not permit such proceedings, and why should we? Let us have, at least, as much courage as this. Of course, we shall sacrifice ourselves; but we will try to make such misdeeds impossible." This argument was put into practice at Odessa by Koval'skii and his friends, and afterwards by others at Kiev and St. Petersburg. How the government answered this new manifestation of the party is a matter of history. It proclaimed a state of seige and began to hang revolutionists by scores.

It is obvious that the movement has ever since been growing more and more militant and aggressive. The watchword becomes self-defense against the spies who denounce; against the officials who hang (even boys of nineteen, and on simple suspicion); against governors of provinces who cruelly mistreat the prisoners; against those who induce the tsar to double the severity of sentences pronounced in his courts. The secret organ of the party developed the idea, and the new tactics were approved even by moderate liberals. Even those who repudiate the principle of attack, the policy of offense as they call it, approve the policy of defense. It may seem strange in this country; but to one familiar with police raids, arrests on suspicion, and official brutality; to one who knows what a military court, with its ready-made verdicts, really is; to one made

7 Kropotkin speaks of his brother Aleksandr who was arrested and exiled in 1875 for revolutionary activities. After repeated efforts at appeal failed, he shot himself in 1886.—*Editor*.

desperate by stories of women going mad after outrages of the police, or tramping for three months through ice and snow on the march to Nizhne-Kolymsk (now the prison of Cherny-shevskii, the well-known Russian economist and critic); to one knowing what it is to sojourn in northern Siberia in the huts of aborigines, poisoned by the most disgusting diseases; to one who has witnessed the doings of an army of spies; to one, in a word, who has lived the life that we Russians have to live, it is not strange at all.

I cannot linger more on this phase of the movement. It must suffice to say that "nihilists" killed five spies and three officials, and that, in return, seventeen young men were hanged. But it is worth notice that until 1879 the person of the tsar remained inviolable. It was only when the reign of the White Terror was established that the idea of attacking absolutism in the person of the tsar became popular among the revolutionary party, and gradually grew to a conviction.[8] The various incidents which characterize this third phase of the movement are common property: the daily press in all countries has made much of them. Therefore I shall say nothing of them, but endeavor to elucidate the far less known tendencies, aims, and prospects of the party.

The popular notion is, the Russian nihilists do not themselves know what they are fighting for. "They have never said what they want," is the cry, the cuckoo cry, of the press; and current opinion was summed up in the caricature which showed two dreadful "nihilists," laden with dynamite, meditating among heaps of ruins. "Is there anything left?" asks one of them. "The great globe itself? Well, more dynamite, and spring it!" But a few quotations from the publications of the Executive Committee will show how far removed from truth this conception is.

8 Although Kropotkin is speaking of the 1870s, the repressive tactics of the government against revolutionaries known as the White Terror actually began in 1866 after Karakazov's attempt on the tsar's life. Thus the tactic of tsaricide began earlier than 1879, and the White Terror has generally been considered a reaction to this tactic rather than the reverse as Kropotkin argues.—*Editor.*

It must clearly be understood, of course, that the party of the Executive (or terrorist) Committee, whose organ is the *People's Will*, does not represent all aspirations of all Russian revolutionists. There is, besides, the party of the *Chernyi Peredel* ("Black Partition"), which is known also as the *Narodniki*, or People's party, and which differs from the former by its giving more importance to socialistic propaganda in villages and to the economic struggle, and intending rather to institute an organization like the Irish Land League before taking a direct part in the struggle against the government. This party, however, though it has many sympathizers among the youth of Russia, has no strong organization, and is not to be compared for energy and daring activity with the People's Will section. Again, there are the Little Russian (or Ukrainian) groups, as well as several other groups which advocate the liberation and federation of all Little-Russian speaking provinces of Russia and Austria (eastern Galicia), as well as the independence of all major ethnographical subdivisions of the Russian empire, and represent the principles of federated socialist communes. Up to the present time their impulse has been inconsiderable, and their action of little moment; but in the near future, I think, the principles of federalism advocated by them will become a factor of great and lasting importance in resolving the Russian and Slavonic problems. For the moment, though, they have had but little influence on the course of events. The People's Will party is thus the strongest and most influential of all Russian revolutionary organizations, and it has done almost all the fighting that has been done during the last five years; it is therefore to its aspirations and aims that we must give the chief attention. The secret organ of the party, in its first number, exposed its tendencies as follows:

> A party which looks forward to a practical future must, before all, have a clear conception of life. The loftiest ideal is not only useless, but dangerous, if it is incapable of actual realization and diverts the forces from the pursuit of less grand but realizable ameliorations. . . . A party of action must aim at the production of definite, tangible, and immediately useful effects, and to that end it must choose such means

alone as are immediately applicable to existing circumstances. For the moment, the most important practical question is that of the form of government. The anarchist doctrines have too commonly diverted our attention; but for Russia it is of the greatest importance. We have no body of representatives chosen from the governing classes, as is the case in Europe. Our government is but a potent, independent organization, existing for itself alone, a compact and well-disciplined hierarchy which keeps the people in a state of economic and political slavery, and would keep it so, even had we no exploiting classes at all. . . . While engaged in the attainment of this object, we shall acquire a certain influence on the coming revolution; and although we should not achieve the complete emancipation of the people, at least we shall have established the fact of its very sovereignty; we shall have given it a voice in the government; we shall have assured its friends the right of existence; and to serve the nation will no longer be a crime.

In another number of the same periodical the Executive Committee goes on to foreshadow its course of action in the event of this consummation being achieved:

As for ourselves, we are popular socialists. We hold that liberty, equality, and fraternity, the economic welfare of all, and true progress can be established only on a socialistic basis. And we hold that all forms of society must receive their sanction from the will of the people, and that the development of the nation will only be assured when the people's conscience and the people's will shall become the common law of life. . . . As popular socialists, therefore, our first ambition must be: (1) to relieve the people of the burden of the present government, and to bring about a political revolution which shall give power to the people. . . . (2) We believe that the people's will might be adequately expressed by an *assemblée constituante* composed of delegates elected by universal suffrage, and receiving instructions from their electors. Such assembly is not, of course, an ideal representation of the popular will, but it is the only one possible in our time; and, therefore, we think it necessary to advocate its convocation. . . . While ready absolutely to obey the national will, thus expressed, we shall nevertheless, as a party, submit our own program to the consideration of the nation. This we shall preach before the revolution, and we shall advocate its adoption at the elections and before the assembly. It is: (1) The permanent representation of the people on the principles already formulated (universal suffrage and complete freedom in elections), and its sovereignty in all state affairs.

(2) A large self-government for the provinces, guaranteed by the application of election to the appointment of all officials, by the autonomy of rural communes, and by the economic independence of the people. (3) The autonomy of the rural assembly (*Mir*) as an economic and administrative unity. (4) The right of the people to the land (nationalization of land). (5) The introduction of a system of measures tending towards the transfer of manufactures to the working classes. (6) Absolute liberty of religion, of thought, of association, of meeting, and of electoral agitation. (7) Universal suffrage. (8) The substitution for the standing army of a system of territorial defense. (*Narodnaia volia*, no. 3, January 1, 1880.)

It is seen from these quotations that, while boldly advocating political reform, the Executive Committee is very cautious as to social reforms, and submits them completely to the will of a freely elected constituent assembly. The political change is considered thus as a first step, and the economic change as a second step which may follow the former after a certain period of time. This point of view is still better set forth in a recent number of the secret organ of the Executive Committee.

It cannot be too clearly understood that it is impossible to apply to Russian parties such names as are in vogue in Western Europe ("Political Radicals," "Socialists," and so forth). In our program are included the elements of both political radicalism and of socialism, intimately connected one with another. . . . The sovereignty of the people is everywhere a necessary thing. But in Europe it already exists, if not in so complete a form as might be desired, but to such an extent, at least, that *de facto* it is only for economic causes that people are unable to make complete use of their political rights. Economic independence is therefore the question of the day in Western Europe; and the social question appears there chiefly under an economic aspect. But in Russia, things are otherwise. For us, the solution of the political question is as important as the solution of the economic question. . . . Not only do we consider the achievement of a political change to be our first duty; we also affirm that a party which does not understand the necessity of such a change would not be capable of effecting any practical improvements. Our first need is to break the chains of slavery which bind the hands of the people, to the end that it may become its own master, at least as regards the main conditions of life. Unless we do this, we shall have, in our economic spheres, not Owens, but Arakcheevs. Of course, we do not think that political liberty can be consolidated without economic independence. But in any case, this last could only be a second step, closely following on the first, but utterly impossible while the present form of government remains unchanged. (*Narodnaia volia*, no. 7, January, 1882).

The tendencies of the terrorist party are still better laid down in the letter of the Executive Committee to the Tsar Alexander III, published a few days after his accession to the throne. It gives a complete idea of the practical program of the Executive Committee, and I may add that if its voice had only been heard *at that time*, many sections of the Russian revolutionary party would have joined the Executive Committee in its promises to work for the peaceful development of the political institutions of Russia. After discussing the situation generally, and proving that the revolutionary agitation, far from being the result of the ill-will of a few, is a natural effect of general causes, the Executive Committee says:

To this situation there are but two issues: either revolution which cannot be put back by executions, or appeal from the emperor to the nation. In the interests of our country, to avoid the useless waste of strength and the dreadful calamities inseparable from revolution, the Executive Committee advises your majesty to choose the second. Be sure that as soon as the supreme power shall cease from being despotic, as soon as it shall take a firm resolution to accomplish the wishes of the conscience of the people, you may safely dismiss the spies—the shame of government—send your escorts quietly to the barracks, and burn the gallows. The Executive Committee itself will stop its task, and the forces organized about it will scatter for peaceful civilizing work throughout the country. Peaceful discussion will take the place of brute force, the use of which is even more hateful to us than to your officials, and is only resorted to by us out of a miserable necessity.

We address ourselves directly to you, putting aside prejudices that are the growth of centuries. We forget that you are the representative of that power which has so long deceived and wronged the people. We speak to you as citizens and honest men. We hope that no feeling of personal anger will stifle in you the sentiment of moral obligations and the desire to know the truth. We, too, have the right of being angry. You have lost your father. We have lost, not our fathers only, but our brothers, our wives, our children, and our best friends. But we will not take our personal feelings into account, if it is necessary for the welfare of our country. And we expect the same from you.

We are not imposing conditions on you. Do not, we pray, be shocked by our proposals. The conditions which must be fulfilled to put an end to the revolutionary agitation, and make peaceful development possible, are not of our dictating. We do not impose conditions; we only remember them.

These conditions we see to be two:

(1) A general amnesty for all past political crimes, inasmuch as they were not crimes, but performance of civil duties.

(2) The convocation of delegates representing the whole Russian people, for the revision of all fundamental laws in conformity with the people's will."

The Executive Committee adds that a national sanction of the supreme power will be valid only if the elections are free, which cannot be realized unless they are brought about by means of universal suffrage and accompanied by absolute liberty of the press, by freedom of speech and meeting, and of electoral programs.

By no other means can a process of natural and peaceful development be initiated. We solemnly declare before our country and the world that our party will unconditionally submit to the conditions of a national assembly thus elected, and will never allow itself unlawfully to oppose a government thereby sanctioned.

Such were, one year ago, the aims and tendencies of the "terrorists," supported by many Russian revolutionary organizations, and, in fact, by the majority of the educated men of the wealthy classes, with the exception of the reactionaries represented by the *Moscow Gazette* of Mr. Katkov. If a national assembly had been convoked in the above-said conditions, the representatives of the peasantry, who constitute ninety per cent of our population, would form an influential part of it. And to everyone who knows the Russian peasant, with his eminently practical mind and with his many centuries' experience of the difficult questions that are debated before the assemblies of the rural communes—it is obvious that, were the elections fair, and were the autonomous and federalist tendencies of the great natural subdivisions of the Russian empire to have free play, such peasant delegates would be elected as, for practical ability and business qualities, would put most lawyers and newspapermen to shame. The hope that the new tsar would understand that, and make the concessions asked, was maintained until the last. But there is now no room for doubt that Alexander III has chosen the other way, and has elected to stake the existence of the principle of hereditary absolutism on the governmental capacities of the same party whose counsels have provoked the desperate struggle now going on in Russia, and prepared the violent death of his father.

One year ago there was an easy way of escape from the difficulty. But now the difficulty is intensified by the intervention of a new and important element. During the first ten years after the emancipation the peasants remained quiet. But the famines of the last two years have fully revealed to them their miserable fate, and they have begun to protest once more. The outbreaks against Jews in the southwest and against the Russian bourgeoisie in the southeast as well as the incendiarism and "no-rent" movement in the central provinces are but a foreshadowing of far more intense movements which are growing in the villages. The people already talk of the general partition of land, of "the great war and bloodshed" which are to begin sometime in the spring. Until now the revolutionary party has scarcely applied its forces at all to a serious agrarian agitation, but it is easy to foresee the quality and momentum of forces that will rise ready to their hands among the peasantry if Russian revolutionists should only apply to agrarian agitation the determination and the capacities of organization they have shown in their struggle against the government; and this will be done, the People's Will says, if the necessary improvements cannot be obtained otherwise. Of course, there are many among the tsar's advisers to hint that, the whole agitation being the work of a few men, nothing would be easier than to hang and to banish it into nothingness. But the fact is that the revolutionary party cannot be hanged out of existence. Its ramifications are too wide and too deep, its objects are too popular, it has everywhere too many sympathizers ever to be in want of men ready to fill up the thinned ranks of the active group. Men may change, but the idea will remain. The party has been too steadily and bitterly prosecuted not to attract the most devoted, the most self-denying, and the most intelligent of the young men and women of this generation. It will not be destroyed until it has fulfilled its historical mission; and even the men in power understand this so perfectly well that they are ready to expose Russia to all the perils of a desperate war in order to maintain for a few years more the absolutism which they cherish for base personal and egotistic reasons.

"Expropriation" remains one of Kropotkin's most detailed discussions of the process of revolution leading to anarchist communism. In his narrative, he weaves historical precedent together with what he sees as the practical details of the organization of the coming revolution. He emphasizes the supreme role of the masses in making the revolution and in arranging the postrevolutionary society which will ensure the future of anarchism.

The essay was originally published in *Le Révolté* on November 25, 1882 and republished in *Paroles d'un Révolté* (Paris: Flammarion, 1885), Several years later, Kropotkin expanded the original article for an English translation. The article was later included in *The Conquest of Bread* (New York: Vanguard Press, 1924). The following version is republished from *Expropriation*, Freedom Pamphlets, no. 7 (London: W. Reeves, n.d. [1895]) with permission of the publisher.

Expropriation

It is told of Rothschild that, seeing his fortune threatened by the revolution of 1848, he hit upon the following stratagem. "I am quite willing to admit," said he, "that my fortune has been accumulated at the expense of others, but if it were divided among the millions of Europe tomorrow the share of each would only amount to five shillings. Very well then, I undertake to render to each his five shillings if he asks me for it."

Having given due publicity to his promise, our millionaire proceeded as usual to stroll quietly through the streets of Frankfort. Three or four passersby asked for their five shillings, which he disbursed with a sardonic smile. His stratagem succeeded and the family of the millionaire is still in possession of its wealth.

It is in much the same fashion that the shrewd heads among the middle classes reason when they say "Ah, expropriation; I know what that means. You take all the overcoats and lay them in a heap, and every one is free to help himself and fight for the best."

But such jests are irrelevant as well as flippant. What we want is not a redistribution of overcoats. Besides, is it likely that in such a general scramble the shivering folk would come off any better? Nor do we want to divide up the wealth of the Rothschilds. What we do want is to arrange things so that every human being born into the world shall be ensured the opportunity in the first instance of learning some useful occupation and of becoming skilled in it; next, that he shall be free to work at his trade without asking leave of master or owner, and without handing over to landlord or capitalist the lion's share of what he produces. As to the wealth held by the Rothschilds or the Vanderbilts, it will serve us to organize our system of communal production.

The day when the laborer may till the ground without paying away half of what he produces, the day when the machines necessary to prepare the soil for rich harvests are at the free disposal of the cultivators, the day when the worker in the factory produces for the community and not for the monopolist—that day will see the workers clothed and fed; and there will be no more Rothschilds or other exploiters.

No one will then have to sell his working power for a wage that only represents a fraction of what he produces.

"So far, good," say our critics, "but you will have Rothschilds coming in from outside. How are you to prevent a person from amassing millions in China and then settling among you? How are you going to prevent such a person from surrounding himself with lackeys and wage slaves—from exploiting them and enriching himself at their expense?"

"You cannot bring about a revolution all over the world at the same time. Well then, are you going to establish custom houses on your frontiers, to search all who enter your country, and confiscate the money they bring with them? Anarchist policemen firing on travelers would be a fine spectacle!"

But at the root of this argument there is a great error. Those who propound it have never paused to inquire whence come the fortunes of the rich. A little thought would suffice to show them that these fortunes have their beginnings in the poverty of the poor. When there are no longer any destitute there will no longer be any rich to exploit them.

Let us glance for a moment at the Middle Ages, when great fortunes began to spring up.

A feudal barron seizes a fertile valley. But as long as the fertile valley is unpopulated our baron is not rich. His land brings him nothing; he might as well possess property on the moon. Now what does our baron do to enrich himself? He looks for peasants!

But if every peasant-farmer had a piece of land, free from rent and taxes, if he had in addition the tools and the stock necessary for farm labor, who would plow the lands of the baron? Each would look after his own. But there are whole tribes of destitute persons ruined by wars, or drought, or pestilence. They have neither horse nor plow. (Iron was costly in the Middle Ages, and a draft horse still more so.)

All these destitute creatures are trying to better their condition. One day they see on the road at the confines of our baron's estate a notice board indicating by certain signs adapted to their comprehension that the laborer who is willing to settle on this estate will receive the tools and materials to build his cottage and sow his fields, and a portion of land rent free for a certain number of years. The number of years is represented by so many crosses on the sign board, and the peasant understands the meaning of these crosses.

So the poor wretches swarm over the baron's lands, making roads, draining marshes, building villages. In nine years he begins to tax them. Five years later he levies rent. Then he doubles it. The peasant accepts these new conditions because he cannot find better ones elsewhere; and little by little, by the aid of laws made by the oppressors, the poverty of the peasants becomes the source of the landlord's wealth. And it is not only the lord of the manor who preys upon him. A whole host of usurers swoop down upon the villages, increasing as the wretchedness of the peasants increases. That is how things went in the Middle Ages; and today is it not still the same thing? If there were free lands which the peasant could cultivate if he pleased, would he pay fifty pounds to some "Monsieur le Vicomte" for condescending to sell him a scrap?

Would he burden himself with a lease which absorbed a third of the produce? Would he—on the métayer system—consent to give the half of his harvest to the landowner?

But he has nothing. So he will accept any conditions, if only he can keep body and soul together, while he tills the soil and enriches the landlord.

So in the nineteenth century, just as in the Middle Ages, the poverty of the peasant is a source of wealth to the landed proprietor.

II

The landlord owes his riches to the poverty of the peasants, and the wealth of the capitalist comes from the same source.

Take the case of a citizen of the middle class who, somehow or other, finds himself in possession of twenty thousand pounds. He could, of course, spend his money at the rate of two thousand pounds a year, a mere trifle in these days of fantastic, senseless luxury. But then he would have nothing left at the end of ten years. So, being a "practical person," he prefers to keep his fortune intact, and win for himself a snug little annual income as well.

That is very easy in our society, for the good reason that the towns and villages swarm with workers who have not the wherewithal to live for a month, or even a fortnight. So our worthy citizen starts a factory: the banks hasten to lend him another twenty thousand pounds, especially if he has a reputation for "business ability"; and with this round sum he can command the labor of five hundred hands.

If all the men and women in the countryside had their daily bread assured and their daily needs already satisfied, who would work for our capitalist, or be willing to manufacture for him, at a wage of half a crown a day, commodities selling in the market for a crown or even more?

Unhappily—we know it all too well—the poor quarters of our towns and the neighboring villages are full of needy wretches, whose children clamor for bread. So, before the factory is well finished, the workers hasten to offer themselves. Where a hundred are required a thousand besiege the doors and from the time his mill is started the owner, if he is not more than commonly stupid, will clear forty pounds a year out of each millhand he employs.

He is thus able to lay hold of a snug little fortune, and if he chooses a lucrative trade, and if he has "business talents," he will increase his income by doubling the number of the men he exploits.

So he becomes a personage of importance. He can afford to give dinners to other personages, to the local magnates, the civic, legal, and political dignitaries. With his money he can "marry money," eventually he may pick and choose places for his children, and later on perhaps get something good from the government—a contract for the army or for the police. His gold breeds gold; till at last a war, or even a rumor of war, or a specualtion on the stock exchange, gives him his great opportunity.

Nine-tenths of the huge fortunes made in the United States are (as Henry George has shown in his *Social Problems*) the result of deceit on a large scale, assisted by the state. In Europe nine-tenths of the fortunes made in our monarchies and republics have the same origin. There are not two ways of becoming a millionaire.

This is the secret of wealth; find the starving and destitute, pay them half a crown, and make them produce ten shillings worth in the day, amass a fortune by these means, and then increase it by some lucky hit, made with the help of the state.

Need we go on to speak of small fortunes attributed by the economists to forethought and frugality, when we know that mere saving in itself brings in nothing, so long as the pence saved are not used to exploit the deprivation?

Take a shoemaker, for instance. Grant that his work is well paid, that he has plenty of custom, and that by dint of strict frugality he contrives to increase his income from eighteen pence to two shillings a day, perhaps two pounds a month.

Grant that our shoemaker is never ill, that he does not half starve himself, in spite of his passion for economy; that he does not marry or that he has no children; that he does not die of consumption; suppose anything and everything you please!

Well, at the age of fifty he will not have scraped together eight hundred pounds; and he will not have enough to live on during his old age, when he is past work. Assuredly this is not how great fortunes are made. But suppose our shoemaker, as soon as he has earned a few pence, thriftily conveys them to the savings bank, and that the savings bank lends them to the capitalist who is just about to "employ labor"—that is, to exploit the poor. Then our shoemaker takes an apprentice, the child of some poor wretch who will think himself lucky if in five years time his son has learned the trade and is able to earn his living.

Meanwhile our shoemaker does not lose by him; and if trade is brisk he soon takes a second, and then a third apprentice. Eventually he will take two or three journeymen—poor wretches, thankful to receive half a crown a day for work that is worth five shillings, and if our shoemaker is "in luck," that is to say, if he is keen enough and mean enough, his journeymen and apprentices will bring him in nearly a pound a day over and above the product of his own toil. He can then enlarge his business. He will gradually become rich, and no longer have any need to deny himself the necessities of life. He will leave a snug little fortune to his son.

That is what people call "being economical and having frugal temperate habits." At bottom it is nothing more nor less than grinding the face of the poor.

Commerce seems an exception to this rule. "Such a man," we are told, "buys tea in China, brings it to France and realizes a profit of thirty per cent on his original outlay. He has exploited nobody."

Nevertheless, the case is analogous. If our merchant had carried his bales on his back, well and good! In early medieval times that was exactly how foreign trade was conducted, and so no one reached such giddy heights of fortune as in our days. Very few and very hard earned were the gold coins which the medieval merchant gained from a long and dangerous voyage. It was less the love of money than the thirst of travel and adventure that inspired his undertakings.

Nowadays the method is simpler. A merchant who has some capital need not stir from his desk to become wealthy. He telegraphs to an agent telling him to buy a hundred tons of tea, he freights a ship, and in a few weeks, in three months if it is a sailing ship, the vessel brings him his cargo. He does not even take the risks of the voyage, for his tea and his vessel are insured, and if he has expended four thousand pounds he will receive more than five thousand; that is to say, if he has not attempted to speculate in some novel commodities, in which case he runs a chance of either doubling his fortune or losing it altogether.

Now, how could he find men willing to cross the sea, to travel to China and back, to endure hardship and slavish toil to risk their lives for a miserable pittance? How could he find dock laborers willing to load and unload his ships for "starvation wages?" How? Because they are needy and starving. Go to the seaports, visit the cookshops and taverns on the quays, and look at these men who have come to hire themselves crowding around the dock gates, which they beseige from early dawn hoping to be allowed to work on the vessels. Look at these sailors, happy to be hired for a long voyage after weeks and months of waiting. All their lives long they have gone down to the sea in ships, and they will sail in others still until the day when they perish in the waves.

Enter their cabins, look at their wives and children in rags, living one knows not how till the father's return, and you will have the answer to the question. Multiply examples, choose them where you will, consider the origin of all fortunes, large or small, whether arising out of commerce, finance, manufactures, or the land. Everywhere you will find that the wealth of the wealthy springs from the poverty of the poor. An anarchist society need not fear the advent of an unknown Rothschild who would seek to settle in its midst. If every member of the community knows that after a few hours of productive toil he will have a right to all the pleasures that civilization procures, and to those deeper sources of enjoyment which art and science offer to all who seek them, he will not sell his strength for a starvation wage. No one will volunteer to work for the enrichment of your Rothschild. His golden guineas will be only so many pieces of metal—useful for various purposes, but incapable of breeding more.

In answering the above objection we have at the same time indicated the scope of expropriation. It must extend to all that permits anyone, no matter whom—financier, millowner, or landlord—to appropriate the produce of others' toil. Our formula is simple and comprehensive.

We do not want to rob anyone of his coat, but we wish to give to the workers all those things the lack of which makes them fall an easy prey to the exploiter, and we will do our utmost to see that no one shall lack anything, that not a single man shall be forced to sell the strength of his right arm to obtain a bare subsistence for himself and his children. That is what we mean when we talk of expropriation; that will be our duty during the revolution, for whose coming we look, not two hundred years hence, but soon, very soon.

III

The ideas of anarchism in general and of expropriation in particular find much more sympathy than we are apt to imagine among men of independent character and those for whom idleness is not the supreme ideal. "Still," our friends often warn us, "take care you do not go too far! Humanity cannot be changed in a day, so do not be in too great a hurry with your schemes of expropriation and anarchy, or you will be in danger of achieving no permanent result."

Now, what we fear with regard to expropriation is exactly the contrary. We are afraid of not going far enough, of carrying out expropriation on too small a scale to be lasting. We would not have the revolutionary impulse arrested in mid career, to exhaust itself in half measures which would content no one, and which, while producing a tremendous upheaval of society and stopping its customary activities, would have no power of life in themselves, and would merely spread general discontent and inevitably prepare the way for the triumph of reaction.

There are, in fact, in a modern state established relations which it is practically impossible to modify if one attacks them only in detail. There are wheels within wheels in our economic organization—the machinery is so complex and interdependent that no one part can be modified without disturbing the whole. This will become clear as soon as an attempt is made to expropriate anything.

Let us suppose that in a certain country a limited form of expropriation is effected; for example, that, as recently suggested by Henry George, only the property of the great landlords is confiscated while the factories are left untouched; or that, in a certain city, house property is taken over by the commune but merchandise is left in private ownership; or that, in some manufacturing center, the factories are communalized but the land is not interfered with.

The same result would follow in each case—a terrible shattering of the industrial system, without the means of reorganizing it on new lines. Industry and commerce would be at a deadlock, yet a return to the first principles of justice would not have been achieved, and society would find itself powerless to construct a harmonious whole.

If agriculture could free itself from great landowners, while industry still remained the bond slave of the capitalist, the merchant, and the banker, nothing would be accomplished. The farmer suffers today not only in having to pay rent to the landlord; he is oppressed on all sides by existing conditions. He is exploited by the tradesman, who makes him pay half a crown for a spade which, measured by the labor spent on it, is not worth more than sixpence. He is taxed by the state, which cannot do without its formidable hierarchy of officials, and finds it necessary to maintain an expensive army, because the traders of all nations are perpetually fighting for the markets, and any day a little quarrel arising from the exploitation of some part of Asia or Africa may result in war.

Then again farmer and laborer suffer from the depopulation of country places; the young people are attracted to the large factory towns by the bait of high wages paid temporarily by the manufacturers of articles of luxury, or by the attractions of a more stirring life. The artificial protection of industry, the industrial exploitation of foreign countries, the prevalence of stockjobbing, the difficulty of improving the soil and the machinery of production—all these are causes which work together against agriculture, which indeed is burdened not only by rent, but by the whole complexity of conditions developed in a society based on exploitation. Thus, even if the expropriation of land were accomplished, and everyone were free to till the soil and cultivate it to the best advantage without paying rent, agriculture, even though it should enjoy—which can by no means be taken for granted—a momentary prosperity, would soon fall back into the slough in which it finds itself today. The whole thing would have to be begun over again, with increased difficulties.

The same holds true of industry. Take the converse case. Make over the factories to those who work in them, but leave the agricultural laborers slaves to farmer and landlord. Abolish the master manufacturers, but leave the landowner his land, the banker his money, the merchant his exchange, maintain still the swarm of idlers who live on the toil of the workmen, the thousand and one middlemen, the state with its numberless officials, and industry would come to a standstill. Finding no purchasers in the mass of country people still as poor as ever, having no raw material, unable to export its products, and embarrassed by the stoppage of trade, industry could only struggle on feebly, and thousands of workers would be thrown upon the streets. These starving crowds would be ready and willing to submit to the first schemer who came to exploit them; they would even consent to return to the old slavery, if only under promise of work.

Or, finally, suppose you oust the landowners and hand over the mills and factories to the worker without interfering with the swarm of middlemen who drain off the produce of our manufacturers and speculate in corn and flour, meat and groceries in our great centers of commerce. Well, when exchange is arrested and products cease to circulate, when London is without bread, and Yorkshire finds no buyers for her cloth, a terrible counterrevolution will take place—a counterrevolution trampling upon heaps of the slain, sweeping the towns and villages with shot and shell; there will be proscriptions, panic, flight, perhaps all the terrors of wholesale judicial massacre of the guillotine, as in France in 1815, 1848, and 1871.

All is interdependent in a civilized society; it is impossible to reform any one thing without altering the whole. On that day when we strike at private property, under any one of its forms, territorial or industrial, we shall be obliged to attack all its manifestations. The very success of the revolution will demand it.

Besides, we could not even if we would confine ourselves to a partial expropriation. Once the principle of the "divine right of property" is shaken, no amount of theorizing will prevent its overthrow, here by the slaves of the soil, there by the slaves of the machine.

If a great town, Paris for example, were to confine itself to taking possession of the houses or the factories, it would still be forced to deny the right of the bankers to levy upon the commune a tax amounting to two million pounds, in the form of interest for former loans. The great city would be obliged to put itself in touch with the rural districts, and its influence would inevitably urge the peasants to free themselves from the landowner. It would be necessary to communalize the railways that the citizens might get food and work, and lastly, to prevent the waste of supplies, and to guard against the deception of corn speculators like those to whom the commune of 1793 fell prey; it would place in the hands of the citizens the work of stocking their warehouses with commodities and apportioning the produce.

Nevertheless, some socialists still seek to establish a distinction. "Of course," they say, "the soil, the mines, the mills, and factories must be expropriated; these are the instruments of production, and it is right we should consider them public property. But articles of consumption, food, clothes, and dwellings should remain private property."

Popular common sense has got the better of this subtle distinction. We are not savages who can live in the woods without other shelter than the branches. The civilized man needs a roof and a hearth, a room and a bed. It is true that the bed, the room and the house of the nonproducer are only part of the paraphernalia of idleness. But for the worker a room, properly heated and lighted, is as much an instrument of production as the tool or the machine. It is the place where the nerves and sinews gather strength for the work of the morrow. Rest for the workman is the daily repairing of the machine.

The same argument applies even more obviously to food. The so-called economists of whom we speak would hardly deny that the coal burned in a machine is as necessary to production as the raw material itself. How then can food, without which the human machine could do no work, be excluded from the list of things indispensable to the producer? Such hair-splitting is worthy of the metaphysic of the schoolmen. The rich man's feast is indeed a matter of luxury, but the food of the worker is just as much a part of production as the fuel burned by the steam engine.

The same with clothing: if the economists who draw this distinction between articles of production and of consumption dressed themselves in the fashion of New Guinea we could understand their objection. But men who could not write a word without a shirt on their back are not in a position to draw such a hard and fast line between their shirt and their pen. And though the dainty gowns of their ladies must certainly rank as objects of luxury, there is nevertheless a certain quantity of linen, cotton, and woolen stuff which is a necessity of life to the producer. The shirt and shoes in which he goes to his work, his cap and the jacket he slips on after the day's toil is over, these are as necessary to him as the hammer to the anvil.

Whether we like it or not, that is what the people mean by a revolution. As soon as they have made a clean sweep of the government, they will seek first of all to ensure to themselves decent dwellings and sufficient food and clothes—free of rent and taxes.

And the people will be right. The methods of the people will be much more in accordance with science than those of the economists who draw so many distinctions between instruments of production and articles of consumption. The people understand that this is just the point where the revolution ought to begin; and they will lay the foundations of the only economic science worthy the name—a science which might be called "the study of the needs of humanity, and of the economic means to satisfy them."

IV

If the coming revolution is to be a social revolution, it will be distinguished from all former uprisings not only by its aim, but also by its methods. To attain a new end new means are required.

The three great popular movements which we have seen in France during the last hundred years differ from each other in many ways, but they have one common feature.

In each case, the people strove to overturn the old regime, and spent their heart's blood for the cause. Then, after having borne the brunt of the battle, they sank again into obscurity. A government, composed of men more or less honest, was formed and undertook to organize the republic in 1793, labor in 1848, and the free commune in 1871.

This government was filled with Jacobin ideas, and concerned almost exclusively with political questions such as the reorganization of the machinery of government, the purifying of the administration, the separation of church and state, civic liberty and such matters. It is true the workmen's clubs kept an eye on the members of the new government, and often imposed their ideas on them. But even in these clubs, whether the leaders belonged to the middle or to the working classes, it was always middle-class ideas which prevailed. They discussed various political questions at great length, but forgot to discuss the question of bread.

At those times great ideas sprang up, ideas that have moved the world; words were spoken which still stir our hearts at the interval of a century. But the people were starving in the streets.

From the very commencement of the revolution industry stopped of necessity, the circulation of produce was checked, and capital was withdrawn. The master—the employer—had nothing to fear at such times, he fattened on his dividends if indeed he did not speculate on the wretchedness around; but the wage earner was reduced to live from hand to mouth. Want knocked at the door.

Famine was abroad in the land—such famine as had hardly been seen under the old regime.

"The Girondists are starving us!" was the cry in the workmen's quarters in 1793, and thereupon the Girondists were guillotined, and full powers were given to "the Mountain" and to the Commune. The Commune indeed concerned itself with the question of bread, and made heroic efforts to feed Paris. At Lyons, Fouché and Collot d'Herbois established plenty of granaries, but the sums spent on filling them were woefully insufficient. The town councils made great efforts to procure corn; the bakers who hoarded flour were hanged—and still the people lacked bread.

Then they turned on the royalist conspirators and laid the blame at their door. They guillotined a dozen or fifteen a day—servants and duchesses alike, especially servants, for the duchesses had gone to Coblentz. But if they had guillotined a hundred dukes and viscounts a day it would have been equally futile.

The want only grew. For the wage earner cannot live without his wage, and the wage was not forthcoming. What difference could a thousand corpses more or less make to him?

Then the people began to grow weary. "So much for your vaunted revolution! You are more wretched than ever before," whispered the reactionary in the ears of the worker. And little by little the rich took courage, emerged from their hiding places, and flaunted their luxury in the face of the starving multitude. They dressed themselves up in fantastic fashions, and bade the worker to abandon his folly—this revolution which had left him worse off than before. "It is time to make an end of this," they said.

Sick at heart and weary of patience in vain, the revolutionary had at last to admit to himself that the cause was lost once more. He retreated into his hovel and awaited the worst.

Then reaction proudly reasserted itself. The political counter-revolution was accomplished. The revolution was dead. Nothing remained now but to spurn its corpse and trample it underfoot.

The White Terror began. Blood flowed like water, the guillotine was never idle, the prisons were crowded, while the pageant of rank and fashion resumed its old course, and went on merrily as before.

This picture is typical of all our revolutions. In 1848 the workers of Paris placed "three months of starvation" at the service of the Republic, and then having reached the limit of their powers, they made one last desperate effort—an effort which was drowned in blood. In 1871 the Commune perished for lack of combatants. It had taken measures for the separation of church and state, but it neglected, alas, until too late, to take measures for providing the people with bread. And so it came to pass in Paris that exquisites and fine gentlemen could spurn the confederates, and bid them go sell their lives for a miserable pittance, and leave their "betters" to feast at their ease in fashionable restaurants.

At last the Commune saw its mistake, and opened communal kitchens. But it was too late. Its days were already numbered, and the troops of Versailles were on the ramparts.

"Bread, it is bread that the revolution needs!"

Let others spend their time in issuing pompous proclamations, in decorating themselves lavishly with official gold lace, and in ranting about political liberty!

Be it ours to see, from the first day of the revolution to the last, in all the provinces fighting for freedom, that there is not a single man who lacks bread, not a single woman compelled to stand with the weary crowd outside the bakehouse door that a coarse loaf may be thrown to her in charity, not a single child pining for want of food.

It has always been the middle-class idea to harangue about "great principles"—great lies rather!

The idea of the people will be to provide bread for all. And while middle-class citizens and workmen infested with middle-class ideas admire their own rhetoric in the "talking shops," and "practical people" are engaged in endless discussions on forms of government, we the "utopian dreamers"—we must consider the question of daily bread.

We have the temerity to declare that all have a right to bread, that there is bread enough for all, and that with this watchword of "Bread for All" the revolution will triumph.

V

That we are utopians is well known. So utopian are we in fact, that we go the length of believing that the revolution can and ought to assure shelter, food and clothes to all—an idea extremely displeasing to middle-class citizens, whatever their party color, for they are quite alive to the fact that it is not easy to keep the upper hand of a people whose hunger is satisfied.

All the same, we maintain our contention: bread must be found for the people during the revolution, and the question of bread must take precedence over all other questions. If it is settled in the interests of the people, the revolution will be on the right road; for in solving the question of bread we must accept the principle of equality, which will force itself upon us to the exclusion of every other solution.

It is certain that the coming revolution—similar in that respect to the revolution of 1848—will burst upon us in the middle of a great industrial crisis. Things have been seething for more than a dozen years now, and can only go from bad to worse. Everything tends that way; new nations entering the lists of international trade and fighting for possession of the world's markets, wars, taxes ever increasing; national debts, the insecurity of the morrow, and huge commercial undertakings in every quarter of the globe.

There are millions of unemployed workers in Europe at this moment. It will be still worse when revolution has burst upon us and spread like fire put to a grain of gunpowder. The number of the unemployed will be doubled as soon as the barricades are erected in Europe and the United States. What is to be done to provide these multitudes with bread?

We do not know whether the folk who call themselves "practical people" have ever asked themselves this question in all its nakedness. But we do know that they wish to maintain the wage system, and we must therefore expect to have "national workshops" and "public works" vaunted as a means of giving food to the unemployed.

Because national workshops were opened in 1789 and in 1793; because the same means were resorted to in 1848; because Napoleon III succeeded in contenting the Parisian proletariat for eighteen years by giving them public works—which cost Paris today its debt of eighty million pounds—and its municipal tax of three or four pounds a head; because this excellent method of "taming the beast" was customary in Rome, and even in Egypt four thousand years ago; and lastly because despots, kings and emperors have always employed the ruse of throwing a scrap of food to the people to gain time to snatch up the whip— it is natural that "practical" men should extol this method of perpetuating the wage system. What need to rack our brains when we have the time-honored method of the Pharaohs at our disposal!

Well, should the revolution be so misguided as to start on this path, all would be lost.

In 1848, when the national workshops were opened on February 27, the unemployed of Paris numbered only 8,000; a fortnight later they had already increased to 49,000. They would soon have been 100,000, without counting those who crowded in from the provinces.

Yet, at that time trade and manufactures in France only employed half as many hands as today. And we know that in time of revolution exchange and industry suffer most from the general upheaval.

To realize this, we have only to think for a moment of the number of workmen whose labor depends directly or indirectly upon export trade, or of the number of hands employed in producing luxuries whose consumers are the middle-class minority.

A revolution in Europe means the immediate stoppage of at least half the factories and workshops. It means millions of workers and their families thrown on the streets.

And your "practical men" would seek to avert this truly terrible situation by means of national relief works, that is to say, by means of new industries created on the spot to give work to the unemployed!

It is evident, as Proudhon has already pointed out, that the smallest attack upon property will bring in its train the complete disorganization of the system based upon private enterprise and wage labor. Society itself will be forced to take production in hand, in its entirety, and to reorganize it to meet the needs of the whole people. But this cannot be accomplished in a day or a month; it must take a certain time thus to reorganize the system of production, and during this time millions of men will be deprived of the means of subsistence—what then is to be done?

There is only one really practical solution of the problem— boldly to face the great task which awaits us, and instead of trying to patch up a situation which we ourselves have made untenable, to proceed to reorganize production on a new basis.

Thus the really practical course of action, in our view, would be that the people should take immediate possession of all the food of the insurgent districts, keeping strict account of it all, that none might be wasted and that by the aid of these accumulated resources everyone might be able to weather the crisis. During that time an agreement would have to be made with the factory workers, the necessary raw material given them and the means of subsistence assured to them while they worked to supply the needs of the agricultural population. For we must not forget that while France weaves silks and satins to deck the wives of German financiers, the empress of Russia and the queen of the Sandwich Islands, and while Paris fashions wonderful trinkets and playthings for rich folk all the world over, two-thirds of the French peasantry have not proper lamps to give them light, or the implements necessary for modern agriculture. Lastly, unproductive land, of which there is plenty, would have to be turned to the best advantage, poor soils enriched, and rich soils, which yet, under the present system, do not yield a quarter, no, nor a tenth of what they might produce, submitted to intensive culture and tilled with as much care as a market garden or a flower plot. It is impossible to imagine any other practical solution of the problem, and, whether we like it or not, sheer force of circumstances will bring it to pass.

VI

The most prominent characteristic of capitalism is the wage system, which in brief amounts to this:

A man, or a group of men, possessing the necessary capital, starts some industrial enterprise; he undertakes to supply the factory or workshops with raw material, to organize production, to pay the employees a fixed wage, and lastly to pocket the surplus value or profits under pretext of reimbursing himself for managing the concern, for running the risks it may involve, and for the fluctuations of price in the market value of the wares.

To preserve this system, those who now monopolize capital would be ready to make certain concessions: to share, for example, a part of the profits with the workers, or rather to establish a "sliding scale," which would oblige them to raise wages when prices were high; in brief, they would consent to certain sacrifices on condition that they were still allowed to direct industry and to take its first fruits.

Collectivism, as we know, does not abolish wages, though it introduces considerable modifications into the existing order of things. It only substitutes the state, that is to say, representative government, national or local, for the individual employer of labor. Under collectivism, it is the representatives of the nation or of the district and their deputies and officials who are to have the control of industry. It is they who reserve to themselves the right of employing the surplus of production— in the interests of all. Moreover, collectivism draws a very subtle but very far-reaching distinction between the work of the laborer and of the man who has learned a craft. Unskilled labor in the eyes of the collectivist is *simple* labor, while the work of the craftsman, the mechanic, the engineer, the man of science and so forth is what Marx calls *complex* labor, and is entitled to a higher wage. But laborers and craftsmen, weavers and men of science, are all wage servants of the state—"all officials," as has been said lately, to gild the pill.

The coming revolution can render no greater service to humanity than to make the wage system in all its forms an impossibility, and to render communism, which is the negation of wage slavery, the only possible solution.

For even admitting that the collectivist modification of the present system is possible, if introduced gradually during a period of prosperity and peace—though for my part I question its practicability even under such conditions—it would become impossible in a period of revolution, when the need of feeding hungry millions springs up with the first call to arms. A political revolution can be accomplished without shaking the foundations of industry, but a revolution where the people lay hands upon property will inevitably paralyze exchange and production. Millions of public money would not suffice for wages to the millions of unemployed.

This point cannot be too much insisted upon: the reorganization of industry on a new basis (and we shall presently show how tremendous this problem is) cannot be accomplished in a few days, nor, on the other hand, will the people submit to be half starved for years in order to oblige the theorists who uphold the wage system. To tide over the period of stress, they will demand what they have always demanded in such cases—communization of supplies—the giving of rations.

It will be in vain to preach patience. The people will be patient no longer, and if food is not put in common they will plunder the bakeries.

If the people are not strong enough to carry all before them, they will be shot down to give collectivism a fair field for experiment. To this end "order" must be maintained at any price—order, discipline, obedience! And as the capitalists will soon realize, when the people are shot down by those who call themselves revolutionists the revolution itself will become hateful in the eyes of the masses. The capitalists will certainly lend their support to the champions of "order"—even though they are collectivists. In such a line of conduct, the capitalists will see a means of hereafter crushing the collectivists in their turn. If "order is established" in this fashion, the consequences are easy to foresee. Not content with shooting down the "marauders," the faction of "order" will search out the "ring-leaders of the mob." They will set up again the law courts and reinstate the hangman. The most ardent revolutionists will be sent to the scaffold. It will be 1793 over again.

Do not let us forget how reaction triumphed in the last century. First the Hébertists, "the madmen," were guillotined —those whom Mignet, with the memory of the struggle fresh upon him, still called anarchists. The Dantonists soon followed them; and when the party of Robespierre had guillotined these revolutionaries, they in their turn had to mount the scaffold; whereupon the people, sick of bloodshed, and seeing the revolution lost, threw up the sponge, and let the reactionaries do their worst.

If "order is restored," we say, the social democrats will hang the anarchists; the Fabians will hang the social democrats, and will in their turn be hanged by the reactionaries, and the revolution will have to be begun all over again.

But everything confirms us in the belief that the energy of the people will carry them far enough, and that, when the revolution takes place, the idea of anarchist communism will have gained ground. It is not an artificial idea. The people themselves have breathed it in our ear, and the number of communists is ever increasing as the impossibility of any other solution becomes more and more evident.

And if the impetus of the people is strong enough, affairs will take a very different turn. Instead of plundering the bakers' shops one day and starving the next, the people of the insurgent cities will take possession of the warehouses, the cattle markets, in fact of all the provision stores and of all the food to be had. The well-intentioned citizens, men and women both, will form themselves into bands of volunteers, and address themselves to the task of making a rough general inventory of the contents of each shop and warehouse. In twenty-four hours the revolted town or district will know what Paris has not found out yet, in spite of the statistical commission, and what it never did find out during the seige—the quantity of provisions it contains. In forty-eight hours, millions of copies will be printed of the tables giving a sufficiently exact account of the available food, the places where it is stored, and the means of distribution.

In every block of houses, in every street, in every town ward, bands of volunteers will have been organized. These commissariat volunteers will work in unison and keep in touch with each other. If only the Jacobin bayonets do not get in the way; if only the self-styled "scientific" theorists do not thrust themselves in to darken counsel! Or rather let them expound their muddleheaded theories as much as they like, provided they have no authority, no power! And that admirable spirit of organization inherent in the people, above all in every social grade of the French nation, but which they have so seldom been allowed to exercise, will initiate, even in so huge a city as Paris, and in the midst of a revolution, an immense guild of free workers, ready to furnish to each and all the necessary food.

Give the people a free hand, and in ten days the food service will be conducted with admirable regularity. Only those who have never seen the people hard at work, only those who have passed their lives buried among documents can doubt it. Speak of the organizing genius of the "great misunderstood," the people, to those who have seen it in Paris in the days of the barricades, or in London during the last great strike, when half a million starving people had to be fed, and they will tell you how superior it is to official ineptness.

And even supposing we had to endure a certain amount of discomfort and confusion for a fortnight or a month; surely that would not matter very much. For the mass of the people it could not but be an improvement of their former condition, and, besides, in times of revolution one can dine contentedly enough on a bit of bread and cheese, while eagerly discussing events.

In any case, a system which springs up spontaneously, under stress of immediate need, will be infinitely preferable to anything invented between four walls by hidebound theorists sitting on any number of committees.

VII

The people of the great towns will be driven by force of circumstances to take possession of all the provisions, beginning with the barest necessaries and gradually extending communism to other things in order to satisfy the needs of all the citizens.

The sooner it is done the better; the sooner it is done the less misery there will be and the less strife.

But upon what basis must society be organized in order that all may share and share alike? That is the question that meets us at the outset.

We answer that there are no two ways. There is only one way in which communism can be established equitably, only one way which satisfies our instincts of justice, and is at the same time practical, namely, the system already adopted by the agrarian communes of Europe.

Take, for example, a peasant commune, no matter where, even in France, where the Jacobins have done their best to destroy all communal usage. If the commune possesses woods and shrubbery, for instance, as long as brushwood is plentiful, everyone can take as much as they want, without other let or hindrance than the public opinion of their neighbors. As to the timber trees, which are always scarce, they have to be carefully apportioned.

The same with the communal pastureland; while there is enough to spare, no limit is put to what the cattle of each homestead may consume nor to the number of beasts grazing upon the pastures. Grazing grounds are not divided nor fodder doled out unless there is scarcity. All the Swiss communes and many of those in France and Germany also, wherever there is communal pastureland, practice this system.

And in the countries of Eastern Europe, where there are great forests and no scarcity of land, you find the peasants felling the trees as they need them, and cultivating as much of the soil as they require, without any thought of limiting each man's share of timber or of land. But the timber will be divided and the land parcelled out to each household according to its needs, as soon as either becomes scarce, as is already the case in Russia.

In a word, then, the system is this: no stint or limit to what the community possesses in abundance, but equal sharing and dividing of those commodities which are scarce or apt to run short. Of the 350 millions who inhabit Europe, 200 millions still follow this system of natural communism.

It is a fact worth remarking that the same system prevails in the great towns in the distribution of one commodity at least which is found in abundance, the water supplied to each house.

As long as there is no fear of the supply running short, no water company thinks of checking the consumption of water in each house. Take what you please! In Paris during the great droughts if there is any fear of supply failing, the water companies know that all they have to do is to make known the fact by means of a short advertisement in the papers, and the citizens will reduce their consumption of water and not let it run to waste.

But if water were actually scarce, what would be done? Recourse would be had to a system of rations. Such a measure is so natural, so inherent in common sense, that Paris twice asked to be put on rations during the two sieges which it supported in 1871.

Is it necessary to go into details, to prepare tables, showing how the distribution of rations will work, to prove that it is just and equitable, infinitely more just and equitable than the existing state of things? All these tables and details will not serve to convince those of the middle classes, nor, alas, those of the workers tainted with middle-class prejudices, who regard the people as a mob of savages ready to fall upon and devour each other when the government ceases to direct affairs. Only one who has never seen the people resolve and act on their own initiative can doubt for a moment that if they were masters of the situation they could and would distribute rations to each and all in the strictest accordance with justice and equity.

If you were to give utterance, in any gathering of people, to the opinion that delicacies should be reserved for the fastidious palates of aristocratic idlers and black bread given to the sick in the hospitals, you would be hissed. But say at the same gathering, preach at the street corners and in the marketplaces that the most tempting delicacies ought to be kept for the sick and feeble—especially for the sick. Say that if there are only five partridges in the whole of Paris, and only one case of sherry wine, they should go to sick people and convalescents. Say that after the sick come the children. For them the milk of the cows and goats should be reserved if there is not enough for all. To the children and the aged the last piece of meat, and to the strong man dry bread, if the community be reduced to that extremity.

Say, in a word, that if this or that article of consumption runs short, and has to be doled out, those who have most need should be given most: say that and see if you do not meet with universal agreement.

The man who is fully fed does not understand this, but the people do understand, have always understood it; and even the child of luxury if he is thrown on the street and comes into contact with the masses, even he will learn to understand.

The theorists—for whom the soldier's uniform and the barrack mess table are civilization's last word—would like no doubt to start a regime of national kitchens and "Spartan broth." They will point out the advantages thereby gained, the economy in fuel and food if huge kitchens were established where everyone could come for their rations of soup and bread and vegetables.

We do not question these advantages. We are well aware that important savings have already been achieved in this direction

—as for instance when the handmill and the baker's oven attached to each house were abandoned. We can see perfectly well that it would be more economical to cook broth for a hundred families at once instead of lighting a hundred separate fires. We know, besides, that there are a thousand ways of doing up potatoes, but that cooked in one huge pot for a hundred families they would be just as good.

We know, in fact, that variety in cooking is a matter of the seasoning introduced by each cook or housewife, the cooking together of a hundredweight of potatoes would not prevent each cook or housewife from dressing and serving them in any way she pleased. And we know that stock made from meat can be converted into a hundred different soups to suit a hundred different tastes.

But though we are quite aware of all these facts, we still maintain that no one has a right to force the housewife to take her potatoes from the communal kitchen ready-cooked if she prefers to cook them herself in her own pot on her own fire. And, above all, we should wish each one to be free to take his meals with his family, or with his friends, or even in a restaurant, if that seemed good to him.

Naturally large public kitchens will spring up to take the place of the restaurants, where people are poisoned nowadays. Already the Parisian housewife gets the stock for her soup from the butcher and transforms it into whatever soup she likes, and London housekeepers know that they can have a joint roasted or an apple or rhubarb tart baked at the bakers for a trifling sum, thus economizing time and fuel. And when the communal kitchen—the common bakehouse of the future—is established, and people can get their food cooked without the risk of being cheated or poisoned, the custom will no doubt become general of going to the communal kitchen for the fundamental parts of the meal, leaving the last touches to be added as individual taste shall suggest.

But to make a hard and fast rule of this, to make a duty of taking home our food ready-cooked, that would be as repugnant to our modern minds as the ideas of the convent or the barrack, morbid ideas born in brains warped by tyranny or superstition.

Who will have a right to the food of the commune? will assuredly be the first question which we shall have to ask ourselves. Every township will answer it for itself, and we are convinced that the answers will all be dictated by the sentiment of justice. Until labor is reorganized, as long as the disturbed period lasts, and while it is impossible to distinguish between inveterate idlers and genuine workers thrown out of work, the available food ought to be shared by all without exception. Those who have been enemies to the new order will hasten of their own accord to rid the commune of their presence. But it seems to us that the people, who have always proved themselves magnanimous and have nothing of vindictiveness in their composition, will be ready to share their bread with all who remain with them, conquered and conquerors alike. It will be no loss to the revolution to be inspired by such an ideal, and, when work is set going again, the antagonists of yesterday will stand side by side in the same workshops. A society where work is free will have nothing to fear from idlers.

"But provisions will run short in a month," our critics at once exclaim.

So much the better, we say. It will prove that for the first time on record the people have had enough to eat. As to the means of keeping up the supply of food, that is the very question we are going to attack next.

VIII

We have now to consider by what means a city in a state of revolution could supply itself with food. Before answering this question it should be pointed out that obviously the means resorted to will depend on the character of the revolution in the provinces and in neighboring countries. If the entire nation, or, better still, all of Europe should accomplish the social revolution simultaneously, and start with thoroughgoing communism, our procedure would be simplified; but if only a few communities in Europe make the attempt, other means will have to be chosen. The circumstances will dictate the measures.

We are thus led, before proceeding further, to glance at the state of Europe, and, without pretending to prophesy, we ought to be able to foresee what course the revolution will take, or at least what will be its essential features.

Certainly it would be very desirable that all Europe should rise at once, that expropriation should be general, and that communistic principles should inspire all and sundry. Such a universal rising would do much to simplify the task of our century.

But all the signs lead us to believe that it will not take place. That the revolution will embrace Europe we do not doubt. If one of the four great continental capitals—Paris, Vienna, Brussels or Berlin—rises in revolution and overturns its government, it is almost certain that the three others will follow its example within a few weeks' time. It is, moreover, highly probable that the peninsulas and even London and St. Petersburg would not be long in following suit. But whether the revolution would have everywhere the same character is quite another question.

Though it is more than probable that expropriation will be everywhere carried into effect on a larger or smaller scale, and that this policy carried out by anyone of the great nations of Europe will influence all the rest, yet the beginnings of the revolution will exhibit great local differences, and its course will vary in different countries. In 1789-1793, the French peasantry took four years to finally rid themselves of the redemption of feudal rights, and the bourgeois to overthrow royalty. Let us keep in mind, therefore, and be thus prepared to see the revolution develop itself somewhat gradually. Let us not be disheartened if here and there its steps should move less rapidly. Whether it would take an avowedly socialistic character in all European nations, at any rate at the beginning, is doubtful. Germany, be it remembered, is still realizing its dream of a united empire. Its advanced parties see visions of a Jacobin republic like that of 1848, and of the organization of labor according to Louis Blanc; while the French people, on the other hand, want above all things a free commune, whether it be a communist commune or not.

There is every reason to believe that when the coming revolution takes place, Germany will go further than France. The middle-class revolution in France in the eighteenth century was an advance on the English revolution of the seventeenth, abolishing as it did at once the power of the throne and of the landed aristocracy, whose influence still survives in England. But, if Germany goes further and does greater things than the France of 1848, there can be no doubt that the ideas which will foster the birth of the revolution will be those of 1848, as the ideas which will inspire the revolution in Russia will be those of 1789, modified somewhat by the intellectual movements of our own century.

Without, however, attaching to these forecasts a greater importance than they merit, we may safely conclude this much: the revolution will take a different character in each of the different European nations; the point attained in the socialization of wealth will not be everywhere the same.

Will it therefore be necessary, as is sometimes suggested, that the nations in the vanguard of the movement should adapt their pace to those who lag behind? Must we wait till the communist revolution is ripe in all civilized countries? Clearly not! Even if it were a thing to be desired it is not possible. History does not wait for the idlers.

Besides we do not believe that in any one country the revolution will be accomplished at a stroke, in the twinkling of an eye, as some socialists dream. It is highly probable that if one of the five or six large towns of France—Paris, Lyons, Marseilles, Lille, Saint Etienne, Bordeaux—were to proclaim the commune, the others would follow its example, and that many smaller towns would do the same. Probably also various mining districts and industrial centers would hasten to rid themselves of owners and masters and form themselves into free groups.

But many country places have not advanced to that point. Side by side with the revolutionized communes such places would remain in an expectant attitude and would go on living on the individualist system. Undisturbed by visits of the bailiff or the tax collector, the peasants would not be hostile to the revolutionaries, and thus, while profiting by the new state of affairs, they would defer the settlement of accounts with the local exploiters. But with that practical enthusiasm which always characterizes agrarian uprisings (witness the passionate toil of 1792) they would throw themselves into the task of cultivating the land, which, freed from taxes and mortgages, would become so much dearer to them.

As to foreign countries, there would be revolution everywhere, but revolution under various aspects; here state socialism, there federation; everywhere more or less of socialism, but uniformity nowhere.

IX.

Let us now return to our city in revolt and consider how its people are to be fed. How are the necessary provisions to be obtained if the nation as a whole has not accepted communism? That is the question to be solved. Take for example one of the large French towns—take the capital itself, for that matter. Paris consumes every year thousands of tons of grain, 350,000 head of oxen, 200,000 calves, 300,000 swine, and more than 2 million sheep, besides great quantities of game. This huge city devours besides, 18 million pounds of butter, 172 million eggs, and other produce in like proportion.

It imports flour and grain from the United States and Russia, Hungary, Italy, Egypt and the Indies; livestock from Germany, Italy, Spain—even Rumania and Russia; and, as for groceries, there is not a country in the world that it does not lay under contribution. Now, let us see how Paris or any other great town could be restocked by homegrown produce, supplies of which would be readily and willingly sent in from the provinces.

To those who put their trust in "authority" the question will appear quite simple. They would begin by establishing a strongly centralized government, furnished with all the machinery of coercion: the police, the army, the guillotine. This government would draw up a statement of all the produce contained in France. It would divide the country into districts of supply, and then *command* that a prescribed quantity of some particular foodstuff be sent to such a place on such a day and delivered at such a station to be there received on a given day by a specified official and stored in particular warehouses.

Now, we declare with the fullest conviction, not merely that such a solution is undesirable, but that it never could by any possibility be put into practice. It is wildly utopian!

Pen in hand, one may dream such a dream in the study, but in contact with reality it comes to nothing; for, like all such theories, it leaves out of account the spirit of independence that is in man. The attempt would lead to a universal uprising, three or four Vendées in one, the villages warring against the towns, all France up in arms defying the city for its arrogance in attempting to impose such a system upon the country.

But enough of Jacobin utopias! Let us see if some other form of organization will fit the case.

In 1793 the provinces starved the large towns and killed out the revolution. And yet it is a known fact that the production of grain in France during 1792-93 had not diminished, indeed the evidence goes to show that it had increased. But after having taken possession of the manorial lands, after having reaped a harvest from them, the peasants would not part with their grain for paper money. They withheld their produce, waiting for a rise in the price or the introduction of gold. The most rigorous measures of the National Convention were without avail, and even the fear of death failed to break up the ring or force its members to sell their corn. For it is a matter of history that the district commissaries did not scruple to guillotine those who withheld their grain from the market, and the populace of Paris strung them up to the lampposts at the street corners. All the same the corn was not forthcoming and the towns suffered from famine.

But what was offered to the farmer in exchange for the fruit of his toil? Assignats, scraps of paper decreasing in value every day, nominal twenty-pound notes of no real worth! A forty-pound note would not purchase a pair of boots, and the peasant, very naturally, was not anxious to barter a year's toil for a piece of paper with which he could not even buy a shirt.

As long as worthless paper money—whether called assignats or labor notes—is offered to the peasant-producer it will always be the same. The country will withhold its produce, and the towns will suffer want, even if the recalcitrant peasants are drowned and guillotined as before.

We must offer to the peasant in exchange for his toil not worthless paper money, but the manufactured articles of which he stands in immediate need. He lacks the proper implements to till the land, clothes to protect him properly from the inclemencies of the weather, lamps and oil to replace his miserable candle or tallow dip, spades, rakes, plows. All these things, under present conditions, the peasant is forced to do without, not because he does not feel the need of them, but because, in his life of struggle and privation, a thousand useful things are beyond his reach; because he has no money to buy them.

Let the town apply itself without loss of time to manufacturing all that the peasant needs instead of fashioning useless trinkets for the wives of rich citizens. Let the sewing machines of Paris be set to work on clothes for the country folk; everyday clothes and clothes for Sunday too, instead of costly evening dresses for the wives of English and Russian landlords. Let the factories and foundries turn out agricultural implements, spades, rakes, and the like, instead of waiting till the English send them in exchange for French wines!

Let the towns send no more inspectors to the villages with red, blue, or rainbow-colored scarves, to convey to the peasant orders to take his produce to this place or that, but let them send friendly embassies to the country folk and bid them in brotherly fashion: "Bring us your produce, and take from our stores and shops all the manufactured articles you please." Then provisions would pour in on every side. The peasant would only withhold what he needed for his own use, and would send the rest into the cities, feeling *for the first time in the course of history*, that these toiling townsfolk were his comrades—his brethren, and not his exploiters.

We shall be told, perhaps, that this would necessitate a complete transformation of industry. Well, yes, that is true of certain departments; but there are other branches which could be rapidly modified in such a way as to furnish the peasant with clothes, watches, furniture, and the simple implements for which the towns make him pay such exorbitant prices at the present time. Weavers, tailors, shoemakers, tinsmiths, cabinet makers, and many other trades and crafts could easily direct their energies to the manufacture of useful and necessary articles, and abstain from producing mere luxuries. All that is needed is that the public mind should be thoroughly convinced of the necessity of this transformation, and should come to look upon it as an act of justice and of progress, and that it should no longer allow itself to be cheated by that dream so dear to the theorists—the dream of a revolution confining itself to taking possession of the profits of industry, and leaving production and commerce just as they are now.

This, then, is our view of the whole question. Cheat the peasant no longer with scraps of paper—be the sums inscribed upon them ever so large—but offer him in exchange for his produce the very things of which he, the tiller of the soil, stands in need. Then the fruits of the land will be poured into the towns. If this is not done there will be famine in our cities, and reaction and despair will follow in its train.

X.

All the great towns, we have said, buy their grain, their flour, and their meat not only from the provinces, but also from abroad. Foreign countries send Paris spices, fish, and various delicacies, besides immense quantities of corn and meat.

But when the revolution comes we must depend on foreign countries as little as possible. If Russian wheat, Italian or Indian rice, and Spanish or Hungarian wines abound in the markets of western Europe, it is not that the countries which export them have a superabundance, or that such produce grows there of itself, like the dandelion in the meadows. In Russia, for instance, the peasant works sixteen hours a day and half starves from three to six months every year in order to export the corn with which he pays the landlord and the state. Today the police appear in the Russian village as soon as the harvest is gathered in, and sell the peasant's last horse and last cow for arrears of taxes and rent due to the landlord, unless the victim immolates himself of his own accord by selling the corn to the exporters. Usually, rather than part with his livestock at a disadvantage, he keeps only nine months' supply of grain and sells the rest. Then, in order to sustain life until the next harvest, he mixes birchbark and tares with his flour for three months if it has been a good year, and for six if it has been bad, while in London they are eating biscuits made of his wheat.

But as soon as the revolution comes, the Russian peasant will keep bread enough for himself and his children, the Italian and Hungarian peasants will do the same, and the Hindu, let us hope, will profit by these good examples as well as the workers on the farms of America, if indeed these domains are not immediately disorganized by the crisis. So it will not do to count on contributions of wheat and maize coming from abroad.

Since all our middle-class civilization is based on the exploitation of inferior races and countries with less advanced industrial systems, the revolution will confer a boon at the very outset, by menacing that "civilization," and allowing so-called inferior races to free themselves.

But this great benefit will manifest itself by a steady and marked diminution of the food supplies pouring into the great cities of western Europe.

It is difficult to predict the course of affairs in the provinces. On the one hand the slave of the soil will take advantage of the revolution to straighten his bowed back. Instead of working fourteen or fifteen hours a day, as he does at present, he will be at liberty to work only half that time, which of course would have the effect of decreasing the production of the principal articles of consumption, grain and meat.

But, on the other hand, there will be an increase of production as soon as the peasant realizes that he is no longer forced to support the idle rich by his toil. New tracts of land will be cleared, new and improved machines set going.

"Never was the land so energetically cultivated as in 1792, when the peasant had taken back from the landlord the soil which he had coveted so long," Michelet tells us, speaking of the Great Revolution.

Before long, intensive culture would be within the reach of all. Improved machinery, chemical manures, and all such matters would be common property. But everything tends to indicate that at the outset there would be a falling off in agricultural products, in France as elsewhere.

In any case it would be wisest to count upon such a falling off of contributions from the provinces as well as from abroad.

And how is this falling off to be made good? Why, in heaven's name, by setting to work ourselves! No need to rack our brains for farfetched panaceas when the remedy lies close at hand!

The large towns and villages must undertake to till the soil. We must return to what biology calls the integration of functions: after the division of labor, the integration—that is the plan followed all through nature. Besides, philosophy apart, the force of circumstances would bring about this result. Let Paris see at the end of eight months that it is running short of corn, and Paris will set to work to grow corn.

Is land the difficulty? That will not be wanting, for it is around the great towns, and around Paris especially, that the parks and pleasure grounds of the landed gentry are to be found. These thousands of acres only await the skilled labor of the husbandman to surround Paris with fields infinitely more fertile and productive than the steppes of southern Russia, where the soil is dried up by the sun. Nor will labor be lacking. To what do you suppose will the two million citizens of Paris turn their attention, when they are no longer catering for the luxurious fads and amusements of Russian princes, Rumanian grandees, and wives of Berlin financiers?

With all the mechanical inventions of the century, with all the intelligence and technical skill of the workers accustomed to deal with complicated machinery, with inventors, chemists, botanists, the professors of the *Jardin des plantes* and the market gardeners of Gennevilliers, besides the factories necessary for multiplying and improving machinery, and, finally, with the organizing spirit of the Parisian people, their courage and energy—with all these at its command, the agriculture of the anarchist commune of Paris would be a very different thing from the rude husbandry of the Ardennes.

Steam, electricity, the heat of the sun, and the breath of the wind will before long be pressed into service. The steam harrow and the steam plow will quickly do the rough work of preparation, and the soil thus cleaned and enriched will only need the intelligent care of man, and of woman even more than man, to be clothed with luxuriant vegetation, not once but three or four times in the year.

Thus, learning the art of horticulture from experts, and trying experiments in different methods on small patches of soil reserved for the purpose, vying with each other to obtain the best returns, finding in physical exercise, without exhaustion or overwork, the health and strength which so often weakens in cities, men, women and children will gladly turn to the labor of the fields when it is no longer a slavish drudgery but has become a pleasure, a festival, a renewal of health and joy.

"There are no barren lands; the earth is worth what man is worth"—that is the last word of modern agriculture. Ask of the earth and she will give you bread, provided that you ask correctly.

A district, though it were as small as the departments of the Seine and the Seine-et-Oise, and with so great a city as Paris to feed, would be practically sufficient to fill the gaps which the revolution had made around it.

The combination of agriculture and industry, the farmer and the mechanic one and the same individual—this is what anarchist communism will inevitably lead us to, if it starts fair with expropriation.

Let the revolution only get so far, and famine is not the enemy it will have to fear. No, the danger which will menace it lies in timidity, prejudice, and half measures. The danger is where Danton saw it when he cried to France: "Be bold, be bold, and yet again, be bold!" The bold thought first, and the bold deed will not fail to follow.

XI.

Those who have watched at all closely the growth of certain ideas among the workers must have noticed that on one momentous question—the housing of the people, namely—a unanimous conclusion has been unconsciously arrived at. It is a known fact that in the large towns of France, and in many of the smaller ones also, the workers are coming gradually to the conclusion that dwelling houses are in no sense the property of those whom the state recognizes as their owners.

This idea has evolved naturally in the minds of the people, and nothing will ever convince them again that the "rights of property" ought to extend to houses.

The house was not built by its owners. It was erected, decorated, and furnished by innumerable workers, in the timber yard, the brickfield, and the workshop, toiling for dear life at an inadequate wage.

The money spent by the owner was not the product of his own toil. It was amassed, like all other riches, by paying the workers two-thirds or only a half of what was their due.

Moreover—and it is here that the enormity of the whole proceeding becomes most glaring—the house owes its actual value to the profit which the owner can make out of it. Now, this profit results from the fact that his house is built in a town possessing bridges, quays, and fine public buildings, and affording to its inhabitants a thousand comforts and conveniences unknown in villages; a town paved and lighted with gas, in regular communication with other towns, and itself a center of industry, commerce, science, and art; a town which the work of twenty or thirty generations has gone to render habitable, healthy, and beautiful.

A house in certain parts of Paris may be valued at thousands of pounds sterling, not because thousands of pounds' worth of labor have been expended on that particular house, but because it is in Paris; because for centuries workmen, artists, thinkers, and men of learning and letters have contributed to make Paris what it is today—a center of industry, commerce, politics, art, and science; because Paris has a past; because, thanks to literature, the names of its streets are household words in foreign countries as well as at home; because it is the fruit of eighteen centuries of toil, the work of fifty generations of the whole French nation.

Who then can appropriate to himself the tiniest plot of ground, or the smallest building, without committing a flagrant injustice? Who then has the right to sell to any bidder the smallest portion of the common heritage?

On that point, as we have said, the workers are agreed. The idea of free dwellings showed its existence very plainly during the siege of Paris, when the cry was that the landlords should remit the rent altogether. It appeared again during the Commune of 1871, when the Paris workmen expected the Communal Council to decide boldly on the abolition of rent. And when the new revolution comes it will be the first question with which the poor will concern themselves.

Whether in time of revolution or in time of peace, the worker must be housed somehow or other; he must have some sort of roof over his head. But, however tumbledown and squalid your dwelling may be, there is always a landlord who can evict you. True, during the revolution he cannot find bailiffs and police sergeants to throw your rags and chattels into the street, but who knows what the new government will do tomorrow? Who can say that it will not call in the aid of force again, and set the police pack upon you to hound you out of your hovels? We have seen the commune proclaim the remission of rents due up to April 1 only![1] After that, rent had to be paid, though Paris was in a state of chaos and industry at a standstill, so that the

1 The decree of March 30: by this decree quarterly rents due in October 1870, and January and April 1871, were annulled.

revolutionist had absolutely nothing to depend on but his allowance of fifteen pence a day!

Now the worker must be made to see clearly that in refusing to pay rent to a landlord or owner he is not simply profiting by the disorganization of authority. He must understand that the abolition of rent is a recognized principle, sanctioned, so to speak, by popular assent; that to be housed rent-free is a right proclaimed aloud by the people.

Are we going to wait until the measure, which is in harmony with every honest man's sense of justice, is taken up by the few socialists scattered among the middle-class elements, of which the provisionary government will be composed? We should have to wait long—until the return of reaction, in fact!

That is why, refusing uniforms and badges (those outward signs of authority and servitude) and remaining people among the people, the earnest revolutionists will work side by side with the masses, that the abolition of rent and the expropriation of houses may become an accomplished fact. They will prepare the soil and encourage ideas to grow in this direction, and when the fruit of their labors is ripe the people will proceed to expropriate the houses without giving heed to the theories which will certainly be thrust in their way—theories about paying compensation to landlords, and finding first the necessary funds.

On the day that the expropriation of houses takes place, on that day, the exploited workers will have realized that the new times have come, that they will no longer have to bear the yoke of the rich and powerful, that equality has been proclaimed on the housetops in clear truth, that this revolution is a real fact and not a theatrical make-believe like too many others which went before.

XII.

If the idea of expropriation is adopted by the people it will be carried into effect in spite of all the "insurmountable" obstacles with which we are menaced.

Of course the good folk in new uniforms, seated in the official armchairs of the *Hôtel de Ville*, will be sure to busy themselves in heaping up obstacles. They will talk of giving compensation to the landlords, of preparing statistics, and drawing up long reports. Yes, they would be capable of drawing up reports long enough to outlast the hopes of the people, who, after waiting and starving in enforced idleness and seeing nothing come of all these official researches, would lose heart and faith in the revolution and abandon the field to the reactionaries. The new bureaucracy would end by making expropriation hateful in the eyes of all.

Here, indeed, is a rock which might shipwreck our hopes. But if the people turn a deaf ear to the specious arguments used to dazzle them and realize that new life needs new conditions, and if they undertake the task themselves, then expropriation can be effected without any great difficulty.

"But how? How can expropriation be achieved?" you ask us. We are about to reply to that question, but with a reservation. We have no intention of tracing out the plans of expropriation in their smallest details. We know beforehand that all that any man, or group of men, could suggest today would be far surpassed by the reality when it comes. The human spirit will accomplish greater things and accomplish them better and in a simpler way than anyone could dictate beforehand. Thus we are content to indicate the methods by which expropriation *might* be accomplished without the intervention of government. We do not propose to go out of our way to answer those who declare that the thing is impossible. We confine ourselves to replying that we are not the upholders of any particular method of organization. We are only concerned to demonstrate that expropriation *could* be effected by popular initiative, and *could not* be effected by any other means whatever.

It seems very likely that as soon as expropriation is started, groups of volunteers will spring up in every district, street, and block of houses and undertake to inquire into the number of flats and houses which are empty and of those which are overcrowded, the unwholesome slums and the houses which are too spacious for their occupants and might well be used to house those who are stifled in swarming tenements. In a few days, these volunteers would have drawn up complete lists for the street and the district of all the flats, tenements, family mansions, and villa residences, all the rooms and suites of rooms, healthy and unhealthy, small and large, odious dens and homes of luxury.

Freely communicating with each other, these volunteers would soon have their statistics complete. False statistics can be manufactured in boardrooms and offices, but true and exact statistics must begin with the individual, and mount up from the simple to the complex.

Then, without waiting for anyone's leave, those citizens will probably go and find their comrades who were living in miserable garrets and hovels and will say to them simply: "It is a real revolution this time, comrades, and no mistake about it. Come to such a place this evening; all the neighborhood will be there; we are going to redistribute the dwelling houses. If you are tired of your slum garret come and choose one of the flats of five rooms that are to be disposed of, and when you have once moved in you shall stay, never fear. The people are up in arms, and he who would venture to evict you will have to answer to them."

"But every one will want a fine house or a spacious flat!" we are told. No, you are mistaken. It is not the people's way to clamor for the moon. On the contrary, every time we have seen them set about repairing a wrong we have been struck by the good sense and instinct for justice which animate the masses. Have we ever known them to demand the impossible? Have we ever seen the people of Paris fighting among themselves while waiting for their rations of bread or firewood during the two sieges? The patience and resignation which prevailed among them was constantly held up to admiration by the foreign press correspondents, and yet these patient waiters knew full well that the last comers would have to pass the day without food or fire.

We do not deny that there are plenty of egoistic instincts in isolated individuals in our societies. We are quite aware of it. But we contend that the very way to revive and nourish these instincts would be to confine such questions as the housing of the people to any board or committee, in fact to the tender mercies of officialism in any shape or form. Then indeed all the evil passions spring up, and it becomes a case of who is the most influential person on the board. The least inequality causes wranglings and recriminations. If the smallest advantage is given to anyone a tremendous hue and cry is raised—and not without reason!

But if the people themselves, organized by streets, districts, and parishes, undertake to move the inhabitants of the slums into the half-empty dwellings of the middle classes, the trifling inconveniences, the little inequalities will be easily tided over. Rarely has appeal been made to the good instincts of the masses—only as a last resort, to save the sinking ship in times of revolution—but never has such an appeal been made in vain; the heroism, the self-devotion of the toiler has never failed to respond to it. And thus it will be in the coming revolution.

But when all is said and done, some inequalities, some inevitable injustices will remain. There are individuals in our societies whom no great crisis can lift out of the deep ruts of egoism in which they are sunk. The question, however, is not whether there will be injustices, but rather how to limit the number of them.

Now all history, all the experience of the human race, and all social psychology unite in showing that the best and fairest way is to trust the decision to those whom most it concerns. It is they alone who can consider and allow for the hundred and one details which must necessarily be overlooked in any merely official redistribution.

XIII.

Moreover, it is by no means necessary to make immediately an absolutely equal redistribution of all the dwellings. There will no doubt be some inconveniences at first, but matters will soon be corrected in a society which has adopted expropriation.

When the masons, and carpenters, and all who are concerned with house building know that their daily bread is secured to them, they will ask nothing better than to work at their old trades a few hours a day. They will adapt the fine houses which absorbed the time of a whole staff of servants, and in a few months homes will have sprung up, infinitely healthier and more conveniently arranged than those of today. And to those who are not yet comfortably housed the anarchist commune will be able to say: "Patience comrades! Palaces fairer and finer than any the capitalists built for themselves will spring from the ground of our enfranchised city. They will belong to those who have most need of them. The anarchist commune does not build with an eye to revenues. These monuments erected to its citizens, products of the collective spirit, will serve as models to all humanity; they will be yours."

If the people of the revolution expropriate the houses and proclaim free lodgings, the communalizing of houses and the right of each family to a decent dwelling, then the revolution will have assumed a communistic character from the first and started on a course from which it will be by no means easy to turn it. It will have struck a fatal blow at individual property.

For the expropriation of dwellings contains in germ the whole social revolution. On the manner of its accomplishment depends the character of all that follows. Either we shall start on a good road leading straight to anarchist communism or we shall remain sticking in the mud of despotic individualism.

It is easy to see the numerous objections—theoretical on the one hand, practical on the other—with which we are sure to be met. As it will be a question of maintaining iniquity at any price, our opponents will of course protest "in the name of justice." "Is it not a crying shame," they will exclaim, "that the people of Paris should take possession of all these fine houses, while the peasants in the country have only tumbledown huts to live in?" But do not let us make a mistake. These enthusiasts for justice forget, by a lapse of memory to which they are subject, the "crying shame" which they themselves are tacitly defending. They forget that in this same Paris the worker, with his wife and children, suffocates in a rancid garret, while from his window he sees the rich man's palace. They forget that whole generations perish in crowded slums, starving for air and sunlight, and that to redress this injustice ought to be the first task of the revolution.

Do not let these disingenuous protests hold us back. We know that any inequality which may exist between town and country in the early days of the revolution will be transitory and of a nature to right itself from day to day; for the village will not fail to improve its dwellings as soon as the peasant has ceased to be the beast of burden of the farmer, the merchant, the money-lender, and the state. In order to avoid an accidental and transitory inequality, shall we stay our hand from righting an ancient wrong?

The so-called practical objections are not very formidable either. We are bidden to consider the hard case of some poor fellow who by dint of privation has contrived to buy a house just large enough to hold his family. And we are going to deprive him of his hard-earned happiness to turn him into the street! Certainly not. If his house is only just large enough for his family, by all means let him stay there. Let him work in his little garden too; our "boys" will not hinder him—on the contrary, they will lend him a helping hand if need be. But suppose he rents lodgings, suppose he has empty rooms in his house. The people will make the lodger understand that he is not to pay his former landlord any more rent. Stay where you are, but rent-free. No more collectors and insistent demands for payments of debts; socialism has abolished all that!

Or again, suppose that the landlord has a score of rooms all to himself and some poor woman lives nearby with five children in one room. In that case the people would see whether, with some alterations, these empty rooms could not be converted into a suitable home for the poor woman and her five children. Would not that be more just and fair than to leave the mother and her five little ones languishing in a garret, while Sir Gorgeous Midas sat at his ease in an empty mansion? Besides, good Sir Gorgeous would probably hasten to do it of his own accord; his wife will be delighted to be freed from half her big unwieldy house when there is no longer a staff of servants to keep it in order.

"So you are going to turn everything upside down, it seems, and set everybody by the ears. There will be no end to the evictions and removals. Would it not be better to start fresh by turning everybody out of doors and redistributing the houses by lot?" Thus our critics; but we answer we are firmly persuaded that if only there is no sort of government interference in the matter, if all the changes are entrusted to those free groups which have sprung up to undertake the work, the evictions and removals will be less numerous than those which take place in one year under the present system, owing to the rapacity of landlords.

In the first place, there are in all large towns almost enough empty houses and flats to lodge all the inhabitants of the slums. As to the palaces and suites of fine apartments, many working people would not live in them if they could. One could not "keep up" such houses without a large staff of servants. Their occupants would soon find themselves forced to seek less luxurious dwellings. The fine ladies would find that palaces were not well adapted to self-help in the kitchen. Gradually people would become acclimated. There would be no need to conduct Dives to a garret at the bayonet's point, or install Lazarus in Dives's palace by the help of an armed escort. People would become accustomed amicably to the available dwellings with the least possible friction and disturbance. Have we not the example of the village communes' redistributing fields and disturbing the owners of the allotments so little that one can only praise the intelligence and good sense of the methods they employ. Fewer fields change hands under the management of the Russian commune than where personal property holds sway and is forever carrying its quarrels into courts of law. And we are to believe that the inhabitants of a great European city would be less intelligent and less capable of organization than Russian or Hindu peasants?

Moreover, we must not deny the fact that every revolution means a certain disturbance to everyday life, and those who expect this tremendous lift out of the old patterns to be accomplished without so much as jarring the dishes on their dinner tables will find themselves mistaken. It is true that governments can change without disturbing worthy citizens at dinner, but the crimes of society towards those who have nourished and supported it are not to be redressed by any such political deception of parties.

Undoubtedly there will be a disturbance, but it must not be of pure destruction; it must be minimized. And again—it is impossible to lay too much stress on this maxim—it will be by addressing ourselves to the interested parties, and not to boards and committees, that we shall best succeed in reducing the sum of inconveniences for everybody.

The people commit blunder on blunder when they have to choose by ballot some harebrained candidate who solicits the honor of representing them, and takes upon himself to know all, to do all, and to organize all. But when they take upon themselves to organize what they know, what touches them directly, they do it better than all the "talking-shops" put together. Is not the Paris Commune an instance in point, and the last London strike, and have we not constant evidence of this fact in every village commune?

XIV.

When the houses have become the common heritage of the citizens, and when each man has his daily rations of food, another forward step will have to be taken. The question of clothing will of course demand consideration next, and again the only possible solution will be to take possession, in the name of the people, of all the shops and warehouses where clothing is sold or stored and to throw open the doors to all, so that each can take what he needs. The communalization of clothing—the right of each to take what he needs from the communal stores, or to have it made for him at the tailors and outfitters—is a necessary corollary of the communalization of houses and food.

Obviously, we shall not need, for that, to despoil all citizens of their coats, to put all the garments in a heap and draw lots for them, as our critics, with equal wit and ingenuity, suggest. Let him who has a coat keep it still—indeed, if he has ten coats it is highly improbable that any one will want to deprive him of them, for most people would prefer a new coat to one that has already graced the shoulders of some fat bourgeois; and there will be enough new garments and to spare without having recourse to secondhand wardrobes.

If we were to take an inventory of all the clothes and material for clothing accumulated in the shops and stores of the large towns, we should find probably that in Paris, Lyons, Bordeaux, and Marseilles there was enough to enable the commune to offer garments to all the citizens of both sexes; and if all were not suited at once, the communal outfitters would soon make good these shortcomings. We know how rapidly our great tailoring and dressmaking establishments work nowadays, provided as they are with machinery specially adapted for production on a large scale.

"But every one will want a sable-lined coat or a velvet gown!" exclaim our adversaries.

Frankly, we do not believe it. Every woman does not dote on velvet, nor does every man dream of sable linings. Even now, if we were to ask each woman to choose her gown, we should find some to prefer a simple, practical garment to all the fantastic trimmings the fashionable world affects.

Tastes change with the times, and the fashions in vogue at the time of the revolution will certainly make for simplicity. Societies, like individuals, have their hours of cowardice, but also their heroic moments; and though the society of today cuts a very poor figure sunk in the pursuit of narrow personal interest and second-rate ideas, it wears a different air when great crises come. It has its moments of greatness and enthusiasm. Men of generous nature will gain the power which today is in the hand of jobbers. Self-devotion will spring up and noble deeds beget their like; even the egoists will think shame to hang back, and will be drawn in spite of themselves to admire, if not to imitate, the generous and brave.

The great revolution of 1793 abounds in examples of this kind, as it is always during such times of spiritual revival—as natural to societies as to individuals—that the spring tide of enthusiasm sweeps humanity onward.

We do not wish to exaggerate the part played by such noble passions, nor is it upon them that we would found our ideal of society. But we are not asking too much if we expect their aid in tiding over the first and most difficult moments. We cannot hope that our daily life will be continuously inspired by such exalted enthusiasms, but we may expect their aid at the first, and that is all we need.

It is just to wash the earth clean, to sweep away the wreckage and refuse accumulated by centuries of slavery and oppression, that the new anarchist society will have need of this wave of brotherly love. Later on it can exist without appealing to the spirit of self-sacrifice, because it will have eliminated oppression and thus created a new world instinct with all the feelings of solidarity.

Besides, should the character of the revolution be such as we have sketched here, the free initiative of individuals would find an extensive field of action in thwarting the efforts of the egoists. Groups would spring up in every street and quarter to undertake the charge of the clothing. They would make inventories of all that the city possessed, and would find out approximately what were the resources at their disposal. It is more than likely that in the matter of clothing, the citizens would adopt the same principle as in the matter of provisions—that is to say, they would offer freely from the common store everything which was to be found in abundance, and dole out whatever was limited in quantity.

Not being able to offer to each man a sable-lined coat and to every woman a velvet gown, society would probably distinguish between the superfluous and the necessary, and, provisionally at least, class sable and velvet among the superfluities of life, ready to let time prove whether what is a luxury today may not become common to all tomorrow. While the necessary clothing would be guaranteed to each inhabitant of the anarchist city, it would be left to private beneficence to provide for the sick and feeble those things provisionally considered as luxuries, to procure for the less robust such special articles as would not enter into the daily consumption of ordinary citizens.[2]

2 After the experience of the Russian revolution, Kropotkin revised his view that modern capitalist society possessed enough of life's necessities to go around, if only properly distributed by the masses. In 1919, he wrote: "We should understand that as soon as a revolutionary movement begins in any country, the only possible way out [to avoid shortages and famine] will consist in the workingmen and peasants from the beginning taking the whole national economy into their hands and organizing it themselves with a view to a rapid increase in production." This, he hoped, would offset shortages that might be encountered when the revolution succeeded in overturning the capitalist ownership of the means of production. See Roger N. Baldwin, ed., *Kropotkin's Revolutionary Pamphlets*, (New York: Vanguard Press, 1927), pp. 75–78.—*Editor*.

"The State: Its Historic Role" surveys modern history from an anarchist perspective. In this article, Kropotkin finds an evolutionary pattern which every civilization has undergone, beginning with tribal communities and ending with the domination of the state. He forcefully argues that the free towns and communes of the Middle Ages represented the period of greatest liberty to man. These institutions were, however, systematically crushed by the emerging nation-state in the fifteenth and sixteenth centuries. They did not, as is commonly believed, die a natural death due to their archaic structure and uselessness in the modern world. Kropotkin sees the struggle between the commune and the state as one involving the survival of liberty against tyranny and looks ahead to the victory of the social revolution as the fulfillment of man's quest for freedom.

Originally a lecture to have been delivered on March 7, 1896, in Paris, "The State: Its Historic Role" was first published in *Les temps nouveaux*, December 19, 1896. This version has been newly translated from the original French by Vernon Richards. The footnotes are Kropotkin's.

The State:
Its
Historic
Role

I.

In taking the state and its historic role as the subject for this study, I think I am satisfying a need much felt at the present time: to examine in depth the very concept of the state; to study its essence, its past role, and the part it may be called upon to play in the future.

It is above all over the question of the state that socialists are divided. Two main currents can be discerned in the factions that exist among us, which correspond to differences in temperament as well as in ways of thinking, but above all to the extent that one believes in the coming revolution.

There are those, on the one hand, who hope to achieve the social revolution through the state by preserving and even extending most of its powers to be used for the revolution. And there are those like ourselves who see in the state, both in its present form, in its very essence, and in whatever guise it might appear, an obstacle to the social revolution, the greatest hindrance to the birth of a society based on equality and liberty, as well as the historic means designed to prevent this blossoming. The latter work to abolish the state and not to reform it.

It is clear that the division is a deep one. It corresponds with two divergent currents which in our time are manifest in all philosophical thought, in literature as well as in action. And if the prevailing views on the state remain as obscure as they are today, there is no doubt whatsoever that when—and we hope, soon—communist ideas are subjected to practical application in the daily life of communities, it will be on the question of the state that the most stubborn struggles will be waged.

Having so often criticized the state as it is today it becomes necessary to seek the reason for its emergence, to study in depth its past role, and to compare it with the institutions that it has replaced.

First of all let us be agreed as to what we wish to include in the term the state.

There is, of course, the German school which enjoys confusing state with society. The best German thinkers and many among the French are guilty of this confusion because they cannot conceive of society without a concentration of the state; and because of this anarchists are usually accused of wanting to "destroy society" and of advocating a return to "the permanent war of each against all."

Yet to argue thus is to overlook altogether the advances made in the domain of history during the last thirty-odd years; it is to overlook the fact that man lived in societies for thousands of years before the state had been heard of; it is to forget that so far as Europe is concerned the state is of recent origin— it barely goes back to the sixteenth century; finally, it is to ignore that the most glorious periods in man's history are those in which civil liberties and communal life had not yet been destroyed by the state, and in which large numbers of people lived in communes and free federations.

The state is only one of the forms adopted by society in the course of history. Why then make no distinction between what is permanent and what is accidental?

Then again the state has also been confused with government. Since there can be no state without government, it has sometimes been said that what one must aim at is the absence of government and not the abolition of the state.

However, it seems to me that in state and government we

have two concepts of a different order. The state idea means something quite different from the idea of government. It not only includes the existence of a power situated above society, but also of a territorial concentration as well as the concentration of many functions of the life of societies in the hands of a few. It carries with it some new relationships between members of society which did not exist before the establishment of the state. A whole mechanism of legislation and of policing has to be developed in order to subject some classes to the domination of others.

This distinction, which at first sight might not be obvious, emerges especially when one studies the origins of the state.

Indeed, there is only one way of really understanding the state, and that is to study its historic development, and this is what we will try to do.

The Roman Empire was a state in the real sense of the word. It remains to this day the legist's ideal. Its organs covered a vast domain with a tight network. Everything flowed toward Rome: economic and military life, wealth, education, even religion. From Rome came the laws, the magistrates, the legions to defend the territory, the prefects, and the gods. The whole life of the empire went back to the senate—later to the Caesar, the all-powerful, omniscient god of the empire. Every province, every district had its capitol in miniature, its small portion of Roman sovereignty to govern every aspect of daily life. A single law, imposed by Rome, dominated the empire which did not represent a confederation of fellow citizens but was simply a herd of subjects.

Even now, the legist and the authoritarian still admire the unity of that empire, the unitarian spirit of its laws and, as they put it, the beauty and harmony of that organization.

But the disintegration from within, hastened by the barbarian invasion; the extinction of local life, which could no longer resist the attacks from outside on the one hand nor the cancer spreading from the center on the other; the domination by the rich who had appropriated the land to themselves and the misery of those who cultivated it—all these causes reduced the empire to a shambles, and on these ruins a new civilization was developed which is ours.

So, if we ignore the civilizations of antiquity, and concentrate our attention on the origins and developments of this young barbarian civilization, right up to the times when, in its turn, it gave birth to our modern states, we will be able to capture the essence of the state. This is better than if we had directed our studies to the Roman Empire or to that of Alexander of Macedonia, or to the despotic monarchies of the East.

In taking these powerful barbarian overthrowers of the Roman Empire as our point of departure, we will be able to retrace the evolution of our whole civilization from its beginnings up to the stage of the state.

II

Most eighteenth-century philosophers had very elementary ideas on the origin of societies.

According to them, in the beginning men lived in small isolated families, and perpetual warfare between them was the normal state of affairs. But one fine day, realizing at last the disadvantages that resulted from their endless struggles, men decided to join forces. A social contract was concluded among the scattered families who willingly submitted themselves to an authority which—need I say?—became the starting point as well as the initiator of all progress. And does one have to add what we have all been told at school, that our present governments have so far kept within the limits of this fine role of being the salt of the earth, the pacifiers and civilizers of the human race?

The idea dominated the eighteenth century, a period in which very little was known about the origins of man; and one must add that in the hands of the encyclopedists and of Rousseau, the idea of the "social contract" became a weapon with which to fight against the divine right of kings. Nevertheless, in spite of the services it may have rendered in the past, this theory must be seen to be false.

The fact is that all animals, with the exception of some carnivores and birds of prey and some species which are becoming extinct, live in societies. In the struggle for life, the gregarious species have an advantage over those that are not. In every animal classification they are at the top of the ladder, and there cannot be the slightest doubt that the first beings with human attributes were already living in societies. Man did not create society; society existed before man.

We now also know—and it has been convincingly demonstrated by anthropology—that the point of departure for mankind was not the family but the clan, the tribe. The patriarchal family as we know it or as it is portrayed in Hebrew traditions did not appear until very much later. Man spent tens of thousands of years in the clan or tribal phase—let us call it the primitive or, if you will, savage tribe—during which he developed all kinds of institutions, habits and customs all much earlier than the institutions of the patriarchal family.

In these tribes, the separate family existed no more than it exists among so many other sociable mammals. Any division within the tribe was rather between generations; and from a far distant age, going right back to the dawn of the human race, limitations had been imposed to prevent sexual relations between the different generations, which however were allowed between those of the same generation. One can still find traces of that period in some contemporary tribes as well as in the language, customs, and superstitions of peoples of a much higher culture.

Hunting and food gathering were engaged in by the whole tribe in common, and once their hunger was satisfied, they gave themselves up with passion to their dramatized dances. To this day one still finds tribes who are very close to this primitive phase living on the periphery of the large continents or in the vicinity of mountainous regions in the least accessible parts of the world.

The accumulation of private property could not then take place, since anything that had been the personal possession of a member of the tribe was destroyed or burned where his body was buried. This is still done, in England too, by the gypsies, and funeral rites of "civilized" people still bear the imprint of this custom; thus the Chinese burn paper models of the dead person's possessions, and at the military leader's funeral his horse, his sword, and decorations accompany him as far as his grave. The meaning of the institution has been lost though the form has survived.

Far from expressing contempt for human life, those primitive people hated murder and blood. To spill blood was considered such a grave matter that every drop spilled—not only human blood but also that of some animals—required that the aggressor should lose an equal amount of his own blood.

Furthermore, murder within the tribe is something quite unknown. For instance among the Inoits or Eskimos—those survivors of the Stone Age who inhabit the Arctic regions—or among the Aleuts and others one definitely knows that there has not been a single murder within the tribe for fifty, sixty or more years.

But when tribes of different origin, color, and language met in the course of their migrations, it often ended in war. It is true that even then men were seeking to make these encounters more pacific. Tradition, as Maine, Post, and Ernest Nys have so well demonstrated, was already developing the germs of what in due course became international law. For instance, a village could not be attacked without warning the inhabitants. Never would anyone dare to kill on the path used by women to reach the spring. And often to make peace it was necessary to balance the numbers of men killed on both sides.

However, all these precautions and many others besides were not enough: solidarity did not extend beyond the confines of the clan or tribe; quarrels arose between people of different clans and tribes, which could end in violence and even murder.

From that period a general law began to be developed between the clans and tribes. "Your members have wounded or killed one of ours; we have a right therefore to kill one of you or to inflict a similar wound on one of you." And it did not matter who, since the tribe was always responsible for the individual acts of its members. The well-known biblical verse: "Blood for blood, an eye for an eye, a tooth for a tooth, a wound for a wound, a life for a life"—but no more! as Koenigswarter so well put it—owe their origin to them. It was their concept of justice; and we have no reason to feel superior since the principle of a life for a life which prevails in our codes is only one of its many survivals.

Clearly, a whole series of institutions (and many others I have not mentioned) as well as a whole code of tribal morality were already developed during this primitive phase. And this nucleus of sociable customs was kept alive by usage, custom, and tradition only. There was no authority with which to impose it.

There is no doubt that primitive society had temporary leaders. The sorcerer, the rainmaker—the learned men of that age—sought to profit from what they knew about nature in order to dominate their fellow beings. Similarly, he who could more easily memorize the proverbs and songs in which all tradition was embodied became influential. At popular festivities he would recite these proverbs and songs in which were incorporated the decisions that had been taken on such and such an occasion by the people's assembly in such a connection. In many small tribes this is still done. And dating from that age, these "educated" members sought to ensure a dominant role for themselves by communicating their knowledge only to the chosen few, to the initiates. All religions, and even the arts and all trades have begun with "mysteries," and modern research demonstrates the important role that secret societies of the initiates play to maintain some traditional practices in primitive clans. Already the germs of authority are present there.

It goes without saying that the courageous, the daring, and above all the prudent also became the temporary leaders in the struggles with other tribes or during migrations. But there was no alliance between the bearer of the "law" (the one who knew by heart the tradition and past decisions), the military chief, and the sorcerer; and the state was no more part of these tribes than it is of the society of bees or ants, or of our contemporaries the Patagonians and the Eskimos.

Nevertheless that phase lasted for many thousands of years, and the barbarians who overran the Roman Empire had also gone through this phase and were only just emerging from it.

In the early centuries of our era there were widespread migrations of the tribes and confederations of tribes that inhabited central and northern Asia. Whole waves of small tribes were driven by more or less civilized peoples who had come down from the high tablelands of Asia—they themselves had probably been driven away by the rapid desiccation of these plateaus[1]—and spread all over Europe, each driving the other and being assimilated in their push toward the west.

In the course of these migrations, in which so many tribes of different origins became assimilated, the primitive tribe which still existed among most of the savage inhabitants of Europe could not avoid disintegration. The tribe was based on a common origin and the cult of common ancestors; but to which common origin could these agglomerations of people appeal when they emerged from the confusion of migrations, drives, intertribal wars, during which here and there one could already observe the emergence of the paternal family—the nucleus formed by the exclusive possession by some of women won over or carried off from neighboring tribes?

The old ties were broken, and to avoid disruption (which, in fact, did occur for many tribes, which disappeared forever) new links had to be established. And they were established through the communal possession of the land—of the territory on which each agglomeration had finally settled.[2]

1 The reasons which lead me to this hypothesis are put forward in a paper, "Desiccation of Eur-Asia," compiled for the Research Department of the Geographical Society of London, and published in its *Geographical Journal* for June 1904.

2 The reader interested in this subject, as well as in that of the communal phases and of the free cities, will find more detailed information and source references in my book *Mutual Aid*.

The possession in common of a particular area—of this small valley or those hills—became the basis for a new understanding. The ancestral gods lost all meaning; so then local gods, of that small valley or this river or that forest, gave their religious sanction to the new agglomerations by replacing the gods of the original tribe. Later Christianity, always willing to adjust to pagan survivals, made them into local saints.

Henceforth, the village community, consisting entirely or partly of individual families—all united, however, by the possession in common of the land—became the essential link for centuries to come.

Over vast areas of eastern Europe, Asia, and Africa it still survives. The barbarians—Scandinavians, Germans, Slavs, and others—who destroyed the Roman Empire lived under such an organization. And by studying the codes of the barbarians of that period, as well as the confederations of village communities that exist today among the Kabyles, the Mongols, the Hindus, the Africans, and others, it has been possible to reconstruct in its entirety that form of society which was the starting point of our civilization as it is today.

Let us therefore have a look at this institution.

III

The village community consisted then, as it does now, of individual families. But all the families of the same village owned the land in common. They considered it as their common heritage and shared it out among themselves on the basis of the size of each family—their needs and their potential. Hundreds of millions of human beings still live in this way in Eastern Europe, India, Java, etc. It is the same kind of system that has been established in our time by Russian peasants, freely in Siberia, as soon as the state gave them a chance to occupy the vast Siberian territory in their own way.

Today the cultivation of the land in a village community is carried out by each household independently. Since all the arable land is shared out between the families (and further shared out when necessary) each cultivates its fields as best it can. But originally, the land was also worked in common, and this custom is still carried on in many places—at least on a part of the land. As to the clearing of woodland and the thinning of forests, the construction of bridges, the building of small forts and turrets for use as places of safety in the event of invasion— all these activities were carried out on a communal basis, just as hundreds of millions of peasants still do where the village commune has held out against the encroachments of the state. But "consumption"—to use a modern term—was already operating on a family basis, each family having its cattle, its kitchen garden, and stores. The means both for hoarding and for handing down goods and chattels accumulated through inheritance had already been introduced.

In all its affairs the village commune was sovereign. Local custom was the law, and the plenary assembly of all the heads of family, men and women, was the judge, the only judge, in civil and criminal matters. When an inhabitant had lodged a complaint against another and stuck his knife in the ground in the place where the commune normally assembled, the commune had to "find the sentence" according to local custom once the fact of an offense had been established by the juries of the two parties in litigation.

Were I to recount all the interesting aspects of this phase, I would not have the space in which to do so. I must therefore refer the reader to *Mutual Aid*. It will suffice to mention here that all the institutions which states were to seize later for the benefit of minorities, that all notions of law that exist in our codes (which have been mutilated in favor of minorities) and all forms of judicial procedure, insofar as they offer guarantees to the individual, had their beginnings in the village commune. So when we imagine that we have made great advances in introducing, for instance, the jury, all we have done is to return to the institution of the so-called "barbarians" after having changed it to the advantage of the ruling classes. Roman law was simply grafted to customary law.

The sense of national unity was developing at the same time

through large free federations of village communes.

The village commune, being based on the possession in common and very often of the cultivation in common of the land and being sovereign both as judge and legislator of customary law, satisfied most of the needs of the social being.

But not all its needs: there were still others that had to be satisfied. Now, the spirit of the times was not to appeal to a government as soon as a new need was making itself felt. On the contrary the individuals themselves would take the initiative and come together, to join forces, and to federate; to create an entente, large or small, numerous or restricted, which was in keeping with the new need. And society then was literally covered as if by a network of sworn brotherhoods, of guilds for mutual aid, of "con-jurations," in the village as well as outside it, in the federation.

We may observe this phase and spirit at work, even today, among many barbarian federations which have remained outside the modern states copied on the Roman or rather the Byzantine model.

Thus, to take one example among many, the Kabyles have maintained their village community, with the characteristics I have just mentioned: land in common, communal tribunals, and so forth. But man feels the need for action beyond the narrow confines of his hamlet. Some rove the world seeking adventure as peddlers. Others take up some kind of trade—or "art." And those peddlers and artisans join together in "fraternities," even when they belong to different villages, tribes, or confederations. Union is needed for mutual succor on voyages to distant lands, for the mutual exchange of the mysteries of one's trade, and so they join forces. They swear brotherhood and practice it in a way that makes a deep impression on Europeans; it is a real brotherhood and not just empty words.

Furthermore, misfortune can overtake anyone. Who knows but that tomorrow in a brawl a normally gentle and quiet man may exceed the established limits of decorum and sociability? Who knows whether he might inflict blows and wounds? It may be necessary to pay heavy compensation to the offended or wounded party; it may be necessary to plead one's cause before the village assembly, and to reconstruct the facts on the testimony of six, ten or twelve "sworn brothers." All the more reason to enter a fraternity.

Besides, man feels the need to meddle in politics, to engage in intrigue perhaps, or to propagate a particular moral opinion or a particular custom. Finally, external peace has to be safeguarded; alliances with other tribes to be concluded; federations to be constituted far and wide; elements of intertribal law to be spread abroad. Well then, to gratify all these needs of an emotional or intellectual order, the Kabyles, the Mongols, and the Malays do not appeal to a government; they haven't one. Being men of customary law and individual initiative, they have not been perverted from acting for themselves by the corrupting force of government and church. They unite spontaneously. They form sworn brotherhoods, political and religious associations, craft associations—guilds as they were called in the Middle Ages, and *cofs* as they are called today by the Kabyles. And these *cofs* extend beyond the boundaries of the hamlet; they extend far and wide into the desert and to foreign cities; and brotherhood is practiced in these associations. To refuse help to a member of one's *cof*—even at the risk of losing all one's possessions and one's life—is to commit an act of treason to the brotherhood; it is to be treated as one's brother's murderer.

What we find today among the Kabyles, Mongols, Malays, and others was the very essence of life of the barbarians in Europe from the fifth to the twelfth and even until the fifteenth century. Under the name of guilds, friendships, brotherhoods, and so forth, associations abounded for mutual defense, to avenge affronts suffered by some members of the union and to express solidarity, to replace the "eye for an eye" vengeance by compensation, followed by the acceptance of the aggressor in the brotherhood; for the exercise of trades, for aid in case of illness, for defense of the territory; to prevent the encroachments of a nascent authority; for commerce, for the practice of "good neighborliness"; for propaganda—in a word for all that

Europeans, educated by the Rome of the Caesars and the Popes, nowadays expect from the state. It is even very doubtful whether there was a single man in that period, free man or serf, apart from those who had been banned by their own brotherhoods, who did not belong to a brotherhood or some guild as well as to his commune.

The Scandinavian sagas extol their achievements; the devotion of sworn brothers is the theme of the most beautiful poems. Of course, the church and the nascent kings, representatives of the Byzantine (or Roman) law which reappeared, hurl their excommunications and their rules and regulations at the brotherhood, but fortunately they remained a dead letter.

The whole history of the epoch loses its meaning and is quite incomprehensible if one does not take those brotherhoods into consideration, these unions of brothers and sisters, which sprang up everywhere to deal with the many needs in the economic and personal lives of the people.

In order to appreciate the immense progress achieved by this double institution of village communities and freely sworn brotherhoods—outside any Roman, Christian or statist influence—take for instance Europe as it was at the time of the barbarian invasion, and compare it with what it became in the tenth and eleventh centuries. The untamed forest is conquered and colonized; villages cover the country and are surrounded by fields and hedges and protected by small forts interlinked by paths crossing the forests and the marshes.

In these villages one finds the seeds of industrial arts and one discovers a whole network of institutions for maintaining internal and external peace. In the event of murder or woundings the villagers no longer seek, as in the tribe, to eliminate or to inflict an equivalent wound on the aggressor, or even one of his relatives or some of his fellow villagers. Rather is it the brigand-lords who still adhere to that principle (hence their wars without end), whereas among villagers, *compensation*, fixed by arbiters, becomes the rule after which peace is re-established, and the aggressor is often, if not always, adopted by the family who has been wronged by his aggression.

Arbitration for all disputes becomes a deeply rooted institution in daily use—in spite of and against the bishops and the nascent kinglets who would wish that every difference should be laid before them or their agents that they might benefit from the *fred*—the fine formerly levied by the villagers on violators of the peace when they brought their dispute before them, and which the kings and bishops now appropriate.

And finally, hundreds of villages are already united in powerful federations sworn to internal peace, who look upon their territory as a common heritage, and are united for mutual protection. This is the seed of European *nations*. And to this day one can still study these federations in operation among the Mongol, the Turko-Finnish, and Malayan tribes.

Meanwhile black clouds are gathering on the horizon. Other unions—of dominant minorities—are also established, which seek slowly to make these free men into serfs, into subjects. Rome is dead, but its tradition is reborn; and the Christian church, haunted by the visions of Eastern theocracies, gives its powerful support to the new powers that seek to establish themselves.

Far from being the bloodthirsty beast he was made out to be in order to justify a need to dominate, man has always preferred peace and quiet. Quarrelsome rather than fierce, he prefers his cattle, the land, and his hut to soldiering. For this reason, no sooner had the hordes and the tribes fortified themselves more or less in their respective territories than we see that defense of the territory against new waves of migrants is entrusted to someone who engages a small band of adventurers —hardened warriors or brigands who follow him, while the overwhelming majority engages in rearing cattle, in working the land. And that defender soon begins to accumulate riches; he gives horses and iron (then very expensive) to the miserable cultivator who has neither horse nor plow, and reduces him to servitude. He also begins to lay down the bases for military power.

And at the same time, little by little, the tradition that makes the law is being forgotten by the majority. In each village only a few old folk can remember the verses and song containing the "precedents" on which customary law is based, and on festive occasions they repeat these before the community. And slowly, certain families make it their speciality, transmitted from father to son, of remembering these songs and verses, of preserving the purity of the law. Villagers would go to them to adjudicate on complicated disputes, especially when two confederations could not agree to accept the decisions of the arbiters chosen from among themselves.

Princely and royal authority is already germinating in these families, and the more I study the institutions of that period the more I see that customary law did much more to create that authority than did the power of the sword. Man allowed himself to be enslaved much more by his desire to "punish" the aggressor "according to the law" than by direct military conquest.

And gradually the first "concentration of powers," the first mutual assurance for domination—by judge and military leader —is made against the village community. A single man assumes these two functions. He surrounds himself with armed men to carry out the judicial decisions; he fortifies himself in his turret; he accumulates for his family the riches of the time—bread, cattle, iron—and slowly imposes his domination over the peasants in the vicinity.

The learned man of the period, that is, the sorcerer or the priest, soon gives him his support either to share his power or, by adding force and the knowledge of customary law to his powers as a feared magician, the priest takes it over himself. From this stems the temporal authority of the bishops in the ninth, tenth and eleventh centuries.

I would need a whole series of lectures rather than a chapter to deal in depth with this subject which is so full of new lessons, and to recount how free men gradually became serfs, forced to work for the lord of the manor, temporal or clerical; of how authority was built up over the villages and boroughs in a tentative, groping manner; of how the peasants leagued together, rebelled, struggled to oppose this growing domination; of how they perished in those attacks against the thick walls of the castle and against the men clad in iron defending it.

It will be enough for me to say that about the tenth and eleventh centuries the whole of Europe appeared to be moving toward the constitution of those barbarian kingdoms similar to the ones found today in the heart of Africa or of those theocracies one learns of in Oriental history. This could not happen in a day; but the seeds for those petty royalties and for those petty theocracies were already there and were increasingly manifesting themselves.

Fortunately the "barbarian" spirit—Scandinavian, Saxon, Celtic, German, Slavic—which for seven or eight centuries had incited men to seek the satisfaction of their needs through individual initiative and through free agreement between the brotherhoods and guilds—fortunately that spirit persisted in the villages and boroughs. The barbarians allowed themselves to be enslaved, they worked for the master, but their feeling for free action and free agreement had not yet been broken down. Their brotherhoods were more alive than ever, and the crusades had only succeeded in arousing and developing them in the West.

And so the revolution of the urban communities, resulting from the union of the village community and the sworn brotherhood of the artisan and the merchant—which had been prepared long since by the federal mood of the period—exploded in the eleventh and twelfth centuries with striking effect in Europe. It had already started in the Italian communities in the tenth century.

This revolution, which most university historians prefer to ignore altogether or to underestimate, saved Europe from the disaster with which it was threatened. It arrested the development of theocratic and despotic kingdoms in which our civilization might well have ended by foundering after a few centuries of pompous splendor, just as did the civilizations of Mesopotamia, Assyria, and Babylon. It opened the way for a new way of life: that of the free communes.

IV

It is easy to understand why modern historians, trained in the Roman way of thinking and seeking to associate all institutions with Rome, should have such difficulty in appreciating the communalist movement that existed in the eleventh and twelfth centuries. This movement, with its virile affirmation of the individual, and which succeeded in creating a society through the free federation of men, villages, and towns, was the complete negation of the unitarian, centralizing Roman outlook with which history is explained in our university curriculum. Nor is it linked to any historic personality, or to any central institution.

It is a natural development, belonging, just as did the tribe and the village community, to a certain phase in human evolution, and not to any particular nation or region. This is the reason why academic science cannot be sensitive to its spirit and why the Augustin Thierrys and the Sismondis, historians who really understood the mood of the period, have not had followers in France, where Luchaire is still the only one to take up—more or less—the tradition of the great historian of the Merovingian and communalist periods. It further explains why, in England and Germany, the research into this period as well as an appreciation of its motivating forces are of very recent origin.

The commune of the Middle Ages, the free city, owes its origin on the one hand to the village community, and on the other, to those thousands of brotherhoods and guilds which were coming to life in that period independently of the territorial union. As a federation between these two kinds of unions, it was able to assert itself under the protection of its fortified ramparts and turrets.

In many regions it was a peaceful development. Elsewhere— and this applied in general to Western Europe—it was the result of a revolution. As soon as the inhabitants of a particular borough felt themselves to be sufficiently protected by their walls, they made a "conjuration." They mutually swore an oath to drop all pending matters concerning slander, violence, or

The State:
Its Historic
Role

wounding, and undertook, so far as disputes that might arise in the future, never again to have recourse to any judge other than the syndics which they themselves would nominate. In every art, or good neighborly guild, in every sworn brotherhood, it had been normal practice for a long time. In every village community, such had been the way of life in the past, before the bishop and the petty king had managed to introduce and later to impose on it their judges.

Now, the hamlets and parishes which made up the borough, as well as the guilds and brotherhoods which developed within it, looked upon themselves as a single *amitas*, nominated their judges and swore permanent union between all those groups.

A charter was soon drawn up and accepted. If need be, someone would be sent off to copy the charter of some neighboring small community (we know of hundreds of such charters) and the community was set up. The bishop or the prince, who had been until then the judge in the community and often more or less its master, could in such circumstances only recognize the *fait accompli*—or oppose the new conjuration by force of arms. Often the king—that is the prince who sought to be a cut above the other princes and whose coffers were always empty—would "grant" the charter for ready cash. Thus he refrained from imposing *his* judge on the community, while at the same time gaining prestige in the eyes of the other feudal lords. But this was by no means the rule; hundreds of communes remained active with no other authority than their goodwill, their ramparts, and their lances.

In the course of a hundred years, this movement spread in an impressively harmonious way throughout Europe—by imitation, to be sure—covering Scotland, France, the Low Countries, Scandinavia, Germany, Italy, Poland and Russia. And when we now compare the charters and the internal organization of all these communities we are struck by their virtual uniformity and the organization that grew in the shadow of these "social contracts." What a striking lesson for the Romanists and the Hegelians for whom servitude before the law is the only means of achieving conformity in institutions!

From the Atlantic to the middle course of the Volga, and from Norway to Sicily, Europe was being covered with such communities—some becoming populated cities such as Florence, Venice, Amiens, Nuremburg, or Novgorod, others remaining struggling villages of a hundred or as few as some twenty families treated nevertheless as equals by their more prosperous sisters.

As organisms bubbling with life, communities obviously developed in different ways. Geographical location, the nature of external commerce, and resistance to external interference all gave to each community its own history. But for all of them the basic principle was the same. The same friendship (*amitas*) of the village communities and the guilds associated within the precincts whether it was Pskov in Russia or Bruges in Flanders, a village of three hundred inhabitants in Scotland or prosperous Venice with its islands, a village in the north of France or one in Poland, or even *Florence la Belle*. Their constitutions, broadly speaking, were the same.

In general, the town—whose walls grew longer and thicker with the growth of population, and was flanked by towers which grew taller and taller, and were each raised by this or that district, or guild, and consequently displayed individual characteristics—the town was divided into four, five or six sections, or sectors, which radiated from the citadel or the cathedral toward the city ramparts. Each of these sectors was inhabited mainly by an "art" or trade, whereas the new trades—the "young arts"—occupied the suburbs, which in due course were enclosed by a new fortified wall.

The *street*, or the parish, represented the territorial unit, corresponding to the earlier village community. Each street or parish had its popular assembly, its forum, its popular tribunal, its priest, its militia, its banner, and often its seal, the symbol of its sovereignty. Though federated with other streets it nevertheless maintained its independence.

The professional unit which often was more or less identified with the district or with the sector, was the guild—the trade union. The latter also had its saints, its assembly, its forum, and its judges. It had its fund, its landed property, its militia, and its banner. It also had its seal, symbol of its *sovereignty*. In the event of war, its militia joined, assuming it was considered expedient, with the other guilds and placed its own banner alongside the large banner of the city.

Thus the city was the union of districts, streets, parishes and guilds, held its plenary assembly in the grand forum, and had its large belfry, its elected judges, and its banner to rally the militias of the guilds and districts. It dealt with other cities as sovereign, federated with whomever it wished, concluded alliances either nationally or outside the national territory. Thus the Cinque Ports around Dover were federated with French and Dutch ports across the Channel; the Russian Novgorod was the ally of the Germanic-Scandinavian Hansa, and so on. In its external relations each city possessed all the attributes of the modern state, and from that period onward there was formed, by free contracts, what was to be known later as international law, which was subject to the sanctions of public opinion in all the cities, as later it was to be more often violated than respected by the states.

On how many occasions would a particular city, unable "to find the sentence" in a particularly complicated case, send someone to "seek the sentence" in a neighboring city! How often was that dominating spirit of the period—arbitration rather than the judge's authority—demonstrated with two communes taking a third one as arbitrator!

The trades also acted in this way. Their commercial and craft relations went beyond the city, and their agreements were made without taking into account nationality. And when in our ignorance we boast of our international workers' congresses, we forget that already by the fifteenth century international congresses of trades and even apprentices were being held.

Lastly, the city either defended itself against aggressors and itself waged fierce war against the feudal lords in the neighborhood, naming each year one or two military commanders for its militias; or it accepted a "military defender"—a prince or a duke which it selected for one year and dismissed at will.

For the maintenance of his soldiers, he would be given the receipts from judicial fines; but he was forbidden to interfere in the affairs of the city.

Or if the city were too weak to free itself from its neighbors the feudal vultures, it kept as its more or less permanent military defender the bishop or the prince of a particular family—Guelph or Ghibelline in Italy, the Riurik family in Russia, or the Olgerds in Lithuania—but was jealously vigilant in preventing the authority of the bishop or the prince extending beyond the men encamped in the castle. They were even forbidden to enter the city without permission. To this day the king of England cannot enter the city of London without the permission of the lord mayor.

The economic life of the cities of the Middle Ages deserves to be recounted in detail. The interested reader is referred to what I have written on the subject in *Mutual Aid* in which I rely on a vast quantity of up-to-date historical research on the subject. Here it must suffice simply to note that internal commerce was dealt with entirely by the guilds—not by the individual artisans—prices being established by mutual agreement. Furthermore, at the beginning of that period external commerce was dealt with *exclusively by the city*. It was only later that it became the monopoly of the merchants' guild, and later still of individual merchants. Furthermore, nobody worked on Sundays, nor on Saturday afternoons (bath day). The provisioning of the principal consumer goods was always handled by the city, and this custom was preserved in some Swiss towns for corn until the middle of the nineteenth century.

In conclusion, it is shown by an immense documentation from many sources, that never, either before or since, has mankind known a period of relative well-being for all as in the cities of the Middle Ages. The poverty, insecurity, and physical exploitation of labor that exist in our times were then unknown.

V

With these elements—liberty, organization growing from the simple to the complex, production and exchange by the different trades (guilds), foreign trade handled by the whole city and not by individuals, and the purchase of provisions by the city for resale to the citizens at cost price—with such elements, the towns of the Middle Ages for the first two centuries of their free existences, became centers of well-being for all the inhabitants, centers of wealth and culture such as we have not seen since.

One has but to consult the documents which make it possible to compare the rates at which work was remunerated and the cost of provisions—Rogers has done this for England and a great number of German writers have done so for Germany—to see that the labor of an artisan and even of a simple day laborer was paid at a rate not reached in our time, not even by the elite among workers. The account books of colleges of Oxford University (which cover seven centuries beginning at the eleventh) and of some English landed estates, as well as those of a large number of German and Swiss towns, are there to bear witness.

If one also considers the artistic finish and amount of decorative work the craftsman of that period put into not only the objects of art he produced, but also into the simplest of household utensils—a railing, a candlestick, a piece of pottery—one realizes that he did not know what it meant to be hurried in his work or overworked as is the case in our time; that he could forge, sculpt, weave, or embroider as only a very small number of worker-artists among us can manage to do nowadays.

And in addition one should go through the list of donations made to the churches and the communal houses of the parish, the guild, or the city, both in works of art—decorative panels, sculptures, wrought iron and cast metal—and in money, to realize the degree of well-being attained by those cities; one also had an insight into the spirit of research and invention which manifested itself, and of the breath of freedom which inspired their works, the feeling of brotherly solidarity that grew up in those guilds in which men of the same trade were united not simply for commercial and technical reasons, but by bonds of sociability and brotherhood. Was it not in fact the rule of the guild that two brothers should sit at the bedside of each sick brother—a custom which certainly required devotion in those times of contagious diseases and the plague—and to follow him as far as the grave, and then look after his widow and children?

Abject poverty, misery, uncertainty of the morrow for the majority, and the isolation in poverty which are the characteristics of our modern cities were quite inknown in those "free oases which emerged amidst the feudal jungle in the twelfth century."

In those cities, sheltered by their conquered liberties, inspired by the spirit of free agreement and of free initiative, a whole new civilization grew up and flourished in a way unparalleled to this day.

All modern industry comes to us from these cities. In three centuries, industries and the arts attained such perfection that our century has only been able to surpass them in speed of production, but rarely in quality, and very rarely in the intrinsic beauty of the product. All the arts we seek in vain to revive now —the beauty of a Raphael, the strength and boldness of a Michelangelo, the art and science of a Leonardo da Vinci, the poetry and language of a Dante, and not least, the architecture to which we owe the cathedrals of Laon, Rheims, Cologne, Pisa, Florence—as Victor Hugo so well put it *le peuple en fut le maçon* ("they were built by the people")—the treasures of sheer beauty of Florence and Venice, the town halls of Bremen and Prague, the towers of Nuremberg and Pisa, and so on ad infinitum, all were the product of that age.

Do you wish to measure the progress of that civilization at a glance? Then compare the dome of St. Mark in Venice with the rustic arch of the Normans; the paintings of Raphael with the embroidery of the Bayeux tapestry; instruments of mathematics and physics, and the clocks of Nuremberg with the hourglasses of the preceding centuries; the rich language of a Dante with the uncouth Latin of the tenth century. A new world was born between the two!

With the exception of that other glorious period—once more of free cities—of ancient Greece, never had humanity made such a giant step forward. Never, in the space of two or three centuries, had man undergone such far-reaching changes, nor so extended his power over the forces of nature.

You are perhaps thinking of the civilization and progress of our century which comes in for so much boasting? But in each of its manifestations it is only the child of the civilization that grew up within the free communes. All the great discoveries made by modern science—the compass, the clock, the watch, printing, maritime discoveries, gunpowder, the laws of gravitation, atmospheric pressure of which the steam engine is a development, the rudiments of chemistry, the scientific method already outlined by Roger Bacon and applied in Italian universities—where do all these originate if not in the free cities, in the civilization which was developed under the protection of communal liberties?

It will perhaps be pointed out that I am forgetting the internal conflicts, the domestic struggles, with which the history of these communes is filled, the street riots, the bitter wars waged against the lords, the insurrections of the "young arts" against the "old arts," the blood spilled in those struggles and in the reprisals that followed.

No, in fact I forget nothing. But like Leo and Botta—the two historians of medieval Italy—and Sismondi, Ferrari, Gino Capponi, and so many others, I see that those struggles were the very guarantee of a free life in the free city. I perceive a renewal, a new impetus toward progress after each one of those struggles.

After having recounted in detail these struggles and conflicts, and after having measured also the greatness of the progress achieved while blood was being shed in the streets, well-being assured for all the inhabitants, and civilization renewed—Leo and Botta concluded with this idea which is so just and of which I am frequently reminded; I would wish to see it engraved in the mind of every modern revolutionary. "A commune [they said] does not present the picture of a moral whole, does not appear universal in its manner of being, like the human mind itself, *except when it has admitted conflict, opposition.*"

Yes, conflict, freely debated, without an outside force—the

state—adding its immense weight to the balance in favor of one of the forces engaged in the struggle.

I believe with these two writers, that often "more harm has been done by *imposing* peace, because it linked together opposites, in seeking to create a general political order, and sacrificed individualities and small organisms, in order to absorb them in a vast colorless and lifeless whole."

It is for this reason that the communes—so long as they did not themselves seek to become states and to impose around them "submission in a vast colorless and lifeless whole"—for this reason they grew and gained a new lease on life from each struggle, and blossomed to the clatter of swords in the streets; whereas two centuries later that same civilization collapsed in the wake of wars fathered by the states.

In the commune, the struggle was for the conquest and defense of the liberty of the individual, for the federative principle, for the right to unite and to act; whereas the states' wars had as their objective the destruction of these liberties, the submission of the individual, the annihilation of the free contract, and the uniting of men into a universal slavery to king, judge and priest—to the state.

Therein lies all the difference. There are struggles and conflicts which are destructive. And there are those which drive humanity forward.

VI

In the course of the sixteenth century, the modern barbarians were to destroy all that civilization of the cities of the Middle Ages. These barbarians did not succeed in annihilating it, but in halting its progress for at least two or three centuries. They launched it in a different direction, in which humanity is struggling at this moment without knowing quite how to escape.

They subjugated the individual. They deprived him of all his liberties, they expected him to forget all his unions based on free agreement and free initiative. Their aim was to level the whole of society to a common submission to the master. They destroyed all ties between men, declaring that the state and the church alone must henceforth form the union between their subjects; that the church and the state alone have the task of watching over the industrial, commercial, judicial, artistic, and emotional interests for which men of the twelfth century were accustomed to meet directly.

And who are these barbarians? It is the state: the triple alliance, finally constituted, of the military chief, the Roman judge, and the priest—the three constituting a mutual assurance for domination—the three, united in one power which will command in the name of the interests of society—and will crush that same society.

One naturally asks oneself how these new barbarians were able to overcome the communes, hitherto so powerful? Where did they find the strength to conquer?

They found it in the first place in the village. Just as the communes of ancient Greece proved unable to abolish slavery and for that reason perished—so the communes of the Middle Ages failed to free the peasant from serfdom at the same time as the townsman.

It is true that almost everywhere, at the time of his emancipation, the townsman—himself a farming craftsman—had sought to carry the country along with him to help it to free itself. For two centuries, the townsmen in Italy, Spain, and Germany were engaged in a bitter war against the feudal lords. Feats of heroism and perseverance were displayed by the burghers in that war on the castles. They bled themselves white to become masters of the castles of feudalism and to cut down the feudal forest that surrounded them.

But they only partially succeeded. War-weary, they finally made peace over the heads of the peasants. To buy peace, they handed over the peasants to the lord as long as he lived outside the territory conquered by the commune. In Italy and Germany they ended by accepting the lord as burgher, on condition that he come to live in the commune. Elsewhere they finished by sharing his dominion over the peasant. And the lord took his revenge on this "low rabble" of the towns, whom he hated and despised, making blood flow in the streets in struggles resulting from the practice of retaliation among noble families, which did not bring their differences before the syndics and the communal judges but settled them with the sword, in the street, driving one section of town dwellers against another.

The lord also demoralized the commune with his favors, by intrigues, his lordly way of life, and by his education received at the court of the bishop or the king. He induced it to share his ambitions. And the burgher ended by imitating the lord. He became in his turn a lord, he too getting rich from distant commerce or from the labor of the serfs penned up in the villages.

After which, the peasant threw in his lot with the kings, the emperors, budding tsars, and the popes when they set about building their kingdoms and subjecting the towns. Where the peasant did not march under his order, he did nothing about it.

It was in the country, in a fortified castle situated in the middle of rural communities that monarchy slowly came to be established. In the twelfth century, it existed in name only, and we know today what to think of the rogues, leaders of small bands of brigands, who adorned themselves with that name—a name which in any case (as Augustin Thierry has so well observed) didn't mean very much at the time, when there were "the king (the superior, the senior) of the law courts," the "king of the nets" (among fishermen), the "king of the beggars."

Slowly, gropingly, a baron who was favorably situated in one region, who was more powerful or more cunning than the others, would succeed in raising himself above his confreres. The church hastened to support him. And by force, scheming, money, sword, and poison if need be, one such feudal baron would grow in power at the expense of the others. But royal authority never succeeded in constituting itself in any of the free cities, which had their noisy forum, their Tarpeian Rock, or their river for the tyrants; it succeeded in the towns which had grown in the bosom of the country.

After having sought in vain to constitute this authority in Rheims or in Laon, it was in Paris—an agglomeration of villages and boroughs surrounded by a rich countryside which had not yet known the life of free cities; it was in Westminster, at the gates of the populous city of London; it was in the Kremlin, built in the center of rich villages on the banks of the Moskva after having failed in Suzdal and in Vladimir—but never in Novgorod, Pskov, Nuremberg, Laon, or Florence—that royal authority was consolidated.

The peasants from the surrounding areas supplied the nascent monarchies with food, horses, and men; commerce—royal and not communal in this case—added to their wealth. The church surrounded them with its attention. It protected them, came to their aid with its wealth, invented for them their local saint and his miracles. It surrounded with its veneration the Notre Dame of Paris or the Image of the Virgin of Iberia in Moscow. And while the civilization of the free cities, freed from the bishops, gathered its youthful momentum, the church worked relentlessly to reconstitute its authority through the intermediary of the nascent monarchy, surrounding with its attention, incense, and money the royal cradle of the one it had finally chosen, in order to reestablish with and through the monarchy its ecclesiastical authority. In Paris, Moscow, Madrid, and Prague you see her bending over the cradle of royalty, a lighted torch in her hand, the executioner by her side.

Hardworking and tenacious, strengthened by her statist education, leaning on the man of strong will or cunning whom she would look for in no matter what class of society, made for intrigue and versed in Roman and Byzantine law—you can see her unrelentingly marching toward her ideal: the absolute Judaic king who nevertheless obeys the high priest—the secular arm at the orders of the ecclesiastical power.

In the sixteenth century, this slow labor of the two conspirators is already operating at full force. A king already dominates his rival fellow barons, and this power will soon be directed against the free cities to crush them in their turn.

Besides, the towns of the sixteenth century were no longer what they had been in the twelfth, thirteenth, and fourteenth centuries.

Born of the libertarian revolution, they nevertheless lacked the courage or the strength to spread their ideas of equality to the neighboring countryside, not even to those who had come later to settle in the city precincts, those sanctuaries of freedom, where they created the industrial crafts.

In every town one finds a distinction being drawn between the families who made the revolution of the twelfth century (simply known as "the families") and those who came later and established themselves in the city. The old merchant guild would not hear of accepting newcomers. It refused to absorb the "young arts" into the commercial field. And from the simple steward to the city that it was in former times, when it carried out the external trade for the whole city, it became the middleman who got rich on his own account through foreign trade. It imported oriental ostentation, it became moneylender to the city, and later joined the city lord and the priest against "the lower orders"; or instead it looked to the nascent king for support of its right to enrichment and its commercial monopoly. When commerce became a personal matter, the free city was destroyed.

Moreover, the guilds of the old trades, which at the beginning made up the city and its government, did not wish to recognize the same rights for the young guilds, established later by the new crafts. The latter had to conquer their rights by a revolution. And this is what they did everywhere. But whereas in some cities that revolution was the starting point for a renewal of all aspects of life as well as the arts (this is so clearly seen in Florence), in other cities it ended in the victory of the *popolo grasso* over the *popolo basso*—by a crushing repression with mass deportations and executions, above all when the seigneurs and priests interfered.

And need one add that the king will use as a pretext the defense of the "lower classes" in order to crush the "fat classes" and to subjugate both at once? He had become master of the city!

And again, the cities had to die, since *the very ideas of men had changed*. The teaching of canonic law and Roman law had modified people's way of thinking.

The twelfth-century European was fundamentally a federalist. As a man of free enterprise and free understanding, of *associations* which were freely sought and agreed to, he saw in himself the point of departure for the whole of society. He did not seek safety through obedience nor did he ask for a savior for society. The idea of Christian and Roman discipline was unknown to him.

But under the influence of the Christian church—always in love with authority, always anxious to be the one to impose its dominion over the souls, and above all the work of the faithful; and on the other hand, under the influence of Roman law which by the twelfth century had already appeared at the courts of the powerful lords, the kings, and the popes and soon became the favorite subject at the universities—under the influence of these two teachings which are so much in accord even though originally they were bitter enemies, minds became corrupted as the priest and the legislator took over.

Man fell in love with authority. If a revolution of the lower trades took place in a commune, the commune would call for a savior, thus saddling itself with a dictator, a municipal Caesar; it would grant him the full powers to exterminate the opposition party. And he took advantage of the situation, using all the refinements in cruelty suggested to him by the church or those borrowed from the despotic kingdoms of the Orient.

He would no doubt have the support of the church. Had she not always dreamed of the biblical king who will kneel before the high priest and be his docile instrument? Has she not always hated with all her force those rationalist ideas which breathed in the free towns at the time of the first renaissance, that of the twelfth century? Did she not lay her curse on those "pagan" ideas which brought man back to nature under the influence of the rediscovery of Greek civilization? And later did she not get the princes to stifle these ideas which, in the name of primitive Christianity, raised up men against the pope, the priest, and religion in general? Fire, the wheel and the gibbet—those weapons so dear at all times to the church—were used to crush the heretics. It mattered not what the instrument might be, pope, king or dictator, so long as fire, the wheel, and the gibbet were in operation against her enemies.

And in the shadow of this double indoctrination of the Roman jurist and the priest, the federalist spirit which had created the free commune, the spirit of initiative and free association, was dying out and giving place to the spirit of discipline and to pyramidal authoritarian organization. Both the rich and the poor were asking for a savior.

And when the savior appeared—when the king, enriched far from the turmoil of the forum in some town of his creation, propped up by the inordinately wealthy church and followed by defeated nobles and by their peasants, knocked at the gates of the city, promising the "lower classes" royal protection against the rich and to the submissive rich his protection against the rebellious poor—the towns, already undermined by the cancer of authority, lacked the strength to resist him.

The great invasions of Europe by waves of people who had come once more from the East, assisted the rising royalty in this work of the concentration of powers.

The Mongols had conquered and devastated eastern Europe in the thirteenth century, and soon an empire was founded there, in Moscow, under the protection of the Tartar khans and the Russian Christian Church. The Turks had come to impose themselves in Europe and pushed forward as far as Vienna, destroying everything in their way. As a result a number of powerful states were created in Poland, Bohemia, Hungary and in central Europe to resist these two invasions. Meanwhile at the other extremity, the wars of extermination waged against the Moors in Spain allowed another powerful empire to be created in Castille and Aragon, supported by the Roman Church and the Inquisition—by the sword and the stake.

These invasions and wars inevitably led Europe to enter a new phase—that of military states.

Since the communes themselves were becoming minor states, these were bound in due course to be swallowed up by the large ones.

The victory of the state over the communes of the Middle Ages and the federalist institutions of the time was nevertheless not sudden. There was a period when it was sufficiently threatened for the outcome to be in doubt.

A vast popular movement—religious in its form and expressions but eminently equalitarian and communist in its aspirations—emerged in the towns and countryside of central Europe.

Already in the fourteenth century (in 1358 in France and in 1381 in England) two similar movements had come into being. The two powerful uprisings of the Jacqueries and of Wat Tyler had shaken society to its very foundations. Both however had been principally directed against the nobility, and though both had been defeated, they had broken feudal power. The uprising of peasants in England had put an end to serfdom and the Jacquerie in France had so severely checked serfdom in its development that from then on the institution simply vegetated, without ever reaching the power that it was to achieve later in Germany and throughout eastern Europe.

Now, in the sixteenth century, a similar movement appeared in central Europe. Under the name of the Hussite uprising in Bohemia, Anabaptism in Germany, Switzerland, and in the Low Countries, it was—apart from the revolt against the lords— a complete revolt against the state and church, against Roman and canon law, in the name of primitive Christianity.[3] For a long time misrepresented by statist and ecclesiastical historians, this movement is only beginning to be understood today.

The absolute freedom of the individual, who must only obey the commands of his conscience, and communism were the watchwords of this uprising. And it was only later, once the state and church had succeeded in exterminating its most

---

3 The "troubled times" in Russia at the beginning of the seventeenth century represent a similar movement, directed against serfdom and the state but without a religious basis.

ardent defenders and directing it to their own ends, that this movement, reduced in importance and deprived of its revolutionary character, became the Lutheran Reformation.

With Luther the movement was welcomed by the princes; but it had begun as communist anarchism, advocated and put into practice in some places. And if one looks beyond the religious phraseology which was a tribute to the times, one finds in it the very essence of the current of ideas which we represent today: the negation of laws made by the state or said to be divinely inspired, the individual conscience being the one and only law; the commune, absolute master of its destiny, taking back from the lords the communal lands and refusing to pay dues in kind or in money to the state; in other words communism and equality put into practice. Thus when Denck, one of the philosophers of the Anabaptist movement, was asked whether nevertheless he recognized the authority of the Bible, he replied that only the rule of conduct which each individual finds *for himself* in the Bible is obligatory for him. And meanwhile, these very formulas which are so vague—they are derived from ecclesiastical jargon—that authority "of the book," from which one can so easily draw arguments for and against communism, for and against authority, and so indefinite when it is a question of clearly affirming freedom—did not this religious tendency alone contain the germ for the certain defeat of the uprising?

Born in the towns, the movement soon spread to the countryside. The peasants refused to obey anybody, and fixing an old shoe on a pike in the manner of a flag they would go about recovering the land from the lords, breaking the bonds of serfdom, driving away priest and judge, and forming themselves into free communes. And it was only by the stake, the wheel, and the gibbet, by the massacre of a hundred thousand peasants in a few years, that royal or imperial power, allied to the papal or reformed church—Luther encouraging the massacre of the peasants with more virulence than the pope—that put an end to those uprisings which had for a period threatened the consolidation of the nascent states.

The Lutheran Reformation, which had sprung from popular Anabaptism, was supported by the state, massacred the people, and crushed the movement from which it had drawn its strength in the beginning. Then, the remnants of the popular wave sought refuge in the communities of the Moravian Brethren, who in their turn were destroyed a century later by the church and the state. Those among them who were not exterminated went to seek sanctuary, some in the southeast of Russia (the Mennonite community has since emigrated to Canada), some to Greenland where they have managed ever since to live in communities, refusing all service to the state.

Henceforth the state was assured of its existence. The jurist, the priest, and the warlord, formed into an alliance around the thrones, were able to pursue their work of annihilation. How many lies have been accumulated by statist historians, in the pay of the state, on that period!

Indeed have we not all learned at school for instance that the state had performed the great service of creating, out of the ruins of feudal society, national unions which had previously been made impossible by the rivalries between cities? Having learned this at school, almost all of us have gone on believing this to be true in adulthood.

And yet now we learn that in spite of all the rivalries, medieval cities had already worked four centuries toward building those unions, through federation, freely consented, and that they had succeeded.

For instance, the union of Lombardy comprised the cities of northern Italy with its federal treasury in Milan. Other federations such as the union of Tuscany, the union of the Rhineland (which comprised sixty towns), the federations of Westphalia, of Bohemia, of Serbia, Poland and of Russian towns, covered Europe. At the same time, the commercial union of the Hanse included Scandinavian, German, Polish and Russian towns in all the Baltic basin. There were there already all the elements, as well as the fact itself, of large human groupings freely constituted.

Do you require the living proof of these groupings? You have it in Switzerland! There, the union first asserted itself among the village communes (the old cantons), just as at the same time in France it was constituted in the Laonnais. And since in Switzerland the separation between town and village had not been as far-reaching as in the countries where the towns were engaged in large-scale commerce with distant areas, the towns gave assistance to the peasant insurrection of the sixteenth century and thus the union included towns and villages to constitute a federation which continues to this day.

But the state, by its very nature, cannot tolerate a free federation: it represents that nightmare of all jurists, "a state within the state." The state cannot recognize a freely formed union operating within itself; it only recognizes *subjects*. The state and its sister the church arrogate to themselves alone the right to serve as the link between men.

Consequently, the state must, perforce, wipe out cities based on the direct union between citizens. It must abolish all unions within the city, as well as the city itself, and wipe out all direct union between the cities. For the federal principle it must substitute the principle of submission and discipline. Such is the stuff of the state, for without this principle it ceases to be state.

And the sixteenth century—a century of carnage and wars—can be summed up quite simply by this struggle of the nascent state against the free towns and their federations. The towns were beseiged, stormed, and sacked, their inhabitants decimated or deported.

The state in the end wins total victory. And these are the consequences: in the sixteenth century Europe was covered with rich cities, whose artisans, masons, weavers, and engravers produced marvellous works of art; their universities established the foundations of modern empirical science, their caravans covered the continents, their vessels plowed the seas and the rivers.

What remained two centuries later? Towns with anything from fifty thousand to a hundred thousand inhabitants and which (as was the case of Florence) had had a greater proportion of schools and, in the communal hospitals, beds, in relation to the population than is the case with the most favored towns today, became rotten boroughs. Their populations decimated or deported, the state and church took over their wealth, industry died out under the rigorous control of the state's employees. Commerce was dead. Even the roads, which had hitherto linked these cities, became impassable in the seventeenth century.

The state is synonymous with war. Wars devastated Europe, and managed to finish off the towns which the state had not yet directly destroyed.

With the towns crushed, at least did the villages gain something from the concentration of state power? Of course not! One has only to read what the historians tell us of life in the Scottish countryside, or in Tuscany and in Germany in the sixteenth century, and compare these accounts with those of extreme poverty in England in the years around 1648, in France under Louis XIV—the "*Roi Soleil*"—in Germany, in Italy, everywhere, after a century of state domination.

The historians are unanimous in declaring that extreme poverty existed everywhere. In those places where serfdom had been abolished, it was reconstituted under a thousand new guises; and where it had not yet been destroyed, it emerged under the aegis of the state, as a fierce institution, displaying all the characteristics of ancient slavery or worse. In Russia it was the nascent state of the Romanovs that introduced serfdom and soon gave it the characteristics of slavery.

But could anything else come out of statist wretchedness since its first concern, once the towns had been crushed, was to destroy the village commune and all the ties between the peasants, and then to surrender their lands to sacking by the rich and to bring them all individually into subjection to the official, the priest, or the lord?

VIII

The role of the nascent state in the sixteenth and seventeenth centuries in relation to the urban centers was to destroy the independence of the cities; to pillage the rich guilds of merchants and artisans; to concentrate in its hands the external commerce of the cities and ruin it; to lay hands on the internal administration of the guilds and subject internal commerce as well as all manufacturers totally to the control of a host of officials—and in this way to kill industry and the arts; by taking over the local militias and the whole municipal administration, crushing the weak in the interest of the strong by taxation, and ruining the countries by wars.

Obviously the same tactic was applied to the villages and the peasants. Once the state felt strong enough it eagerly set about destroying the village commune, ruining the peasants in its clutches and plundering the common lands.

Historians and economists in the pay of the state teach us, of course, that the village commune having become an outdated form of land possession—which hampered progress in agriculture—had to disappear under "the action of natural economic forces." The politicians and the bourgeois economists are still saying the same thing now; and there are even some revolutionaries and socialists who claim to be scientific socialists who repeat this stock fable learned at school.

Well, never has such an odious lie been uttered by science. A calculated lie since history abounds with documents to prove for those who want to know—and for France it would virtually suffice to consult Dalloz—that the village commune was in the first place deprived of all its powers by the state; of its independence, its juridical and legislative powers; and that afterward its lands were either simply stolen by the rich with the connivance of the state or confiscated by the state directly.

In France the pillage was started from the sixteenth century, and followed its course at a greater pace in the following century. From 1659 the state started taking the communes under its wing, and one has only to refer to Louis XIV's edict of 1667 to appreciate on what a scale communal goods were already being pillaged during that period. "Men have taken the land for their own best interests; . . . lands have been divided; . . . to fleece the communes, fictitious debts have been devised," the "*Roi Soleil*" said in that edict, and two years later he confiscated all the communes' income to his own advantage. Such is the meaning of "a natural death" in the language which claims to be scientific.

In the following century, at a low estimate half of the communally owned lands were simply taken over by the nobility and the clergy under the aegis of the state. And nevertheless the commune continued in existence until 1787. The village assembly met under the elm tree, apportioned the lands, distributed the tax demands—documentary evidence can be found in Babeau (*Le village sous l'ancien régime*). Turgot, in the province in which he was the administrator, had already found the village assemblies "too noisy," and under his administration they were abolished and replaced by assemblies elected from among the village bigwigs. In 1787, on the eve of the revolution, the state generalized that measure. The commune had been abolished, and its affairs thus came into the hands of a few syndics, elected by the richest bourgeois and peasants.

The Constituent Assembly lost no time in confirming this law in December 1789, and the bourgeois took the place of the lords to divest the communes of what communal lands remained to them. It therefore needed one jacquerie after another in 1793 to confirm what the peasants in revolt had just achieved in eastern France. That is to say the Constituent Assembly gave orders for the return of the communal lands to the peasants—which was in fact only done when *already achieved by revolutionary action*. This is the fate of all revolutionary laws, and it is time that it was understood. They are only enacted after the *fait accompli*.

But while recognizing the right of the communes to the lands that had been taken away from them since 1669, the law had to add some of its bourgeois venom. Its intent was that the communal lands should be shared in equal parts only among the "citizens"—that is among the village bourgeoisie. By a stroke of the pen it wanted to dispossess the "inhabitants" and the bulk of the impoverished peasants, who were most in need of these lands. Whereupon, fortunately, there were new jacqueries

and in July 1793, the Convention authorized the distribution
of the land among all the inhabitants individually—and again
this was carried out only here and there, and served as a pretext
for a new pillage of communal lands.

Were these measures not already enough to provoke what
those gentlemen call "the natural death" of the commune? Yet
for all that the commune went on living. So on August 24, 1794,
reaction having seized power, it struck the major blow. The
state confiscated all the communal lands and used them as a
guarantee fund for the national debt, putting them up for
auction and surrendering them to its creatures, the Thermi-
dorians.

This law was happily repealed on 2 Prairial, year V, after
three years of rushing after the spoils. But by the same stroke
of the pen the communes were abolished and replaced by
cantonal councils, in order that the state could the more easily
pack them with its creatures. This lasted until 1801 when the
village communes were reintroduced; but then the government
itself undertook to appoint the mayors and syndics in each of the
thirty-six thousand communes! And this absurdity lasted until
the revolution of July 1830, after which the law of 1789 was
reintroduced. And in the meantime, the communal lands were
again confiscated entirely by the state in 1813 and pillaged for
the next three years. What remained was not returned to the
communes until 1816.

Do you think that was the end? Not at all! Each new regime
saw in the communal lands a means of compensation for its
henchmen. Thus from 1830, on three different occasions—the
first in 1837 and the last under Napoleon III—laws were
promulgated to *force* the peasants to share what remained to
them of the communal forests and pastures, and three times was
the state obliged to abrogate these laws because of the resistance
of the peasants. Nevertheless, Napoleon III took advantage
of this situation to seize a few large estates and to make presents
of them to his creatures.

Such are the facts. And this is what those gentlemen call in
"scientific" language the natural death of communal ownership

"under the influence of economic laws." One might as well call the massacre of a hundred thousand soldiers on the battlefield natural death.

Now, what was done in France was also done in Belgium, in England, Germany, and in Austria—everywhere in Europe except in the Slav countries.[4] But then, the periods of outbreaks of the pillaging of the communes are linked throughout Europe. Only the methods vary. Thus, in England they dared not proceed with general measures; they preferred to pass through parliament some thousands of separate enclosure acts by which, in every special case, parliament sanctioned confiscation— *it does so to this day*—and gave the squire the right to keep the communal lands that he had ring-fenced. And whereas nature had until now respected the narrow furrows by which the communal fields were divided temporarily among the families of a village in England, and though we have in the books of Marshal clear descriptions of this form of possession at the beginning of the nineteenth century, and though communal economy has survived in some communes[5] up to the present time, there is no lack of scholars (such as Seebohm, worthy emulator of Fustel de Coulanges) to maintain and teach that the commune never existed in England except in the form of serfdom!

In Belgium, in Germany, in Italy, and Spain we find the same methods being used. And in one way or another the individual seizure of the lands that were once communal was almost completed in western Europe by the 1850s. Of their communal lands the peasants only retain a few scraps.

This is the way the mutual alliance between the lord, the priest, the soldier, and the judge, that we call the "state," acted towards the peasants, in order to strip them of their last guarantee against extreme poverty and economic bondage.

But while the state was condoning and organizing this pillage,

4 It is already being done in Russia, the government having authorized the pillaging of communal lands under the law of 1906 and favored this pillage by its own functionaries.

5 See Dr. Gilbert Slater "The Inclosure of Common Fields" in the *Geographical Journal of the Geographical Society of London*, with plans and maps, January 1907. Later published in volume form.

could it respect the institution of the commune as the organ of local affairs? Obviously, it could not. For to admit that some citizens should constitute a federation which takes over some of the functions of the state would have been a contradiction in principle. The state demands from its subjects a direct, personal submission without intermediaries; it demands equality within slavery; it cannot admit of a "state within a state."

Thus as soon as the state began to be constituted in the sixteenth century, it sought to destroy all the links which existed among the citizens both in the towns and in the villages. Where it tolerated, under the name of municipal institutions, some remnants of autonomy—never of independence—it was only for fiscal reasons, to reduce correspondingly the central budget; or also to give the bigwigs of the province a chance to get rich at the expense of the people, as was the case in England, quite legally until recent years.

This is understandable. Local affairs are a matter of customary law whereas the centralization of powers is a matter of Roman law. The two cannot live side by side; the latter had to destroy the former.

It is for this reason that under the French regime in Algeria, when a Kabyle *djemmah*—a village commune—wants to plead for its lands, each inhabitant of the commune must lodge a personal complaint with the tribunals, who will deal with fifty or two hundred isolated cases rather than accept the commune's collective plea. The Jacobin code developed in the Code Napoleon hardly recognizes customary law, preferring Roman law or rather Byzantine law.

It is for this reason, again in France, that when the wind blows down a tree onto the national highway, or a peasant whose turn it is to repair the communal lane prefers to pay two or three francs to a stone breaker to do it—from twelve to fifteen employees of the ministries of the interior and of finance have to be involved *and more than fifty documents* passed between these austere functionaries before the tree can be sold, or before the peasant can receive permission to hand over his two or three francs to the communal treasury.

Those who may have doubts as to the veracity of this statement will find these fifty documents listed and duly numbered by Mr. Tricoche in the *Journal des Economistes* (April 1893).

That was of course under the Third Republic, for I am not talking about the barbaric procedure of the *ancien régime* which was satisfied with five or at the most six documents. But the scholars will tell you that in more barbaric days, the control by the state was fictitious.

And if it were only paper work! It would only mean, after all, twenty thousand officials too many, and another billion added to the budget. A mere trifle for the lovers of "order" and alignment! But at the bottom of all this is something much worse. There is the *principle* that destroys everything.

Peasants in a village have a large number of interests in common: household interests, neighborhood, constant relationships. They are inevitably led to come together for a thousand different things. But the state does not want this, nor can it allow them to join together! After all the state gives them the school and the priest, the gendarme and the judge— this should be sufficient. And if other interests arise they can be dealt with through the usual channels of the state church!

Thus until 1883 villagers in France were strictly prohibited from combining be it only for the purpose of bulk buying of chemical fertilizers or the irrigation of their meadows. It was not until 1883-1886 that the republic made up its mind to grant the peasants this right, by voting in the law on the trade unions which however was hedged in with provisos and conditions.

And because we are stupified by state education, we can rejoice in the sudden advances made by agricultural unions, without blushing at the thought that this right which has been denied the peasants until now was one enjoyed without question by every man—free or serf—in the Middle Ages. We have become such slaves that we already look upon it as a "victory for democracy." This is the stage we have reached in brainwashing thanks to our education deformed and vitiated by the state, and our state prejudices!

IX

"If in the town and the village you have common interests, then ask the state or the church to deal with them. But for you to get together and deal with these interests is prohibited." This is the formula that echoes through Europe from the sixteenth century onward.

Already at the end of the sixteenth century an edict by Edward III, king of England, stated that "every alliance, connivance, gatherings, meetings, enactments, and solemn oaths made or to be made between carpenters and masons, are null and void." But it was only after the defeat of the villages and of the popular uprisings, to which we have already referred, that the state dared to interfere with all the institutions—guilds, brotherhoods, and so forth—which bound the artisans together, to disband and destroy them. This is what one sees so clearly in England since the vast documentation available allows one to follow this movement step by step. Little by little the state takes over the guilds and the brotherhoods. It besets them, abolishes their conjurations, their syndics, which they replace by their offices, their tribunals and their banquets; and at the beginning of the sixteenth century under Henry VIII, the state simply confiscates all that the guilds possess without bothering with formalities or procedure. The heir of the great Protestant king completes the job.

It is daylight robbery without apologies, as Thorold Rogers so well put it. And again, it is this theft that the so-called scientific economists describe as the "natural" death of the guilds under the influence of "economic laws"!

Indeed, could the state tolerate the guild, the trade corporation, with its tribunal, its militia, its treasury, its sworn organization? It was "the state within the state"! The real state *had* to destroy it and this it did everywhere: in England, in France, in Germany, Bohemia, and Russia, maintaining only the pretense for the sake of the tax collector and as part of its huge administrative machine. And surely there is no reason to be surprised that the guilds and guild masterships were deprived of all that hitherto had been their lives; were put under the orders of the royal officials and had simply become cogs in the machinery of administration; that by the eighteenth century they were a hindrance, an obstacle to industrial development, in spite of the fact that for four centuries before that they represented life itself. The state had destroyed them.

But the state was not satisfied with putting a spoke in the wheels of life of the sworn brotherhoods of trades which had embarrassed it by placing themselves between it and its subjects. It was not satisfied with confiscating their funds and their properties. The state had to take over their functions as well as their assets.

In a city of the Middle Ages, when there was a conflict of interests within a trade or where two different guilds were in disagreement, the only recourse was to the city. They were obliged to come to an agreement, to any kind of compromise arrangement, since they were all mutually tied up with the city. And the latter never failed to assert itself, either by arbitration or, if necessary, by referring the dispute to another city.

From then on, the state was the only judge. All local conflicts including insignificant disputes in small towns with only a few hundred inhabitants, had to pile up in the form of documents in the offices of the king or of parliament. The English parliament was literally inundated by thousands of minor local squabbles. As a result thousands of officials were required in the capital—most of them were corruptible—to read, classify, and form an opinion on all this litigation and adjudicate on the smallest details: for example how to shoe a horse, to bleach linen, to salt herrings, to make a barrel, and so on ad infinitum; and the wave of questions went on increasing in volume!

But this was not all. In due course the state took over export trade, seeing it as a source of profit. Formerly, when a difference arose between two towns on the value of cloth that had been exported, or of the quality of wool or over the capacity of herring barrels, the towns themselves would remonstrate with each other. If the disagreement dragged on, more often than not they would invite another town to arbitrate. Alternatively a congress of the weavers' or coopers' guilds would be summoned to decide on an international level the quality and value of cloth and the capacity of barrels.

But henceforth it was the state in London or in Paris which undertook to deal with these disputes. Through its officials it controlled the capacity of barrels, defined the quality of cloth, allowing for variations as well as establishing the number of threads and their thickness in the warp and the woof, and by its ordinances meddling with the smallest details in every industry. You can guess the result. Under this control, industry in the eighteenth century was dying.

What had in fact come of Benvenuto Cellini's art under state tutelage? It had disappeared! And the architecture of those guilds of masons and carpenters whose works of art we still admire? Just observe the hideous monuments of the statist period and at one glance you will come to the conclusion that architecture was dead, to such an extent that it has not yet recovered from the blows it received at the hands of the state.

What was happening to the textiles of Bruges and the cloth from Holland? Where were these ironsmiths, so skilled in handling iron and who, in every important European village, knew how to make this ungrateful metal lend itself to transformation into the most exquisite decorations? Where were those turners, those watchmakers, those fitters who had made Nuremberg one of the glories of the Middle Ages for precision instruments? Talk about it to James Watt who two centuries later spent thirty years in vain, looking for a worker who could produce a more or less circular cylinder for his steam engine. Consequently his machine remained at the project stage for thirty years because there were no craftsmen able to construct it.

Such was the role of the state in the industrial field. All it was capable of doing was to tighten the screw for the worker, depopulate the countryside, spread misery in the towns, reduce millions of human beings to a state of starvation and impose industrial serfdom.

And it is these pitiful remains of the old guilds, these

organisms which have been battered and overtaxed, these use-less cogs of the administrative machine, of which the ever "scientific" economists are so ignorant as to confuse with the guilds of the Middle Ages. What the Great French Revolution swept away as harmful to industry was not the guild, nor even the trade union, but the useless and harmful cog in the machinery of state.

But what the revolution was at pains to sweep away was the power of the state over industry, over the factory serf.

Do you remember the discussion which took place at the Convention—at the terrible Convention—apropos of a strike? To the complaints of the strikers the Convention replied: "The state alone has the duty to watch over the interests of all citizens. By striking, you are forming a coalition, you are creating a state within the state. So—death!"

In this reply only the bourgeois nature of the revolution has been discerned. But has it not, in fact, a much deeper significance? Does it not sum up the attitude of the state, which found its complete and logical expression with regard to society as a whole in the Jacobinism of 1793? "Have you something to complain about? Then address your complaint to the state! It alone has the mission to redress the wrongs to its subjects. As for a coalition to defend yourselves—[that] never!" It was in this sense that the republic called itself one and *indivisible*.

Does not the modern socialist Jacobin think in the same way? Did not the Convention express the gist of Jacobin thought with the cold logic that is typical of it?

In this answer of the Convention was summed up the attitude of all states with regard to all coalitions and all private societies, whatever their aim.

In the case of the strike, it is a fact that in Russia it is still considered a crime of high treason. In most of Germany too where Wilhelm would say to the miners: "Appeal to me; but if ever you presume to act for yourselves you will taste the swords of my soldiers."

Such is still almost always the case in France. And even in England, only after having struggled for a century by means of secret societies, by the dagger for traitors and for the masters, by explosive powders under machines (as late as 1860), by emery powder poured into grease boxes and so on, did British workers begin to win the right to strike, and will soon have it altogether—if they don't fall into the traps already set for them by the state, which seeks to impose compulsory arbitration in exchange for the law for an eight-hour day.

More than a century of bitter struggles! And what misery; how many workers died in prison, were transported to Australia, were shot or hanged, in order to win back the right to combine which—let it be remembered once more—every man free or serf practiced freely so long as the state did not lay its heavy hand on societies.

But then, was it only the workman who was treated in this way?

Let us only recall the struggles that the bourgeoisie had to wage against the state to win the right to constitute itself into commercial societies—a right which the state only began to concede when it discovered a convenient way of creating monopolies for the benefit of its creatures and of filling its coffers. Think of the struggle for the right to speak, think or write other than the way the state decrees through the academy, the university and the church! Think of the struggles that have to be waged to this day in order to be able to teach children to read —a right which the state possesses but does not use! Even of the struggles to secure the right to enjoy oneself in public! Not to mention those which should be waged in order to dare to choose one's judge and one's laws—a thing that was in daily use in other times—nor the struggles that will be needed before one will be able to make a bonfire of that book of infamous punishments, invented by the spirit of the Inquisition and of the despotic empires of the Orient known under the name of the penal code!

Observe next taxation—an institution originating purely with the state—this formidable weapon used by the state, in Europe as in the young societies of the two Americas, to keep the masses under its heel, to favor its minions, to ruin the majority for the benefit of the rulers and to maintain the old divisions and castes.

Then take the wars without which states can neither constitute themselves nor maintain themselves; wars which become disastrous, and inevitable, the moment one admits that a particular region—simply because it is part of a state—has interests opposed to those of its neighbors who are part of another state. Think of past wars and of those that oppressed people will have to wage to conquer the right to breathe freely; of the wars for markets; of the wars to create colonial empires. And in France we unfortunately know only too well that every war, victorious or not, is followed by slavery.

And finally what is even worse than all that has just been enumerated, is the fact that the education we all receive from the state, at school and after, has so warped our minds that the very notion of freedom ends up by being lost and disguised in servitude.

It is a sad sight to see those who believe themselves to be revolutionaries unleashing their hatred on the anarchist—just because his views on freedom go beyond their petty and narrow concepts of freedom learned in the state school. And meanwhile, this spectacle is a reality. The fact is that the spirit of voluntary servitude was always cleverly cultivated in the minds of the young, and still is, in order to perpetuate the subjection of the individual to the state.

Libertarian philosophy is stifled by the Roman and Catholic pseudophilosophy of the state. History is vitiated from the very first page, where it lies when it speaks of the Merovingian and Carlovingian monarchies, up to the last page, where it glorifies Jacobinism and refuses to recognize the role of the people in creating its own institutions. Natural sciences are perverted in order to be put at the service of the double idol church-state. Individual psychology, and even more, that of societies, are falsified in each of their assertions in justifying the triple alliance of soldier, priest, and judge. Finally, morality, after having preached for centuries obedience to the church, or the book, only gains its emancipation today to preach servitude to the state: "No direct moral obligations towards your neighbor, nor even any feeling of solidarity; all your obligations are to the state" we are told, we are taught, in this new cult of the old Roman and Caesarian divinity. "The neighbor, the comrade, the companion—forget them. You will henceforth only know them through the intermediary of some organ or other of your state. And every one of you will make a virtue out of being equally subjected to it."

And the glorification of the state and of its discipline, for which the university and the church, the press and the political parties labor, is propagated so successfully that even revolutionaries dare not look this fetish straight in the eye.

The modern radical is a centralist, statist, and rabid Jacobin. And the socialists fall in step. Just like the Florentines at the end of the fifteenth century who knew no better than to call on the dictatorship of the state to save themselves from the patricians, so the socialists only can call upon the same gods, the dictatorship of the state, to save themselves from the horrors of the economic regime, created by that very same state!

X

If one goes a little deeper into these different categories of phenomena which I have barely touched upon in this short outline, one will understand why—seeing the state as it has been in history, and as it is in essence today—and convinced that a social institution cannot lend itself to all the desired goals, since, like every organ, it developed according to the function it performed, in a definite direction and not in all possible directions—one will understand, I say, why the conclusion we arrive at is for the abolition of the state.

We see in it the institution, developed in the history of human societies, to prevent direct association among men, to shackle the development of local and individual initiative, to crush existing liberties, to prevent their new blossoming—all this in order to subject the masses to the will of the minorities.

And we know an institution which has a long past going back several thousand years cannot lend itself to a function opposed to the one for which and by which it was developed in the course of history.

To this unshakable argument for anybody who has reflected on history the reply we receive is almost infantile: "The state exists and it represents a powerful ready-made organization. Why not use it instead of wanting to destroy it? It operates for evil ends—agreed; but the reason is that it is in the hands of the exploiters. If it were taken over by the people, why would it not be used for better ends, for the good of the people?"

Always the same dream—that of the Marquis de Posa in Schiller's drama, seeking to make an instrument of emancipation out of absolutism; or again the dream of the gentle Abbé Pierre in Zola's *Rome* seeking to make of the church the lever for socialism.

Take a concrete example in France. All thinking people must have noticed the striking fact that the Third Republic, in spite of its republican form of government, has remained monarchist in essence. We all have reproached it for not having republicanized France—I do not only say that it has done nothing for the *social* revolution, but that it has not even introduced the morality or simply the *republican* outlook. For the little that has been done in the past twenty-five years to democratize social attitudes or to spread a little education has been done everywhere, in all the European monarchies, under pressure from the times through which we are passing. Then where does this strange anomaly of a republic which has remained a monarchy come from?

It arises from the fact that France has remained a state, and just where it was thirty years ago. The holders of power have changed the name but all that huge ministerial scaffolding, all that centralized organization of white-collar workers, all this aping of the Rome of the Caesars which has developed in France, all that huge organization to assure and extend the exploitation of the masses in favor of a few privileged groups, which is the essence of the state institution—all that has remained. And those cogs continue as in the past to exchange their fifty documents when the wind has blown down a tree onto the highway and to transfer the millions deducted from the nation to the coffers of the privileged. The official stamp on the documents has changed; but the state, its spirit, its organs, its territorial centralization, its centralization of functions, its favoritism, its role as creator of monopolies have remained. Like an octopus they go on spreading their tentacles over the country.

The republicans, and I am speaking of the sincere ones—had cherished the illusion that one could "utilize the organization of the state" to effect a change in the republican direction, and these are the results. Whereas it was necessary to break up the old organization, *shatter the state* and rebuild a new organization, by beginning from the very foundations of society—the liberated village commune, federalism, groupings from simple to compound, free workingmen's associations—they thought of using the "organization that already existed." And, not having understood that one does not make an historical institution follow in the direction which one seeks to indicate—in the opposite direction to the one it has taken over the centuries—they were swallowed up by the institution.

And this happened, though in this case it was not even a question yet of changing the whole of the economic relations in society! The aim was merely to reform only some aspects of political relations between men.

But after such complete failure, and in the light of such a pitiful experiment, there are those who still insist on telling us that the conquest of powers of the state by the people will suffice to accomplish the social revolution!—that the old machine, the old organism, slowly developed in the course of history to crush freedom, to crush the individual, to establish oppression on a legal basis, to create monopolists, to lead minds astray by accustoming them to servitude—will lend itself perfectly to its new functions: that it will become the instrument, the framework for the germination of a new life, to found freedom and equality on economic bases, for the destruction of monopolies, the awakening of society and the advance toward a future freedom and equality!

What a sad and tragic mistake! To give full scope to socialism entails rebuilding from top to bottom a society dominated by the narrow individualism of the shopkeeper. It is not as has sometimes been said by those indulging in metaphysical woolliness just a question of giving the worker "the total product of his labor"; it is a question of completely reshaping all relationships, from those which exist today between every individual and his churchwarden or his stationmaster to those which exist between neighborhoods, hamlets, cities, and regions. In every street, in every hamlet, in every group of men gathered around a factory or along a section of the railway line, the creative, constructive, and organizational spirit must be awakened in order to rebuild life—in the factory, in the village, in the store, in production, and in distribution of supplies. All relations between individuals and great centers of population have to be made all over again, from the very day, from the very moment one alters the existing commercial or administrative organization.

And they expect this immense task, requiring the free expression of popular genius, to be carried out within the framework of the state and the pyramidal organization which is the essence of the state! They expect the state whose very *raison d'être* is the crushing of the individual, the hatred of initiative, the triumph of *one* idea which must be inevitably that of mediocrity—to become the lever for the accomplishment of this immense transformation! . . . They want to direct the revival of a society by means of decrees and electoral majorities. . . . How ridiculous!

Throughout the history of our civilization, two traditions, two opposing tendencies have confronted each other: the Roman and the popular traditions; the imperial and the federalist; the authoritarian and the libertarian. And this is so, once more, on the eve of the social revolution.

Between these two currents, always manifesting themselves, always at grips with each other—the popular trend and that which thirsts for political and religious domination—we have made our choice.

We seek to recapture the spirit which drove people in the twelfth century to organize themselves on the basis of free agreement and individual initiative as well as of the free federation of the interested parties. And we are quite prepared to leave the others to cling to the imperial, the Roman, and canonical tradition.

History is not an uninterrupted natural development. Again and again development has stopped in one particular territory only to emerge somewhere else. Egypt, the Near East, the Mediterranean coasts, central Europe have all in turn been centers of historical development. But every time the pattern has been the same, beginning with the phase of the primitive tribe, followed by the village commune, then by the free city, finally to die with the advent of the state.

In Egypt, civilization begins with the primitive tribe. It advances to the village commune and later to the period of the free cities, later still to the state which, after a period in which it flourishes, leads to death.

Development starts afresh in Syria, in Persia, and in Palestine. It follows the same pattern: the tribe, the village commune, the free city, the all-powerful state and . . . death!

A new civilization then comes to life in Greece. Always through the tribe. Slowly it reaches the level of the village commune and then of the republican cities. In these cities civilization reaches its heights. But the East communicates its poisonous breath, its despotic traditions. War and conquests build up the empire of Alexander of Macedonia. The state asserts itself, grows, destroys all culture and again . . . it is death!

In its turn Rome starts civilization over again. Once more one finds at the beginning the primitive tribe, then the village commune followed by the city. At this phase Rome was at the height of its civilization. But then come the state and the empire and then . . . death!

On the ruins of the Roman Empire, Celtic, Germanic, Slavonic and Scandinavian tribes once more take up the threads of civilization. Slowly the primitive tribe develops it institutions and manages to build up the village commune. It lingers in this phase until the twelfth century when the republican city arises, and this brings with it the blossoming of the human spirit, proof of which are the masterpieces of architecture, the grandiose development of the arts, the discoveries which lay the foundations of natural sciences. But then the state emerges . . . and then—death!

Yes: death—or renewal! *Either* the state forever, crushing individual and local life, taking over in all fields of human activity, bringing with it its wars and its domestic struggles for power, its palace revolutions which only replace one tyrant by another, and inevitably at the end of this development there is . . . death! *Or* the destruction of the state, and new life starting again in thousands of centers on the principle of the lively initiative of the individual and groups and that of free agreement.

The choice lies with you!

After the outbreak of revolution in Russia in January 1905, Kropotkin carefully studied the course of events. Though his vantage point in England was far from the actual developments, he received personal, firsthand reports and, in addition, followed the accounts in the Russian press. He believed that this upheaval might inaugurate the social revolution leading to anarchism. In November, he wrote "The Revolution in Russia" in which he described the situation and interpreted the significance of the nascent revolution. For Kropotkin, 1905 was a revolution not of radical parties but of the masses.

The following is reprinted with permission of Associated Book Publishers Ltd. from the original publication of the article in *Nineteenth Century,* vol. 58, no. 346 (December 1905). The notes are Kropotkin's except where otherwise indicated.

The
Revolution
in Russia

I.

Events in Russia are following one another with that rapidity which is characteristic of revolutionary periods. Eleven months ago when I wrote in this review about the constitutional agitation in Russia, the Congress of the Zemstvos, which had timidly expressed the desire of having some sort of representative institutions introduced in Russia, was the first open step that had been made by a collective body in the struggle which was going to develop itself with such an astounding violence.[1] Now, autocracy, which then seemed so solid as to be capable of weathering many a storm, has already been forced to recognize that it must cease to exist. But between these two events so many others of the deepest importance have taken place that they must be recalled to memory, before any safe conclusion can be drawn as to the probable further developments of the revolution in Russia.

On August 10, 1904, the omnipotent minister of the interior Plehve was killed by the revolutionary socialist Sazonov. Plehve had undertaken to maintain autocracy for another ten years,

---

1 *Nineteenth Century*, January 1905. On the zemstvo movement at this time, see George Fischer, *Russian Liberalism* (Cambridge, Mass.: Harvard University Press, 1958), pp. 159-204.—*Editor*.

provided that he and his police were invested with unlimited powers; and having received these powers, he had used them so as to make of the police the most demoralized and dangerous body in the state. In order to crush all opposition, he had not recoiled from deporting at least thirty thousand persons to remote corners of the empire by mere administrative orders.

He was spending immense sums of money for his own protection, and when he drove in the streets, surrounded by crowds of policemen and detective bicyclists and automobilists, he was the best-guarded man in Russia—better guarded than even the tsar. But all that proved to be of no avail. The system of police rule was defeated, and nobody in the tsar's surroundings would attempt to continue it. For six weeks the post of minister of the interior remained vacant, and then Nicholas II reluctantly agreed to accept Sviatopolk-Mirskii, with the understanding that he would allow the zemstvos to work out some transitional form between autocracy pure and simple, and autocracy mitigated by some sort of national representation. This was done by the zemstvos at their congress in November of last year, when they dared to demand "the guarantee of the individual and the inviolability of the private dwelling," "the local autonomy of self-administration," and "a close intercourse between the government and the nation," by means of a specially elected body of representatives of the nation who would "participate in the legislative power, the establishment of the budget, and the control of the administration."[2]

Modest though this declaration was, it became the signal for a general agitation. True, the press was forbidden to discuss it, but all the papers, as well as the municipal councils, the scientific societies, and all sorts of private groups discussed it nevertheless. Then, in December last, the "intellectuals" organized themselves into vast unions of engineers, lawyers, chemists, teachers, and so on—all federated in a general union of unions. And amid this agitation, the timid resolutions of the zemstvos were soon outdistanced. A constituent assembly, elected by universal, direct, and secret suffrage, became the watchword of all the constitutional meetings. This demand was soon as popular as the paragraphs of the charter were during the Chartist agitation.[3]

The students were the first to carry these resolutions into the streets, and they organized imposing demonstrations in support of these demands at St. Petersburg, Moscow, and in all the university towns. At Moscow the Grand Duke Sergei [Aleksandrovich Romanov] ordered the troops to fire at the absolutely peaceful demonstration. Many were killed and from that day he became a doomed man.

Things would have probably dragged if the St. Petersburg workingmen had not at this moment lent their powerful support to the young movement—entirely changing by their move the very face of events. To prevent by any means the "intellectuals" from carrying on their propaganda amid the workingmen and the peasant had been the constant preoccupation of the Russian government; while, on the other side, to join hands with the workers and the peasants and to spread among them the ideas of freedom and socialism had always been the goal of the revolutionary youth for the last forty years—since 1861.[4] Life itself worked on their side. The labor movement played so prominent a part in the life of Europe during the last half-century, and it so much occupied the attention of all the European press, that the infiltration of its ideas into Russia could not be prevented by repression. The great strikes of 1896-1900 at St. Petersburg and in central Russia, the growth of the labor organizations in Poland, and the admirable success of the Jewish labor organization, the Bund, in western and southwestern Russia proved, indeed, that the Russian workingmen had joined hands in their aspirations with their Western brothers.

3 Democratic movement for political and social reform in England, 1836-48. The Peoples' Charter was drafted in 1838.—*Editor*.

4 See Kropotkin's article, "The Russian Revolutionary Party," included in this volume.—*Editor*.

There is no need to repeat here what Father Gapon has told already in his autobiography[5]—namely, how he succeeded in grouping in a few months a considerable mass of the St. Petersburg workers around all sorts of lecturing institutes, tea restaurants, cooperative societies, and the like, and how he, with a few workingmen friends, organized within that mass and linked together several thousands of men inspired by higher purposes. They succeeded so well in their underground work that when they suggested to the workingmen that they should go en masse to the tsar, and unroll before him a petition asking for constitutional guarantees as well as for some economic changes, nearly seventy thousand men took in two days the oath to join the demonstration, although it had become nearly certain that the demonstration would be repulsed by force of arms. They more than kept word, as they came out in still greater numbers—about two hundred thousand—and persisted in approaching the Winter Palace notwithstanding the firing of the troops.

It is now known how the emperor, himself concealed at Tsarskoe Selo, gave orders to receive the demonstrators with volley-firing; how the capital was divided for that purpose into military districts, each one having at a given spot its staff, its field telephones, its ambulances . . . The troops fired at the dense crowds at a range of a few dozen yards, and no less than two to three thousand men, women, and children fell: the victims of the tsar's fears and obstinacy.

The feeling of horror with which eyewitnesses, Russian and English, speak of this massacre surpasses description. Even time will not erase these horrible scenes from the memories of those who saw them, just as the horrors of a shipwreck remain engraved forever in the memory of a rescued passenger. What Gapon said immediately after the massacre about *the viper's brood* of the whole dynasty was echoed all over Russia, and went as far as the valleys of Manchuria. The whole character of the movement was changed at once by this massacre. All illusions

5 *The Strand Magazine* (July to November 1905).

were dissipated. As the autocrat and his supporters had not shrunk from that wanton, fiendish, and cowardly slaughtering, it was evident that they would stop at no violence and no treachery. Since that day the name of the Romanov dynasty began to become odious among the workingmen of Russia. The illusion of a benevolent autocrat who was going to listen paternally to the demands of his subjects was gone forever.

Distrust of everything that might come from the Romanovs took its place; and the idea of a democratic republic, which formerly was adopted by a few socialists only, now found its way even into the relatively moderate program. To let the people think that they might be received by the tsar, to lure them to the Winter Palace, and there to mow them down by volleys of rifle fire—such crimes are never pardoned in history.

If the intention of Nicholas II and his advisers had been to terrorize the working classes, the effect of the January slaughter was entirely in the opposite direction. It gave a new force to the labor movement all over Russia. Five days after the terrible "Vladimir" Sunday, a mass strike broke out at Warsaw, and was followed by mass strikes at Lodz and in all the industrial and mining centers of Poland. In a day or two the Warsaw strike was joined by a hundred thousand operatives and became general. All factories were closed, no tramways were running, no papers were published. The students joined the movement, and were followed by the pupils of the secondary schools. The shop assistants, the clerks in the banks and in all public and private commercial establishments, the waiters in the restaurants—all gradually came out to support the strikers. Lodz joined Warsaw, and two days later the strike spread over the mining district of Dombrowo. An eight-hour day, increased wages, political liberties, and home rule, with a Polish Diet sitting at Warsaw were the demands of all the strikers. We thus find in these Polish strikes all the characteristics which, later on, made of the general strikes of October last so powerful a weapon against the crumbling autocratic system.

If the rulers of Russia had had the slightest comprehension of what was going on, they would have perceived at once that a new factor of such potency had made its appearance in the movement, in the shape of a strike in which all classes of the population joined hands, that nothing remained but to yield to their demands; otherwise the whole fabric of the state would be shattered down to its deepest foundations. But they remained as deaf to the teachings of modern European life as they had been to the lessons of history; and when the strikers appeared in the streets, organizing imposing demonstrations, they knew of no better expedient than to send the order: "Shoot them!" In a couple of days more than three hundred men and women were shot at Warsaw, one hundred at Lodz, forty-three at Sosnowice, forty-two at Ostrowiec, and so on, all over Poland!

The result of these new massacres was that all classes of society drew closer together in order to face the common enemy, and swore to fight till victory should be gained. Since that time governors of provinces, officers of the police, gendarmes, spies, and the like have been killed in all parts of Poland, not one day passing without some such act being recorded; so it was estimated in August last that ninety-five terrorist acts of this sort had taken place in Poland, and that in very few of them were the assailants arrested. As a rule they disappeared—the whole population evidently helping to conceal them.

II.

In the meantime the peasant uprisings, which had already begun a couple of years ago, were continuing all over Russia, showing, as is usually the case with peasant uprisings, a recrudescence at the beginning of the winter and a falling off at the time when the crops have to be taken in. They now took serious proportions in the Baltic provinces, in Poland, and Lithuania, in the central provinces of Chernigov, Orel, Kursk, and Tula, on the middle Volga, and especially in western Transcaucasia. There were weeks when the Russian papers would record every day from ten to twenty cases of peasant uprisings. Then, during crop time, there was a falling off in these numbers, but now that the main field work is over, the peasant revolts are beginning with a renewed force. In all these uprisings the peasants display a most wonderful unity of action, a striking calmness, and remarkable organizing capacities. In most cases their demands are even very moderate. They begin by holding a solemn assembly of the *mir* ("village community"); then they ask the priest to sing a Te Deum for the success of the enterprise; they elect as their delegates the wealthiest men of the village, and they proceed with their carts to the landlord's grain stores. There they take exactly what they need for keeping alive till the next crop, or they take the necessary fuel from the landlord's wood, and if no resistance has been offered they take nothing else, and return to their houses in the same orderly way, or else they come to the landlord and signify to him that unless he agrees to rent all his land to the village community at some price—usually a fair price—nobody will be allowed to rent his land or work for him as a hired laborer, and that the best he can do is therefore to leave the village. In other places, if the landlord has been a good neighbor, they offer to buy all his land on the responsibility of the commune, for the price which land, sold in a lump, can fetch in that neighborhood; or alternatively they offer such a yearly rent; or, if he intends to cultivate the land himself, they are ready to work at a fair price, slightly above the now current prices. But rack-renting, renting to middlemen, or renting to other villages, in order to force his nearest neighbors to work at lower wages—all this must be given up forever.

As to the Caucasus, the peasants of Guria (western portion of Georgia) proceeded even in a more radical way. They refused to work for the landlords, sent away all the authorities, and, nominating their own judges, they organized such independent village communities, embodying a whole territory, as the old cantons of Schwyz, Uri, and Unterwalden represented for several centuries in succession.

All these facts point in one direction. Rural Russia will *not* be pacified so long as some substantial move has not been made toward land nationalization. The theoreticians of the mercantile school of economists may discuss this question with no end of argument, coming to no solution at all; but the peasants are evidently decided *not* to wait any more. They see that the landlords not only do not introduce improved systems of agriculture on the lands which they own, but simply take advantage of the small size of the peasant allotments and the heavy taxes which the peasants have to pay, for imposing rack-rents, and very often the additional burden of a middleman, who sublets the land. And they seem to have made up their minds all over Russia in this way: "Let the government pay the landlords, if it be necessary, but *we* must have the land. We shall get out of it, under improved methods, much more than is obtained now by absentee landlords, whose main income is derived from the civil and military service."

It may therefore be taken as certain that such insignificant measures as the abandonment of arrears or a reduction of the redemption tax, which were promulgated by the tsar on the eighteenth of this month (November), will have *no effect whatever* upon the peasants. They know that, especially with a new famine in view, no arrears can be repaid. On the other hand, it is the unanimous testimony of all those who know the peasants that the general spirit—the *mentalité*, as the French would say—of the peasant nowadays is totally changed. He realizes that while the world has moved he has remained at the mercy of the same *uriadnik* ("village constable") and the same district chief, and that at any moment, for the mere exposition of his griefs, he can be treated as a rebel, flogged to death in the teeth of all laws, or shot down by the Cossacks. Therefore he will not be lulled into obedience by sham reforms or mere promises. This is the impression of all those who know the peasants from intercourse with them, and this is also what appears both from the official peasant congress which was held last summer, and from the unofficial congresses organized by revolutionary socialists in more than one hundred villages of eastern Russia. Both have expressed the same views: "We want the land, and we shall have it."

III

The peasants uprising alone, spreading over wide territories, rolling like waves which flood today one part of the country and tomorrow another, would have been sufficient to entirely upset the usual course of affairs in Russia. But when the peasant insurrection is combined with a general awakening of the working-men in towns, who refuse to remain in the old servile conditions; when all the educated classes enter into an open revolt against the old system; and when important portions of the empire, such as Finland, Poland, and the Caucasus, strive for complete home rule, while other portions, such as Siberia, the Baltic provinces, and Little Russia, and in fact every province, claim autonomy and want to be freed from the St. Petersburg bureaucrats—then it becomes evident that the time has come for a deep, complete revision of all the institutions. Every reasoning observer, everyone who has learned something in his life about the psychology of nations, would conclude that if any concessions are to be made to the new spirit of the time, they must be made with an open mind, in a straightforward way, with a deep sense of responsibility for what is done—not as a concession enforced by the conditions of a given moment, but as a quite conscious reasoned move, dictated by a comprehension of the historical phase which the country is going through.

Unfortunately, nothing of that consciousness and sense of responsibility is seen among those who have been the rulers of Russia during the last twelve months. I have told in my memoirs how certain moderate concessions, if they had been granted towards the end of the reign of Alexander II or at the advent of his son, would have been hailed with enthusiasm and would have paved the way for the gradual and slow passage from absolutism to representative government.[6] Even in 1895, when Nicholas II had become emperor, it was not too late for such concessions. But it was also evident to everyone who was not blinded by that artificial atmosphere of bureaucracy created in

6 See Kropotkin's *Memoirs of a Revolutionist* (Garden City, New York: Doubleday Anchor, 1962), pp. 273-79.—*Editor.*

all capitals, that ten years later—that is, in November last—such halfhearted concessions as a "Consultative Assembly" were already out of the question. The events of the last ten years, with which the readers of this review are familiar—the students' affair of 1901, the rule of Plehve, and so on, to say nothing of the abominable blunders of the [Russo-Japanese] war—had already created too deep a chasm between Russia and Nicholas II. The January massacres widened that chasm still more. Therefore only an open recognition of the right of the nation to frame its own constitution, and a complete *honest* amnesty, granted as a pledge of good faith, could have spared Russia all the bloodshed of the last ten months. Every intelligent statesman would have understood it. But the cynical courtier, Bulygin, whom Nicholas II and his mother considered a statesman, and to whom they had pinned their faith, was not the man to do so. His only policy was to win time, in the hope that something might turn the scales in favor of his masters.

Consequently, vague promises were made in December 1904, and next in March 1905, but in the meantime the most reckless repression was resorted to—not very openly, I must say, but under cover, according to the methods of Plehve's policy. Death sentences were distributed by the dozen during the last summer.[7] The worst forms of police autocracy, which characterized the rule of Plehve, were revived in a form even more exasperating than before, because governors-general assumed now the rights which formerly were vested in the minister of the interior. Thus, to give one instance, the governor-general of Odessa exiled men by the dozen by his own will, including the old ex-dean of the Odessa University, Professor Yaroshenko, whom he ordered (on July 26) to be transported to Vologda! And this went on at a time when all Russia began to take fire, and lived through such a series of events as the uprising of the Musulmans, and the massacres at Baku and Nakhichevan; the uprising at Odessa, during which all the buildings in the port were burned; the

---

7 A number of these are enumerated in *La Tribune Russe*, published in Paris, no. 33, p. 497.

mutiny on the ironclad *Kniaz Potemkin*; the second series of strikes in Poland, again followed by massacres at Lodz, Warsaw, and all other chief industrial centers; a series of uprisings at Riga, culminating in the great street battles of July 28—to say nothing of a regular, uninterrupted succession of minor agrarian revolts. All Russia had thus to be set into open revolt, blood had to run freely in the streets of all the large cities, simply because the tsar did not want to pronounce the word which would put an end to his sham autocracy and to the autocracy of his camarilla. Only towards the end of the summer could he be induced to make some concessions which at last took the shape of a convocation of a state's Duma, announced in the manifesto of August 19.

IV.

General stupefaction and disdain are the only words to express the impression produced by this manifesto. To begin with, it was evident to anyone who knew something of human psychology that no assembly elected to represent the people could be maintained as a merely *consultative* body, with no legislative powers. To impose such a limitation was to create the very conditions for producing the bitterest conflicts between the crown and the nation. To imagine that the Duma, if it ever could come into existence in the form under which it was conceived by the advisers of Nicholas II, would limit itself to the functions of a mere consulting board, that it would express its wishes in the form of mere *advices*, but not in the form of *laws*, and that it would not defend these laws as such, was absurd on the very face of it. Therefore the concession was considered as a mere desire to bluff, to win time. It was received as a new proof of the insincerity of Nicholas II.

But in proportion as the real sense of the Bulygin "Constitution" was discovered, it became more and more evident that such a Duma would never come together; never would the Russians be induced to perform the farce of the Duma elections under the Bulygin system. It appeared that under this system the city of St. Petersburg, with its population of nearly 1,500,000 and its immense wealth, would have only about 7,000 electors, and that large cities having from 200,000 to 700,000 inhabitants would have an electoral body composed of but a couple of thousand, or even a few hundred electors; while the 90,000,000 peasants would be boiled down, after several successive elections, to a few thousand men electing a few deputies. As to the nearly 4,000,000 Russian workingmen, they were totally excluded from any participation in the political life of the country. It was evident that only fanatics of electioneering could be induced to find interest in so senseless a waste of time as an electoral campaign under such conditions. Moreover, as the press continued to be gagged, the state of siege was maintained, and the governors of the different provinces continued to rule as absolute satraps, exiling whom they disliked, public opinion in Russia gradually came to the idea that, whatever some moderate zemstvoists might say in favor of a compromise, the Duma would never come together.

Then it was that the workingmen again threw the weight of their will into the contest and gave quite a new turn to the movement. A strike of bakers broke out at Moscow in October last, and they were joined in their strike by the printers. This was not the work of any revolutionary organization. It was entirely a workingmen's affair, but suddenly what was meant to be a simple demonstration of economic discontent grew up, invaded all trades, spread to St. Petersburg, then all over Russia, and took the character of such an imposing revolutionary demonstration that the autocracy had to capitulate before it.

When the strike of the bakers began, troops were, as a matter of course, called out to suppress it. But this time the Moscow workingmen had had enough of massacres. They offered an armed resistance to the Cossacks. Some three hundred men barricaded themselves in a garret, and a regular fight between the besieged workingmen and the besieging Cossacks followed. The latter took, of course, the upper hand, and butchered the besieged, but then all the Moscow workingmen joined hands with the strikers. A general strike was declared. "Nonsense!

A general strike is impossible!" the fools said, even then. But the workingmen set earnestly to stop all work in the great city, and fully succeeded. In a few days the strike became general. What the workingmen must have suffered during these two or three weeks, when all work was suspended and provisions became extremely scarce, one can easily imagine; but they held out. Moscow had no bread, no meat coming in, no light in the streets. All traffic on the railways had been stopped, and the mountains of provisions which, in the usual course of life, reach the great city every day, were lying rotting along the railway lines. No newspapers except the proclamation of the strike committees appeared. Thousands upon thousands of passengers who had come to that great railway center which Moscow is could not move any further, and were camping at the railway stations. Tons and tons of letters accumulated at the post offices, and had to be stored in special storehouses. But the strike, far from abating, was spreading all over Russia. Once the heart of Russia, Moscow, had struck, all the other towns followed. St. Petersburg soon joined the strike, and the workingmen displayed the most admirable organizing capacities. Then, gradually, the enthusiasm and devotion of the poorest class of society won over the other classes. The shop assistants, the clerks, the teachers, the employees at the banks, the actors, the lawyers, the chemists, even the judges gradually joined the strikers. A whole country had struck against its government, all but the troops; but even from the troops separate officers and soldiers came to take part in the strike meetings, and one saw uniforms in the crowds of peaceful demonstrators who managed to display a wonderful skill in avoiding all conflict with the army.

In a few days the strike had spread over all the main cities of the empire, including Poland and Finland. Moscow had no water, Warsaw no fuel; provisions ran short everywhere; the cities, great and small, remained plunged in complete darkness. No smoking factories, no railways running, no tramways, no stock exchange, no banking, no theaters, no law courts, no schools. In many places the restaurants, too, were closed, the waiters having left, or else the workers compelled the owners to extinguish all lights after seven o'clock. In Finland even the house servants were not allowed to work before seven in the morning or after seven in the evening. All life in the towns had come to a standstill. And what exasperated the rulers most was that the workers offered no opportunity for shooting at them and reestablishing "order" by massacres. A new weapon, more terrible than street warfare, had thus been tested and proved to work admirably.

The panic in the tsar's entourage had reached a high pitch. He himself, in the meantime, was consulting in turn the conservatives (Ignat'ev, Goremykin, Stürmer, Stishinskii), who advised him to concede nothing, and Witte, who represented the liberal opinion. It is said that if he yielded to the advice of the latter, it was only when he saw that the conservatives refused to risk their reputations, and maybe their lives, in order to save the autocracy. He finally signed on October 30, a manifesto in which he declared that his "inflexible will" was

(1) To grant the population the immutable foundations of civic liberty based on real inviolability of the person and freedom of conscience, speech, union, and association.

(2) Without deferring the elections to the state Duma already ordered, to call to participation in the Duma, as far as is possible in view of the shortness of the time before the Duma is to assemble, those classes of the population now completely deprived of electoral rights, leaving the ultimate development of the principle of the electoral right in general to the newly established legislative order of things.

(3) To establish it as an immutable rule that no law can come into force without the approval of the state Duma, and that it shall be possible for the elected of the people to exercise a real participation in the supervision of the legality of the acts of the authorities appointed by us.

On the same day Count Witte was nominated the head of a ministry, which he himself had to form, and the tsar approved by his signature a memorandum of the minister-president in which it was said that "straightforwardness and sincerity in the confirmation of civil liberty," "a tendency towards the abolition of exclusive laws," and "the avoidance of repressive measures in respect to proceedings which do not openly menace society and the state" must be binding for the guidance of the ministry. The government was also "to abstain from any interference in the elections to the Duma," and "not resist its decisions as long as they are not inconsistent with the historic greatness of Russia."

At the same time a general strike had also broken out in Finland. The whole population joined in supporting it with a striking unanimity; and as communication with St. Petersburg was interrupted, the wildest rumors about the revolution in the Russian capital circulated at Helsinki. Pressed by the Finnish population, the governor-general undertook to report to the tsar the absolute necessity for full concessions, and, the tsar agreeing with this demand, a manifesto was immediately issued, by which all repressive measures of the last few years, including the unfortunate manifesto of the year 1899, by which the Finnish Constitution had been violated, were rescinded, the Diet was convoked, and a complete return to the *status quo ante* Bobrikov was promulgated. What a pity for the future development of Russia that on this very same day an identical measure, establishing and convoking a Polish Diet at Warsaw, was not taken! How much bloodshed would have been saved! And how much safer the further development of Russia would have been, if Poland had then known that she would be able to develop her own life according to her own wishes!

V.

Count Witte having been invested on October 30 with wide powers as minister-president, and the further march of events undoubtedly depending to a great extent upon the way in which he will use his extensive authority, the question, "What sort of man is Witte?" is now asked on all sides.

The present prime minister of Russia is often described as the Necker of the Russian revolution; and it must be owned that the resemblance between the two statesmen lies not only in the situations which they occupy with regard to their respective monarchies. Like Necker, Witte is a successful financier, and he is also a "mercantilist": he is an admirer of the great industries, and would like to see Russia a moneymaking country, with its Morgans and Rockefellers making colossal fortunes in Russia itself and in all sorts of Manchurias. But he has also the limited political intelligence of Necker, and his views are not very different from those which the French minister expressed in his work *Pouvoir Exécutif* published in 1792. Witte's ideal is a liberal, half absolute and half constitutional monarchy, of which he, Witte, would be the Bismarck, standing by the side of a weak monarch and sheltered from his whims by a docile middle-class parliament. In that parliament he would even accept a score of labor members—just enough to render inoffensive the most prominent labor agitators and to have the claims of labor expressed in a parliamentary way.

Witte is daring, he is intelligent, and he is possessed of an admirable capacity for work; but he will not be a great statesman because he scoffs at those who believe that in politics, as in everything else, complete honesty is the most successful policy. In the polemics which Herbert Spencer carried on some years ago in favor of "principles" in politics, Witte would have joined, I suppose, his opponents, and I am afraid he secretly worships the "almighty dollar policy" of Cecil Rhodes. In Russia he is thoroughly distrusted. It is very probable that people attribute to him more power over Nicholas II than he has in reality, and do not take sufficiently into account that Witte must continually be afraid of asking too much from his master, from fear that the master will turn his back on him and throw himself at the first opportunity into the hands of his reactionary advisers, whom he certainly understands and likes better than Witte. But Witte, like his French prototype, has retained immensely the worship of bureaucracy and autocratic power, and distrust of the masses. With all his boldness he has not that boldness of doing things thoroughly, which is gained only by holding to certain fundamental principles. He prefers vague promises to definite acts, and therefore Russian society applies to him the saying: *Timeo danaos et dona ferentes.* And if the refusal he has met with on behalf of all prominent liberals to collaborate with him has been

caused by their complete disapproval of the policy which refuses
home rule for Poland, there remains besides the widely spread
suspicion that Witte is capable of going too far in the way of
compromises with the palace party. At any rate, even the
moderate zemstvoists could not agree—we learn now—with his
policy of half measures, both as regards the popular representation, and even such a secondary question as the amnesty. He
refused to accept universal suffrage and to grant a complete
amnesty, upon which the zemstvo delegation was ordered to
insist.

That "straightforwardness and sincerity in the confirmation
of civil liberty" which—the prime minister wrote—had to be
accepted as binding for the guidance of his ministry, surely are
not yet seen. The state of siege not only continues to be maintained
in many parts of Russia, but it has been spread over Poland; and
as to the amnesty, its insincerity is such that it might be envied
by Pobedonostsev. An honest amnesty is never couched in
many words: it is expressed in four or five lines. But Witte's
amnesty is a long document written with an obvious intention of
deceiving the reader as to its real tenor, and therefore it is full of
references to numbers of articles of the code, instead of naming
things by their proper names. Thousands of contests must arise,
Russian lawyers say, out of this muddled document. At any
rate, one thing is evident. Those who were confined at
Schlüsselburg since 1881-1886—immured in secrecy would be
the proper term—and whose barbarous treatment is known to
the readers of this review, will *not* be liberated, according to the
terms of the amnesty. They will have to be exiled as *posselentsy*
("criminal exiles") for another four years to Siberia, probably
to its most unhealthy parts, before they are allowed to enter
Russia! This, after a twenty-four years' cellular confinement, in
absolute secrecy, without any communication whatever with the
outer world! As to those who were driven to desperate action by
the police rule of Plehve, they all must remain for ten to twelve
years more in the Russian bastille of Schlüsselburg; the
amnesty does not apply to them. And as regards the exiles
abroad, they are offered the right to obtain certificates of

admission to Russia from the Russian state police! All over the world, each time that a new departure has been made in general policy, an honest *general* amnesty was granted as a guarantee of good faith. Even that pledge was refused to Russia. And so it is all around. All that has hitherto been done are words, words, and words! And every one of these words can be crossed with a stroke of the pen, just as the promises of a constitution given by the Austrian emperor after the Vienna revolution of March 13, 1848 were cancelled a few months later, and the population of the capital was massacred as soon as its revolutionary spirit cooled down. Is it not the same policy that is coveted at Tsarskoe Selo? Unfortunately, the first step in the way of reaction has already been made by proclaiming the state of siege in Poland.

VI.

The first victory of the Russian nation over autocracy was met with the wildest enthusiasm and jubilation. Crowds, composed of hundreds of thousands of men and women of all classes, all mixed together, and carrying countless red flags, moved about in the streets of the capitals, and the same enthusiasm rapidly spread to the provinces, down to the smallest towns. True that it was not jubilation only; the crowd also expressed three definite demands. For three days after the publication of the manifesto in which autocracy had abdicated its powers, no amnesty manifesto had yet appeared, and on November 3, in St. Petersburg, a crowd a hundred thousand men strong was going to storm the House of Detention, when, at ten in the evening, one of the Workmen's Council of Delegates addressed them, declaring that Witte had just given his word of honor that a general amnesty would be granted that same night. The delegate therefore said: "Spare your blood for graver occasions. At eleven we shall have Witte's reply, and if it is not satisfactory, then tomorrow at six you will all be informed as to how and where to meet in the streets for further action." And the immense crowd— I hold these details from an eyewitness—slowly broke up and dispersed in silence, thus recognizing the new power—the labor delegates—which was born during the strike.

Two other important points, beside amnesty, had also to be cleared up. During the last few months the Cossacks had proved to be the most abominable instrument of reaction, always ready to whip, shoot, or bayonet unarmed crowds, for the mere fun of the sport and with a view to subsequent pillage. Besides, there was no guarantee whatever that at any moment the demonstrators would not be attacked and slaughtered by the troops. The people in the streets demanded therefore the withdrawal of the troops, and especially of the Cossacks, the abolition of the state of siege, and the creation of popular militias which would be placed under the management of the municipalities.

It is known how, first at Odessa and then all over Russia the jubilant crowds began to be attacked by bands, composed chiefly of butcher assistants, and partly of the poorest slum dwellers, sometimes armed, and very often under the leadership of policemen and police officials in plain clothes; how every attempt on behalf of the radical demonstrators to resist such attacks by means of revolver shots immediately provoked volleys of rifle fire from the Cossacks; how peaceful demonstrators were slaughtered by the soldiers after some isolated pistol shot—maybe a police signal—was fired from the crowd; and how finally at Odessa an organized pillage and the slaughter of men, women, and children in some of the poorest Jewish suburbs took place, while the troops fired at the improvised militia of students who tried to prevent the massacres or to put an end to them. In Moscow, the editor of the *Moscow Gazette*, Gringmut, and part of the clergy, stimulated by a pastoral letter of Bishop Nikon, openly preached "to put down the intellectuals by force," and improvised orators spoke from the platform in front of the Iberia Virgin, preaching the killing of the students. The result was that the university was besieged by crowds of the "defenders of order," the students were fired at by the Cossacks, and for several nights in succession isolated students were assailed in the dark by the *Moscow Gazette* men, so that in one night twenty-one were killed or mortally wounded.

An inquest into the origin of these murders is now being made by volunteer lawyers; but this much can already be said. If race hatred has played an important part at Odessa and in other southern towns, no such cause can be alleged at Moscow, Tver (the burning of the house of the zemstvo), Tomsk, Nizhni Novgorod, and a great number of towns having a purely Russian population. And yet outbreaks having the same savage character took place in all these towns and cities at about the same time. An organizing hand is seen in them, and there is no doubt that this is the hand of the Monarchist party. It sent a deputation to Peterhof, headed by Prince Shcherbatov and Count Sheremetev, and after the deputation had been most sympathetically received by Nicholas II, they openly came forward in the *Moscow Gazette* and in the appeals of the bishops Nikon and Nikandr, calling upon their sympathizers to declare an open war on the radicals.

Of course it would be unwise to imagine that autocracy, and the autocratic habits which made a little tsar of every police official in his own sphere, would die out without showing resistance by all means, including murder. The Russian revolution will certainly have its Feuillants and its Muscadins. And this struggle will necessarily be complicated in Russia by race hatred. It has always been the policy of the Russian tsardom to stir national hatred, setting the Finns and the Karelian peasants against the Swedes in Finland, the Letts against the Germans in the Baltic provinces, the Polish peasants (partly Ukranian) against the Polish landlords, the Orthodox Russians against the Jews, the Musulmans against the Armenians, and so on. Then, for the last twenty years it has been a notable feature of the policy of Ignat'ev, and later on of Plehve, to provoke race wars with a view of checking socialist propaganda. And the police in Russia have always taken advantage of all such outbreaks for pilfering and plundering. . . . Consequently, a few hints from above were enough—and several reactionary papers and two bishops went so far as to *openly* give such hints—to provoke the terrible massacres at Odessa and the smaller outbreaks elsewhere.

Such conflicts between the representatives of a dark past and the young forces representing the future will certainly continue for some time before the mighty floods raised by the storm of the revolution will subside. The revolution in England lasted from 1639 to 1655, that of France from 1788 till 1794, and both were followed by an unsettled period of some thirty years' duration. So we cannot expect that the Russian revolution should accomplish its work in a few months only. One extremely important feature has, however, to be noted now. Up to the present moment, "bloodshed has come, not from the revolutionists, but from the defenders of absolutism." It is estimated that more than twenty-five thousand persons have already been killed in Russia since January last. But *all this mass of murders lies on the side of the defenders of autocracy.* The victory over absolutism which compelled it to abdicate was obtained by a strike, unique in the annals of history by its unanimity and the self-abnegation of the workers; but no blood was shed to win this first victory. The same is true of the villages. It may be taken as certain that the landlord ownership of the land *has* already sustained a blow which renders a return to the *status quo ante* in land-ownership *materially impossible.* And this other victory—a very great one, in my opinion—is being obtained again without bloodshed on behalf of the revolting peasants. If blood is shed, it is shed by the troops called in for the defense of the monopoly in land—not by those who endeavor to get rid of it. As to the peasants, they have even pronounced themselves against retaliation.

Another prominent feature of the Russian revolution is the ascendency which labor has taken in it. It is not social democrats, or revolutionary socialists, or anarchists, who take the lead in the present revolution. It is labor—the workingmen. Already during the first general strike, the St. Petersburg workingmen had nominated 132 delegates, who constituted a "Council of the Union of Workingmen," and these delegates had nominated an executive of eight members. Nobody knew their names or their addresses, but their advice was obeyed like orders. In the streets they appeared surrounded by fifty or sixty workingmen, armed, and linked together so as to allow no one to approach a delegate. Now, the workingmen of St. Petersburg have apparently extended their organization, and while their delegates confer with representatives of the revolutionary parties, they nevertheless retain their complete independence. Similar organizations most probably have sprung up at Moscow and elsewhere, and at this moment the workingmen of St. Petersburg are systematically arming themselves in order to resist the absolutist "black gangs." As to the powers of the labor organization, they are best seen from the fact that while the bureaucrat lawyers are still concocting some crooked press law, the workingmen have abolished preventive censorship in St. Petersburg by publishing a short-worded resolution in their clandestine daily, the *Izvestia* of the Council of Labor Delegates. "We declare," they said, "that if the editor of any paper continues to send his sheet to the censor before issuing it, the paper will be confiscated by us in the streets, and the printers will be called out from the printing office (they will be supported by the strike committee). If the paper continues nevertheless to appear, the scabs will be boycotted by us, and the presses will be broken."[8] This is how preliminary censorship has ceased to exist in St. Petersburg. The old laws remain, but *de facto* the daily press is free.

Many years ago the general strike was advocated by the Latin workingmen as a weapon which would be irresistible in the hands of labor for imposing its will. The Russian revolution has demonstrated that they were right. Moreover, there is not the slightest doubt that if the general strike has been capable of forcing the centuries-old institution of autocracy to capitulate, it will be capable also of imposing the will of the laborers upon capital; and that the workingmen, with the common sense of which they have given such striking proof, will find also the means of solving the labor problem, so as to make industry the means not of personal enrichment but of satisfying the needs of the community. That the Russian revolution will not limit itself to a mere reform of political institutions, but like the revolution of 1848, will make an attempt at least, to solve the social problem, has always been my opinion. Half a century of socialist evolution

8 I take this resolution, slightly condensing it, from the *Russ* of November 4—the day when the first free papers appeared openly at St. Petersburg.

in Europe cannot remain without influence upon the coming events. And the dominant position taken by labor in the present crisis seems to yield support to that foresight. How far the social change will go, and what concrete forms it will take, I would not undertake to predict without being on the spot, in the midst of the workers; but steps in that direction are sure to be made.

To say that Russia has begun her great revolution is no longer a metaphor or a prophecy; it is a fact. And one is amazed to discover how history repeats itself: not in the events, of course, but in the psychology of the opposed forces. The governing class, at any rate, has learned nothing. They remain incapable of understanding the real significance of events which are screened from their eyes by the artificiality of their surroundings. Where a timely yielding, a frank, open-minded recognition of the necessity of new forms of life would have spared the country torrents of blood, they make concessions at the last moment, always in a halfhearted way, and always with the secret intention of soon returning to the old forms. Why have they massacred at least twenty-five thousand men during these ten months, when they had to recognize in October what they refused to recognize last December?

Why do they continue repression and provoke new massacres, when "they will have to recognize in a few months hence universal suffrage as the basis of representative government in Russia, and the legislative autonomy of Poland as the best, the only possible means for keeping the two countries, Russia and Poland, firmly linked together," just as they were compelled, after having set all the country on fire, to recognize that the honest recognition of Finland's autonomy was the only means of maintaining her bonds with Russia? But no, they will not recognize what is evident to everyone as soon as he frees himself from the fools' paradise atmosphere of the St. Petersburg bureaucracy. They will stir up the bitterest civil wars.

Happily enough, there is a more hopeful side to the Russian revolution. The two forces which hitherto have played the leading part in the revolution—namely, the workingmen in the towns, fraternizing with the younger "intellectuals," and the peasants in the countryside—have displayed such a wonderful unanimity of action, even where it was not concerted beforehand, and such a reluctance for useless bloodshed, that we may be sure of their ultimate victory. The troops have already been deeply impressed by the unanimity, the self-sacrifice, and the consciousness of their rights displayed by the workmen in their strikes; and now that the St. Petersburg workmen have begun to approach in a spirit of straightforward propaganda those who were enrolled in the "black gangs," that other support of autocracy will probably soon be dissolved as well. The main danger lies now in that the statesmen, enamored of "order" and instigated by timorous landlords, might resort to massacres for repressing the peasant rebellions, in which case retaliation would follow to an extent and with consequences which nobody could foretell.

The first year of the Russian revolution has already proved that there is in the Russian people that unity of thought without which no serious change in the political organization of the country would have been possible, and that capacity for united action which is the necessary condition of success. One may already be sure that the present movement will be victorious. The years of disturbance will pass, and Russia will come out of them a new nation; a nation owning an unfathomed wealth of natural resources and capable of utilizing them; ready to seek the ways for utilizing them in the best interest of all; a nation averse to bloodshed, averse to war, and ready to march towards the higher goals of progress. One of her worst inheritances from a dark past, autocracy, lies already mortally wounded, and will not revive; and other victories will follow.

Letters

In the spring of 1902, Kropotkin sent the following letter to Max Nettlau, the distinguished historian of anarchism. The letter was provoked by a published letter of Nettlau's which appeared in 1900 in a London anarchist paper, and, more immediately, by a résumé of a manuscript composed in 1901 which Nettlau mailed to Kropotkin for comments. The aspects of Nettlau's views which Kropotkin chose to criticize reflect the complexity and diversity of anarchist ideology at the turn of the century.

Nettlau's résumé seems to have been lost, but his position is clearly stated in the earlier letter, anonymously published in *Freedom* (September-October 1900, pp. 42-43). Responding to an open appeal from several anarchists that the movement should attempt to reorganize itself, Nettlau argued for "collective action which corresponds to our present ideas of individual liberty." He proposed that the anarchist movement broaden its scope in order to appeal to a wider sector of the population and thereby increase its strength. He saw no value in the tendency toward exclusive party organization on doctrinal grounds. His suggestions were: (1) that the idea of freedom be stressed over economic questions, (2) that anarchists seek to attract people in society who were not anarchists strictly speaking but who shared similar notions about liberty, atheism, antistatism, and voluntary association, and (3) that anarchists should increase their publications and reevaluate their local propaganda in order to embrace the problems of the new generation. Such efforts, he believed, would lift the movement out of its impasse and move it to the forefront of the revolutionary struggle.

Kropotkin's response centered on the problem of the composition of the movement. He tried to show that a blind expansion of the anarchist ranks with youthful individual rebels would not necessarily strengthen the movement but, on the contrary, might weaken it. His fears were based on the Nietzschean vogue then attracting youth which was of no value to anarchism. Rather than looking for the proper individualism among intellectuals, who were too frequently concerned ultimately with destructive egoism and bourgeois hedonism, Kropotkin argued for increased emphasis on the masses. He reiterated his cherished faith in the necessity of a working-class-motivated revolutionary constituency. Anarchists should be guided by working-class ethics and should try to awaken the solidarity of the lower classes in general. The sincerely dedicated youth would offer his services to the cause of his own accord; the others ought to be left to remain within the framework of the old order to which they were so attached.

This translation, by Pauline Baggio, has been taken from "Une lettre inédite de Pierre Kropotkine à Max Nettlau," edited by Derry Novak, *International Review of Social History*, vol. 9, pt. 2 (1964), pp. 268-285. The letter was first published in *Golos Truda* (Buenos Aires), nos. 260-263 (1926).

Letter
to
Nettlau

Viola, Bromley, Kent
March 5, 1902

My dear friend,

I read your letter with a great deal of personal and general interest, and I would like to be able to answer it at length, as well as to discuss one of its essential points, individualism. Maybe someday I will write a few articles on individualism. At any rate, I will try to answer you now without entering into lengthy details.

I will start with the central point of your letter, in which you ask why youth is not the same now as it was in 1890-94. According to you, "it is because at the time, we were affected by the libertarian movement in art and literature . . ." and so forth.

Well, we still are. The only difference is that it is they who no longer want us, and that, after having given us several comrades, they are now what they have always been, Epicurians and very bourgeois individualists who evidently find in Nietzsche (as their predecessors found in Darwin) ideas which suit them better or possibly offer them more justification than anarchy.

In my opinion, the 1890-94 movement can be explained in this manner: with the Boulangist agitation[1] creating an alarming atmosphere, the young working class believed that a few heroic and devoted persons would be sufficient to provoke the revolution. Some serious and learned members of the bourgeoisie thought the same thing. Since then we have realized that this was an illusion, and have been forced, in France as elsewhere, to join the slow process of organization and preparatory propaganda among the working classes. This is the point where we are now.

As for the French bourgeois youth, it has always liked bold and striking affirmations, particularly between the ages of nineteen and thirty. The negativism, the "nihilism" of anarchy enticed them. On the other hand, they were impressed by the devotion and the self-sacrificing spirit of the young working class. And finally, a movement similar to that of the nihilism of Bazarov[2] is flourishing in France, a movement concerned with mores (*moeurs*), a *Kulturbewegung*, whose object is to reject conventional lies. It has happened, with this difference: in Russia, the nihilist movement (1859-69) was followed by the populist movement, *v narod* ("to the people"), whereas in France, nothing like this occurred. This is why the revolutionary movement has not gained anything directly from it. Where are the Mirabeaus? Where are the authors of dithyrambs to Ravachol? Who came forward to work for the revolutionary cause? Has this young generation produced a single person who could relieve the old one? *Nihil.*

The youth of today is Nietzschean because, as you so aptly put it, Nietzscheanism is a "spurious" individualism. It is a bourgeois individualism which cannot exist unless the masses are oppressed and—note this well—without lackeyism, servility towards tradition and the *obliteration of the individualism* of the oppressor, as well as in the oppressed masses. The "beautiful

---

1 Antirepublican followers of General Georges Boulanger (1837-91).—*Editor.*

2 A reference to the nihilistic philosophy of Bazarov, the central character in Turgenev's *Fathers and Sons.—Editor.*

blond beast" is, after all, a *slave*, a slave to the king, to the priest, to law and tradition, another possession of the exploiting clique, without individuality.

It is not because we became *trade unionists* that youth has left us. Attracted by the picturesque, they lost interest as soon as the picturesque and the dramatic became less forceful and they had to apply themselves to pedestrian tasks. "I came to you because I thought the revolution was near at hand, but I see now that a long period of educational work is needed." How often have I heard this said in the last twenty-five years!!! They enjoyed the flamboyance of Ravachol, of Vaillant, of Pauwels, and as soon as they realized that they were being asked to prove their thirst for *liberty* with sacrifices, they returned to their petty concerns. I am not demanding individual acts of revolt from them; Epicurians would be incapable of that. But when it comes to defending the cause of the oppressed (remember the last plea of Grave), the libertarian school, the small daily efforts of propaganda, where are they? We must find more workers! Do you know of a movement, a call to arms that produced fewer leaders than the aforesaid movement?

Why? Because a narrow and selfish individualism such as that offered from Mandeville (*Fable of the Bees*) to Nietzsche and the young French anarchists, *cannot inspire anyone.* It does not offer anything great and inspiring.

I will go still further—and this seems to me of the greatest importance (a new philosophy to be developed): what has been called "individualism" up to now has been only a foolish egoism which belittles the individual. Foolish because it was not individualism at all. It did not lead to what was established as a goal; that is the complete, broad, and most perfectly attainable development of individuality. It seems to me that nobody except Ibsen has been able to reach the conception of true individualism; and even he, having foreseen it by an inspiration of genius, did not succeed in expressing it in a comprehensible way. All the same, there is in Ibsen a certain vision of future individualism, which I foresee, and which will be the superior affirmation of individuality. This will be as different from misanthropic bourgeois individualism as from Christian communism and equally hostile to both since they are impediments to the full development of individuality.

I think that the individualism which will become the ideal of philosophy in the near future will not lead anyone to appropriate to himself more than the part which is due him from the common patrimony of production (the only one that the bourgeoisie has understood). Individualism will not consist in the creation throughout the world of a mass of slaves serving the chosen nation (*individualismus* or *pro sibi Darwinianum* or rather *Huxleianum*). Nor will it be a sensual type of individualism and the "liberation from the notion of good and evil" that a few French anarchists have preached—vague reminders of our fathers, the "aesthetes," the "lovers of beauty," the Byronic and Don Juan-like poets who preached it as well. It will not consist either in the oppression of one's neighbor (*individualismus Nietzscheanum*) which reduces the "beautiful blond beast" to the level of an animal in a herd. It will consist, rather, in a sort of *individualismus* or *personalismus* or *pro sibi communisticum*, which I see coming and which I would try to define well if I had the necessary time.

That which has been represented as individualism so far has been pathetic and skimpy—and what is worse, contains in itself the negation of its goal, the impoverishment of individuality, or in any case the denial of what is necessary for obtaining the most complete flowering of the individual. We saw kings who were rich and filled their paunches and we immediately represented individualism as the tendency to become a king, surrounded by slaves like a king, pampered by women like a king (and what women! who would want them?), eating nightingales' tongue (cold and always served with the same sauce!) on gold or silver plates like a king! And yet, is there anything in the world more typically bourgeois than a king! And, worse still, more *enslaved* than a king!

Nietzsche's "blond beast" makes me laugh. Yet, due to a warped representation established in literature during the era (1820–1830) when these people, the aesthetes, wanted you

to believe that they represented a superior type of humanity—
we still continue to believe naïvely that these people who only
asked to be left to their excessive pleasures ("All pleasures
are mine!" goes the tune from Gounod's *Faust*) represented a
superior development of individuality, a progress, a desideratum
—the pearls of the human race!

Up to now, these so-called advocates of individualism have
had as opponents only Christian preachers who proclaimed
the annihilation of the personality. Fate has dealt them a
good hand. In undermining Christianity, Nietzsche, next to
Fourier, is unequalled. The same thing happens when one
contrasts the *altruist* and *egoist*. It is easy for the latter to prove
that the altruist is also guided by egoism—while the stupid
egoist is incapable of understanding his own interest and is like
the Zulu king who thought he was "asserting his personality"
while eating a quarter of a steer a day. The stupid egoist should
be contrasted (as was done by Chernyshevskii) with the *perfect
egoist*—the "thinking realist" of Pisarev who became capable
of infinitely more social good than the staunchest of the Christian
or Comtian altruists. One should say and know at the same
time that he is guided only by egoism.

With these few brief remarks, you can probably understand
what I mean by *personalismus* or *pro sibi communisticum*: the
individuality which attains the greatest individual development
possible through practicing the highest communist sociability
in what concerns both its primordial needs and its relationships
with others in general. The bourgeoisie has asserted that the
flowering of the personality demands slaves and the sacrifice
of others (not himself, etc. . . .) and the result of this was the
weakening of individuality which characterizes modern bourgeois society. Is that individualism?!! Oh, wouldn't Goethe's
"individuality" have put it to shame! But let us consider the
same Goethe with his strong personality. If he had had a share
in work with others, would he have balked at it? No. He would
have been a delight to his co-workers; he would have brought
with him so much enthusiasm, gaiety, zest, and a sociable and
communist spirit. And at the same time, he would have lost none

of his great personal poetry or philosophy: he would even have gained from it the enjoyment of ordinary things in a communal *work*, while learning about a new aspect of the human genius (consider his joy in discovering mutual reliance!). His whole being and personality having developed in this new direction (since nothing human was unfamiliar to him), another aspect would have been added to his genius. In the communal life in Russia, I knew people who, while remaining what the Russians call *mirskoi chelovek* (a communal man) in the fullest sense, were also individual *personalities* breaking with all the narrowness of their village and continuing alone, isolated on *their* way—whether that involved an individual political revolt or a personal moral revolt or a revolt against religion. . . .

This is why I find the individualism of which the young French anarchists spoke to us for a while petty and false, *because it fails to achieve its chosen goal*. This sounds all the more false to me when I consider that there are men who, at this very moment, consciously march to the gallows for the common cause, after having strongly affirmed their own personalities. It is only because the concept of individualism is so poorly understood that others, calling themselves individualists, believed that they belonged to the same intellectual and political group as these heroes. Those who called themselves "individualists" (in the bourgeois sense) have as little right to claim them for "their own" as the [early] Christians would have had. They belong to a type of man who I see coming and who Ibsen has tried to create in his plays.

This letter is getting so long that I must skip over some very important points brought up in your letter. As I said before, if the movement has slowed down in France, it is because the general situation is not as revolutionary as it was before 1894-95, and we have realized that one cannot *begin* a revolution with a handful of people. It was foolish to imagine that the strong effort of a few could succeed in inciting the revolution: things did not happen that way, and it was necessary to organize the *preparatory* movement which precedes all revolutions. It was necessary, in addition, to have an ideal for the revolution. Could *bourgeois individualism have been the one?* No! And as for *anarchist communism, was it strong enough,* not among the millions, but more especially *among the anarchists themselves?* No! (Force only comes from practical experience in life). As in this preparatory movement that we have been engaged in for five or six years, the absence of debate on such matters as the Boulangist and Dreyfus questions will force us to start this work again (but only for a few years).

If only we could explain our idea, as you say, during this lull! But we are faced with a problem that has not existed until now: *the ethic of a society of equals, who are completely free.* Christian ethics only had to copy the Buddhist ethic, the one of Lao-tse, and so forth, diluting it and minimizing it. We have to create the *new* ethic of the socialist society of the future. *The anarchist working class is creating this ethic.* Their work involves a thousand aspects. The general idea is taking shape. But whether we lack a *great mind* or whether that work is still too unfinished is difficult to distinguish. Yes, we have to follow the path, not only of the few "individualists" of 1890, but also of the ancient Greeks. We still have a long way to go, as you see.

As for your comments on the past and present role of the workers, I won't take too seriously the point you made about exaggeration—an inevitable exaggeration in brevity. I only fear that even in granting much importance to this inevitable exaggeration, there remains a substratum on which it will be difficult for us to agree. You pointed out the lack of solidarity among workers. Fine. And then? As far as I am concerned— and I think the same is true for thousands of anarchists and a hundred thousand socialists—I did not need to overrate the qualities of the workers in order to espouse the cause of the social, predominantly workers' revolution. But it was in order to forge solidarity gradually among various trades, and later among nations, to expand the notion of solidarity, to enable you to expand it today as you did before, that the International was founded. It is precisely to awaken this solidarity—without which progress would be difficult—that we must work to insure that the syndicates and the trade unions not be pushed aside by the bourgeois who, after having failed as moderates, are trying to reach power through more radical ways.

My purpose is not to determine "which is better—the bourgeois or the worker?" It does not interest me any more than the question of determining "which is better—man or woman?" — a question which fascinated the heroes in a Russian short story in a very amusing way. All I know is that the worker at least is accustomed to doing a certain amount of unpleasant work—*real work*, not only amusement—which is an important point for the future. In addition, the worker is used to manual labor; in his dreams of the future he does not seek a place among the governing class, as the social democrats do. Being exploited today at the bottom of the social ladder, it is to his advantage to demand equality. He has never ceased demanding it, he has fought for it and will fight again for it again, whereas the bourgeois, greedy and stupid, thinks it is to his advantage to maintain inequality. The *bourgeois* creates his politics and science, and forges his power with this interest in mind. And each time that we fought for equality, the bourgeois was for inequality for the right to govern, while the working class was on the other side. No amount of reasoning or statistics will do anything to change this, and as I already told you in my last letter, it was again *the people, the worker* who fought in the last skirmish that you were able to cite (1871); and I see no reason for it to be any different the next time than it was in 1871 in Milan, in Barcelona, in Trieste—everywhere!

As for the tolerance you mention, I can only repeat that in my opinion, the side which is in the right has exercised too much tolerance. I support aggressiveness and I think that preaching *passivity*, as Christianity did and as you seem to desire (but I remember in time the correction made about the exaggeration inevitable in any short letter), is an impediment to progress. Yes, there are in present society survivals of cannibalism, the savage period of the Stone Age, the Bronze Age, the abominations of the oriental despots—absolutely everything since the beginning of history. You will see a beautiful example of these survivals if you come to England in June: Huxley's kneeling before the queen to receive the investiture of the Grand Cross was already quite a sight to see. But we are going to see some even more spectacular ones around Edward VII, with this revival of the most savage and cannibalistic periods. Who knows? Should I see all that with a condescending eye? No, dear friend, eclecticism is death, the worst death, the death of the intellect.

Your understanding of revolution seems to me *absolutely* wrong. You probably speak *with* the historians when you say: "Then in the aftermath of the overthrow of the government in Russia, the peasants will burn the estates, and so forth." But I think I have shown that this conception is *completely erroneous*.

If the manors had not been burned starting in May 1789, the Bastille would not have been taken in July, nor would there have been a night like the fourth of August. And saying this, I have the advantage of Taine's opinion, and Taine was the only person (except maybe Kareev, who is of the same opinion) who has studied the movements *preceding* the revolution of July 14. "I know of three hundred outbreaks before July 14," wrote Taine, who necessarily knows of only a few since most of the "feudal documents" have been burned. The jacquerie, begun in 1788 and lasting until 1793 (that is, the six jacqueries mentioned by Taine), was the basis on which the revolution developed and *without which there would have been no revolution*.

Individuals?! Do you think that Bakunin was not equal to Danton and that Guillaume was worth less than Robespierre? It is only because they lacked the foundations of a jacquerie of the peasants and workers in all the large cities of the northeast, east, and southeast that they did not become great historical figures like their predecessors.

Your conception of the Commune is also absolutely contrary to everything I have heard said by the communards. On March 18, they had all of Paris. Between the elections—let us say between April 1 and May 21, the day of the coming of the troops of Versailles—the number of the defenders of the Commune decreased and never did the Commune have *more than ten thousand men in April and May to defend Paris.* (I questioned Lefrançais and Pindy, etc. on this particular point and they were very positive about it.) On May 21, when the people heard the news of the coming of the armies of Versailles, they rose up with a word from Delescluze. "Enough courtiers!" etc. And since at least 35,000 were slaughtered, there must have been a minimum of 50,000 men on the barricades.

All revolutions, everywhere, always, those in deed and those involving intellectual ideas, are made by minorities. But where do these minorities come from? Who initiates the first skirmish in the streets? Certainly not the bourgeois! Always the working class—the same holds true for Barcelona.

This might lead to misunderstanding.[3] Here is my idea: *outbreaks* always come from the oppressed class, from the people. There comes a moment when the discontent of the people (ready to become active) corresponds to the discontent of the "intelligentsia," of the bourgeoisie (never ready to become active). Then there is revolution.

The jacqueries, the peasants' war, Stenka Razin, Pugachev, also Milan, Trieste, Lyon in 1830, and so forth—those were the great insurrections. All these incidents added to the force of the discontented bourgeoisie—not to mention the revolution of 1789.

This is natural. I thought it was taken for granted by every socialist and every anarchist. You make me think that I should write everything down.

Going on to another subject, I see no reason for your pessimism. Revolution, like industrialism, has been moving since 1648 from the west to the east: England, France . . . It is Germany's turn now, as it approaches its 1848, just as Russia is approaching its 1789 (a little more advanced). In the meantime, England and France profit from the fruits of revolutions in the countries that lag behind them in making revolutions, so as to make progress of their own.

---

3 Kropotkin later added the following two paragraphs in the margin.—*Editor*.

Besides, a new factor must be considered in the nineteenth century: progress in transportation, which encourages world trade, thriving domestic trade (in America, in France, in Russia), and the conquest of millions of slaves in Africa and the Far East.

In addition, the defeat of France and the proximity of Metz to Paris has made France militaristic. All this prevents revolution.

I know that the period we are going through in England invites pessimism. But do you know that our sadness, our pessimism due to the failure of England is only the result of our ignorance? Elisée [Reclus] must see in modern England only what he had seen a long time ago when he predicted England's death like Spain's death. Out of ignorance, I protested when he mentioned it to me one day in 1881. But that was due to my ignorance. When has England had a less abominable attitude toward her foreign policy than at present? The Ionian Isles (Gladstone) and Pretoria (the same Gladstone) are the only exceptions.[4] Pitt paid Russia, Prussia, and Austria to fight Napoleon and supported the bombardment of Copenhagen and Alexandria. England paid for Poland's insurrection and for Turkey's fight with Russia, and let both be crushed, and so forth. Among Pitt, Palmerston, Disraeli and Chamberlain—in what way is the fourth worse than the other three? In what way has there been any decline? [Kropotkin adds in a note: "And don't forget the rise of the stock market, like in sixteenth century Genoa, in Venice, in Rome and in Carthage!"]

England *must* perish, unless she accomplishes "the revolution of the communes," which would mean the disintegration of the state; and she must take the initiative (or follow France) in repeating the revolution of the seventeenth century.

As for America—go and see it; it is worth the effort, and I think you will change your ideas completely. "America—land of the dollar" is as false an assertion as saying that the

---

4 On these two occasions, England abandoned territories which she had occupied or annexed earlier.—*Editor.*

Pont Neuf is the oldest bridge in Paris. Elie Reclus once told me: "If everyone says that something is one way you can be certain in advance that it is completely incorrect!" Land of the dollar? It is more like a land of cranks. And the cranks are you and me—all of us, the rebels. They buy libraries and paintings, but they need a *few* models for their art, which, although young, is already so developed in sculpture and architecture. Here is my opinion: from among a hundred men taken at random in Europe, you will not find as many enthusiasts, ready to set forth on untraveled paths, as in America. The dollar is nowhere given so little importance: it is won or it is lost. In England, one values and worships the pound, but definitely not in America. That is America. *Any village in Oregon is better than the smallest hamlet in Germany.*

But, coming back to the subject of your letter, you say that the method changed in 1894? Is it really true?

The *tone* is definitely calmer than it was then—just as the tone in the years 1884–90 was calmer than it had been in 1881–82. It is one of those fluctuations which accompany any development. We will find this tone again, heightened (but already more profound and thorough), as soon as we enter a more tormented period. I really don't see any change.

I myself have always been a communist. From the *Jura Bulletin* to *La Révolte*, I have always preached active participation in the workers' movement, in the *revolutionary workers' movement*. Recently, I made a collection of *La Révolte*. And in each issue, I found one and often two of my articles dealing with the revolutionary workers' movement. From *La Révolte*, at least one cannot say that we have changed. Are you referring to Pouget, who wrote *La Voix du Peuple* instead of *Peinard*?[5] So, he is perfectly right when, after having worked on the *elaboration of the idea*, he works on *diffusing* it, on instilling anarchist and revolutionary ideas in the milieu which, alone, will take arms and make the revolution. As for the young people who

---

5 Pouget in April 1900 stopped publishing *Pére Peinard*, an anarchist weekly in Parisian slang; from December 1900, he collaborated on *La Voix du Peuple*. —*Editor*.

have written articles which are sometimes very anarchistic (while remaining out of touch with reality), some continue to help us in newspapers and schools; others I suppose, will soon offer their services in order to attain the "perfect" development of their individuality. To these people—bon voyage!

We ought to aim never to make any concession to the bourgeois and authoritarian principle. But to pretend that anyone at all can remain a prouder libertarian by limiting himself to writing on or speaking of individualist anarchy, than by taking part in the syndicalist movement, is, my dear friend, simply an aberration. For the worker who *must sell* his labor, it is impossible to remain *free*, and it is precisely because it is impossible that we are anarchists and communists. Nietzsche was able to remain very free—and yet!—what if he had had serfs to keep him alive and what if he had profited from their work to live. Furthermore, precisely for this reason, he did not understand anything about the economic workers' revolt. The great Nietzsche, for he was great in a certain revolt, remained a *slave* to bourgeois prejudice. What a terrible irony! As for the bourgeois who claims to be free and to keep his full independence while he sells his mind, his brush, or his pen to other bourgeois, he ends up one day by selling himself body and soul to Rhodes or to Waldeck [-Rousseau], and while he is writing touching articles on Ravachol and the right of theft, he *is* already more of a slave (in mind and in deed) that the cooper of Barcelona enlisted in the organization which signs itself *Salud y Anarquia* and numbers a hundred thousand workers.

Your utopia is very fine. We might pass through such a similar period. But *to get there, we will need a revolution*, just as the Anabaptist and Lutheran revolutions of the sixteenth century, the Cromwellian revolution of 1648 and the beginnings of the French Revolution were necessary preludes to the tolerance which prevailed at the time of the encyclopedists. I think that your principal error is in attributing the gains which were really conquered by the force of the popular revolution to an evolution created by an elite. At least *a hundred thousand Anabaptists were decapitated* in Holland and northern Germany (the number is given by *recent* historians of the Reformation), almost a hundred thousand peasants were killed in the uprising in 1515—that is far from an evolution made by the elite! That they profited from what the peasant and workers' movement had won, that they had the intelligence to force Europe to make the next step, is true beyond question. But in order to get there, the rising of the masses was necessary. Without that, the elites would have been thrown into jail.

Yes, to get to your idyll, *the revolution is still necessary*—and the question is to know what will facilitate its preparation. That is the whole question, and you will agree that Barcelona, Trieste, and Milan are preparing its way: they are giving it the element which was missing in 1890-94—the people.

That is why I find your comparison of the unionist anarchist movement with the social democratic movement very unfair. Obviously, the Spanish movement or the French syndicalist movement represents a limitation of the ideal, not theoretically, but insofar as it was embodied in certain men at a certain time. Clearly every realization in actuality does not live up to the ideal from which it derives its origin (this letter, for example, does not live up to the ideal that made me write it). But there the resemblance ends. One of these two movements is, in theory and in practice, in favor of tradition, the opposite of revolutionary. The one seeks to accelerate the course of events, the other to stop them!

Given our ideal, we should aim to stamp all that we do with the mark of this ideal: we must be inspired by it. Without this, we can no more reproach the movement in Barcelona than we can criticize all the activities of 1890-94, including the publication of individualist articles in newspapers, or even individual acts. (That is, although it didn't inspire in me the ideal expressed in the beginning of this letter, the individualism which was preached at that time, due to a series of misunderstandings, was not sufficiently differentiated from the pseudoindividualism of the bourgeoisie which leads to the weakening of the individual).

As for Tolstoy, if he had not been a *Christian* while at the same time being a communist and an anarchist he would not have had any more success than the anarchists—not to mention his great talent which permitted the acceptance of ideas coming from him (for example, the negation of justice) which could never be accepted from us.

But enough! I have to end this letter and I will do so abruptly. Tomorrow I have to start working and will not be able to write to you.

Best wishes from all of us.

Peter

The following letter was published in *Freedom*, October 1914, pp. 76–77, shortly after the outbreak of World War I. Gustav Steffen, a Swedish professor, had asked for Kropotkin's opinion on the war, and the anarchist leader replied with this open letter. Aside from providing one of the clearest formulations of Kropotkin's controversial war position, this letter was for many anarchists the first evidence of his dramatic ideological shift to supporting the Allied cause. His position forced all anarchists to take sides and consequently split the movement. Reprinted by permission of Freedom Press.

Letter
to
Steffen

Dear Steffen,

You ask my opinion about the war. I have expressed it on several occasions in France, and the present events, unfortunately, only reinforced it.

I consider that the duty of everyone who cherishes the ideals of human progress altogether, and especially those that were inscribed by the European proletarians on the banner of the International Workingmen's Association, is to do everything in one's power, according to one's capacities, to crush down the invasion of the Germans into Western Europe.

The cause of this war was *not* Russia's attitude toward the Austrian ultimatum, as the German government, true to Bismarck's traditions, has tried to represent it. *As early as July 19* it was known among the West European continental statesmen that the German government had definitely made up its mind to declare war. The Austrian ultimatum was the *consequence*, not the cause of that decision. We thus had a repetition of Bismarck's well-known trick of 1870.[1]

---

1 I mean the falsified "Ems telegram" which he published to make people believe it was the French who were the cause of the war. Later on, he himself boasted of that trick.

The cause of the present war lies in *the consequences of the war of 1870–71*. These consequences had already been foreseen in 1871 by Liebknecht and Bebel, when they protested against the annexation of Alsace and parts of Lorraine to the German empire, for which protest they went to prison for two years. They foresaw that this annexation would be the cause of new wars, the growth of Prussian militarism, the militarization of all Europe, and the arrest of all social progress. The same was foreseen by Bakunin,[2] by Garibaldi, who came with his volunteers to fight for France as soon as the republic was proclaimed, and, in fact, by all the representatives of advanced thought in Europe.

We, who have worked in the different fractions, social democratic and anarchist, of the great socialist movement in Europe, know perfectly well how the menace of a German invasion paralyzed all advanced movements in Belgium, France, and Switzerland, as the workers knew that the moment an internal struggle would begin in these countries, German invasion would immediately follow. *Belgium had been warned of that.* France knew it perfectly well without warning.

The French knew that Metz, of which the Germans had made *not* a fortress for the defense of the territory they had appropriated but *a fortified camp for aggressive purposes*, was within less than ten days' march from Paris, and that on the day of a declaration of war (or even before that day) an army of 250,000 men could march out of Metz against Paris, with all its artillery and train.

Under such conditions a country cannot be free, and France was not free in her development, just as Warsaw is not free under the guns of the Russian citadel and the surrounding fortresses, and Belgrade was not free under the Austrian guns of Zemlin.

Since 1871 Germany had become a standing menace to European progress. All countries were compelled to introduce obligatory military service on the lines it had been introduced

2 In his "Lettres à un Français" and "L'Empire Knouto-Germanique et la Révolution Sociale."

in Germany, and to keep immense standing armies. All were living under the menace of a sudden invasion.

More than that, for Eastern Europe, and especially for Russia, Germany was the chief support and protection of reaction. Prussian militarism, the mock institution of popular representation offered by the German Reichstag and the feudal Landtags of the separate portions of the German empire, and the ill-treatment of the subdued nationalities in Alsace, and especially in Prussian Poland, where the Poles were treated lately as badly as in Russia (without protest from the advanced political parties), these fruits of German imperialism were the lessons that modern Germany, the Germany of Bismarck, taught her neighbors and, above all, Russian absolutism. Would absolutism have maintained itself so long in Russia, and would that absolutism ever have dared to ill-treat Poland and Finland as it has ill-treated them, if it could not produce the example of "cultured Germany," and if it were not sure of Germany's protection?

Let us not be so forgetful of history as to forget the intimacy that existed between Alexander II and Wilhelm I, the common hatred they displayed for France on account of her efforts to free Italy, and their opposition to the Italians themselves when in 1860 they sent away the Austrian rulers of Florence, Parma, and Modena; and Florence became the capital of Italy. Let us not forget the reactionary advices which Wilhelm I gave to Alexander III in 1881, and the support his son gave to Nicholas II in 1905. Let us not forget either that if France granted the loan of 1906 to the Russian autocracy, it was because she saw that unless Russia succeeded in reforming her armies after the Manchurian defeat, she would be doomed to be torn to pieces by Germany, Italy, and Austria leagued against her. The events of the last few weeks have proved already how well-founded were these apprehensions.

The last forty-three years were a confirmation of what Bakunin wrote in 1871, namely, that if French influence disappeared from Europe, Europe would be thrown back in her development for half a century. And now it is self-evident that if the present invasion of Belgium and France is not beaten back by the common effort of all nations of Europe, we shall have another half century or more of general reaction.

During the last forty years, a Franco-German war was always hanging over Europe. Bismarck was not satisfied with the crushing defeat inflicted upon France. He found that she was recovering too rapidly from her wounds. He regretted not having annexed the province of Champagne, and not having taken an indemnity of fifteen billion francs instead of five billion. On three different occasions Alexander II and Alexander III had to interfere in order to prevent the German imperialists from assailing France once more. And the moment they began to feel themselves strong as a sea power, the Germans took it into their heads to destroy the maritime power of Britain, to take a strong footing on the southern shores of the Channel, and to menace England with an invasion. The German "reptile press" is saying now that by sending their wild hordes to sack and burn the cities of Belgium and France they are fighting Russia; but I hope there is nobody stupid enough to believe this absurdity. They conquer Belgium and France, and they fight England.

Their purpose is to force Holland to become part of the German empire, so that the passages leading from the Indian Ocean into the Pacific, which are now held by the Dutch, should pass into German hands; to take possession of Antwerp and Calais; to annex the eastern portion of Belgium, as well as the French province of Champagne, so as to be within a couple of days only from the capital of France. This has been the dream of the German "Kaiserists" since the times of Bismarck, long before there was a *rapprochement* between France and Russia, and this remains their dream.

It was not to fight Russia that Germany in 1886 laid her hands upon Denmark and annexed the province of Schleswig-Holstein. It was not against Russia, but against France and England, that Germany has built her enormous navy, that she dug and fortified the Kiel Canal, and established the military seaport of Wilhelmshafen, where an invasion of England or a raid upon Brest and Cherbourg can be prepared in full security and secrecy. The tale of fighting Russia on the plains of France and Belgium, which is now repeated by the German press, has been concocted for export to Sweden and the United States; but there is not a single intelligent man in Germany itself who does not know that the foes who were aimed at lately were Britain and France. The Germans themselves made no secret of it in their conversations and their works on the coming war.

The decision of declaring the present war was taken in Germany, as soon as the works on the enlargement and the fortification of the Kiel Canal had been terminated in a great hurry this summer, on June 20. But the war nearly broke out in June 1911 —we knew it well here. It would have broken out last summer, if Germany had been ready. Last February, the coming of the present war was so evident that, being at Bordighera, I told my French friends that it was foolish of them to oppose the three years' military law while Germany was busily preparing for war; and I advised my Russian friends not to remain too late in the German watering places, because war would begin as soon as the crops were ready in France and in Russia. In fact, only those who buried their heads in the sand, like ostriches, could go on without seeing it themselves.

Now we have learned what Germany wants, how extensive are her pretensions, how immense and detailed were her preparations for this war, and what sort of "evolution" we have to expect from the Germans if they are victorious. What their dreams of conquest are we have been told by the German emperor himself, his son, and his chancellor. And now we have heard, not only what a drunken German lieutenant or general can say to justify the atrocities committed in Belgium by the German hordes, but what a leader of the German Social Democratic party, Dr. Südekum, *delegated by his own party* to the workers of Sweden and Italy, had the impudence to say to excuse the barbarities committed by the German Huns in the Belgian villages and cities. They committed these atrocities because civilian inhabitants had fired upon the invaders in defense of their territory!! For a German Social Democrat this is quite enough! When Napoleon III gave the same excuse to account for the shooting of the Parisians on the day of his *coup d'état*, all Europe named him a scoundrel. Now the same excuse is produced to account for infinitely more abominable atrocities, by a German pupil of Marx!

This gives us the measure of the degradation of the nation during the last forty years.

And now let everyone imagine for himself what would be the consequences if Germany came victorious out of this war.

Holland—compelled to join the German empire, because she holds the passages from the Indian Ocean to the Pacific, and "the Germans need them."

Most of Belgium annexed to Germany—*it is already annexed.* An immense, ruinous contribution levied, in addition to the already accomplished pillage.

Antwerp and Calais becoming military ports of Germany, in addition to Wilhelmshafen. Denmark—at the mercy of Germany, to be annexed the moment she would dare not to serve the aggressive plans of the Germans, which plans are bound to extend as they have extended since the successes of 1871.

Eastern France—annexed to Germany, whose new fortresses will then be within two or three days' march from Paris. France will be thus at the mercy of Germany for the next fifty years. All French colonies—Morocco, Algiers, Tonkin—taken by Germany: "We have no colonies worth twopence: we must have them," said the elder son of Wilhelm the other day. It is so simple—and so candid!

Having opposite her shores a string of German military ports along the south coast of the Channel and the North Sea, what can be the life of the United Kingdom, but a life entirely ruled by the idea of a new war to be fought in order to get rid of the standing menace of an invasion—an invasion being no longer impossible now, as the aggressor would have at his service big liners, submarine boats, and the aircraft.

Finland—becoming a German province. *Germany has been working at that since 1883,* and her first steps in the present campaign show where she is aiming at. Poland—compelled definitely to abandon all dreams of national independence. Are not the rulers of Germany now treating the Poles of Pozen as badly as, if not worse than, the Russian autocrat? And are not the German Social Democrats already considering the Polish dreams of national revival as stupid bosh! *Deutschland über Alles!* Germany above all!

But enough! Everyone who has any knowledge of European affairs and the turn they have taken during the last twenty years will himself complete the picture.

"But what about the danger of Russia?" my readers will probably ask.

To this question, every serious person will probably answer, that when you are menaced by a great, very great danger, the first thing to do is to combat this danger, and then see to the next. Belgium and a good deal of France *are* conquered by Germany, and the whole civilization of Europe is menaced by its iron fist. Let us cope first with this danger.

As to the next, is there anybody who has not thought himself that the present war, in which all parties in Russia have risen unanimously against the common enemy, will render a return to the autocracy of old materially impossible? And then, those who have seriously followed the revolutionary movement of Russia in 1905 surely know what were the ideas which dominated in the first and second, approximately freely elected Dumas. They surely know that complete home rule for all the component parts of the empire was a fundamental point of all the liberal and radical parties. More than that: Finland then actually *accomplished* her revolution in the form of a democratic autonomy, and the Duma approved it.

And finally, those who knew Russia and her last movement certainly feel that *autocracy will never more be reestablished in the forms it had before 1905, and that a Russian constitution could never take the imperialist forms and spirit which parliamentary rule has taken in Germany.* As to us, who know Russia from the inside, we are sure that the Russians never will be capable of becoming the aggressive, warlike nation Germany is. Not only the whole history of the Russians shows it, but with the federation Russia is bound to become in the very near future, such a warlike spirit would be absolutely incompatible.

But even if I were wrong in all these previsions, although every intelligent Russian would confirm them—well, then there would be time to fight Russian imperialism in the same way as all freedom-loving Europe is ready at this moment to combat that vile warlike spirit which has taken possession of Germany since it abandoned the traditions of its former civilization and adopted the tenets of the Bismarckian imperialism.

It is certain that the present war will be a great lesson to all nations. It will have taught them that war cannot be combatted by pacifist dreams and all sorts of nonsense about war being so murderous now that it will be impossible in the future. Nor can it be combatted by that sort of antimilitarist propaganda which has been carried on till now. Something much deeper than that is required.

The causes of war must be attacked at the root. And we have a great hope that the present war will open the eyes of the masses of workers and of a number of men amid the educated middle classes. They will see the part that capital and state have played in bringing about the armed conflicts between nations.

But for the moment we must not lose sight of the main work of the day. *The territories of both France and Belgium* MUST *be freed of the invaders.* The German invasion *must* be repulsed— no matter how difficult this may be. All efforts must be directed that way.

Peter Kropotkin

Once Kropotkin arrived in Russia during the summer of 1917, communication with his European friends became difficult because of the war. After the October Revolution, the flow of letters to and from the West was reduced still further. Concern for Kropotkin's well-being grew as the silence lengthened, particularly because his hostility to Bolshevism was well known. In 1918, rumors began to circulate in Europe that Kropotkin had been arrested under order from Lenin. Some of Kropotkin's friends began to issue public protests. One of these was an article by Georg Brandes, the eminent Danish literary critic and friend of Kropotkin's, which stated that the arrest of "the most celebrated Russian revolutionary in the entire world" can be regarded only as "insensitive and revolting."[1] To calm these rumors, Kropotkin wrote a letter to Brandes explaining that he was not under arrest. Since he discussed various aspects of life under the revolutionary regime, the letter was published in *L'Humanité* on October 10, 1919 and other European papers. This letter is one of the most revealing documents of Kropotkin's attitudes toward the Bolshevik revolution.

The following translation, by Pauline Baggio, is from *Les temps nouveaux*, nos. 19-21 (March 1921), p. 14.

---

1 Originally published in *Politiken*, September 15, 1918. Reprinted in *Correspondance de Georg Brandes*, 3 vols., ed. Paul Kruger (Copenhagen: Rosenkilde og Bagger, 1956-66) 2:290.

Letter
to
Brandes

My very dear friend,

Finally I have an opportunity to write to you and I hasten to take advantage of it without being sure, however, that this letter will reach you.

We both[2] thank you cordially for the interest you took in your old friend when the rumor of my arrest began to circulate. This rumor was absolutely false as well as the stories about the state of my health.

The person who will deliver this letter to you will tell you about the secluded life that we lead in this small provincial town.[3] At my age it is practically impossible to take part in public affairs during a revolution and it is not in my nature to do things in an amateurish way. When we were in Moscow last winter, I drew up the elements of a federalist republic with a group of collaborators. But we had to disperse and I returned to a work on ethics which I had started in England some fifteen years ago.

All I can do now is to give you a general idea of the situation

2 Kropotkin refers to his wife and himself. —*Editor*.

3 Dmitrov, about forty miles north of Moscow. —*Editor*.

in Russia which in my opinion is not very well known in the West. Possibly an analogy will explain it.

We are now at the same stage as France was during the Jacobin revolution from September 1792 to July 1794, except that now a social revolution is seeking expression.

The dictatorial method of the Jacobins was wrong. It was unable to create a stable organization and necessarily produced a reactionary movement. But in June 1793, the Jacobins effected nevertheless the abolition of feudal rights begun in 1789 which neither the Constituent nor the Legislative Assemblies wanted to complete. They also exalted the political equality of all citizens. These are two great fundamental changes which spread through Europe during the nineteenth century.

A similar situation now exists in Russia. Through the dictatorship of a fraction of the Social Democratic party, the Bolsheviks are striving to introduce the socialization of land, industry, and commerce. This change which they are striving to effect is the fundamental principle of socialism. Unfortunately, the method by which they seek to establish a communism like Babeuf's in a strongly centralized state makes success absolutely impossible and paralyzes the constructive work of the people. This situation is nourishing a strong and potentially dangerous reaction, which is already organized to reestablish the old regime. They hope to profit from the general state of exhaustion produced first by the war and then by the famine that we are experiencing in central Russia and also by the complete disorganization of production and trade. These effects are inevitable during such a large-scale revolution accomplished by decree.

One speaks in the West of reestablishing "order" in Russia by the armed intervention of the Allies. Well, dear friend, you know how harmful to the entire social progress of Europe was, in my opinion, the attitude of those who worked to disorganize the power of resistance of Russia. This prolonged the war for a year, brought us the German invasion in the guise of a treaty, and cost us rivers of blood to prevent conquering Germany from crushing Europe under its imperial heel. You know very well my feelings in this matter.

And nevertheless I protest with all my strength against any type of armed intervention by the Allies in Russian affairs. This intervention would produce an outburst of Russian chauvinism. It would bring back to us a chauvinistic monarchy—the signs are already evident—and, note this well, it would produce a hostile attitude toward Western Europe among the majority of the Russian people, an attitude which would have the most lamentable consequences. The Americans have already understood that very well.

They imagine perhaps that in supporting Admiral Kolchak and General Denikin they support a liberal republican party, but this is already an error. Whatever might have been the personal intentions of these two military leaders, the great number of those who have grouped around them have other aims. Necessarily, what they propose would bring us back to monarchy, reaction, and rivers of blood.

Those among the Allies who understand the events ought therefore to repudiate all armed intervention. Especially since, if they really come to the aid of Russia, they will find an enormous amount of work to do in a different way.

People in the great expanse of the central and northern provinces are lacking in bread.

In Moscow or here in Dmitrov, each person can get a pound or a quarter of a pound of bread delivered by the state at the very high but still relatively modest price of a ruble sixty a pound (which formerly represented four francs). But to procure an additional pound of black bread or rye, you must pay from twenty-five to thirty rubles (that is sixty-two to seventy-five francs) for a pound. And besides, it is almost impossible to find! This is famine, with all its consequences. A whole generation is wasting away . . . And we are not granted the right to buy bread in the West!—Why? Could it be to bring a Romanov back to us?

Throughout Russia, there is a want of manufactured products.

The peasant pays outlandish prices for a scythe, an ax, a few nails, for a needle, a tape measure and any fabric; he pays for example a thousand rubles (which was formerly twenty-five hundred francs) for the four iron-rimmed wheels of a miserable Russian cart. In the Ukraine, it is still worse: you cannot find any products at any price.

Instead of taking the role that Austria, Prussia, and Russia took toward France in 1793, the Allies should have done everything to aid the Russian people to get out of this terrible situation. Besides, had rivers of blood been shed to bring the Russian people back to their past, it would not have been successful.

It is in building a new future by the constructive elaboration of a new life which is taking shape already, in spite of everything, that the Allies ought to help us. Without delay, come to the aid of our children! Come and help us in the constructive work that is necessary! And may they send us, not diplomats and generals, but bread, the tools to produce it, and the organizers who knew so well how to help the Allies during these five terrible years in preventing economic disorganization and in repelling the barbarian invasions of the Germans . . .

I am reminded that I have to end this letter which is already too long. In so doing, I send you my most friendly regards.

Peter Kropotkin

Kropotkin
and
Lenin

In the spring of 1919, Vladimir Bonch-Bruevich, an acquaintance of Kropotkin's and a close associate of Lenin's in the Soviet government, arranged a meeting between Kropotkin and Lenin. Bonch-Bruevich had visited Kropotkin shortly after the latter's return to Russia in June 1917. During their conversation Kropotkin spoke of Lenin and of those conceptions of revolution propounded by Marx and Lenin with which he concurred. Kropotkin said that he had heard about (but had not read) Lenin's *State and Revolution* and that he regarded it highly because it emphasized the necessity of the withering away of the state. For Kropotkin, this was one of the most important aspects of Marx's thinking and he believed that Lenin was closer to Marx's original theoretical position on the state than most social democrats. He expressed an interest in discussing these ideas with the Bolshevik leader. Somewhat later, Bonch-Bruevich mentioned the talk with Kropotkin to Lenin and found him responsive to the idea of a meeting.

The account of the meeting and the entire conversation as recorded by Bonch-Bruevich follows. All ellipses here are as they appear in the Russian text. The translation by Martin A. Miller, is from Vladimir D. Bonch-Bruevich, "Moi vospominaniia o Petre Alekseeviche Kropotkine," *Zvezda*, no. 4 (1930), pp. 189–194. An abbreviated version of this memoir is included in the more recent Soviet edition of Bonch-Bruevich's writings: "Vstrecha V. I. Lenina s P. A. Kropotkinym," Vladimir D. Bonch-Bruevich, *Izbrannye sochineniia* (Moscow, 1963), 3: 339–406. One article in English deals with the relationship between the Bolshevik and anarchist leaders (D. Shub, "Kropotkin and Lenin," *The Russian Review*, October 1953, pp. 227–234), and contains brief excerpts from this conversation and from the letters of Kropotkin to Lenin. However, none of the material is documented. Part of the original memoir by Bonch-Bruevich contains polemical portions where he attacks Kropotkin's anarchism and staunchly defends Leninism. Those wishing to consult the memoir should also see the anarchist rebuttal in Petr Arshinov, "P. A. Kropotkin i Bol'sheviki," *Delo truda* (Paris), no. 62–63 (January-February 1931), pp. 7–13.

Conversation
with
Lenin

I can almost certainly date the meeting of Vladimir Ilich and Peter Alekseevich as having taken place between May 8 and 10 [1919]. Vladimir Ilich set a time after the business hours of the *Sovnarkom*[1] and informed me that he would be at my apartment around 5 P.M. I told Peter Alekseevich by telephone the day and the hour of the meeting and sent a car for him at that time. Vladimir Ilich arrived at my place earlier than Peter Alekseevich. We spoke about the works of the revolutionaries in preceding eras; during this discussion, Vladimir Ilich expressed his opinion that undoubtedly the time would soon come when we would see complete editions of our émigré literature and its leading authors, with all the necessary notes, prefaces, and all other research material.

"This is extremely necessary," Vladimir Ilich said. "Not only must we ourselves study the past history of our revolutionary movement but we must also give young researchers and scholars the opportunity of writing a multitude of articles based on these documents and materials, in order to familiarize the

1 Council of Peoples' Commissars, of which Lenin was chairman and Bonch-Bruevich was secretary at this time. —*Editor*.

widest possible masses with everything that existed in Russia during the last generation. Nothing could be more pernicious than thinking that the history of our country begins with that day on which the October Revolution occurred. Yet we frequently hear this opinion now. Such a stupidity isn't worth talking about. Our industry is being repaired, the paper and printing crisis is passing, and we will publish a hundred thousand copies of such books as the *History of the French Revolution* by Kropotkin[2] and other works by him; despite the fact that he is an anarchist, we will issue [his] complete works in every way possible, with all the necessary notes for the reader to clearly understand the distinction between the petty bourgeois anarchist and the true communist world view of revolutionary Marxism."

Vladimir Ilich took from my library a book by Kropotkin and another by Bakunin which I had kept since 1905,[3] and rapidly looked through them, page by page. At that moment, I learned that Kropotkin had arrived. I went to greet him. He slowly climbed our fairly steep staircase. I greeted him and we walked into my study. Vladimir Ilich strode across the corridor quickly to meet him and, smiling warmly, welcomed Peter Alekseevich. Peter Alekseevich glowed and said to him immediately:

"How happy I am to see you, Vladimir Ilich! We have differences over a whole series of questions, means of action, and organization. But our goals are identical and what you and your comrades do in the name of communism—that is very near and dear to my aging heart."

Vladimir Ilich took him by the arm and very attentively and politely led him into my study, seated him in the armchair, and then took a place himself on the opposite side of my desk.

2 The actual title of the book referred to by Lenin is Kropotkin's *The Great French Revolution*, first published in 1909 in Paris and London.—*Editor.*

3 Censorship was relaxed in Russia during 1905–1906 as a consequence of the 1905 Revolution. Virtually every press took advantage of the situation and published works that had been forbidden by the government. Among these were the first collected edition of Kropotkin's writings ever issued in Russia and some of Bakunin's books.—*Editor.*

"Well, since our goals are the same, there is much that unites us in our struggle," said Vladimir Ilich. "Of course it is possible to move toward one and the same goal by various paths, but I think that in many respects our paths had to merge."

"Yes of course," Peter Alekseevich interrupted, "but you persecute the cooperatives and I am for cooperatives."

"And we are for them," Vladimir Ilich exclaimed loudly, "but we are against the kind of cooperative which conceals kulaks, landowners, merchants, and private capital in general. We simply want to strip the mask from the dishonest cooperative and to give the broad masses of the population the chance to join a genuine cooperative."

"I won't argue with that," Kropotkin answered, "and of course wherever that [situation] exists, one must fight it with all one's strength as [one opposes] all dishonesty and mystification. We don't need any covers; we must ruthlessly expose each lie, everywhere. But in Dmitrov,[4] I see that they are persecuting the cooperatives which have nothing in common with those which you just mentioned; and this is because the local authorities, perhaps even the revolutionaries of yesterday, like any other authority have become bureaucratized, converted into officials who wish to twist the strings of those subordinate to them—and they think that the whole population is subordinate to them."

"We oppose bureaucrats everywhere at all times," said Vladimir Ilich. "We oppose bureaucrats and bureaucracy, and we must tear out these remnants by the roots if they still nestle in our new system; but after all, Peter Alekseevich, you under-stand perfectly well that it is very difficult to make people over, that, as Marx said, the most terrible and most impregnable fortress is the human skull! We are taking all possible measures

4 Kropotkin, who lived his last years outside of Moscow in the small town of Dmitrov, was closely associated with the formation of a cooperative there. On this period in his life, see the personal memoir written by several participants, "P. A. Kropotkin v Dmitrove," *Byloe*, no. 17 (1921), pp. 81-89. On the cooperative movement, see Sébestien Faure, ed., *Encyclopédie Anarchiste*, 4 vols. (Paris: La Librairie internationale, 1934) 1; 447-450.—*Editor.*

for success in this struggle; indeed, life itself, of course, forces many to learn. Our lack of culture, our illiteracy, our backwardness, naturally, are obvious everywhere and no one can blame us, as a party, as a government power, for what is done incorrectly in the machinery of that power; even less for what happens in the depths of the country, remote from the centers."

"But as a result, it's not any easier for those who are exposed to the influence of this unenlightened authority," exclaimed P. A. Kropotkin, "which is already revealing itself to be an overwhelming poison for each of those who appropriates this authority for himself."

"But there's no other way," added Vladimir Ilich. "You can't make a revolution wearing white gloves. We know perfectly well that we have made and will make a great many mistakes, that there are many irregularities and many people have suffered needlessly. But what can be corrected, we will correct; we will acknowledge our errors, often due to simple stupidity. But it is impossible not to make mistakes during a revolution. Not to make them means to renounce life entirely and do nothing at all. But we have preferred to make errors and thus to act. We want to act and we will, despite all the mistakes, and will bring our socialist revolution to the final and inevitably victorious end. And you can help us in this by communicating to us all the information which you have on all the irregularities. You can be certain that each of us will direct himself to this information most assiduously."

"Excellent," said Kropotkin. "Neither I nor anyone else will refuse to help you and all your comrades as much as possible, but our aid will consist chiefly in reporting to you all the irregularities which are occurring everywhere from which people groan in many places . . ."

"Not the groaning, but the howling of the resisting counter-revolutionaries, toward whom we have been and will be merciless . . ."

"But you say that it is impossible not to have authority," Peter Alekseevich again began to theorize, "and I say it is possible. Anywhere you look around, a basis for nonauthority flares up. I have just received news that in England the dockers in one of the ports have organized an excellent, completely free cooperative into which workers of all other industries continually come. The cooperative movement is enormous and its significance is extremely important . . ."

I watched Vladimir Ilich. His eyes glinted somewhat mockingly and, listening attentively to Peter Alekseevich, he appeared perplexed that in view of the enormous upward flight and sweeping motion of the revolution which had occurred in October, one could speak only of cooperatives and cooperatives . . . And Peter Alekseevich continued to speak incessantly about how in still another place in England a cooperative had also been organized, how in some third place, in Spain, some small federation had been organized, how the syndicalist movement had flared up in France . . . "It is indeed harmful," Vladimir Ilich could not restrain himself from inserting, "not to devote any attention to the political side of life and obviously to demoralize the working masses, distracting them from the immediate struggle . . ."

"But the professional movement is uniting millions; this by itself is a huge factor," Peter Alekseevich said excitedly. "Together with this cooperative movement, this is an enormous step forward . . ."

"This is well and good," Vladimir Ilich interrupted him. "Of course the cooperative movement is important, just as the syndicalist movement is harmful. What can one say about this? This is completely obvious once it becomes a real cooperative movement, connected to the wide masses of the population. But is that really the point? Is it possible to move on to something new just through that? Do you really think that the capitalist world will submit to the path of the cooperative movement? It is trying by every measure and through every means to take the movement into its own hands. And this small cooperative, a heap of English workers without power, will be crushed and transformed most ruthlessly into the servant of capital; this new rising trend in the cooperative movement that you favor so much [will be] in direct and absolute dependence through thousands of threads which will entangle it like a cobweb. This is all petty! You will pardon me, but this is all nonsense! We need direct action of the masses, revolutionary action of the masses, that activity which seizes the capitalist world by the throat and brings it down. For the time being, there is no such activity, to say nothing of either federalism or communism or social revolution. All of these are children's play-things, idle chatter, having no realistic soil underneath, no force, no means, and almost nothing approaching our socialist goals. A direct and open struggle, a struggle to the last drop of blood—that is what we need. Civil war must be proclaimed everywhere, supported by all revolutionary and opposition forces, so far as they can go into such a civil war. There will be much blood spilled and there will be many horrors in such a fight. I am convinced that in Western Europe these horrors will be yet greater than in our country, due to the sharper class struggle there and the greater tension of the opposing forces which will fight up to the last opportunity in this, perhaps the last, skirmish with the imperialist world!"

Vladimir Ilich got up from his chair, having said all this clearly and distinctly, with animation. Peter Alekseevich leaned back in his chair and, with an attentiveness which changed to listlessness, listened to the fiery words of Vladimir Ilich. After that, he ceased speaking about cooperatives.

"Of course you are right," he said. "Without a struggle, nothing can be accomplished in any country, without the most desperate struggle . . ."

"But only a massive one," exclaimed Vladimir Ilich. "We don't need the struggle and violent acts of separate persons. It is high time that the anarchists understood this and stopped scattering their revolutionary energy on utterly useless affairs. Only in the masses, only through the masses and with the masses, from underground work to massive red terror if it is called for, to civil war, to a war on all fronts, to a war of all against all—this is the only kind of struggle that can be crowned with success. All other ways—including those of the anarchists—have been surrendered to history, to the archives, and they are of no use to anyone, ill-suited for everyone; no one is attracted to them and they only demoralize those who for some reason are seduced by this old, worn-out road . . ."

Vladimir Ilich suddenly stopped, smiled kindly and said: "Forgive me. It seems that I've gotten carried away and am tiring you. But that's the way it is with us Bolsheviks. This is our problem, our cognac, and it is so close to us that we cannot speak about it calmly."

"No, no," answered Kropotkin. "It is extremely gratifying for me to hear all that you say. If you and all your comrades think in this way, if they are not intoxicated with power and feel themselves secure from enslavement by state authority, then they will do a lot. Then the revolution is truly in reliable hands."

"We will try," Lenin answered good-naturedly, "and *we will see* (he used his favorite phrase) that none of us becomes conceited and thinks too much of himself. This is a terrible sickness, but we have an excellent cure: we will send those comrades back to work, to the masses."

"This is excellent, excellent," exclaimed Peter Alekseevich. "In my opinion, this must be done for everyone more often. This is useful for all. One must never lose contact with the working masses and one must know that only with the masses is it possible to achieve everything that has been set down in all of our most progressive programs. But social democrats and those people without means in all countries think that in your party there are many nonworkers, and that this nonworker element is corrupting the workers. What is needed is the reverse: that the worker element should prevail and that they, the nonworkers, should only help the working masses in matters of instruction, in the business of mastering some area of knowledge or another; they would be like a service element in one socialist organization or another."

"We need enlightened masses," said Vladimir Ilich, "and it would be desirable, for instance, if your book, *History of the French Revolution*, were to be issued immediately in a very large edition. After all, it is useful to everyone. We would like very much to publish this excellent book and to issue it in a quantity that could satisfy all libraries, village reading rooms and company libraries in the regiments."

"But where can it be published? I will not permit a state-published edition . . ."

"No, no," Vladimir Ilich interrupted Peter Alekseevich, smiling slyly. "Naturally, not in the State Publishing House, but in a cooperative press . . ."

Peter Alekseevich nodded his head approvingly. "Well then," he said, visibly gladdened by this encouragement and by this proposal, "if you find the book interesting and needed, I agree to publish it in an inexpensive edition. Perhaps a cooperative publishing house which will accept it can be found . . ."

"We'll find one, we'll find one," Vladimir Ilich confirmed. "I'm convinced of this . . ."[5]

With this, the conversation between Peter Alekseevich and Vladimir Ilich began to exhaust itself. Vladimir Ilich looked at his watch, stood up and said that he had to prepare for a session of the *Sovnarkom*. He bid farewell to Peter Alekseevich most affectionately, telling him that he would always be glad to receive letters and instructions from him, which would always be given serious attention. Peter Alekseevich bid us farewell and moved to the door where Vladimir Ilich and I saw him off. He departed in the same automobile for his apartment.

5 The book appeared in 1922, the year after Kropotkin's death, published in Petrograd by *Golos truda*, the most well-known and last anarchist press in Soviet Russia. For a sympathetic appraisal of Kropotkin as a historian of the French Revolution, see Nikolai Ivanovich Kareev, "P. A. Kropotkin o velikoi frantsuzskoi revoliutsii," Aleksei Borovoi and Nikolai Lebedev, eds., *Sbornik statei posviashchennyi pamiati P. A. Kropotkina* (Moscow-Petrograd: Golos truda, 1922), pp. 108-138. For a Soviet interpretation, see B. P. Kustov, "Kropotkin, kak istorik frantsuzskoi revoliutsii kontsa XVIII veka, *Istoricheskii sbornik*, ed. N. M. Dobrotvor (Gor'kii, 1939), pp. 185-202. A bibliography on this subject can be found in *Istoriia istoricheskoi nauki v SSSR. Dooktiabr'skoi period.* (Moscow: Nauka, 1965), pp. 541-542.—*Editor.*

Kropotkin took Lenin's offer quite seriously and sent him two letters during the following year. The letters concern specific issues and indicate Kropotkin's deep concern for the fate of the revolution. Kropotkin sharply and frankly criticized Bolshevik centralization, authoritarianism, and bureaucratic tendencies in his discussion of food shortages and the Red Army's treatment of hostages during the civil war. The letters show that Kropotkin wanted the revolution to succeed in freeing, not reenslaving, the Russian people. While he was able to celebrate what he considered the virtues of the revolution, he could not accept certain practices which he felt were survivals of the overthrown state. The letters are translated by Martin A. Miller from Vladimir Bonch-Bruevich, "Moi vospominaniia o Petre Alekseeviche Kropotkine," *Zvezda*, no. 6 (1930), pp. 186-187, 193-194.

Two
Letters to
Lenin

Dmitrov, 4 March, 1920

Esteemed Vladimir Ilich,

Several employees of the postal-telegraph department have come to me with the request that I bring to your attention information about their truly desperate situation. As this problem concerns not only the commissariat of mail and telegraphs alone, but the general condition of everyday life in Russia, I hasten to fulfill their request.

You know, of course, that to live in the Dmitrov district on the salary received by these employees is *absolutely impossible*. It is impossible even to buy a bushel of potatoes with this [salary]; I know this from personal experience. In exchange they ask for soap and salt, of which there is none. Since [the price] of flour has gone up—if you manage to get any—it is impossible to buy eight pounds of grain and five pounds of wheat. In short, without receiving provisions, the employees are doomed to a very real famine.

Meanwhile, along with such prices, the meager provisions which the postal and telegraph employees received from the Moscow postal and telegraph supply center (according to the decree of August 15, 1918: eight pounds of wheat to an employee or to employees, and five pounds of wheat to incapacitated members of a family) *have not been delivered for two months already*. The local supply centers cannot distribute their provisions, and the appeal of the employees (125 persons in the Dmitrov area) to Moscow remains unanswered. A month ago one of the employees wrote you personally, but he has received no answer thus far.

I consider it a duty to testify that the situation of these employees is truly desperate. The majority are *literally starving*. This is obvious from their faces. Many are preparing to leave home without knowing where to go. And in the meantime, I will say openly that they carry out their work conscientiously; they have familiarized themselves with [their jobs] and to lose such workers would not be in the interests of local life in any way.

I will add only that whole categories of other Soviet employees can be found in the same desperate condition.

In concluding, I cannot avoid mentioning something about the general situation to you. Living in a great center—in Moscow—it is impossible to know the true condition of the country. To know the truth about current experiences, one must live in the provinces, in close contact with daily life, with its needs and misfortunes, with the starving—adults and children—with running back and forth to offices in order to get permission to buy a cheap kerosene lamp, and so forth.

There is now one way out of these trials for us. It is necessary to hasten the transition to more normal conditions of life. We will not continue like this for long, and we are moving toward a bloody catastrophe. The locomotives of the Allies, the export of Russian grain, hemp, flax, hides, and other things that are so indispensable to us will not help the population.

One thing is indisputable. Even if the dictatorship of the party were an appropriate means to bring about a blow to the capitalist system (which I strongly doubt), *it is nevertheless harmful for the creation of a new socialist system*. What are necessary and needed are local institutions, local forces; but there are none, anywhere. Instead of this, wherever one turns there are people who have never known anything of real life, who are committing the gravest errors which have been paid for with thousands of lives and the ravaging of entire districts.

Consider the supply of firewood, or that of last season's spring seed . . .

Without the participation of local forces, without an organization from below of the peasants and workers themselves, it is impossible to build a new life.

It would seem that the soviets should have served precisely this function of creating an organization from below. But Russia has already become a Soviet Republic only in name. The influx and taking over of the people by the "party," that is, predominently the newcomers (the ideological communists are more in the urban centers), has already destroyed the influence and constructive energy of this promising institution—the soviets. At present, it is the party committees, not the soviets, who rule in Russia. And their organization suffers from the defects of bureaucratic organization.

To move away from the current disorder, Russia must return to the creative genius of local forces which, as I see it, can be a factor in the creation of a new life. And the sooner that the necessity of this way is understood, the better. People will then be all the more likely to accept [new] social forms of life. If the present situation continues, the very word "socialism" will turn into a curse. This is what happened to the conception of "equality" in France for forty years after the rule of the Jacobins.

With comradely greetings,

P. Kropotkin

Dmitrov (Moscow province)
21 December, 1920

Respected Vladimir Ilich,

An announcement has been placed in *Izvestiia* and in *Pravda* which makes known the decision of the Soviet government to seize as hostages SRs [Social Revolutionary party members] from the Savinkov and Chernov groups, White Guards of the nationalist and tactical center, and Wrangel officers; and, in case of an [assassination] attempt on the leaders of the soviets, to "mercilessly exterminate" these hostages.

Is there really no one around you to remind your comrades and to persuade them that such measures represent a return to the worst period of the Middle Ages and religious wars, and are undeserving of people who have taken it upon themselves to create a future society on communist principles? Whoever holds dear the future of communism cannot embark upon such measures.

Is it possible that no one has explained what a hostage really is? A hostage is imprisoned not as punishment for some crime. He is held in order to blackmail the enemy with his death. "If you kill one of ours, we will kill one of yours." But is this not the same thing as leading a man to the scaffold each morning and taking him back, saying: "Wait awhile, not today . . ."

And don't your comrades understand that this is tantamount to a *restoration of torture* for the hostages and their families.

I hope no one will tell me that people in power also do not lead easy lives. Nowadays even among kings there are those who regard the possibility of assassination as an "occupational hazard."

And revolutionaries assume the responsibility of defending themselves before a court which threatens their lives. Louise Michele chose this way. Or they refuse to be persecuted, as did Malatesta and Voltairine de Cleyre.

Even kings and popes have rejected such barbaric means of self-defense as the taking of hostages. How can apostles of a new life and architects of a new social order have recourse to such means of defense against enemies?

Won't this be regarded as a sign that you consider your communist experiment unsuccessful, and [that] you are not saving the system that is so dear to you but only [saving] yourselves?

Don't your comrades realize that you, communists (despite the errors you have committed), are *working for the future?* And that therefore you must in no case stain your work by acts so close to primitive terror? [You must know] that precisely these acts performed by revolutionaries in the past make the new communist endeavors so difficult.

I believe that for the best of you, the future of communism is more precious than your own lives. And thoughts about this future must compel you to renounce such measures.

With all of its serious deficiencies (and I, as you know, see them well), the October Revolution brought about enormous progress. It has demonstrated that social revolution is not impossible, as people in Western Europe had begun to think. And, for all its defects, it is bringing about progress in the direction of *equality*, which will not be corroded by attempts to return to the past.

Why, then, push the revolution on a path leading to its destruction, primarily because of defects which are not at all inherent in socialism or communism, but represent the survival of the old order and old disturbances, of an unlimited, omnivorous authority?

P. Kropotkin

Glossary
of
Names

The following list contains the names of most of the individuals cited by Kropotkin in the preceding essays. The list stresses Russian names and European scholarly sources mentioned by Kropotkin which may be unfamiliar to the general reader. Names so obvious as to require no biographical note have been omitted.

Arakcheev, Count Aleksei Andreevich (1769–1834). Russian soldier and statesman. Minister of war, 1808–1810, under Alexander I. Established military colonies in Russia which became notorious for rigid discipline and regimentation.

Arnould, Arthur (1833–95). French political figure and writer. Served in ministries of public instruction and finance before collaborating on various journals opposing the regime of Louis-Napoleon. Was twice elected member of the 1871 Paris Commune. Author of numerous books, including *Histoire populaire et parlementaire de la Commune de Paris* (1878).

Azef, Yevno-Meyer Fishelevich (1869–1918). Well-known Russian double agent employed by the police while working as a member of the central committee of the Social Revolutionary party at the same time. Organized numerous assassinations while denouncing his comrades to the police. Was exposed in 1908 by V. I. Burtsev in Paris and sentenced to death by the Social Revolutionary party. Escaped to Russia where he later died.

Babeau, Albert Arséne (1835–1913). French writer and historian of rural France. Author of many studies, including *Le village sous l'ancien régime* (1877).

Bakunin, Michael Aleksandrovich (1814-76). Russian revolutionary leader and anarchist theoretician. Chief rival of Marx in struggle for control of First International. Exercised prominent influence among Russian revolutionaries of 1870s, including Kropotkin. Author of many works on anarchism.

Bobrikov, Nikolai Ivanovich (1839-1904). Russian statesman. Governor-general of Finland, 1898-1904. Subjected Finns to harsh rule, especially after 1902 when journals were censored and opponents of Bobrikov's rule were exiled. He was assassinated by Eugen Schauman (1875-1904), a Finnish worker, on June 16, 1904. Schauman committed suicide.

Bogoliubov (pseud. of Aleksandr Stepanovich Yemel'ianov) (1852-85). Russian revolutionary. Active in various circles in 1870s. Arrested and sentenced to fifteen years' hard labor for participation in demonstration in St. Petersburg in December 1878. Cruelly treated in jail, which motivated Vera Zasulich to shoot the chief of police in protest. After this incident, Bogoliubov was removed to a prison in Kharkov where he went insane. He died in a Kazan asylum in 1885.

Bonch-Bruevich, Vladimir (1873-1955). Secretary of Council of Peoples' Commissars, 1917-1920 and close associate of Lenin's. Long-time member of Russian Social Democratic party before the revolution. After 1920, engaged in scholarship. Arranged meeting between Kropotkin and Lenin in 1919.

Botta, Carlo Giuseppe (1766-1837). Italian physician and historian.

Buckle, Henry Thomas (1821-62). English historian. Stressed climate, topography, etc., of each individual country in the writing of history. Author of many works including *History of Civilization in England* (1856-61).

Bulygin, Aleksandr Grigor'evich (1851-1919). Minister of internal affairs in Russia during the 1905 revolution after serving as deputy governor-general of Moscow, 1900-04. Organized plan for a state consultative assembly, called the "Bulygin Duma," with no legislative authority. Plan was rejected during the revolutionary protest of 1905.

Burtsev, Vladimir L'vovich (1862-1942). Journalist concerned with the Russian revolutionary movement. Instrumental in exposing *agents provocateurs* in the movement. Editor of *Byloe*, a journal devoted to the revolutionary movement. After the 1917 revolution, opposed Bolshevism.

Callot d'Herbois, Jean Marie (1750-96). French revolutionary. Member of the Convention in 1792. Notorious for cruelty in hunting down and judging suspected royalists. Conspired against

Robespierre in 1795. Exiled from France.

Capponi, Gino (1792-1876). Florentine statesman and scholar. Prime minister of Tuscany in 1848 and senator under King Victor Emmanuel. Author of *Storia della repubblica di Firenze* (1875).

Chaikovskii, Nikolai Vasil'evich (1850-1926). Russian revolutionary. In 1869 he helped organize leading revolutionary organization in Petersburg, the Chaikovskii Circle. Later emigrated to western Europe and was active in Russian radical groups. Joined Social Revolutionary party in 1904. After October Revolution in 1917, he formed anti-Bolshevik organizations and supported White Army in Russian civil war.

Cherkezov, Varlaam Nikolaevich (1846-1925). Georgian aristocrat by birth. Active in revolutionary movement in Moscow in 1860s, later emigrated and devoted himself to anarchism. Friend of Kropotkin's. Author of *Pages d'histoire socialiste* (1896) in which he attempted to prove Marx a plagiarist of Considérant.

Chernov, Viktor Mikhailovich (1873-1952). Leader of the Russian Social Revolutionary party, favoring socialization of land among the peasantry. Served briefly in Kerensky's government. Attempted to form Social Revolutionary government in Samara against Bolshevik rule. Fled Russia. Author of several studies which recount his experiences.

Chernyshevskii, Nikolai Gavrilovich (1828-89). Radical journalist, philosopher, and literary critic in Russia. Edited *Sovremennik* until 1862 when he was arrested and exiled. Exercised enormous influence on later generations of Russian revolutionaries.

Cleyre, Voltairine de (1866-1912). American anarchist. Named after Voltaire by her father, who later sent her to a convent after his conversion to Catholicism. After the Haymarket Affair in 1886, she accepted anarchism. Wrote prolifically, lectured across the country, and agitated for anarchism. Her *Selected Works* was published in 1914.

Dalloz, Victor (1795-1869). Well-known French lawyer and author of juridical studies of modern states.

Delescluze, Louis Charles (1809-71). French journalist and revolutionary. Member of the First International and participant in the 1871 Paris Commune. Killed on the barricades on May 28, 1871.

Denck, Johannes (1495-1527). German Anabaptist. Translated Old Testament prophets and published theological treatises.

Denikin, Anton Ivanovich (1872-1947). Commander of anti-Bolshevik White Army until 1920. After being routed by Red Army, he was replaced by General Wrangel. Last years spent writing his five-volume history of the Russian Civil War.

Dolgushin, Aleksandr Vasil'evich (1845-85). Russian revolutionary. Arrested in connection with the Nechaev case in 1870. In 1872, organized revolutionary circle which agitated in the countryside. Arrested in 1873 for encouraging peasant revolts.

Dubrovin, Vladimir Dmitrievich (1855-79). Russian revolutionary. Attended military schools and served in the military before joining terrorist group in St. Petersburg. Condemned to death and executed on April 20, 1879.

Ferrari, Guiseppe (1812-76). Italian philosopher, historian, and statesman. Professor at Turin, Milan, and Rome.

Flerovskii, N. (pseud. of Vasilii Vasil'evich Bervi) (1829-1918). Russian economist and sociologist. After graduation from Kazan University in 1849 was active with revolutionary groups. His most widely read book was his study of the condition of the Russian working class, published in 1869.

Fouché, Joseph (1763-1820). French statesman. Member of the National Convention, 1792-95. Police official at various periods until 1815. Developed highly effective spy system and secret police under Napoleon I. Exiled from France in 1816.

Fustel de Coulanges, Numa Denis (1830-89). French historian and author of various works on the origins of political institutions, property, and cities.

Gapon, Georgii Appollonovich (1870-1906). Combined the disparate professions of priest, revolutionary organizer, and police informer. Led large crowd of workers and peasants to petition the tsar on January 9, 1905, which resulted in troops firing on the unarmed crowd. Known to history as Father Gapon.

George, Henry (1839-97). American economist. Developed single-tax theory. Attacked monopolies and sought egalitarian society. His most famous book is *Progress and Poverty* (1877-79).

Golovachev, Aleksei Andrianovich (1819-1903). Liberal Russian publicist. Worked on peasant emancipation reforms and occupied local administrative posts. From 1858, published series of articles which appeared regularly in liberal press on subject of reform.

Goremykin, Ivan Logginovich (1839-1917). Minister of justice in 1891 in Russia, and prime minister in 1905 during convening of state Duma. Dismissed soon after. Served again as prime minister 1914-16.

Gounod, Charles François (1818-93). French composer and conductor. Achieved success with his opera *Faust* (1859). Also composed *Ave Maria*, based on Bach's prelude, and many other vocal pieces and operas.

Grave, Jean (1854-1939). French anarchist, journalist, and close friend of Kropotkin's. Editor of numerous anarchist organs, including Kropotkin's *Le Révolté* during Kropotkin's imprisonment, 1883-85. Author of many anarchist works, including *Moribund Society and Anarchy* (1893).

Green, John Richard (1837-83). English historian. Author of *The Making of England* (1881) and other works.

Gringmut, Vladimir Andreevich (1851-1907). Russian publicist. Editor of *Moskovskiia vedomosti* from 1897. Was dedicated to defense of absolute monarchy and gentry privilege. Helped organize reactionary Union of the Russian People.

Guillaume, James (1844-1916). One of the leading figures in the Jura Federation of the First International. Philosophy student in Zurich in 1860s, became friend and follower of Bakunin, with whom he worked in the International. Also close to Kropotkin. Author of four-volume memoir on the International.

Gukovskaia, Viktoriia Leont'evna (1864-1881). Russian revolutionary. Arrested for involvement in demonstration protesting the sentence of I. M. Koval'skii in Odessa in 1878. Exiled to Siberia and committed suicide there in 1881.

Helfman, Hesse (Gel'fman, Gesia Meerovna) (1855-82). Russian revolutionary. Left home at 16 to join revolutionaries. Active in leading groups during the 1870s. Arrested after assassination of Alexander II in 1881 and imprisoned. Despite protests on her behalf from European socialists including Kropotkin, she was not released.

Ignat'ev, Count Nikolai Pavlovich (1832-1908). Russian diplomat and statesman. Ambassador to Turkey and, after 1881, minister of internal affairs. Identified with reactionary policies of Alexander III.

Ishutin, Nikolai Andreevich (1840-79). Founder of Russian revolutionary circle during 1860s called "Organization." Arrested in 1866 and sentenced to life imprisonment. Went insane serving hard labor in Siberia and died of tuberculosis in 1879.

Karakazov, Dmitrii Vladimirovich (1840-66). Russian revolutionary. Member of Ishutin's circle. On April 4, 1866, attempted unsuccessful assassination of Alexander II. Arrested and executed on September 3.

Kareev, Nikolai Ivanovich (1850-1931). Russian historian. Professor in St. Petersburg. In 1879, published influential study of the peasants during the French Revolution. In 1905, became prominent liberal leader of Constitutional Democratic party. Author of numerous studies on the French Revolution.

Katkov, Mikhail Nikiforovich (1818-87). Russian journalist. Gave up professorship in Moscow to edit *Moskovskiia vedomosti* in 1851.

Also editor of *Russkii vestnik*, 1856–87. Influential in court circles. Moved from liberal to reactionary and nationalist viewpoint during 1860s.

Kavelin, Konstantin Dmitrievich (1818–85). Russian historian and political philosopher. Professor of history of law in Moscow from 1857 until his death. Advocate of strong monarchy. Believed government to be imposed upon the people for their benefit and not the result of popular initiative.

Koenigswarter, Louis Jean (1814–78). French economist and lawyer. Author of works on the history of legislation and the development of human society.

Kolchak, Aleksandr Vasil'evich (1873–1920). Russian admiral. Monarchist, opposed to Bolshevik revolution. Advocate of Allied intervention against Bolshevik rule during civil war. His efforts to create a counterrevolutionary government in Siberia failed. Arrested and shot by Red Army on February 7, 1920.

Kornilov, Lavr Georgevich (1870–1918). Russian general. Appointed supreme commander of Russian military forces on July 18, 1917. Fearful of Bolsheviks, he sought to abolish army committees organized by the soviets. On August 18 he sent a division to Petrograd presumably to suppress the soviets. Kerensky sensed a right-wing coup developing and dismissed Kornilov. Kornilov died in 1918 fighting in the White Army against the Bolshevik government.

Koval'skii, Ivan Martynovich (1850–78). Russian revolutionary. Arrested in Odessa in 1878 and executed on August 2.

Kravchinskii, Sergei Mikhailovich (1851–95). One of most celebrated Russian revolutionary figures. Member of radical circles in Russia during 1870s. Argued for Bakuninist orientation to revolution. On August 4, 1878, assassinated Mezentsev, chief of police in St. Petersburg, and escaped abroad. Wrote number of books dealing with revolutionary movement in Russia. Close friend of Kropotkin's. Accidentally killed by train on December 23, 1895, in England.

Kryzhanovskii, Nikolai Andreevich (1818–88). Russian military figure. Member of military council, 1865–81. Governor-general and commander of troops in Orenburg district.

Kukel', Boleslar Kazimirovich (1829–69). Major-general in Russian army, commander of forces in Zabaikal district of eastern Siberia. Kropotkin worked closely with Kukel' while in military service. Kukel' was dismissed from his post in 1863 for refusing to participate in military suppression of Poles and for his sympathetic attitude toward political exiles.

Kviatkovskii, Aleksandr Aleksandrovich (1853-80). Directed revolutionary group in Nizhni-Novgorod in late 1870s. Became member of Executive Committee of the People's Will. Arrested and executed in November, 1880.

Lavrov, Petr Lavrovich (1823-1900). Russian philosopher and ideologist of revolutionary populism. Removed from teaching post in artillery school in 1866. In western Europe, he later became editor of *Vpered!* (*Forward!*), revolutionary journal which enjoyed wide circulation. Author of influential *Historical Letters* (now available in English translation).

Lebedeva, Tat'iana Ivanovna (1850-87). Russian revolutionary. Member of Moscow section of Chaikovskii Circle. Later joined the People's Will in 1879. Sentenced to life at hard labor after arrest in 1881. Died in exile.

Lefrançais, Gustav (1826-1901). French revolutionary. Active in 1848 revolution. Expelled from France under Louis-Napoleon, but returned in 1871 to participate in Paris Commune. Member of First International. Author of *Etude sur le mouvement communaliste à Paris en 1871* (1872).

Leo, Heinrich (1799-1878). German historian. Conservative viewpoint. Author of five-volume history of Italy and other works on universal history, religion, and politics.

Liebknecht, Karl (1871-1919). German lawyer and radical leader. Son of Wilhelm Liebknecht. Member of Reichstag, 1912. Against German war policy during World War I. Imprisoned in 1916-18 for his political views. With Rosa Luxemburg, was one of the leaders of the Spartacus party. Arrested and murdered with her after failure of 1919 insurrection.

Liebknecht, Wilhelm (1826-1900). German journalist and radical politician. One of founders of German Social Democratic party. Member of Reichstag, 1867-70. Imprisoned for treason in 1872. Editor of *Volksstaat* and *Vorwarts*.

Loris-Melikov, Count Mikhail Tarielovich (1825-88). Russian statesman. Appointed minister of internal affairs in 1880 and attempted liberalization program. Known to revolutionaries as "dictator of the heart." Project was shelved after assassination of Alexander II and Loris-Melikov was dismissed by his successor, Alexander III.

Loshkarev, General. Official of ministry of interior in Russia. Involved in Tokarev affair (see Tokarev).

Luccheni, Luigi (*d.* 1910). Assassin of Austrian Empress Elizabeth, wife of Emperor Franz Joseph, during her visit to Geneva on September 10, 1898. While serving term of life imprisonment, he wrote open letters proclaiming his anarchist beliefs. Committed suicide in 1910.

Luchaire, Denis Jean (1846-1908). French historian and professor. Author of numerous studies on aspects of the Middle Ages including *Les communes françaises à l'époque des Capétiens directs* (1890).

Maine, Sir Henry James Sumner (1822-88). English jurist. Professor of civil and international law at Cambridge and Oxford. Author of works concerning village communities, law, and social customs.

Malatesta, Errico (1853-1932). Italian anarchist. Member of First International and one of the formulators of the theory of anarchist communism. Led the opposition within the anarchist camp against Kropotkin's support of the Allies during World War I. Edited numerous organs and author of many works on anarchism.

Marshall, Alfred (1842-1924). English economist. Professor at Cambridge, 1885-1908. Author of many works on economics.

Mel'gunov, Sergei Petrovich (1879-1956). Russian historian and journalist. Taught at Moscow University before the revolution. Arrested by Bolsheviks during the civil war, later exiled. Author of numerous studies of Russian history.

Michelet, Jules (1798-1874). French historian. Professor, Collège de France, 1838-51. Best known for his *Introduction à l'histoire universelle* (1831), his monumental *Histoire de France*, and his seven-volume *Histoire de la Révolution française* (completed in 1853). He saw the revolution as the victory of justice over dogma.

Mignet, François Auguste Marie (1796-1884). French historian. Friend and associate of Thiers with whom he edited *Le National*, an anti-Bourbon journal in 1830. Director of national archives until 1848. His two-volume history of the French Revolution was first published in 1824.

Mikhailov, Mikhail Illarionovich (1826-65). Russian poet and radical publicist. Coauthor of the proclamation "To the Young Generation" (1861) which argued for a socialist and egalitarian Russia. Arrested and exiled to Siberia where he died on August 2, 1865.

Morozov, Nikolai Aleksandrovich (1854-1946). Russian revolutionary. Member of Moscow section of Chaikovskii Circle in 1870s and later served on Executive Committee of the People's Will which planned the assassination of Alexander II. Was strong proponent of terrorist tactics. Arrested in 1881 and sentenced to life term of hard labor. Author of two-volume memoir on the revolutionary movement.

Morris, William (1834-96). English poet and socialist. Helped organize the Socialist League and edited its newspaper, *The Commonweal.*

Nechaev, Sergei Gennadievich (1847-82). Russian revolutionary. Leader of radical circle in St. Petersburg which was broken up after the murder of one of its members in 1869. Nechaev escaped abroad. Associated with Bakunin in Switzerland, where he was arrested in 1872. Imprisoned in Peter and Paul Fortress in St. Petersburg where he died in 1882. His unscrupulous tactics inspired Dostoevsky to write *The Possessed*.

Nettlau, Max (1865-1944). German historian of the anarchist movement. His three-volume study of the history of anarchism remains the most detailed and comprehensive to date.

Nikandr (Nikolai Dmitrievich Molchanov) (1852-1910). Russian cleric and author of works on Christianity.

Nys, Ernest (1851-1920). Belgian jurist. Member of the Hague Tribunal. Author of works dealing with international law.

Osinskii, Valerian Andreevich (1853-79). Russian revolutionary. Involved in various terrorist acts in late 1870s. Arrested in Kiev in January 1879 and executed on May 14.

Owen, Robert (1771-1858). Welsh socialist and pioneer of noncompetitive, cooperative industry. Experimented with programs of improving factory conditions for workers and founded cooperative communities in England and America. Author of works which elaborate his ideas.

Pauwels, Jean (*d.* 1894). Belgian anarchist. Died on March 15, 1894, when bomb he was carrying accidentally exploded. Coauthor of *Les ouvriers de la République* (1895).

Perovskaia, Sofia L'vovna (1853-81). Russian revolutionary. Member of leading revolutionary circles in 1870s. As member of Executive Committee of the People's Will she helped plan the assassination of Alexander II. Arrested and executed in April, 1881.

Pindy, Louis (1840-1917). French revolutionary. Active during Paris Commune uprising in 1871. Delegate to congress of First International at St. Imier in 1872 and worked for Jura Federation which maintained a Bakuninist orientation.

Pisarev, Dmitrii Ivanovich (1840-68). Russian radical literary critic. On editorial board of *Russkoe slovo* in 1860s. Exercised strong influence in development of philosophical nihilism, egoism, and materialism in literary criticism. A volume of his selected essays has appeared in English.

Plehve, Viacheslav Konstantinovich von (1846-1904). Reactionary Russian statesman under Nicholas II. Served as chief of security police and was governor-general of Finland before becoming minister of interior. Pursued rigid policy of "Russification" of national minorities. Assassinated in 1904 by a terrorist of the Social Revolutionary party.

Pobedonostsev, Konstantin Petrovich (1827-1907). Russian reactionary statesman. Procurator of Holy Synod, 1880-1905, and was very influential in governments of Alexander III and Nicholas II. Resolute believer in absolute monarchy and morality of the Orthodox church. His *Reflections of a Russian Statesman* has been translated into English.

Post, Albert Hermann (1839-95). German jurist. Regarded as founder of comparative law. Author of many pioneering studies on this subject.

Pouget, Emile (1860-1931). French anarchist. Editor of the Paris anarchist paper, *Le Pére Peinard*, one of the most successful organs of the movement (1889-1900). Later accepted anarcho-syndicalism and collaborated on *La Voix du Peuple*, the daily paper of the Confédération Générale du Travail.

Proudhon, Pierre Joseph (1809-65). French journalist and political figure regarded as one of the first exponents of modern anarchism. Took active part in 1848 revolution. Founded and edited *Le Peuple* and other radical journals. Author of many works on anarchism.

Pugachev, Yemelian Ivanovich (1742-75). Don Cossack leader of peasant uprising during reign of Catherine the Great. Captured and executed on January 10, 1775. Pugachev subsequently became legendary as a popular revolutionary leader.

Ravachol, François-Claudius (1859-92). French terrorist attracted to anarchist ideas. Responsible for series of bomb explosions and murders of officials in Paris in the name of anarchy. Executed in 1892.

Razin, Stenka (*d.* 1671). Cossack leader who attracted a large peasant following and directed an insurrection against the Russian government in Moscow, 1669-71. Movement collapsed with his capture. Executed in 1671. Razin became legendary folk hero as symbol for peasant revolt.

Reclus, Elie (1827-1904). Older brother of Elisée, with whom he worked on many projects both scientific and political. Best known for his *Les primitifs, études d'ethnologie comparée* (1885), an anthropological study. Took part in Paris Commune in 1871 and contributed to various radical journals.

Reclus, Elisée (1830-1905). French geographer and anarchist. One of Kropotkin's closest friends. Author of numerous works on geography, including the nineteen-volume series on world geography. Participant in the Paris Commune of 1871. For his anarchist theory, see his *Evolution, Revolution and the Anarchist Ideal*.

Rhodes, Cecil John (1853-1902). British administrator, colonial statesman and financier in South Africa. Prime minister of Cape

Colony, 1890-96. Sought to establish South African federation under British rule.

Rocker, Rudolf (1873-1958). German socialist, editor of leading left-wing Yiddish papers in England. Prominent in Jewish labor movement prior to World War I. Author of *Nationalism and Culture* (1937), an autobiography, and works on anarcho-syndicalism.

Rogers, James Edwin Thorold (1823-90). English economist and professor at King's College, London, 1859-90. Author of many studies concerning agriculture, industry, and prices.

Rostopchin, Count Fedor Vasil'evich (1763-1826). Military governor of Moscow at time of Napoleon's invasion of Russia in 1812.

Saltykov, Mikhail Yevgrafovich (pseud. of Nikolai Shchedrin) (1826-89). Russian satirical novelist known for his sketches of the gentry. Also edited several progressive journals.

Savinkov, Boris Viktorovich (1879-1925). Russian revolutionary. Member of terrorist section of Social Revolutionary party. Responsible for planning and executing several of the most sensational assassinations prior to 1917. After the October Revolution, became vigorous opponent of Bolshevism and supported reactionary groups. Arrested in 1924 by Bolsheviks. Committed suicide in May 1925.

Sazonov, Yegor (1876-1910). Member of Social Revolutionary party and assassin of Plehve, minister of interior, in 1904. Committed suicide in prison in 1910.

Scheller, Aleksandr Konstantinovich (A. Mikhailov) (1838-1900). Russian writer, of Estonian background. Contributed to leading journals during 1860-80. Author of numerous novels which were critical of the gentry and popular among progressive youth.

Seebohm, Frederic (1833-1912). English economist whose theories altered prevailing views of Anglo-Saxon communal settlements. Among his books are *The English Village Community* (1883) and *Tribal Custom in Anglo-Saxon Law* (1902).

Shakeev, E. A. Magistrate and official in assembly of St. Petersburg nobility. On January 17, 1881, he testified before the St. Petersburg zemstvo on the corruption of local officialdom. His statement was cited by revolutionaries such as Kropotkin to prove the case against the government's tyrannical authority over the people.

Shchedrin, Nikolai. *See* Mikhail Yevgrafovich Saltykov.

Sheremetev, Sergei Dmitrievich (1844-1918). Russian historian, archaeologist, and statesman. Member of state council.

Shishko, Leonid Emmanuilovich (1852-1910). Russian revolutionary. One of leading members of Chaikovskii Circle in St. Petersburg. Arrested in 1874 and exiled to Siberia where he escaped abroad in 1890. Continued his activities in western Europe. Died in Paris.

Shuvalov, Count Pavel Petrovich (1847-1902). Russian stateman, with reactionary political views. Led secret society, The Holy Brotherhood, created in 1881 and dedicated to struggle against revolutionaries. The Brotherhood made an unsuccessful attempt to assassinate Kropotkin.

Sil'vanskii, Nikolai Nikolaevich (Pavlov-Sil'vanskii). Government judicial official in Orenburg. Relieved of his post in 1875 after suspected involvement with radical students. Associated later with revolutionaries in St. Petersburg and was arrested in March 1879.

Sismondi, Jean (1773-1842). Swiss historian and economist. Author of histories of the Italian republics in the Middle Ages and of France, aside from his *Nouveaux principes d'Economie politique* (1819).

'Smith, Joshua Toulmin (1816-69). English constitutional lawyer, geologist, and publicist. Concerned with decentralization in democratic government and with historical principles of local governments. Author of works on these subjects.

Solov'ev, Aleksandr Konstantinovich (1846-79). Russian revolutionary. Affiliated with Land and Freedom group in late 1870s and active in propaganda activities in countryside. Made unsuccessful attempt on life of Alexander II in 1879. Arrested and executed on May 28, 1879.

Stasiulevich, Mikhail Matveevich (1826-1911). Russian historian and journalist. Professor of history in St. Petersburg until 1861. Editor and publisher of *Vestnik yevropy*, the liberal journal, from 1866 to 1908. Favored constitutional monarchy for Russia.

Steffen, Gustav Frederick (1864-1929). Swedish professor of economics and sociology at the University of Göteborg. Member of the Swedish parliament, 1911-16. Belonged to moderate wing of Social Democratic party in Sweden. Sided with Germany during World War I and was expelled from the party. His views on the causes and nature of the war are presented in his four volume work, *War and Culture* (1914-17).

Stishinskii, Aleksandr Semonovich (*b.* 1851). Russian statesman. Served under Plehve in ministry of internal affairs, 1900-04. From 1904, was member of state council and representative of extreme right faction in the council.

Stürmer, Boris Vladimirovich (1848-1917). Russian statesman. In 1904 was appointed to state council. Reactionary political views. In 1916, occupied several high posts in the government including minister of foreign affairs.

Südekum, Albert (1871-1944). German socialist and journalist. Member of Social Democratic party. After World War I, served as minister of finance. During the war, was firm supporter of the policy of defense of the homeland.

Sukhanov, Nikolai Yevgenevich (1852–82). Russian revolutionary. Member of the Executive Committee of the People's Will. Participated in plan to assassinate Alexander II. Arrested and executed on March 19, 1882.

Suvorin, Aleksei Sergeevich (1834–1912). Russian editor. Conservative political viewpoint. Editor of *Novoe vremia*.

Sviatopolk-Mirskii, Prince Petr Danilovich (1857–1914). Russian statesman. Succeeded Plehve as minister of interior in 1904. Dismissed after the violent suppression of workers' demonstration in January 1905.

Taine, Hippolyte Adolphe (1828–93). French literary critic and historian. Professor of aesthetics and art history at Ecole des Beaux-Arts from 1864. His three volume study of the French Revolution was highly critical from a conservative viewpoint.

Thierry, Augustin (1795–1856). French historian. His *Lettres sur l'Histoire de France* (1827) contained information on the rise of communes. His four-volume history of the third estate reflected his support of liberal ideas.

Tiurin, Sergei Petrovich. Professor of political economy at University of Moscow, later professor of Russian economics at University of London. Friend of Kropotkin's. Author of many works on Russia, including *From Peter the Great to Lènin: A History of the Russian Labour Movement* (1935).

Tokarev, Vladimir Nikolaevich. Russian official in ministry of interior. In 1874, as governor-general of Minsk, became center of embezzlement controversy. Received large amounts of land from the governor-general of the Lithuanian provinces, Potapov. After several years of protest by local peasants whose land had been handed over illegally to Tokarev, the government took action. Troops were sent under General Loshkarev to put down disturbances. The results were heavy fines and exile for protesting peasants. The embezzlement became the subject of a public scandal in 1881 as a result of a factional struggle within the government. Enemies of Potapov revealed the facts of the case to the state senate to discredit him.

Tolstoy, Count Dmitrii Andreevich (1823–89). Russian statesman. Reactionary political views. Opposed reforms of 1860s under Alexander II. As minister of education, instituted reform of school system along classical lines. Minister of internal affairs in 1882.

Trepov, Dmitrii Fedorovich (1855-1906). Son of F. F. Trepov. Chief of police in Moscow, 1895-1905. Governor-general of St. Petersburg in 1905. Notorious for tactics of ruthless suppression in dealing with revolutionaries.

Trepov, Fedor Fedorovich (1803-89). Chief of police in St. Petersburg from 1860. In 1878 was shot and wounded by Vera Zasulich, a young revolutionary, for having flogged one of her comrades in prison. She was acquitted in a sensational trial, and Trepov resigned.

Tricoche, George Nestler (*b.* 1859). French historian and writer. Author of numerous works on military affairs including *Les milices des Etats Unis d'Amerique* (1896) and *La vie militaire à l'étranger* (1893).

Turgot, Baron Anne Robert Jacques (1727-81). French statesman and economist. Minister of finance, 1774-76, under Lousi XVI. Author of studies reflecting his physiocratic economic theories.

Tyler, Wat (*d.* 1381). English leader of peasants' revolt in 1381. Protested against poll tax and conditions of workers, led movement of discontented peasants to London. Presented petition demanding abolition of serfdom to Richard II. Executed by order of the lord mayor on June 15, 1381.

Vaillant, Auguste (1861-94). French anarchist-terrorist. Responsible for the sensational bombing carried out during full meeting of the Chamber of Deputies in Paris on December 9, 1893. Condemned to death and executed on February 5, 1894.

Valuev, Count Petr Aleksandrovich (1814-90). Russian statesman. Minister of interior, 1861-68. President of council of ministers, 1877-81. One of most active participants within the government in plans for peasant emancipation reforms. His revealing diary is one of the most important sources for this period.

Voinaral'skii, Porforii Ivanovich (1844-98). Russian revolutionary. Agitated in countryside and worked with members of Chaikovskii Circle. Arrested in 1874 and spent remainder of his life in Siberian exile.

Waldeck-Rousseau, Pierre Marie René (1846-1904). French lawyer and statesman. Counsel for de Lesseps in Panama trial. Premier of France, 1899-1902. In 1899, Alexandre Millerand accepted post of minister of commerce in Waldeck-Rousseau's government, thereby becoming the first socialist to serve in a "bourgeois" cabinet.

Wallace, Alfred Russel (1823-1913). English naturalist. Pioneer, along with Darwin, of theories of natural selection and survival of the fittest. Author of many studies on these subjects.

Weimar, Orest Eduardovich (1845-85). Well-known physician in St. Petersburg. Aided revolutionaries, to whose cause he was very sympathetic, in various ways such as preserving coded material, giving financial support, and permitting revolutionaries to hide in his home. One of organizers of Kropotkin's celebrated escape from prison in 1876. Arrested in 1879 in connection with Solov'ev's assassination attempt on Alexander II (with which he had no involvement) and exiled to Siberia where he died.

Witte, Count Sergei Iul'evich (1849-1915). Russian statesman. After 1892, occupied posts of minister of communications and minister of finance. Responsible for Russia's rapid industrialization in 1890s and for many related policies concerning tariffs and currency. Also, sponsored building of Trans-Siberian Railway. Author of detailed autobiography.

Wrangel, Baron Peter Nikolaevich (1878-1928). General in command of anti-Bolshevik forces during Russian civil war. Succeeded General Denikin as commander of White Army in 1920. See his *Memoirs of General Wrangel* (1930).

Yanson, Iurii Eduardovich (1835-93). Progressive Russian statistician and economist. Occupied various posts related to statistics both in government and academies. In his published studies, he pointed out the impoverished position of the peasantry and called for additional reforms to supplement those of 1861.

Yaroshenko, Semen Petrovich (b. 1864). Professor of mathematics and dean of the university in Odessa. Author of many specialized works on aspects of mathematics.

Yemel'ianov, Yegor Yegorovich (b. 1842). Graduated from Technical Artillery School and served as regiment captain in St. Petersburg before beginning revolutionary activities in 1872. Arrested in 1874 and again in 1876.

Zasulich, Vera Ivanovna (1849-1919). Russian revolutionary. Arrested and imprisoned for two years in connection with the Nechaev affair in 1869. On January 24, 1878, she shot Trepov, chief of police in St. Petersburg, but was acquitted by a sympathetic jury. Joined Marxist groups in 1880s and fled abroad. Translated works of Marx and Engels into Russian. Member of editorial board of *Iskra*, the Russian Social Democratic organ. Supported Menshevik faction after party split in 1903.

Chronology of
Important Dates
in the Life of
Peter Kropotkin

1842   (December 9. November 27 Old Style). Birth of Peter A. Kropotkin in Moscow.

1846   Death of his mother.

1848   Father remarries.

1850   Selected by Emperor Nicholas I as candidate for entrance to the Corps of Pages, an elite military school in St. Petersburg.

1857   Begins formal schooling after several years of private tutors by entering the Corps of Pages in St. Petersburg.

1862   Completes senior year as *page de chambre* of Emperor Alexander II. Graduates first in his class with chance to choose any branch of military service for career. Selects obscure and remote Amur Cossack regiment in eastern Siberia. Assigned to administrative post under liberal General Kukel', who appoints Kropotkin to local committee on prison reform. Begins series of articles for "Sovremennaia letopis'," supplement to *Moskovskiia vedomosti*, as Siberian correspondent for the paper. Articles appear to 1867.

1863   First exploratory trip along the Amur River.

1865   Further travels along the Amur and participates in expeditions to unexplored areas of Manchuria. Results published in geographic journals.

1867   Resigns from military service and returns to St. Petersburg to take post in civil service and to attend classes in the physical-mathematical department of the university.

1868   Elected member of Russian Geographic Society and continues to publish articles on his Siberian expeditions.

1870   Elected secretary of the geological section of the Geographic Society.

1871   Travels to Sweden on geographic trip. Death of father.

1872   Travels to Zurich, Geneva, Neuchâtel in Switzerland and to Belgium. After exposure to anarchist sections of the First International, Kropotkin decides to become affiliated. Returning to St. Petersburg, he joins the radical Chaikovskii Circle and begins full-time career as revolutionary.

1873   Active in various working-class sections of St. Petersburg under pseudonym of Borodin. Drafts manifesto for the Chaikovskii Circle.

1874   Arrested by police and imprisoned in the Peter and Paul Fortress.

1876   Due to illness, is transferred to military prison hospital on outskirts of St. Petersburg. After making contact with friends, Kropotkin draws up escape plan, which is successfully carried out on June 30. Arrives in England after traveling by ship from Finland via Sweden and Norway. Publication of Kropotkin's book on the glacier period, containing an original hypothesis on the formation of the Ice Age.

1877   Attends congress of the International in Verviers and the International Socialist Congress in Ghent, Belgium. Settles in La Chaux-de-Fonds, Switzerland, deciding not to return to Russia. Works on *Bulletin de la Fèdèration jurassienne*, an organ of the anarchist oriented Jura Federation of the International.

1878   Marriage to Sofia Anan'eva, daughter of a Polish Jew exiled to Siberia for revolutionary activities.

1879   Begins publication of his own anarchist paper, *Le Révolté*.

1881   Attends international anarchist congress in London. Publishes series of articles on Russian affairs in *Newcastle Chronicle* and the *Nineteenth Century*. Expelled from Switzerland for revolutionary activities.

1883   Arrested and brought to trial in Lyons for anarchist activities. Sentenced to five years in prison at Clairvaux.

1886   Released from prison. Lectures in France lead to expulsion from that country. Decides to settle in London.

1887   Birth of daughter Alexandra. Publication of *In Russian and French Prisons* which, together with the 1885 publications of *Paroles d'un Révolté*, establishes Kropotkin's reputation as a leading anarchist thinker on international level.

1890   Begins to publish series of articles in the *Nineteenth Century* on hypothesis of mutual aid among animals and human beings in history to counter Darwinian thesis of competition of species.

1897   Travels to United States on lecture tour. Begins publication of his memoirs which are serialized in *Atlantic Monthly*.

1898   Memoirs published in book form as *Memoirs of a Revolutionist*. Publication of *Fields, Factories, and Workshops*.

1901   Second trip to United States. Delivers course of lectures on Russian literature at Lowell Institute in Boston (published as *Ideals and Realities in Russian Literature* in 1905).

1905   Publishes articles on Russian revolution.

1908   Participates in Social Revolutionary party trial to convict Azef as police agent.

1909   Publication of *The Great French Revolution* in both French and English.

1913   Completes *Modern Science and Anarchism*.

1914   Assumes Allied position on war issue and splits anarchist movement.

1917   After February Revolution, Kropotkin decides to return to Russia. Settles in Moscow.

1918   Moves to Dmitrov, about forty miles north of Moscow.

1919   Meeting with Lenin.

1920   Letters to Lenin. Organizes cooperative on federalist principles in Dmitrov.

1921   Death of Kropotkin on February 8. Funeral and burial in Moscow.

Selected
Bibliography

The following bibliography is intended to suggest further study for those interested in pursuing Kropotkin's ideas in more depth. It lists only the most basic published materials in English and makes no pretense at completeness in any category. Where possible, first English language editions have been cited.

I. BOOKS BY KROPOTKIN

The Conquest of Bread. London: Chapman & Hall, 1906.
Ethics: Origin and Development. New York: McVeagh, 1924.
Fields, Factories and Workshops. London: Hutchinson and Co., 1899.
The Great French Revolution. London: Heinemann, 1909.
Ideals and Realities in Russian Literature. New York: Alfred A. Knopf, 1915. Originally published in 1905 as *Russian Literature*.
In Russian and French Prisons. London: Ward & Downey, 1887.
Memoirs of a Revolutionist. Boston: Houghton Mifflin, 1899.
Modern Science and Anarchism. Philadelphia: Social Science Club, 1903.
Mutual Aid. London: Heinemann, 1902
The Terror in Russia. London: Methuen & Co., 1909.

II. ARTICLES AND PAMPHLETS BY KROPOTKIN

"Anarchism," *Encyclopaedia Britannica*, 11th edition (1910).
Anarchism: Its Philosophy and Ideal. Freedom Pamphlets, no. 10. London, 1897.
Anarchist Communism: Its Basis and Principles. Freedom Pamphlets, no. 4. London, 1891.

Anarchist Morality. Freedom Pamphlets, no. 6. London, 1892.
An Appeal to the Young. Translated by H. M. Hyndman. London: Modern Press, 1885.
"The Constitutional Agitation in Russia," *Nineteenth Century*, 57, no. 335 (January 1905).
Law and Authority. London: Freedom Press, 1886.
The Place of Anarchism in Socialist Evolution. Translated by Henry Glasse. London: W. Reeves, 1886.
"The Present Crisis in Russia," *North American Review*, 172 (1901).
"Representative Government," *Commonweal*, 7, nos. 312-321 (1892).
"Revolutionary Government," *Commonweal*, 7, nos. 325-327 (1892).
"Revolutionary Studies," *Commonweal*, 7, nos. 294-300 (1891-1892).
"The Spirit of Revolt," *Commonweal*, 7, nos. 306-310 (1892).
The Wage System. Freedom Pamphlets, no. 1. London, 1889.
War. London: H. Seymour, 1886.

III. ANTHOLOGIES

Baldwin, Roger N., ed. *Kropotkin's Revolutionary Pamphlets.* New York: Vanguard Press, 1927. Reissued in 1968 by Benjamin Blom, Inc., New York.
Horowitz, Irving Louis, ed. *The Anarchists.* New York: Dell, 1964. Contains extract of "Modern Science and Anarchism."
Krimerman, Leonard I. and Perry, Lewis, eds. *Patterns of Anarchy.* Garden City, N.Y.: Doubleday Anchor, 1966. Contains extracts of "Law and Authority" and "Anarchist Communism."
Read, Herbert, ed. *Kropotkin. Selections from his Writings.* London: Freedom Press, 1942.

IV. BIBLIOGRAPHIES

Borovoi, Aleksei and Lebedev, Nikolai, eds. *Sbornik statei posviash-chennyi pamiati P.A. Kropotkina.* Moscow-Petrograd: Golos truda, 1922, pp. 190-249. This is the most complete Kropotkin bibliography to date. It lists his publications year by year in various languages and contains information on Kropotkin's unpublished materials.
Nettlau, Max, *Bibliographie de l'Anarchie.* Paris: P. V. Stock, 1897, pp. 72-86, 238-39. The most complete Western language Kropotkin bibliography. It is particularly good on tracing the editions and translations of various works by Kropotkin.
Stammhammer, Josef, *Bibliographie des Socialismus und Communismus.* 3 vols. Jena: Verlag von Gustav Fischer, 1893-1909, I, 191; II, 173-75; III, 180-81. A fairly thorough list of both books and periodical publications by Kropotkin.

Berneri, Camillo, *Peter Kropotkin. His Federalist Ideas.* London: Freedom Press, 1942.

Cole, G. D. H., *A History of Socialist Thought.* 5 vols. in 7. London: Macmillan, 1953-60, II, 315-60.

Hare, Richard, *Portraits of Russian Personalities Between Reform and Revolution.* London: Oxford University Press, 1959, pp. 342-55.

Masaryk, Thomas, *The Spirit of Russia.* 2 vols. London: G. Allen & Unwin, 1919, II, 378-89. Republished in 1955.

Miller, Martin A., "The Formative Years of P. A. Kropotkin, 1842-1876: A Study of the Origins and Development of Populist Attitudes in Russia." Ph.D. dissertation, University of Chicago, 1967.

Woodcock, George and Avakumovic, Ivan, *The Anarchist Prince.* London and New York: T. V. Boardman, 1950.

Name Index

Alexander of Macedonia, 214, 263
Alexander I, 78
Alexander II, 8, 21, 140, 311, 312
  reign of, 137, 275
Alexander III, 155, 157, 311, 312
Arakcheev, Count A. A., 155
Aristotle, 1
Azef, Y-M. F., 22

Babeuf, F. N., 320
Bacon, R., 234
Bakunin, M., 2, 3, 6, 12, 16, 46, 301,
  310, 311, 326
  followers of, 19, 25
  Marx and, 27
Bebel, A., 310
Bismarck, O. von, 282, 309, 311, 312
  policies of, 26
Blanc, L., 188
Bobrikov, N. I., 281
Bogoliubov (Yemel'ianov, A. S.),
  148-149
Bonch-Bruevich, V., 324-339
Boulanger, General G., 294, 299
Brandes, G., 23, 318
Buckle, H. T., 136
Bulygin, A. G., 276, 277
Burtsev, V. L., 22, 38

Camus, A., 6

Chaikovskii, N. V., 23
Chamberlain, N., 303
Cherkezov, V. N., 3, 27, 34
Chernyshevskii, N. G., 8, 138, 143,
  144, 151, 297
Comte, A., 136
Conrad, J., 4

Dalloz, V., 247
Danton, G. J., 301
Darwin, C. R., 56, 136
de Cleyre, V., 338
Delescluze, L. C., 302
Denck, J., 243
Denikin, General A. I., 321
Diogenes, 1
Disraeli, B., 303
Dobroliubov, N. A., 143
Dubrovin, V. D., 142

Edward III, 253
Edward VII, 301
Elizabeth, Empress, 22-23

Flerovskii, N., 143
Fourier, F. M. C., 297
Fustel de Coulanges, N. D., 250

Gapon, Father G. A., 270
Garibaldi, G., 310

Gauenshtein, I. I., 46
George, H., 169
Gladstone, W. E., 303
Goethe, J. W. von, 297
Goldman, E., 44
Goremykin, I. L., 280
Grave, J., 295
Gringmut, V. A., 285
Guillaume, J., 301
Gukovskaia, V. L., 148

Hegel, G. W. F., 136
Helfman, H., 138
Henry VIII, 253
Hugo, V., 233

Ibsen, H., 295
Ignat'ev, Count N. P., 280, 286
Ishutin, N. A., 138, 144

Karakazov, D. V., 138
Kareev, N. I., 301
Katkov, M. N., 156
Kavelin, K. D., 140
Koenigswarter, L. J., 217
Kolchak, Admiral A. V., 321
Kornilov, L. G., 38
Koval'skii, I. M., 148, 150
Kravchinskii, S. M., 23, 42, 142
Kropotkin, P. A.
    anarchism of, 43–44
    childhood of, 7
    1873 manifesto of, 12–14, 15
    exile of, 35–56
    imprisonment of, 17–18, 24–25
    last years of, 40–41
    military service of, 11
    personality of, 41–42
    schooling of, 7–8
    works of, 6, 12–14, 39, 42, 44
Kukel', General B. K., 9
Kviatkovskii, A. A., 138, 142

Lassalle, F., 143
Lavrov, P. L., 21, 46
Lebedeva, T., 138
Lefrançais, G., 302
Lenin, V. I., 27, 40, 318, 324–339
Liebknecht, W., 27, 310
Louis XIV, 246, 247
Luccheni, L., 23
Luchaire, D. J., 227
Luther, Martin, 243

Maine, H. J. S., 216
Malatesta, E., 3, 34–35, 42, 43, 338
Marshall, A., 250
Marx, K., 143, 324
    Bakunin and, 27
    followers of, 19, 314
    Kropotkin's hostility to, 25–28
Mel'gunov, S., 32
Michele, L., 338
Michelet, J., 129, 195
Mignet, F. A. M., 181
Mikhailov, M. I., 9, 138
Mill, J. S., 136, 143
Mirabeau, H. G. V. R., 294
Morozov, N. A., 138

Napoleon III, 177, 249, 314
Nechaev, S. G., 138, 144
Necker, J., 281, 282
Nettlau, M., 28, 292–307
Nicholas I, reign of, 139
Nicholas II, 36, 268, 271, 275, 276,
    286, 311
    advisers of, 277
    Witte and, 282
Nietzsche, F. W., 293, 305
Nikandr, Bishop, 286
Nikon, Bishop, 285, 286
Nys, A. H., 216

Osinskii, V. A., 142
Owen, R., 155

Palmerston, H. J. T., 303
Pauwels, J., 295
Pericles, 1
Perovskaia, S., 138
Pindy, L., 302
Pisarev, D. I., 297
Pitt, W., 303
Plehve, V. K. von, 267, 276, 283,
    286
Plekhanov, G. V., 27
Post, A. H., 216
Pouget, E., 304
Proudhon, P. J., 2, 9, 12, 58, 61, 178
Pugachev, Y. I., 302

Ravachol, F-C., 5, 21, 294, 295, 305
Razin, S., 302
Reclus, Elie, 304
Reclus, Elisée, 303
Rhodes, C., 282, 305

Robespierre, M. F. M. I. de, 301
Rocker, R., 33–34
Rogers, J. E. T., 232
Rostopchin, Count F. V., 80
Rothschild, L. N., 161, 162, 167, 168
Rousseau, J. J., 214

Saltykov-Shchedrin, M. Y., 21, 141
Sazonov, Y., 5, 267
Scheller, A. K., 143
Schopenhauer, A., 136
Seebohm, F., 250
Sergei (A. Romanov), Grand Duke, 269
Serraux (Egide Spilleux), 21
Shcherbatov, Prince, 286
Sheremetev, Count S. D., 286
Shishko, L. E., 142
Shuvalov, Count P. P., 141
Sil'vanskii, N. N., 141
Solov'ev, A. K., 138
Sismondi, J., 227
Spencer, H., 136, 282
Stasiulevich, M. M., 142
Steffen, G., 308–316
Stishinskii, A. S., 280
Sturmer, B. V., 280
Sudekum, A., 313
Sukhanov, N. Y., 142

Suvorin, A. S., 139
Sviatopolk-Mirskii, Prince P. D., 268

Taine, H. A., 301
Thierry, A., 227, 237
Tiurin, S. P., 37
Tolstoy, Count D. A., 3, 5, 139, 140, 306
Trepov, General F. F., 141, 148–149
Tricoche, G. N., 252
Turgot, A. R. J., 248
Tyler, Wat, 242

Vaillant, A., 295
Vanderbilts, 162
Voinaral'skii, P. I., 142

Waldeck-Rousseau, P. M. R., 305
Wallace, A. R., 56
Weimar, O. E., 142
Wilhelm I, 311
Wilhelm II, 33, 256
Witte, Count S. I., 280, 281–284

Yaroshenko, S. P., 276
Yemel'ianov, Y. Y., 142

Zasulich, V., 138, 148–149

365
Name Index

Subject Index

Absolutism, 151, 157, 158, 275
  Russian, 311
Activism. *See* Agitation
Activists. *See also* Agitators; Organ-
  izers
  populist, 93, 95, 99–100, 102
  protection of, 108
  in Russia, 93, 95
  strikes and, 113
Africans, 219
Aggression, 300
Agitation. *See also* Organization;
  Propaganda
  credibility of, 109
  education and, 102
  electoral, 154
Agitators, 90, 108
  German, 106
  populist, 91, 93, 97, 104, 107. *See
  also* Activists
  propaganda and, 107
Allies, in World War I, 321, 322
Alsace, province of, 310
America, 303–304. *See also* United
  States
Amnesty
  general, 284
  of political prisoners, 156
  Witte's, 283
Anabaptism, 242, 244, 305

Anabaptist commune, 2
Anarchism
  collectivist, 3. *See also* Collectivism
  communist, 243
  economics of, 69–70
  expropriation and, 168
  individualist, 3. *See also* Individualism
  Kropotkin's theory of, 43–44
  morality of, 30
  mutualist, 3
  of nineteenth century, 2, 5, 6
  as science, 29
  theory of, 3, 121
Anarchists. *See also* Jacobins; Revolutionaries
  French, 295, 296, 298
  pacifist, 32
  social democrats and, 27–28
  split between, 308
  state and, 212
Anarcho-syndicalism, 3. *See also*
  Syndicalism
Anarchy
  in commune, 121
  individualist, 305
  Proudhon's vision of, 61
Antiauthoritarianism, 2
Arbitration, 224
Aristocracy. *See* Nobility

Army
  Red, 334
  Russian, 37–38
  state and, 65
  substitution for, 154
Artels, 67, 68, 105
  members of, 74
  organization in, 101
Assassination. *See also* Terrorism
  of Alexander II, 21, 22
  of Empress Elizabeth, 22–23
  as occupational hazard, 338
Assassins, from Versailles, 125
Assemblée constituante, 153
Authority
  Bolshevik, 334
  Church, and, 240
  effect of, 10
  of government, 63
  Lenin and, 328–329
  principle of, 126, 305
  royal, 225, 237, 238
  temporal, 225
  youth and, 87
Autocracy, 267, 315. *See also* Absolutism
  police, 276

Baku, massacres at, 276
Barbarians, 219, 226, 236
  of sixteenth century, 235
Belgium, in World War I, 314
Belgrade, 310
"Blond beast," Nietzsche's, 295, 296–297
Boer War, 31
Bogoliubov, affair, 149
Bohemia, federation of, 244
Bolsheviks, 37, 40, 320, 324, 331, 334
Bourgeoisie, 297, 305
  Russian, 157
  village, 248
Bread, question of, 173, 175
Brotherhoods, 222, 227, 253. *See also* Guilds; Unions
Bund, success of, 269

Capital
  in anarchy, 51
  expropriation of, 67, 113
Capitalism
  in United States, 165

wage system of, 179
Capitalists, 164–165
Caucasus, revolution in, 273
Censorship in Russia, 104, 139n, 143–144, 288, 326n
Chaikovskii Circle, 11, 16, 17, 18, 26, 46
Chartist agitation, 269
Chernyi Peredel ("Black Partition"), 152
Christianity, 219, 223, 240
  Nietzsche's view of, 297
Church, Christian, 225, 237, 240
  Russian, 241
Circles
  of Chaikovskii, 143
  of Nechaev, 138
  socialistic, 146
  unanimity of, 143
  village, 96, 98–100. *See also* Organization
Cities
  free, 237
  of middle ages, 231, 254
  in revolt, 187, 190
Civilization, history of, 262–263
Class
  formation of, 61
  French middle, 123, 125
  inequality of, 55
  of intelligentsia, 56
  lower, 241
  middle, 176
  Russian lower, 145
  Russian upper, 145
  working, 88, 100. *See also* Workers
Clothing, communalization of, 206
Code Napoleon, 251
Cofs, 222
Collectivism, 59, 126. *See also* Communism
  wages and, 179. *See also* Individualism
Commerce, 166
  socialization of, 320
Committees
  city, 75
  district, 73
  Executive. *See* Executive Committee
Communes. *See also Mir; Obshchina*
  abolished, 249
  agrarian, 183

Communes (*continued*)
  Anabaptist, 2
  of ancient Greece, 236
  of 1871, 198
  in France, 184
  free, 226, 241
  function of, 14
  in Germany, 184
  individual and, 235
  of Middle Ages, 227, 236
  of Paris, 119–132
    agriculture of, 196
    defenders of, 301–302
    proclamation of, 189
    revolution of, 303
    of 1793, 171
    Swiss, 183
    village, 220, 221, 247, 251
Communication, as state institution,
    66
Communism, anarchist, 3, 16, 28,
    131, 160, 181
  antiauthoritarian, 130
  application of, 212
  Christian, 296
  of 1848, 126
  establishment of, 183
  free, 126
  spread of, 59
Communities
  urban, 226
  village, 219, 226, 227, 228, 273.
    See also Circles; Communes
Compensation, 223
Congress of the Zemstvos, 267
Constituent Assembly, 248
"Constitution," Bulygin, 277
"Consultative Assembly," 276
Convention, of July 1793, 249
Cooperatives, 327, 329. *See also*
    Communes
Cossacks, 285
Council of Labor Delegates, 288
Council of the Union of Working-
    men, 287
Craftsmanship, 180
Criminals, 4, 74
Czar. *See* Tsar

Daily News, of London, 79
Dantonists, 181
Demands, of masses, 81

Democracy, German social, 26. *See
    also* Social Democratic Party
Democrats, Social, German, 315
Demonstrations, 107
  peaceful, 285
  student, 269
Dissemination, of ideas, 85. *See also*
    Organization; Propaganda
Dmitrov, 38, 41, 335, 336, 338
Dreyfus case, 299
Duma, 280, 315
  convocation of, 277

Economics, of anarchism, 69–70
Economy, local, 70
Education
  agitation and, 102
  compulsory, 58–59
  Count Tolstoy's system of, 140
  public, 141
  in revolution, 143
  state, 65, 252
1873 manifesto, Kropotkin's, 12–14,
    15, 46, 118
Emancipation Act, 137, 157
Emigration, Russian, 116
England
  communication in, 66
  revolution in, 287
  Russia and, 39
Epicurians, 293, 295
Equality, concept of, 49, 54–55
Eskimos, 216, 218
Ethics, 39
Europe
  expropriation in, 188
  military-predatory element in, 84
  sixteenth century, 245
  strikes in, 110, 111–112
  unemployment and, 177
  views of Russia in, 135
  workers of, 82, 100
Evolution, socialist, 119–124
Exchange, problems of, 69–70
Executive Committee, 152–157
Exiles, amnesty for, 283
Exploitation, industrial, 170
Expropriation
  of capital, 67, 113
  of factories, 73, 113
  of food, 185–197
  of housing, 197–206
  of land, 72–73, 113

Expropriation (*continued*)
of private property, 129
of ships, 74

Fabians, 181
Factories, expropriation of, 73, 113
Factory workers, Russian, 83–85.
See also Workers
Famine, 321
of 1867, 138
in Kropotkin's village, 335
peasantry and, 157
politics and, 174
"Fanatics," 135
Federalist League, 38
Federation, barbarian, 221
Feuillants, 286
Finland
general strike in, 281
as German province, 314–315
revolution in, 315
First International, 11, 19, 27. *See
also* International
Food, expropriation of, 185–197
Fortress of Peter and Paul, 147, 148
France
colonies of, 314
of 1848, 189
Germany and, 314
revolution in, 287. *See also* Revolution, French
Fred, 224
Freedom, 34, 308
Freedom
of defense, 139
of individual, 242
of religion, 154
of speech, 79–80

Germany, in World War I, 33–34,
309–316
Ghibelline family, 231
Girondists, 174
Golos truda, 332
Government
absence of, 1. *See also* Anarchism;
Anarchy
absolute, 144. *See also* Absolutism
authority of, 63
centralized, 59
common feature of, 61
communal, 131. *See also* Communes

of provinces, 154
revolution and, 131
revolutionary, 16, 132
"self," 141
state and, 212–213
Great Revolution, 195
Guilds, 222, 227, 232, 239, 253, 254,
255, 256
Gypsies, 216

Hanse, union of, 244
Hébertists, 181
Hebrew tradition, 215
Hegelians, 228
"Heroes of Tashkent," 141
Hindus, 219
Historians, of medieval Italy, 234
History of the French Revolution,
326, 331
Holland, in World War I, 312, 314
Horticulture, 196
Housing, expropriation of, 197–206
Humanité, L', 318
Hussites, 242

Independence, communal, 125
Individualism, 31, 293, 295, 296, 297
"Individualists," 298
Indoctrination, uselessness of, 97.
See also Organization; Propa-
ganda
Industry, socialization of, 320
Inequality, economic, 60
Institutions, state, 65
Insurrection
call for, 83
peasant, 245. *See also* Peasants,
uprising of
social, 76–77. *See also* Revolution
Intelligentsia
class of, 56
as organizers, 90, 93, 109
workers and, 107, 290
union of, 268
International (First), 11, 19, 27,
115
Russian emigration and, 116
International Anarchist Congress, 19
Internationalism, 3
International Socialist Congress, in
Ghent, 19
International Workingmen's Associ-
ation, 120

Irish Land League, 152
Iskra, 27
Izvestia, 288, 338

Jacobin code, 251
Jacobinism, 173, 183, 258, 320
Jacobins, socialist, 256, 337
Jacqueries, 242, 301, 302
January massacres, 270–271, 276
Jesuitism, 109
Jews, outbreaks against, 157
Jura Bulletin, 304
Jura Congress, of 1879, 19
Jura Federation of the International,
    28–29
Justice, conception of, 71

Kabyles, 219, 221, 222
"Kaiserists," German, 312
Kapital, Das, 26
Kerensky government, 38
Kharkov prison, insurrection in, 148
Khozhalyi, Muscovite, 78. *See also*
    Police
Kiel Canal, 312
Kitchens, communal, 106, 175, 185–
    186
Kniaz Potemkin, mutiny on, 277
Kulaks, 327

Labor
    complex, 180
    compulsory, 51–52
    demand for, 52
    division of, 55
    evaluation of, 53
    instruments of, 50
    peasant, 101. *See also* Peasants
    privileged, 48
    problem of, 111
    as product measure, 66
    Russian revolution and, 287
    simple, 180
    voluntary, 89
Land
    communal, 218, 248, 250
    expropriation of, 72–73, 113
    nationalization of, 274
    for peasants, 163
    people's right to, 154
    redivision of, 73
    socialization of, 320
    unproductive, 179

Landholders, 94, 327
    compensation to, 200
    expropriation and, 168, 169
    Russian, 83
    wealth of, 163, 164
Law, Byzantine, 223, 251
    Roman, 223, 240, 251
Leisure, 53
Liberty, infringement of, 60. *See
    also* Freedom
Lodz, massacres at, 277
Lombardy, union of, 244
Lorraine, province of, 310
Lutheran Reformation, 242, 244, 305

Manufactures, transfer of, 154
Marxism, Kropotkin's argument
    with, 25–28, 38
    revolutionary, 326
Marxists, Russian, 38. *See also*
    Bolsheviks
May massacres, 128
Mennonites, 244
Middle Ages, 163
    cities of, 231, 254
    communes in, 227
    towns of, 229, 232
Militarism
    European, 84
    French, 303
    Prussian, 33, 310
Mir, 46, 73, 113, 154
    peasant uprisings and, 273
Monarchy. *See also* Party, mon-
    archist
    Carlovingian, 258
    establishment of, 237
    Merovingian, 258
Mongols, 219, 241
Moravian Brethren, 244
Moscow Gazette, 156, 285, 286
Moscow University, 40
Moskovskiia vedomosti, 8
Movement
    communalist, 227, 228
    cooperative, 329
    of 1871, 124
    French syndicalist, 305, 306
    libertarian, 293
    local, 114
    nihilist, 294
    populist, 294
    reactionary, 320. *See also* Reaction

Movement (*continued*)
revolutionary, history of, 325–326
Russian revolutionary, 46, 150.
See also Party, revolutionary;
Revolution
social democratic, 306
socialist, 115
Spanish, 306
unionist anarchist, 306
workers', 88, 304
youth, 269
Münster, 2
Muscadins, 286
Musulmans, uprising of, 276
Mutual Aid, 220, 231
Mutual aid, Kropotkin's theory of,
9–10

Nakhichevan, massacres at, 276
Narodniki. See Party, People's; Populism
National Convention, 191
Nations, European, 224
Nation-state, progressive role of, 2–3
Nihilism, 294
Russian, 135–136
"Nihilists," 135, 151
Nizhne-Kolymsk prison, 151
Nobility
impotence of, 104
Kropotkin's, 7
renunciation of, 88
revolution and, 114

Obshchina, 13, 14, 46, 48, 63
autonomous, 60, 67
education in, 68
labor in, 52
requirements for, 56
unionization of, 64
October Manifesto, 280
October Revolution, 38, 318, 326, 339
Odessa
massacre at, 285
uprising at, 276–277
Officials, government, 94
Olgerd family, 231
Organization. See also Agitation;
Propaganda
in artels, 101
propaganda and, 96–97, 109
in villages, 96, 98–100
Organizers, 90

Ownership, records of, 75

Parasitism, 54, 63, 127
Paris
in anarchy, 182
Commune of, 119–132, 206, 301–302
history of, 198
siege of, 122, 198
in World War I, 310, 314
Parties, Russian-in-exile, 115–116
Party
Monarchist, 286
nihilist, 135
People's, 152
reactionary, 140, 141, 146
revolutionary, 83, 86
organization of, 105
Russian, 135–158
Social, 338
Social Democratic
German, 37, 313
Russian, 320, 331. See also
Bolsheviks
Peasants
conditions of, 145, 163
exploitation of, 138
inequality of, 109
insurrection and, 84, 86
land for, 163
monarchy and, 238
needs of, 192–193
in nineteenth century, 164
organization of, 85, 115
representatives of, 73
revolutionary activity among, 88–90
Russian, 83–85, 156, 219
self-government of, 139, 141
of sixteenth century, 243, 245
struggle of, 225–226
as unskilled workers, 100
uprisings of, 272–274, 275, 306
People's Will, 152, 157. See also
Executive Committee
Père Peinard, 304n
Police
infiltration by, 21–22
in prerevolutionary Russia, 268
secret, 149
as state institution, 65
Populism, 16
Russian, 20

Populists, revolutionary, 46
Post offices, as state institutions, 66
    desperate condition of employees, 335
Pravda, 338
Press
    anarchist, 5, 8n, 332n
    cooperative, 332
    cuckoo cry of, 151
    European, 136
    German, 313
    "reptile," 312
    Russian, 139–140, 268
Propaganda
    "by the deed," 27–28
    factual, 105
    limitations of, 88
    mass, 98
    newspaper, 79
    organization and, 96–97, 109
    among peasants, 104
    personal, 103
    science and, 101
    social, 107
    of socialists, 79
    stories as, 104
    strikes as, 112
    terror as, 24
    among workers, 104, 269
Propagandists, 90, 144, 145. *See also* Activists
Property
    class views of, 145
    expropriation of, 129. *See also* Expropriation
    private, 172, 215
    public, 172
Psychology, social, 202, 258
Public, opinion of, 139

Races, inferior, 194
Radical, modern, 259
Reaction, 132, 140, 320
    Cossacks and, 285
    of 1793, 175. *See also* Party, reactionary
Redistribution, of housing, 202. *See also* Expropriation
Reforms
    necessity for, 141
    revolution and, 77–78
Reichstag, German, 311

Republic
    federated, 60, 319
    Jacobin, 188
    Soviet, 337
Republicans, 261
Révolte, La, 304
Révolté, Le, 8, 22
Revolution
    Anabaptist, 305
    central government and, 131
    within commune, 124
    Cromwellian, 305
    of 1848, 176
    of 1871, 124
    in England, 287
    in Finland, 315
    French, 256, 287, 305
    goals of, 72, 75
    inevitability of, 120, 142
    Jacobin, 320
    libertarian, 238
    Lutheran, 305
    naturalness of, 30
    necessity of, 306
    October, 38, 318, 326, 339
    promotion of, 88
    Russian, 20n, 40, 267–289. *See also* Party, revolutionary, Russian
    of 1793, 207
    social, 15, 80, 87, 173, 211, 320, 339
        preparation for, 91, 93, 105
    spontaneous, 183
    stage effects of, 119
    success of, 26, 78
    Vienna, 284
Révolution Sociale, La, 21
Revolutionaries
    counter-, 328
    defense of, 338
    hanging of, 150
    imprisonment of, 147–149
    origins of, 141–142
    as outlaws, 149
    of 1793, 175
Rhineland, union of, 244
Riga, uprisings at, 277
Rights, to land, 154
    political, 75, 78. *See also* Freedom
Riurik family, 7, 231
Robespierre, party of, 181
Roman Empire, 213, 218, 219, 263
Romanists, 228

Romanov dynasty, 271
Rostopchin, law of, 80
Russia
    activists in, 93, 95
    army of, 37–38
    dissatisfied elements in, 83
    England and, 39
    illiteracy of, 103
    industrial development of, 141
    prison system in, 36
    revolution in, 266–290
    strikes in, 110
Russo-Japanese War, 31, 276

Sagas, Scandinavian, 223
Sailors
    exploitation of, 167
    in new state, 74
Saint Imier International Congress
    at Verviers, 19
Saint Petersburg Fortress, 148
Schleswig-Holstein, province of, 312
Schlusselburg, bastille of, 283
Secret societies, in England, 256–257
    in Russia, 137–138. See also Circles
Serbia, federation of, 244
Serfdom. See also Peasants
    abolishment of, 137, 138, 157
    records of, 75
Ships, expropriation of, 74
Siberia
    exile to, 147
    occupation of, 219
Siege, of Paris, 122, 198
"Social contract," 214, 228
Social Democratic Party, 37, 313,
    320, 331. See also Bolsheviks
Socialism, 261–262, 337
    diversity of, 190
    Marxist, 33
    Paris commune and, 128–132
    transition of, 126
Socialists
    divisions between, 211
    goals of, 72
    Latin, 121
    of nineteenth century, 126
    popular, 153
    present-day, 48
    propaganda of, 79
Society
    origins of, 214, 215
    postrevolutionary, 160

primitive, 215–216, 217
Soldiers, 74. See also Army
Solidarity, 299
Sovnarkom, 325, 332
"Spartan broth," 185
State
    anarchism and, 1–3
    breakdown of, 126, 132
    as federated republic, 60
    French concept of, 212
    functions of, 65
    German concept of, 212
    government and, 212, 213
    historic role of, 211–264
    institutions of, 65
    labor and, 50
    popular, 121
    reforms and, 84
    in sixteenth century, 246–247
    unions in, 70
    war and, 246, 258
State and Revolution, Lenin's, 324
Stockjobbing, 170
Stoics, 1
Strike, 110
    all-class, 272
    of 1896, 269
    general, 280–281
    in Moscow (1905), 278–279
    as propaganda, 112
    in Russia, 256
Students
    demonstrations by, 269
    killing of, 285
    participation of, 87
    strikes and, 271
Suffrage, universal, 154
Syndicalism, 28, 305, 306

Taxation, 65
    of peasants, 139
    reform of, 141
    as state weapon, 257–258
Telegraphs, as state institutions, 66
Terrorism. See also White Terror
    anarchism and, 4–6, 20, 22
    first act of, 149
    Kropotkin's view of, 23
    in Paris commune, 123–124
    as propaganda, 24
    from Right, 21, 108
Third Republic, 252, 260
Times, London, 36, 79

Towns
  of Middle Ages, 229, 232
  of sixteenth century, 238, 245
Trade, foreign, 232. *See also* Commerce
Trial of the Hundred and Ninety-Three, 146–148
Tribalism, 215. *See also* Society, primitive
Tsar
  absolutism of, 151
  revolution and, 115
  role of, 83–84, 286
Turks, 241
Tuscany, union of, 244

Unions
  agricultural, 252
  of artels, 68
  consumer, 106
  of intellectuals, 268
  workers', 111
United States. *See also* America
  capitalism in, 165
  unemployment in, 177
Utopia, Jacobin, 191

Versailles government, 123
Vienna revolution, 284
Villages, 219, 226, 227, 228
  revolutionary activity in, 95
"Vladimir" Sunday, 271
Voix du Peuple, La, 304
V narod ("to the people"), 144, 294
Vremennik, 8

Wage system, in capitalism, 179
War
  civil, 330
  Franco-Prussian (1870–1871), 65, 310
  peasants', 302. *See also* Peasants, uprisings of

Russo-Japanese, 31, 276
state and, 246, 258
Warsaw, 310
  massacres at, 277
Western International organizations, 115
Westphalia, federation of, 244
White Guards, 338
White Terror, 151
Winter Palace, 270
Women, in Russian revolution, 143
Workers
  community of, 106
  equality of, 73
  exploitation of, 94, 164
  inequality of, 109
  insurrection and, 84, 86
  intelligentsia and, 107
  organization of, 85, 115
  propaganda and, 101, 269
  revolution and, 302
  revolutionary activity among, 88–90
  Russian, 278
  solidarity among, 299
  strikes and, 110, 113
  unemployed, 176–177
  Western European, 82
Workmen's Council of Delegates, 284
Workshops, national, 177
World unity, 104
World War I, Kropotkin's views of, 32–35, 309–316

Youth, 85, 145, 170
  educated, 87, 92. *See also* Students
  French bourgeois, 294
  movement of, 269
  as workers, 100

Zemstvos, 139, 140
  Congress of, 267, 268